PARADIGM
KEYBOARDING
AND
APPLICATIONS

A Mastery Approach for Microcomputers
and Typewriters: *Short Course*

THIRD EDITION

K. A. Mach, Ed.D.

Irvine Valley College, Irvine, California

James E. LaBarre, Ph.D.

University of Wisconsin—Eau Claire

William M. Mitchell, Ed.D.

University of Wisconsin—Eau Claire

Adapted from *Keyboarding: A Mastery Approach*

Paradigm Publishing International

Project Editor	Sharon Bouchard
Editorial Assistant	Paul Larson
Copy Editor	Betty Drury
Text Design	Alex Teshin
Cover Design	Kay Fulton
Composition	Alexander Teshin Associates
Illustrations	Alexander Teshin Associates

Photographs on cover and pages vi–ix and xi: Courtesy of International Business Machines Corporation.

Illustration on page x: Courtesy of *U.S. News & World Report*

Library of Congress Cataloging-in-Publication Data

Mach, K. A. (Kaye A.)
    Paradigm keyboarding and applications: a mastery approach for microcomputers and typewriters: short course / Kaye A. Mach, James E. LaBarre, William Martin Mitchell.
        p. 328 cm.
    ISBN 1-56118-154-4
    1. Electronic data processing—Keyboarding.   2. Typewriting.
I. LaBarre, James E.   II. Mitchell, William Martin.
III. Title.
QA76.9.K48M332   1990   89-25527
004.7'6—dc20   CIP

Originally published as *Keyboarding: A Mastery Approach*. Portions of this book were originally published in the *Beginning, Intermediate,* and *Comprehensive* levels of that series. Some portions also appeared in *College Typewriting: A Mastery Approach* and *Typewriting: A Mastery Approach, For IBM Selectric® Typewriters, Comprehensive Course.*

Printed in the United States of America.

10 9 8 7 6 5 4 3 2

CONTENTS

Module I THE KEYBOARD

Alphabetic Keys

Numeric Keys

10-Key Numeric Keyboard

Specialized Punctuation-Mark/Symbol Keys

Alphabetic Review

Module II BASIC LEVEL PRODUCTIVITY

Composition and Centering

Business Letters and Memorandums

Manuscripts

Tables

PREFACE

The keyboard is one of the most important tools that you will use while pursuing an education and in your field of work. The keyboard is your interface with the electronic machines that provide you with the information needed to function in both environments. If you are just beginning to learn to keyboard, you should know that millions of people have already done so. In the beginning you may find it difficult to use the keyboard without looking at the keys, but in a few sessions you will be on your way to developing and improving your skill. As you work to improve your keyboarding skills, always keep a positive attitude. When you think that you cannot improve your speed and accuracy, try harder—you will be surprised just how easy it can be. Although improving your skill requires hours of practice, the more you practice the better you will be able to keyboard. Concentrate on your practice activities and try to do so for short time periods many times during the week.

Performance Outcomes

The third edition of *A Mastery Approach for Microcomputers and Typewriters* is available in three texts—*Keyboarding Skills* (Module 1); *Keyboarding and Applications, Short Course* (Modules 1 and 2); and *Keyboarding and Applications, Complete Course* (Modules 1–8). Expected performance outcomes for each of the modules in the texts include the following:

Module 1 **The Keyboard:** Key straight-copy alphanumeric material by touch at an average rate of 30 words a minute with two or fewer errors per minute.

Module 2 **Basic Level Productivity:** (1) Key straight-copy alphanumeric material at an average rate of 50 words a minute with two or fewer errors per minute. (2) Key formatted letters, memorandums, tables, and manuscripts at a basic level productivity rate of 15 to 20 words a minute (1.5 to 2.0 lines a minute).

Module 3 **Correspondence Mastery:** Key business correspondence at a productivity rate of 30 to 35 words a minute (3.0 to 3.5 lines a minute).

Module 4 **Table Mastery:** Key tables at a productivity rate of 20 words a minute (2.0 lines a minute).

Module 5 **Manuscript and Business Report Mastery:** Key manuscripts and business reports at a productivity rate of 25 to 30 words a minute (2.5 to 3.0 lines a minute).

Module 6 **Integrated Projects:** Key business correspondence and reports in simulated office settings at a productivity rate of 25 to 30 words a minute (2.5 to 3.0 lines a minute).

Module 7 **In-Basket Project:** Key business correspondence and reports requiring decision-making skills in a simulated office position at a productivity rate of 30 words a minute (3.0 lines a minute).

Module 8 **Job Campaign:** Compose and key the following job-seeking correspondence items: letter of application, personal data sheet, reference request letter, follow-up letter, acceptance letter, and rejection letter.

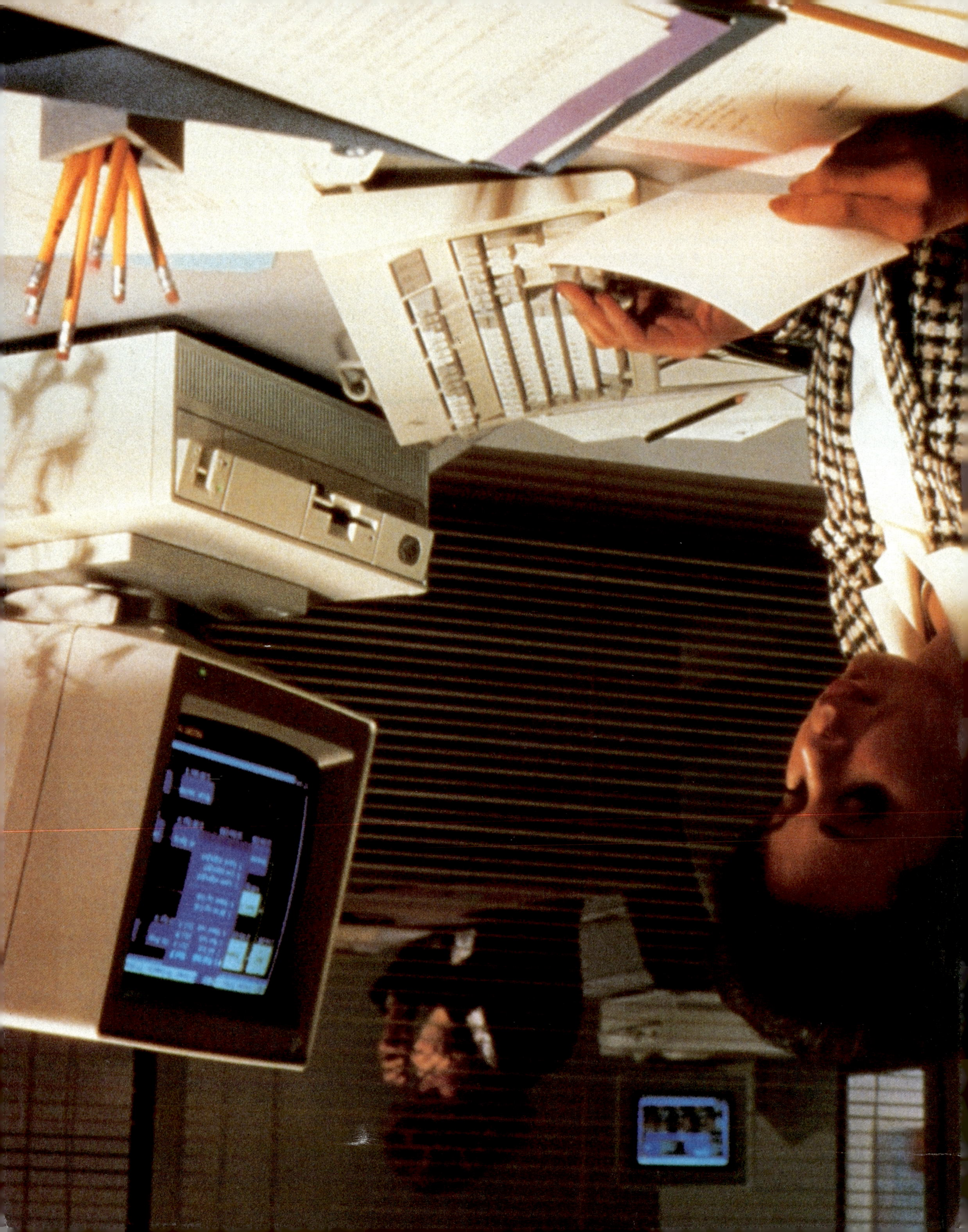

IBM Personal System 2, Model 30

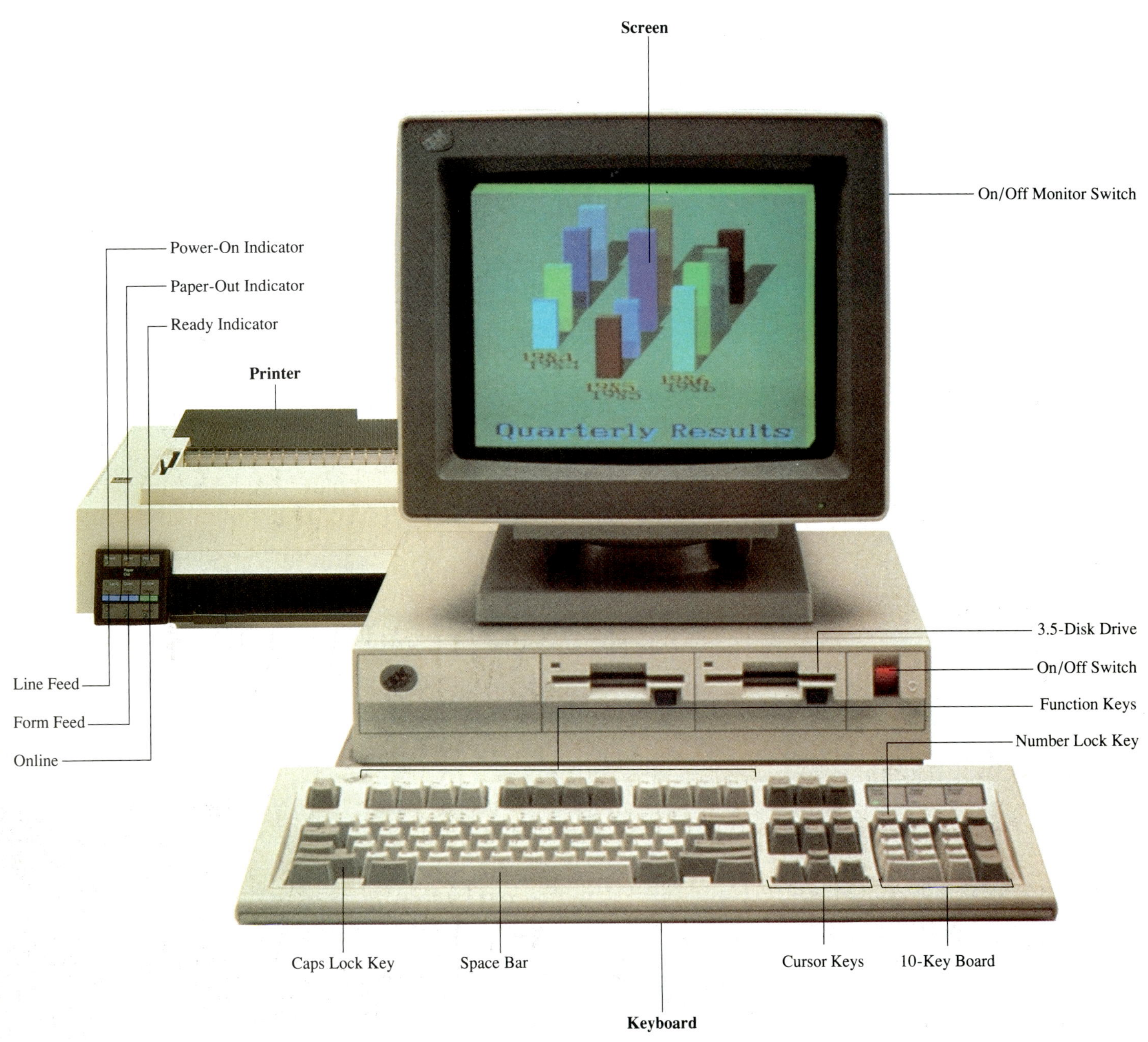

IBM Wheelwriter Series II, Model 30

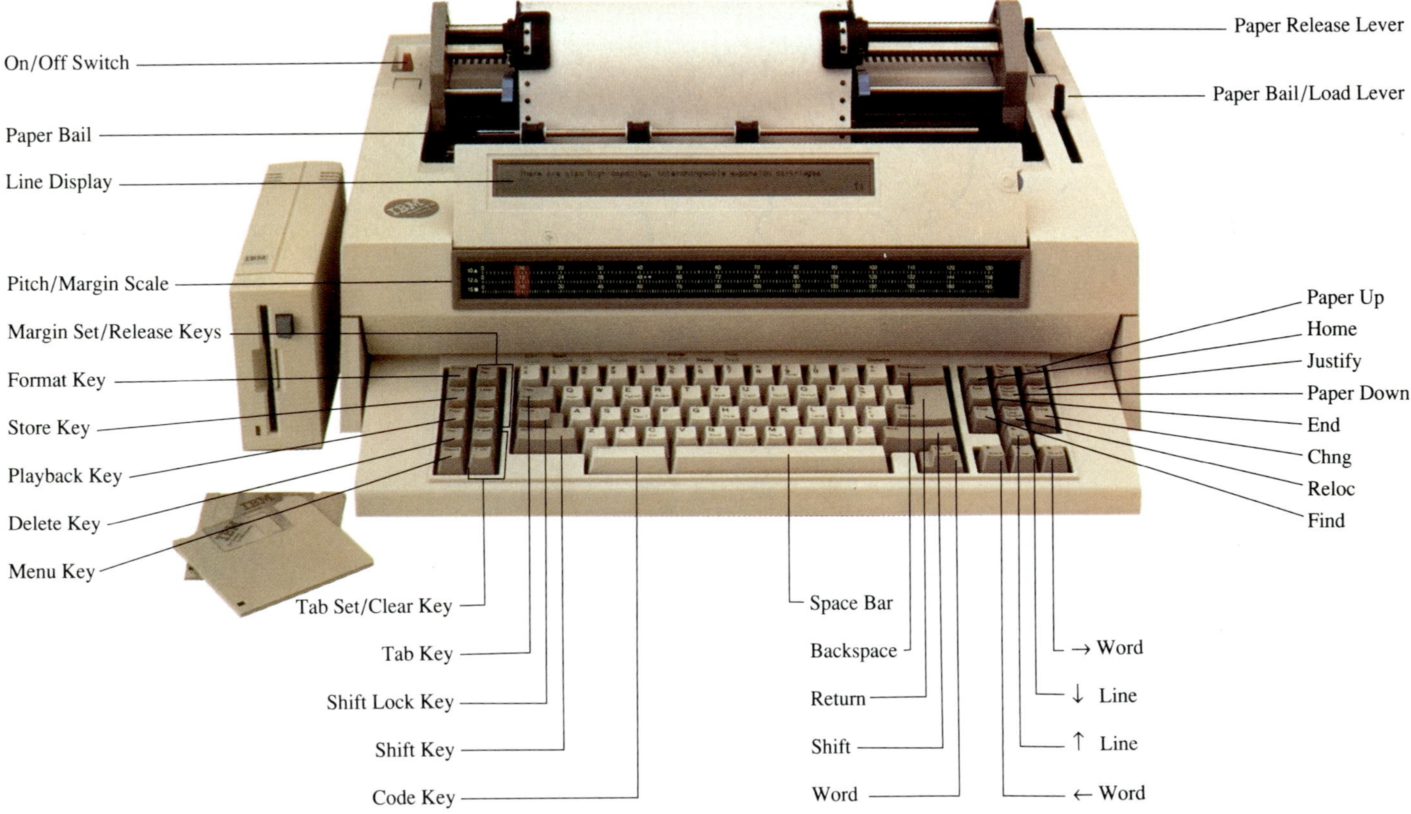

WORKSTATION ERGONOMICS

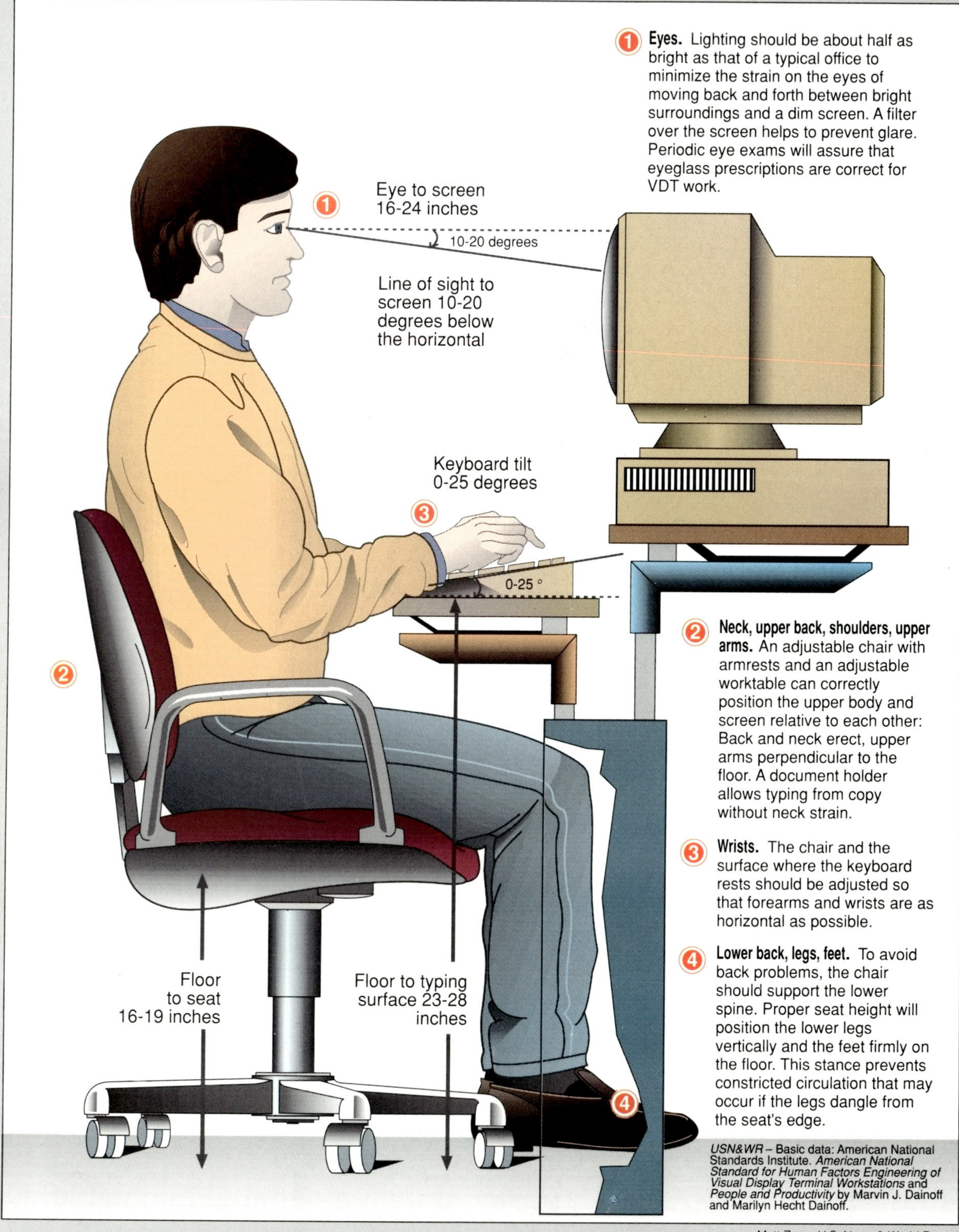

Matt Zang, U.S. News & World Report

Your Position at the Machine

Before beginning to key, check your position at the workstation. After reading the suggestions above, adjust your position at the workstation so that you are comfortable.

YOUR WORKING AREA

The working area should be kept as neat as possible. Remove all items from your working area except the book support, which should be placed on the right side of your machine. Place your book on the support in a position so that you can clearly see the printed material.

PRINTER
Paper Insertion and Removal

Look at your printer and locate the following parts:

1. Paper Table	6. Printer Edge
2. Platen	7. Right Platen Knob
3. Paper Bail	8. Paper Release Lever
4. On Line	9. Form Feed
5. Line Feed	10. On/Off Switch

To insert paper into your printer:

1. Pull paper bail toward you with either your left or right hand.

2. If you are inserting continuous form paper, make sure that you position the paper correctly on the tractor feed. If you are inserting a single page at a time, position the paper between the platen and the paper table.

3. Turn the paper into the printer using either the platen knob or the line feed button. Align the left edge of the paper against the paper-edge guide. Lock the paper guides on the tractor feed. If you are inserting a single page, push the paper release lever back to put pressure on the platen. Press the line feed until the paper is positioned at the print point.

4. To remove the paper, perforate the continuous form paper near the paper table. Press the On Line key and then press the Form Feed key until the paper is out of the printer.

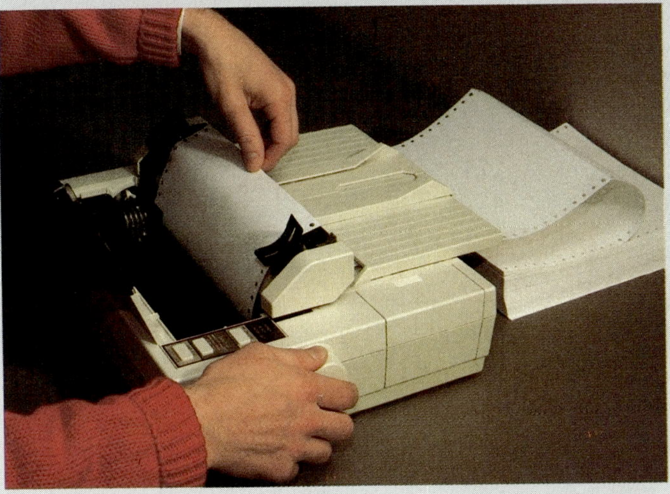

ELECTRONIC TYPEWRITER
Paper Insertion and Removal

Look at your machine and locate the following parts:

1. Paper Table
2. Platen
3. Paper Bail
4. Paper-edge Guide
5. Page-up Key
6. Page-down Key

To insert paper into your machine:

1. Pull paper bail/load lever toward you with your left or right hand, depending on the location of the lever on your machine.

2. Place paper between platen and paper table. Align left edge of paper against paper-edge guide—be sure that the guide is positioned so that the left edge of the paper will be at zero on the line scale.

3. Press the paper-up key—be sure the paper has advanced enough to be covered by the paper bail after completion of the next step.

4. Push paper bail/load lever toward the paper.

5. If your paper is crooked, pull the paper release toward you, straighten the paper, and return the release to the position away from you.

6. To remove the paper from your machine:
   A. Pull paper bail toward you.
   B. Pull paper release toward you with right hand.
   C. Remove paper with left hand.
   Insert and remove a sheet of paper several times until you can do both operations very smoothly and quickly.

CONTROLLING THE LINE SPACING

Line spacing on a printer used with a microcomputer is controlled by the software. Most electronic machines can be set on single, one-and-a-half, or double spacing. If you are using an electronic machine, locate the **line-space** key. You can see the difference in spacing in these examples:

Single Spacing	One-and-a-Half Spacing	Double Spacing
XXXXXXXX	XXXXXXXXXXXXXX	XXXXXXXXXX
XXXXXXXX		
XXXXXXXX	XXXXXXXXXXXXXX	
XXXXXXXX		XXXXXXXXXX
XXXXXXXX	XXXXXXXXXXXXXX	

CONTROLLING THE MARGINS

Generally, software provides for line spacing and margin adjustment via menu-driven options. On an electronic keyboard, you may have to use a series of keystrokes to set the line-space regulator and margins. To set the margins on your machine to the correct line length, it is necessary that you know the type size

(10-pitch or 12-pitch). Ten-pitch letters take up more space on the sheet of paper than 12-pitch letters. There are 10 characters to 1 inch with 10-pitch type and 12 characters to 1 inch with 12-pitch type. Pica is another term for 10-pitch type; elite is another term for 12-pitch type.

12-pitch (Elite) aaaaaaaaaaaa
10-pitch (Pica) aaaaaaaaaa

Before setting your margins, you must locate the center of the paper. A standard sheet of paper is 8-1/2" wide and 11" Long. There are 85 10-pitch spaces (8-1/2" × 10 spaces = 85) and 102 12-pitch spaces (8-1/2" × 12 = 102) across a sheet of paper.

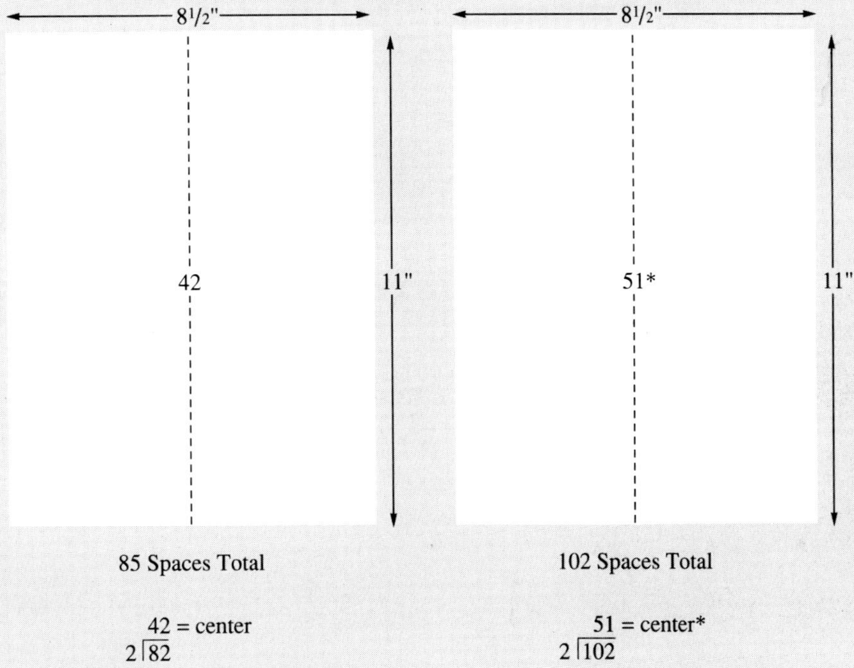

$$\begin{array}{r} 42 = \text{center} \\ 2\,\overline{)82} \end{array} \qquad \begin{array}{r} 51 = \text{center*} \\ 2\,\overline{)102} \end{array}$$

When setting margins, you want to set them so that the left and right margins are approximately even. To do this, **subtract one-half** of the desired line length from the center point to set the left margin. **Add** one-half of the desired line length to the center point to determine the right margin. The following examples show the margins for various length lines:

	10-pitch		12-pitch[†]	
	Left	Right	Left	Right
40-space line	22	62	30	70
50-space line	17	67	25	75
60-space line	12	72	20	80
70-space line	7	77	15	85

Most software packages have both automatic vertical and horizontal centering features. You also can change margin settings after the document has been keyed. This allows you greater flexibility in making your document more presentable. Practice setting the margins for your machine for each of the line lengths given above.

* You may find that using space 50 is more convenient.

† Using space 50 as a center.

HANDS

Place your fingers on the home row (*a s d f j k l ;*) of the keyboard as shown here:

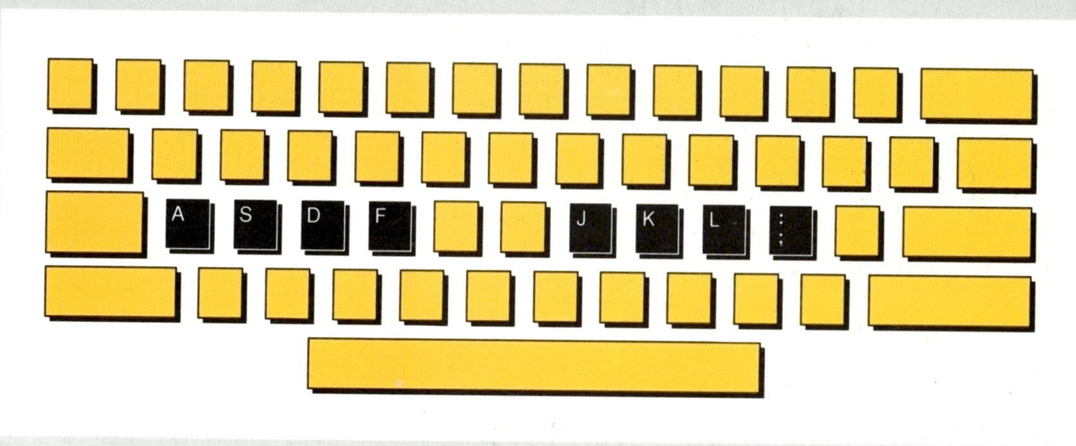

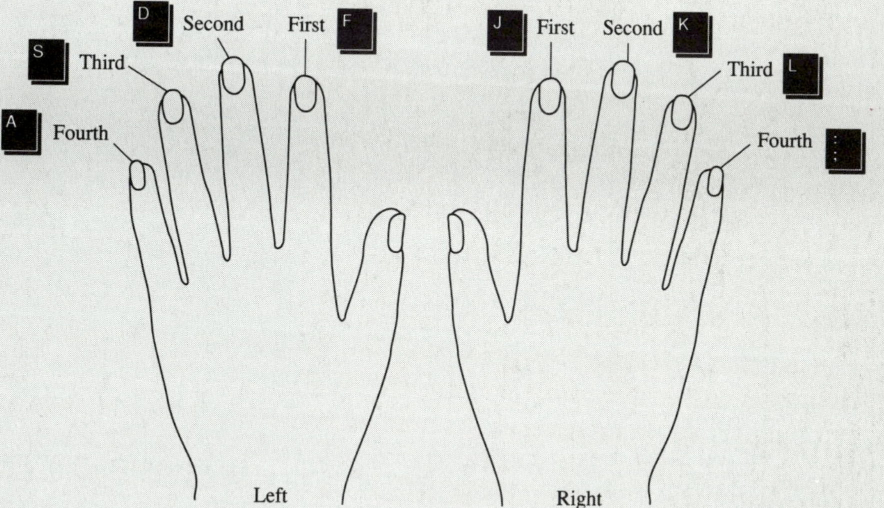

Curve your fingers slightly and let them rest very gently on the home-row keys. "Tap" the keys quickly. Watch your wrists. Keep them straight. Don't let the palms of either hand rest on the machine.

MASTERY SOFTWARE

If you have access to an IBM™ or compatible microcomputer, you will want to take advantage of the **Mastery Software** program that corresponds session-by-session with the text material. Developed with a user-friendly menu structure, the software gives you immediate feedback as you build your skill on speed and accuracy. The automatic checking function gives you constant evaluation of your performance.

Keyboarding Modules

Once you select the **Keyboarding Modules** option from the **Main Menu** (Figure 1), you can choose the session you want to work on. Each session can be accessed at various points—you do not need to complete an entire session in one sitting.

New Key Introduction

During the keyboard introduction, each new alphabetic, numeric, or symbol/punctuation key is presented with a keyboard illustration that highlights the new key. (Figure 2) There is also a special section on the 10-Key numeric keyboard.

Drills

Various types of drills are available to help you build your skill. **Thinking Drills** (Figure 3) are presented early in the sessions to help you learn to think and compose at the keyboard. **Speed Push** drills (Figure 4) challenge you to keep up with the computer as you work to increase your speed while other drills concentrate on accuracy.

Freeform Editor

The **Freeform Editor** option on the **Main Menu** gives you access to the word processing features of the software. After creating or retrieving a document file, (Figure 5) you can key or edit your document. Word processing features can be accessed by pressing special function keys listed at the bottom of the screen. Use these keys to format your document. (Figure 6) A brief description of these features is given below.

F3—Help	Displays Help screens.
F4—Indent	Indents a line of text to the next tab stop. Text will wrap to the indent until the Enter key is pressed.
F5—Spacing	Select single spacing or double spacing.
F6—Center	Centers a line of text.
F7—Ruler	Place the cursor on the ruler line to set margins.
F8—Underline	When printed, the text will be underlined.
F9—Format	Reformats lines or paragraphs to the current margin setting.
F10—Exit	Presents options to resume editing, save text, or exit the editor.

Once you key your document, you can save it to a formatted disk. If you want to make changes in your document, you can retrieve, edit, and save it again.

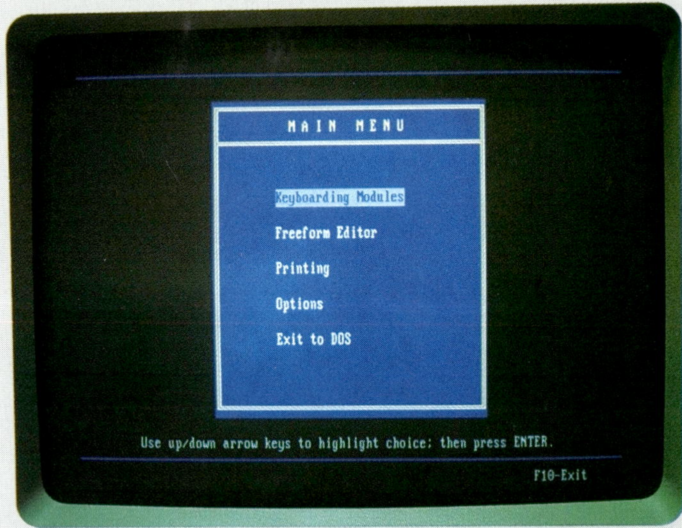

Figure 1

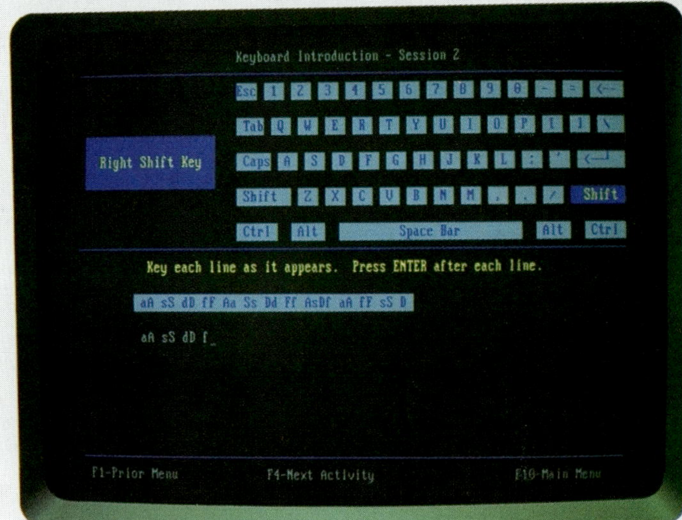

Figure 2

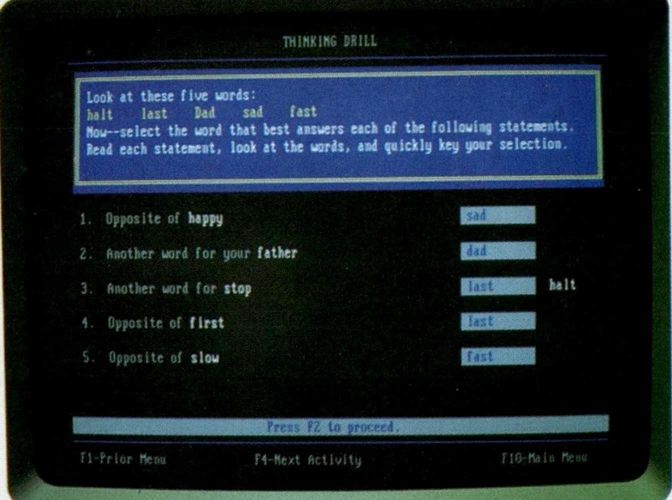

Figure 3

Printing

All drill work and timings are saved and printed by session.
Documents are saved according to the filenames you create and
are printed individually.

Options

By selecting **Options** from the **Main Menu** you can change the
way the software measures your performance. You have a
choice of WAM (words a minute) or LAM (lines a minute).
You also tell the software what type of printer you are using.

Teacher Management

There is a comprehensive **Teacher Management** program
available with the **Mastery Software.** This allows your scores
for checked work to be automatically recorded and used to
calculate your grade.

Flexibility

The **Mastery Software** program is available for the following
texts:

**Keyboarding Skills: A Mastery Approach for Microcompu-
ters and Typewriters**

**Keyboarding and Applications: A Mastery Approach for
Microcomputers and Typewriters, Short Course**

**Keyboarding and Applications: A Mastery Approach for
Microcomputers and Typewriters, Complete Course.**

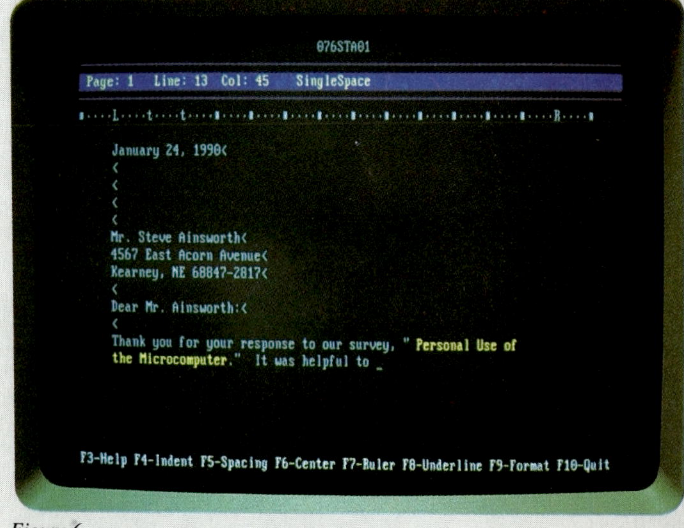

Figure 4

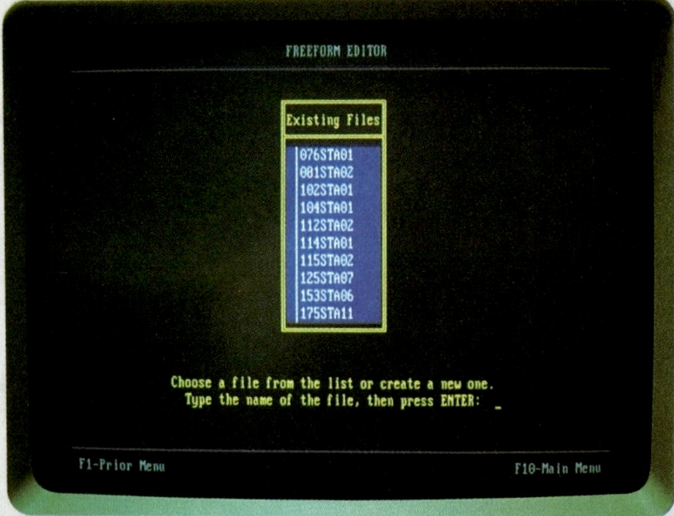

Figure 5

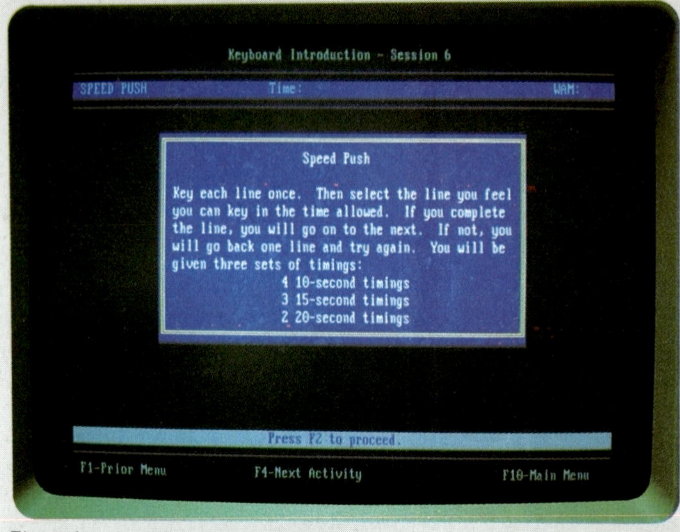

Figure 6

1

T H E
K E Y B O A R D

The KEYBOARD module provides the drill and practice necessary for you to develop keyboarding skills using the touch method. You also are given the opportunity to learn to use the 10-key numeric keyboard available on most electronic keyboards. Upon successful completion of this module, you will be able to key straight-copy alphanumeric material at an average rate of 30 words a minute with two or fewer errors per minute.

SESSION CONTENTS

ALPHABETIC KEYS

Reminder: Your left hand covers *a s d f* and your right hand covers *j k l ;*. Place the outside edge of either your right or left thumb on the **space bar**, depending on which is more natural for you. Curve your fingers slightly, as demonstrated in the photograph.

Strike each key with a firm, quick motion. Practice striking each home-row key several times. At the end of a line, depress the **Enter** or **Return** key with the fourth finger of your right hand. Keep your other fingers on the home row. When completed, continue on to the drill material below. Follow the instructions shown in the left-hand portion of the page.

For the Alphabetic Keys section, use the following margin settings:

12-pitch: 25 and 75
10-pitch: 17 and 67

Lines 1–3 once
Lines 1–3 again

```
1 a s d f j k l ; aa ss dd ff jj kk ll ;;
2 aa ss dd ff jj kk ll ;; asdf jkl; af j;
3 aaa sss ddd fff jjj kkk lll ;;; sd kl ;
```

Lines 4–7 once
Lines 4–7 again

```
4 a ad a ad add add adds adds a ad add ad
5 a as as a ask ask asks asks a all all a
6 a all all a alas alas a as ad add ask a
7 ad add as ask all alas adds asks all ad
```

Lines 8–12 once
Lines 8–12 again

```
8 d dad d dad dads dads s sad sad f fad f
9 fads fads fall fall falls falls fad fad
10 flak flak flask flask lad lad lads lads
11 lass lass lad lad lads dad dads ask ask
12 falls flask alas fads dads asks all sad
```

Mr. Henry Vosen / Roseville Estates, apartment #803 / Charleston, SC 29402-4680 / Dear Hank: Enclosed is a copy of the canceled check for the Sinclair Electric dividend of $65.55. Since the stock was sold prior to the dividend date, we must remit the payment to the proper owner of the stock. You already have a credit in your account of $57.37; therefore, you need only send us a check for $8.18. / Hank, since this payment must also be reported on your income tax statement, it is important that you maintain a record of all dividends that you receive. / We are always pleased to be of service to you. / Sincerely, Robert E. Truax, Senior Vice President

STUDENT MEAL PLANS Many schools require that students who elect to stay in residence halls must also pay for a meal contract of some type. The meal plan is a contract which provides a student a certain number of meals per week for a particular price. Many institutions offer several different types of meal plans. For example, it may be possible to contract for as many meals as 21 per week. Or, the school also may offer an option whereby it is necessary to pay for as few as 15 meals per week. Regardless of the particular meal plan a student has available, many students do not regard the food service at any particular institution too highly. It is quite common to hear a variety of complaints ranging from "the quality of the food is terrible," to "the times of day the meals are served are when I'm not hungry!" It seems it is almost impossible to provide the quality, quantity and serving conditions to satisfy every individual. Most institutions allow professional food service companies to offer bids for providing food service to students. Usually, and perhaps this may be part of the problem, the contract is given to the lowest bidder. The service is contracted to the food service company for a certain number of years, usually two to five. Providing food to students also provides a large number of jobs. Usually the contracting company hires many students as part-time workers. Although the pay is not the highest, it allows the students to earn enough money to help pay for their education.

LOCATIONAL REINFORCEMENT

Lines 1–4 once. At end of each line, press *Enter* quickly and begin next line immediately. Then do again.

```
1 all all
2 sad sad dad dad
3 fad fad alas alas
4 fall fall lad lad add add
```

 | RIGHT SHIFT, H, LEFT SHIFT, COLON

WARM-UP

Lines 1 and 2 once
Lines 1 and 2 again

```
1 a s d f j k l ; aa ss dd ff jj kk ll ;;
2 aa ss dd ff jj kk ll ;; a s d f j k l ;
```

INTRODUCTION TO RIGHT SHIFT KEY

The *right shift* key is used to make capital letters that are keyed with the left hand.

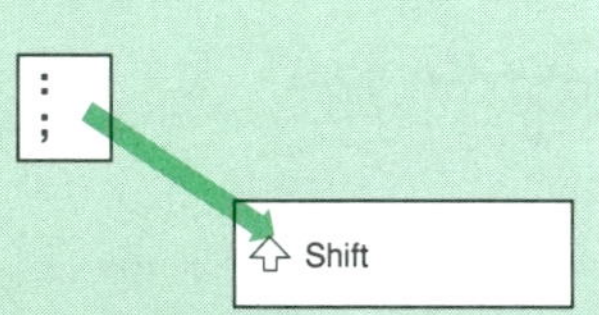

Depress *right shift* key *firmly* with right fourth finger. Key capital letter with correct finger of left hand. Release *right shift* key and return quickly to home-row position.

Lines 1 and 2 once
Lines 1 and 2 again

```
1 aA sS dD fF Aa Ss Dd Ff AsDf aA fF sS D
2 Add Sad Dad Fad Ask Salad Dads Flak All
```

Lines 3–5 once
Lines 3–5 again

```
3 Aa Ss Dd Ff aAa sSs dDd fFf aA sS dD fF
4 a Ask Add Ad As a Alas Alas a All All a
5 Ad All Asks Adds Alas All Ask As Add Ad
```

Lines 6–9 once
Lines 6–9 again

```
6 Fad fad Falls falls Fall fall Fads fads
7 lads lads lad lad Flask Flask Flak Flak
8 Ask lad Dads dad lads Ask Add lass lass
9 Sad All Asks Dads Fads Alas Flask Falls
```

Session 60
Document 1
Filename:
060xxx01

Full sheet;
6 spaces
between
columns;
double-space
body.

COMPUTER SCIENCE
CLASS LIST

<u>Name</u>	<u>Major</u>
Josephine Petrushki	International Studies
Morgan Sutherland	Political Science
Helen Rschzepiejewski	Art, Foreign Languages
Geraldine May Anderson	Computer Science
Hartley Jonathan Smith	Library Science, History
Helen Magdelina Sabrina	Geography, Geology
Charles Robert Tremain	Computer Science
Robert John Rooney	History, Sociology
Patricia Ann Rooney	History, Sociology
Merrill Davis Prissel	Business Administration

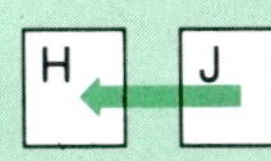

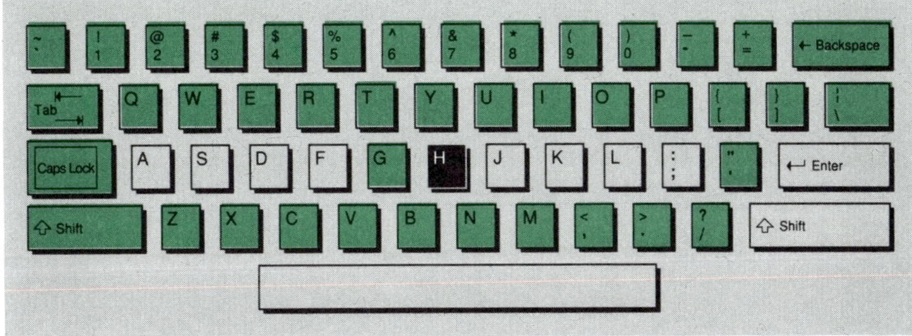

Home-row *j* finger moves left to the letter *h*. Place both hands on the home row and practice the move from *j* to *h*. Look at your hands and watch your finger make the motion. Do this several times; then look away and try the same motion.

H

Line 1 twice

1   jj hh jh jh hj hj jj hh jh jh j h jh jh

Lines 2 and 3 once
Lines 2 and 3 again

2   jh has has has had had had h has had jh

3   jh hall hall hall sash sash has sash jh

Lines 4–7 once
Lines 4–7 again

4   Ash ash Ash ha ha ha jhjh ash ha ash ha

5   half half half lash lash lash half lash

6   Dash dash Dash hash hash hash dash hash

7   Shall Shall Shall Flash Flash Flash Has

INTRODUCTION TO LEFT SHIFT KEY AND COLON

The *left shift* key is used to make capital letters.

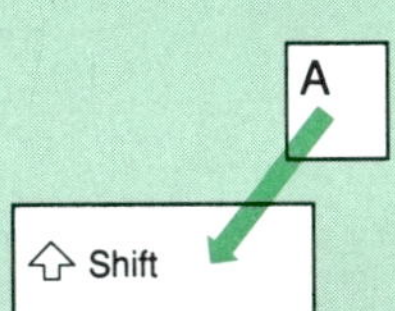

Depress *left shift* key firmly with left fourth finger. Key capital letter with correct finger of right hand. Release *left shift* key and return quickly to home-row position. The shift of the *semi* (;) key will produce a *colon* (:). After keying a colon that follows a word, tap the *space bar* twice.

Lines 1–3 once
Lines 1–3 again

1   jJ kK lL ;; Jj Kk Ll :: JkL; jK lL :;:;

2   jJ hH jH kK lL :: hH jJ kK lL :: jJ hH:

3   Lass Lad Lads Flask: All: Sad: Lads:

WARM-UP

Lines 1–5 once
Lines 1–5 again

1 He enlarged the unlisted analysis of the enlisted men only.

2 The agent insisted that none of the nouns need be censored.

3 A nurse insisted that a ransom note was inserted in a menu.

4 The frenzied inventor unwisely unpacked the bronzed handle.

5 The convicts invaded and conquered a convoy and ran onward.

Lines 6 and 7 once
Lines 6 and 7 again

6 51201304 436 892341176 31,700.73 151,837 515531 1348 319.19

7 631171081 586 34238 10989115 15 5,148.01 538.32 112,831 856

   1   2   3   4   5   6   7   8   9   10   11   12

Timed Short Drills

Turn to pages TSD 1–8 (timed short-drill material) and complete the following:

1. Three 30-second timings for speed
2. Three 30-second timings for control/accuracy
3. Three 1-minute timings for speed
4. Three 1-minute timings for control/accuracy

Number Timings

Take two 30-second timings on Line 7 above.

PRODUCTIVITY CHECK

You have now completed the activities related to letters, memos, manuscripts and reports, and tables for the Basic-Level Productivity Module. In the following sessions, you will master the production of these basic types of documents with more complex formats.

It is now time to determine how quickly you can key basic tables, letters, and manuscripts. Key the following three documents as quickly as possible, correcting your errors. **_Remember:_** You want each task to be "mailable."

Lines 1–3 once. At end of each line, press *Enter* quickly and begin next line immediately. Then do again.

```
1 half:  half:
2 flash:  flash:  shall:  shall:
3 fall:  hall:  alas:  dash:  half:
```

Remember: Tap *space bar* TWICE after a colon.

SESSION 3   PERIOD, T, COMMA

WARM-UP

```
1 aA sS dD fF Aa Ss Dd Ff AsDf aA fF sS D
2 jJ kK lL ;: Jj Kk Ll :; JkL; jK lL :;:;
```

INTRODUCTION TO PERIOD

Lines 1 and 2 once
Lines 1 and 2 again

Home-row *l* finger moves down and to the right to the *period* (.) key. The shift of the period key on a microcomputer keyboard produces a different character. The shift of the period key on a typewriter keyboard produces a period. Locate the period key on your keyboard and compare it to the examples shown below. Place both hands on the home row and practice the move from *l* to *period*. Look at your hands and watch your finger make the motion. Do this several times; then look away and try the same motion.

or

Important: Tap *space bar* TWICE after period at end of sentence. (Note: If a period ends a line, return immediately—there is no need to tap the *space bar*.)

Line 1 twice

```
1 1. 1 1.1 1.1 11.1 11.11 11.11 11.11 11.
```

Lines 2 and 3 once
Lines 2 and 3 again

```
2 All lads shall dash.  A lad shall fall.
3 Ask a lass.  Ask a lad.  Dad asks lads.
```

Lines 4–6 once
Lines 4–6 again

```
4 A lass shall ask a lad.  All lads fall.
5 Dads shall ask.  Lads dash.  Dads dash.
6 Ask a sad lad.  Sad lads fall.  Ask Al.
```

PRODUCTION

Progress Check

You have now completed the activities related to tables for the Basic-Level Productivity Module. It is now time to determine how quickly you can key this type of production document.

Key each of the following documents as quickly as possible, correcting all your errors. Each document should be "mailable." In other words, when you finish each document, it contains no errors.

Required Activity

Session 59
Document 1
Filename:
059xxx01

Full sheet;
4 spaces between columns; double-space body.

OVERSEAS LONG-DISTANCE
TELEPHONE RATES

Country of origin	Direct Dial Station-to-Station	Collect Person-to-Person
Australia	$9.00	$12.00
France	6.75	12.00
Germany	6.75	12.00
Italy	6.75	12.00
Japan	9.00	12.00
Philippines	9.00	12.00
United Kingdom	5.40	9.60

Required Activity

Session 59
Document 2
Filename:
059xxx02

Full sheet;
6 spaces between columns; double-space body.

THE REASONS BUSINESSES
USE TEMPORARY SECRETARIAL HELP

Reasons	Usage
Peakload Periods	86.5 %
Temporary Replacement	48.6 %
Vacation Replacement	70.3 %
One-time Projects	54.1 %
Specialized Work	27.0 %
Possible Permanent Recruitment	18.9 %
Lower Employee Cost	10.8 %
Less Paperwork	2.7 %

INTRODUCTION TO T

Home-row *f* finger moves up and to the right to the *t* key. Place both hands on the home row and practice the move from *f* to *t*. Look at your hands and watch your finger make the motion. Do this several times; then look away and try the same motion.

Line 1 twice	1 ff tt ft ft tf tf ff tt ft ft f t ft ft
Lines 2 and 3 once Lines 2 and 3 again	2 ft at at hat hat hat hat sat sat sat ft
	3 ft fat fat fat aft aft aft t fat aft ft
Lines 4–7 once Lines 4–7 again	4 fast fast fast halt halt halt last last
	5 lath lath lath salt salt salt flat flat
	6 talk talk talk that that that task task
	7 slat slat slat data data data tall tall

LOCATIONAL REINFORCEMENT

Lines 1–3 once. At end of each line, press *Enter* quickly and begin next line immediately. Then do again.	1 staff staff
	2 shaft shaft stalk stalk
	3 stash stash atlas atlas fatal fatal

Build Speed with Control

Try to develop speed with control. Your mind controls your fingers. Try to think *speed.* After you practice setting your "mind" goal several times, you should find that your mind will eventually control your fingers automatically. So think *speed!*

Sentences

Lines 1–3 once Lines 1–3 again	1 A flat flask; a flat hat; a flat atlas.
	2 Half a lath; half a slat; half a flask.
	3 Dad halts a tall lad. A sad lad halts.
Lines 4–6 once Lines 4–6 again	4 Stalk a fast lad; a sad lad has a fall.
	5 Half a lath; half a slat; half a flask.
	6 A dad shall halt. Fat lads shall fall.

Take one 5-minute timing on the following material. Determine your words-a-minute rate. (Divide total words keyed by 5.)

S.I. 1.52

```
When using binoculars, it is better to rest the elbows on a firm   14
surface to steady the glasses.  A telescope is fairly simple to learn   28
to use.  Many telescopes are equipped with a finder.  The finder will   42
assist you in focusing on portions of the sky that you wish to study.   56
Adjusting a finder is a quite simple maneuver.  With little practice,   70
you can become an expert at using all types of optical equipment.  An   84
image will sometimes seem to shimmer.  Any shimmering effect could be   98
due to the fact that you jarred the telescope tube or binoculars; the   112
effect may also be due to a turbulence or an atmospheric disturbance.   126
You will soon discover that the best nights for viewing and observing   140
the stars are those nights when the temperatures have remained fairly   154
steady for several nights.   159

Within our own galaxy, you can observe many beautiful sights.  A   173
lovely domain that you can admire is the satiny stars.  It is easy to   187
see all sorts of patterns in the heavens if you simply relax and turn   201
your imagination loose.  You can obtain diagrams with which to study,   215
observe, and chart the various star patterns.  If you have the equip-   229
ment to look beyond our own galaxy, you will be able to observe stars   243
and galaxies far out into space.  An observatory is a marvelous place   257
to observe the heavens.  The starry displays and changing seasons are   271
not to be missed by an astronomer.  You can develop a very fine hobby   285
through star-gazing, if you care to take the time.   295
```

7 Stalk a fast lad; a sad lad has a fall.

8 A lad talks; a lass talks; a dad talks.

9 Dad halts a tall lad.   A sad lad halts.

INTRODUCTION TO COMMA

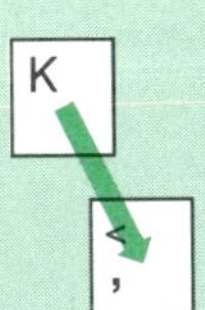

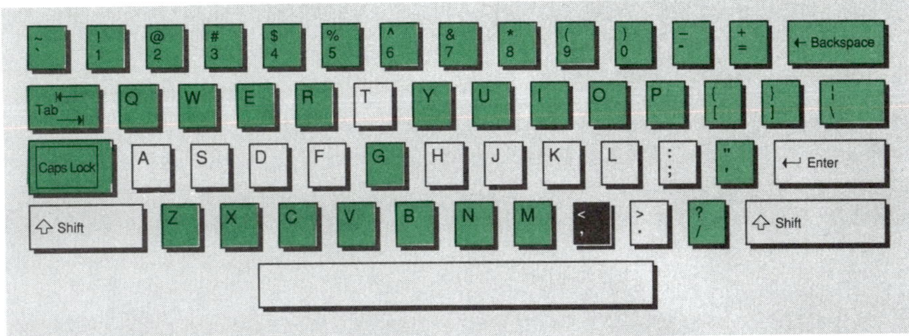

Home-row **k** finger moves down and to the right to the **comma** (,) key. The shift of the comma key on a microcomputer keyboard produces a different character. The shift of the comma key on a typewriter keyboard produces a comma. Locate the comma key on your keyboard and compare it to the examples shown below. Place both hands on the home row and practice the move from **k** to **comma**. Look at your hands and watch your finger make the motion. Do this several times; then look away and try the same motion. **Remember:** Do not space before a comma. Always space once after a comma.

 or 

1 That tall, fat, fast lad shall ask dad.

2 A flat, half lath falls; all lads halt.

3 A flat, fat, sad hall shaft shall fall.

4 Alas, alas, lads fall fast.   Flask, Al.

5 Dad asks, and asks.   Lads shall ask Al.

6 Flat, half, lath shall fall.   Dash, Al.

THINK—AND KEY

One of the most important keyboarding skills that you will want to develop is that of thinking at the machine. After you master the ability to "think" as you key, you will be able to save valuable time by composing directly at the machine rather than having to write your thoughts in longhand and then entering them from your handwritten notes.

You will be given numerous opportunities to develop compositional skills while you are learning the remainder of the letter keys. **Important:** The goal of composing at the machine is to get your thoughts on paper quickly. Don't hesitate—start to key as soon as your thoughts begin. Don't worry about errors; you are composing only in rough-draft form. Later you can concentrate on producing an error-free final copy.

Session 58
Document 3
Filename:
058xxx03

Half sheet;
10 spaces
between
columns;
double-space
body.

Center
horizontally
and vertically.

METRIC CONVERSION TABLE

Fluid Ounces	Milliliters
1 oz	30 ml
4 oz	120 ml
6 oz	180 ml
8 oz	240 ml
10 oz	300 ml
15 oz	450 ml

SESSION 59 — PRODUCTION PROGRESS CHECK — *Assessing Your Performance*

WARM-UP

Lines 1–5 once
Lines 1–5 again

1 A fuzzy buzzard zoomed crazily on that horizon with a zest.

2 Did Buzzy and Hazel realize the prized magazine was seized?

3 A chimpanzee gazed at a bulldozer in amazement and sneezed.

4 Zeb is a lazy zoologist; he snoozes like a zombi in a haze.

5 A dozen frenzied citizens seized the wheezy zither in zest.

Lines 6 and 7 once
Lines 6 and 7 again

6 161176 35017 38131 2924 361.42 101431 166,810 895 13189 456

7 236,731 831464 55565577 3,013,67 4586718 50151672 1893 6718

☐☐☐☐1☐☐☐☐2☐☐☐☐3☐☐☐☐4☐☐☐☐5☐☐☐☐6☐☐☐☐7☐☐☐☐8☐☐☐☐9☐☐☐10☐☐☐11☐☐☐12

Timed Short Drills

Turn to pages TSD 1–8 (timed short-drill material) and complete the following:

1. Three 30-second timings for speed
2. Three 30-second timings for control/accuracy
3. Three 1-minute timings for speed
4. Three 1-minute timings for control/accuracy

Number Timings

Take two 30-second timings on Line 7 above.

LOOK

Look at these five words:

halt   last   Dad   sad   fast

SELECT

Now—select the word that best answers each of the following statements. Read each statement, look at the words, and quickly key your selection.

KEY

1. Opposite of happy

2. Another word for your father

3. Another word for stop

4. Opposite of first

5. Opposite of slow

LOOK

How did you do? Remember—key the appropriate response as quickly as you can. Try these:

SELECT

dash   fat   hat   salt   tall

KEY

6. An object that is worn on your head

7. To move quickly

8. Opposite of short

9. Flavors food

10. Opposite of skinny

SESSION 4   N, E

WARM-UP

Line 1 twice

```
1  a, j, df, kl, j jh jh ;: ;: ft ft jh jh
```

Lines 2 and 3 once
Lines 2 and 3 again

```
2  all sad ask fall lad lass dad ha at ash
3  Add That Has That Shall Dash Last Stall
```

Lines 4–6 once
Lines 4–6 again

```
4  Stalk a fast lad; a sad lad has a fall.
5  Dad halts a tall lad.  A sad lad halts.
6  Half a lath; half a slat; half a flask.
```

13. Repeat the steps for additional columns.

14. Backspace to the left margin, making sure all characters and spaces are deleted.

15. Press *F7* and set your new left margin and tab stop(s). Be sure to delete all old tab stops.

16. Begin keying the body of the table at your new left margin.

Note: If you are using the Mastery Software, do not use the *F9* format function after you reset margins and tabs for the columns under long column headings. All tables will be checked by the software using the guidelines given above.

EMPLOYEE TITLES

Name	Title
Paul Johnson	Accounting Clerk
Carol Zheng	Receptionist
Sabrina Dubrovsky	Office Manager
Aloysius Eull	Data Entry Clerk
Rob Kocher	Personnel Clerk

AUTOMOTIVE EXPORTS FROM U.S.

(Total Value in Millions)

Year	Automobiles	All Vehicles
1990	$9,882	$15,271
1985	9,748	13,561
1980	6,320	11,280
1975	4,580	9,450
1970	1,397	3,652
1965	739	1,929

INTRODUCTION TO N

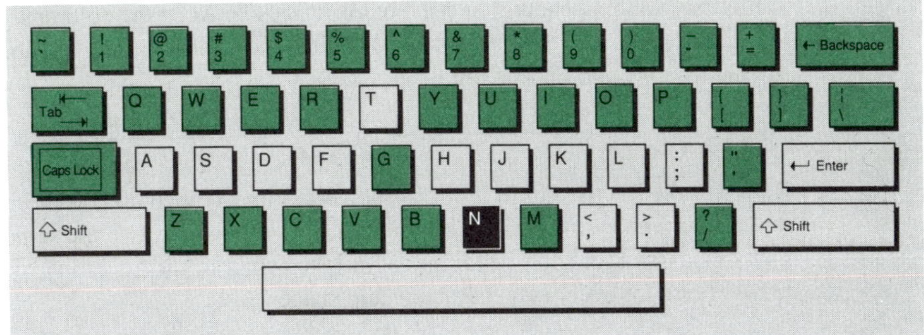

Home-row *j* finger moves down and to the left to the *n* key. Place both hands on the home row and practice the move from *j* to *n*. Look at your hands and watch your finger make the motion. Do this several times; then look away and try the same motion.

Line 1 twice

Lines 2 and 3 once
Lines 2 and 3 again

```
1  jj nn jn jn nj nj jj nn jn jn j n jn jn
2  jn an an an and and and an and an an jn
3  jn ant ant ant fan fan fan hand hand jn
```

Lines 4–7 once
Lines 4–7 again

```
4  land land land sand sand sand tank tank
5  than than than flank flank flank an tan
6  slant slant slant thank thank thank and
7  Nasal nasal Nasal Stand stand Stand Fan
```

LOCATIONAL REINFORCEMENT

Lines 1–3 once. At end of each line, press *Enter* quickly and begin next line immediately. Then do again.

```
1  sand sand
2  sandal sandal shank shank
3  thank thank annal annal hands hands
```

Determine Your Speed Rate

A "word" consists of five letters, digits, symbols, and/or spaces. For example, the words *I see* would be counted as one word, not two.

To determine your speed rate, you must use both the *cumulative* word count (located to the right of the material on the following page) and the *partial-line* word count (located across the bottom of the material). Assume you took a 1-minute timing on lines 1–4 on the next page. You keyed lines 1 and 2 and just finished keying the word *lad* in line 3 when the minute was up. Using the cumulative word count, you find that the last *completed* line you keyed (line 2) shows a word count of 16. Then, looking at the partial-line count, you find that the word *lad* shows a partial-line count of 3. Adding the two (16 plus 3) gives you a total speed rate of 19 words a minute (wam). If you took a 1-minute timing and got to the *s* in *salad*, you would have typed 23 words a minute (16 wam + 7 wam = 23 wam).

2. Set the left margin and space forward *once* for each character and space in the guideline (column heading) and the blank spaces between the columns. Set the tab stop. Return, key the first column heading and underscore it, tab, and key the second heading and underscore it.

<u>Fluid Ounces</u>   <u>Milliliters</u>
123456

3. Return to the left margin. It will now be necessary to move the left margin so that the column entries will be centered under the heading. Use the same process that you learned for short headings to find the center of the guideline; space forward *one* for every *two* characters and spaces.

Fl ui d_ Ou nc es

Your machine is now positioned at the exact center of the guideline.

4. Backspace *once* for each *two* characters and spaces in the longest item in the column.

4_ oz

5. Moved the left margin to this point.

6. Tab to the first stop again and space to the center of the guideline.

Mi ll il it er s

7. Backspace *once* for each *two* characters and spaces in the longest item in the column.

12 0_ ml

8. Set a new tab stop at this point. (Remember to remove the "old" stop.)

When keying *long headings* over columns in Simple Tables that are checked by the software, follow these steps:

1. Use the *F6* automatic centering feature to center table headings and subheadings.

2. Triple space after the table headings.

3. Key the guidelines (the long column headings are your guidelines) with the spaces between columns. Underscore the column headings as you key them.

4. Use the *F6* automatic centering feature to center the guidelines.

5. Double-space to the first line of the body of the table.

6. Space to the location of the first character of the first column heading.

7. Space once for every two characters in the column heading.

8. Backspace once for every two characters in the longest item in the column.

9. Note this position; this will be your new left margin.

10. Space to the first character of the second column heading.

11. Repeat steps 7 and 8.

12. Note this position; it will be your tab setting.

Some timings will be less than 1 minute. Convert these timing rates into your words-a-minute rate. Use the following table to determine your rate when keying for less than 1 minute.

If You Keyed for	Multiply				
5 seconds	number of words	×	12	=	minute stroking rate
10 seconds	number of words	×	6	=	minute stroking rate
15 seconds	number of words	×	4	=	minute stroking rate
30 seconds	number of words	×	2	=	minute stroking rate

Important: Whenever you repeat a timing on the same material, always attempt to

1. Key more words on the second attempt than you did on the first,

or

2. Have fewer errors on the second attempt than you did on the first.

Sentences

1 Jan shall hand a sad lad an atlas fast. 8

2 Slant that fat lath and add tall slats. 16

3 That tall lad sat and had a fast salad. 24

4 Lana and Sal shall stand and talk last. 32

5 Sad dad had a flat hat that falls fast. 8

6 Hal shall thank that tall and lank lad. 16

7 A tall shaft falls and halts that task. 24

8 Hats and sandals shall stand, as a fad. 32

Lines 1–4 once
Lines 1–4 again

Lines 5–8 once
Lines 5–8 again

THINKING DRILL

LOOK

Look at these words:

tan   hand   ant   sand   thanks

SELECT

Now—select the word that best answers each of the following statements. Read each statement, look at the words, and quickly key your selection.

KEY

1. A small insect is an __________.

2. The hot sun may give you a good __________.

3. When you meet someone, you may shake his __________.

4. When you are at the beach you lie on __________.

5. When a person does something nice, say __________.

PRODUCTION

COLUMN HEADINGS

A heading above a column identifies what is contained in that column. To make a heading appear attractive within a table, it is centered over the column and underscored. In some cases, the heading may be shorter than the longest line in the column; in other cases, it may be longer than the longest line.

<u>Short Heading</u>   <u>Long Heading</u>

Washington, D.C.   Johnny

Short Headings

To center a short heading over a column:

1. Key the table heading and then triple-space.

2. Set the left margin and tab stops for columns as usual. Refer to Session 55 to review horizontal centering of tables.

3. Beginning at the left margin, space forward *once* for each *two* characters and spaces in the guideline.

<u>Wa sh in gt on ,_ D. C.</u> →

Your machine is now positioned at the exact center of the first column. Consider this position to be the "centering point" of that column.

4. Backspace *once* for each *two* characters and spaces in the column heading.

← <u>Sh or t_ He ad in g</u>

5. Key the column heading and underscore it. You have now centered the heading over the guideline of the first column.

6. Tab to the next column and repeat the process. Continue until you have centered a heading over each column.

7. Return to the left margin and begin keying the body of the table.

Long Headings

To center a long heading over a column:

1. The column heading becomes the guideline when it is longer than the longest item in the column.

METRIC CONVERSION TABLE

Guideline (longest item in column) ⟨ <u>Fluid Ounces</u>   <u>Milliliters</u> ⟩ Guideline (longest item in column)

4 oz   120 ml

6 oz   180 ml

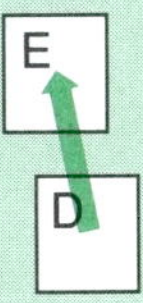

INTRODUCTION TO E

Home-row **d** finger moves up and to the left to the **e** key. Place both hands on the home row and practice the move from **d** to **e**. Look at your hand and watch your finger make the motion. Do this several times; then look away and try the same motion.

Line 1 once

1 d dd de de de dd ed ed de ded ded dd ee de dedede

Lines 2 and 3 once
Lines 2 and 3 again

2 de den den eat eat eel eel ate ate ale ale elf de

3 de let let she she see see the the fee fee elk de

Lines 4–7 once
Lines 4–7 again

4 dead dead date date east east else else deaf deaf

5 deal deal ease ease else else desk desk fell fell

6 fade fade feel feel hate hate head head heal heal

7 Elk Elk Else Ease East End Elf Else Ease End East

LOCATIONAL REINFORCEMENT

Lines 1–3 once. At end of each line, press *Enter* quickly and begin next line immediately. Then do again.

1 He

2 He ate

3 He ate salt.

Lines 4–6 once
Lines 4–6 again

4 She

5 She has

6 She has land.

Lines 7–10 once
Lines 7–10 again

7 He

8 He tested

9 He tested the

10 He tested the saddle.

Lines 11–14 once
Lines 11–14 again

11 Send

12 Send a

13 Send a false

14 Send a false flake.

Timed Short Drills

Turn to pages TSD 1–8 (timed short-drill material) and complete the following:

1. Three 30-second timings for speed
2. Three 30-second timings for control/accuracy
3. Three 1-minute timings for speed
4. Three 1-minute timings for control/accuracy

Number Timings

Take two 30-second timings on Line 7 on the previous page.

Straight-Copy Timings

Take one 3-minute timing on the following material. Determine your words-a-minute rate. (Divide total words keyed by 3.)

S.I. 1.49

```
Plants that have been started can also be purchased at all local    14
nursery or garden shops in the spring.  Usually, these flowers are in    28
full bloom at the period when they are offered for sale; the gardener    42
can then select the colors and kinds of plants that will look best in    56
the specific garden sites and areas.  After the flower garden bed has    70
been prepared, the gardener can simply place the fine blooming plants    84
in the earth and will have an instant garden.                           93

Planning flower displays is a time-consuming but rewarding task.    117
For example, a mass of brilliant colors and textures could brighten a    131
dark corner or highlight darker foliage and shrubs.  Some annuals are    145
better suited for border planting or edging.  Others which grow quite    159
tall can be used for unique backgrounds or screening.  There are many    173
annuals that make gorgeous bouquets of cut flowers.  The gardener can    187
enjoy the fruits of his or her labor with vases of beautiful blossoms    201
placed all around the house.                                            207

Growing annuals in containers has become very popular.  Creative    221
gardeners will move containers from one place to another to highlight    235
the most beautiful plants in bloom.  A movable or mobile green garden    249
allows for the maximum use of color.                                    256

Most gardeners like to write all the detailed plans on paper.  A    270
plan shows them exactly where each new plant is to be located and how    284
many plants should be purchased.                                        290
```

1 2 3 4 5 6 7 8 9 10 11 12 13 14

Sentences

1 Jean shall sell the seashells, saddle, and jeans. 10

2 Taste the lean tea; handle the kettle that leaks. 20

3 The athlete tensed a knee as she dashed and fell. 30

4 The fat hen left the lake. She landed at a nest. 40

☐☐☐☐ 1 ☐☐☐☐ 2 ☐☐☐☐ 3 ☐☐☐☐ 4 ☐☐☐☐ 5 ☐☐☐☐ 6 ☐☐☐☐ 7 ☐☐☐☐ 8 ☐☐☐☐ 9 ☐☐☐☐ 1 0

5 Send the dated lease and halt the endless hassle. 10

6 A talented athlete eats steak and salad at least. 20

7 A flannel hat fell as Allen defended a keen lead. 30

8 The sad attendant halted a theft. He felt tense. 40

☐☐☐☐ 1 ☐☐☐☐ 2 ☐☐☐☐ 3 ☐☐☐☐ 4 ☐☐☐☐ 5 ☐☐☐☐ 6 ☐☐☐☐ 7 ☐☐☐☐ 8 ☐☐☐☐ 9 ☐☐☐☐ 1 0

Take a 1-Minute Timing

Check your stroking rate on the paragraph below. First, key the entire paragraph at a "controlled" rate. A controlled rate is one in which you are keying at a comfortable speed, not concentrating on either speed or accuracy. Second, take a 1-minute timing. Determine your words-a-minute rate. Third, take another 1-minute timing. Attempt to get further in the copy (key more words) than you did on your first attempt. If you finish before time is up, start over. **Remember:** If you get one more letter keyed the second time, you are keying faster!

Timing

Ann and Sal attended a feast at the lake estates. 10

The steaks needed salt and the salad tasted flat. 20

Allen left a sandal and a hat at the tent stakes. 30

☐☐☐☐ 1 ☐☐☐☐ 2 ☐☐☐☐ 3 ☐☐☐☐ 4 ☐☐☐☐ 5 ☐☐☐☐ 6 ☐☐☐☐ 7 ☐☐☐☐ 8 ☐☐☐☐ 9 ☐☐☐ 1 0

THINKING DRILL

LOOK

Look at these words:

heat   handle   eat   fall   lake

SELECT

Now—select the word that best answers each of the following statements. Read each statement, look at the words, and quickly key your selection.

KEY

1. When you are hungry, you usually __________.

2. Grab the mug by the __________.

3. With summer comes __________.

4. Fish live in a __________.

5. If you trip, you might __________.

WORDS INDICATING HAPPINESS

Session 57
Document 1
Filename:
057xxx01

prosperous	favorable	fortunute	successful
bright	wealthy	optimistic	helathy
refreshing	victorious	triumphant	secure
nice	pleasant	charming	elated
cherful	satisfied	joyous	peaceful
gleeful	content	apreciate	atractive
beneficial	jovial	delighted	exhilerated

Full sheet;
6 spaces
between
columns;
double-space
body.

Center
horizontally
and vertically.

Session 57
Document 2
Filename:
057xxx02

Half sheet;
6 spaces
between
columns;
double-space
body.

Center
horizontally
and vertically.

American Painters

Audubon, John	Hart, George	Pierce, Waldo
Cole, Thomas	Henri, Robert	Pyle, Howard
Davis, Stuart	Hicks, Thomas	Shahn, Ben
Earle, Ralph	Kuhn, Walt	Sloan, John
Fuller, George	Marin, John	Stella, Joseph
Grasz, George	Melchers, Gari	Tiffany, Louis
Harding, Chester	Moran, Edward	Weber, Max

SESSION 58 — TABLES WITH COLUMN HEADINGS

WARM-UP

Lines 1–5 once
Lines 1–5 again

1 Shorten the cashmere shirt and finish washing those dishes.

2 The theft of the cathedral heirloom made their hearts ache.

3 A white whale wheezed and was near death in the south tank.

4 The shutters shuddered and thundered during that hurricane.

5 Hammer another lath on that wharf; that whole booth shakes.

Lines 6 and 7 once
Lines 6 and 7 again

6 6,924,083 7.34 98 634,413.77 69397413 81145738571 15164 343

7 7361130 9,368.40 153,986.03 51673451189 9655151 89376 44501

1 2 3 4 5 6 7 8 9 10 11 12

WARM-UP

Lines 1–3 once
Lines 1–3 again

1 dd ee de de asdf jkl; jh ft 1.1 k, et dd ee de de

2 an let see the ale ask and fee fat sad lad all at

3 fell east dated feel desk else deaf eel fade lank

Lines 4–6 once
Lines 4–6 again

4 Elk Elk Else Ease East End Elf Else Ease End East

5 The athlete tensed a knee as she dashed and fell.

6 The sad attendant halted a theft. He felt tense.

INTRODUCTION TO I

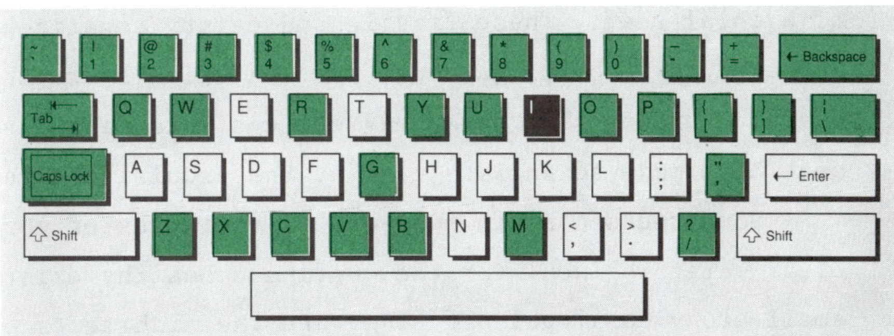

Home-row *k* finger moves up and to the left to the *i* key. Place both hands on the home row and practice the move from *k* to *i*. Look at your hand and watch your finger make the motion. Do this several times; then look away and try the same motion.

Line 1 once

1 k kk ki ki ki kk ik ik ki kik kik kk ii ki kikiki

Lines 2 and 3
Lines 2 and 3 again

2 ki if if in in it it hi hi kid kid his his ail ki

3 ki sit sit ski ski hit lid lid lie lie ill ill ki

Lines 4–7 once
Lines 4–7 again

4 fail fail file file fill fill find find fine fine

5 hill hill tail tail life life said said idea idea

6 this this like like kind kind lift lift dish dish

7 Ill Inside Indeed If Illness Island Indeed Inside

Timed Short Drills

Turn to pages TSD 1–8 (timed short-drill material) and complete the following:

1. Three 30-second timings for speed
2. Three 30-second timings for control/accuracy
3. Three 1-minute timings for speed
4. Three 1-minute timings for control/accuracy

Number Timings

Take two 30-second timings on Line 7 on the previous page.

Straight-Copy Timings

Take one 3-minute timing on the following material. Determine your words-a-minute rate. (Divide total words keyed by 3.)

S.I. 1.50

Nature lovers cannot find words that describe the strange beauty 14
of a coral reef. These fragile and dainty aquatic kingdoms have been 28
compared to colorful gardens; the sea animals are the flowers of this 42
classic garden. The strangely eerie sights beneath the waters of the 56
seas have made scientists gasp at the exquisite coral reef beauty. 69

Some reefs contain hundreds of varieties of coral. The warm and 83
clear water is ideal for the continued healthy existence of all those 97
small stony coral polyps. They are the architects of the coral reef. 111
Others who live in this ocean world are countless invertebrates and a 125
number of different species of fish. The creatures are beautiful and 139
sometimes bizarre in appearance and can be seen in almost every shape 153
and color to be imagined. Each of the tiny creatures has a different 167
and unique form of protective gear. The sea urchin is well-fortified 181
with an arsenal of rock-like, blunt spines. The lionfish exudes some 195
of the most powerful and poisonous venom in the world. The stonefish 209
is a near-perfect replica of a rock; but when an unsuspecting fish is 223
nearby, it is quickly captured by the stonefish. 233

Recently, experts have found that the Crown-of-Thorns variety of 247
starfish has endangered the coral reefs. This fish preys steadily on 261
countless coral polyps. Some experts feel that subtle changes in the 275
water temperature or minerals may have caused the influx of starfish. 289
Regardless of the cause, scientists know that the starfish presents a 303
real danger to the future survival of coral reefs. Experts hope that 317
this underwater warfare will reverse and the reefs will survive. 330

1   2   3   4   5   6   7   8   9   10   11   12   13   14

LOCATIONAL REINFORCEMENT

1 aid
2 aid kid
3 aid kid kin
4 aid kid kin tie
5 aid kid kin tie tin

6 sit
7 sit file
8 sit file kind
9 sit file kind indeed
10 sit file kind indeed inside
11 sit file kind indeed inside listened

12 diet
13 diet dine
14 diet dine dish
15 diet dine dish lien
16 diet dine dish lien link
17 diet dine dish lien link sail
18 diet dine dish lien link sail skit
19 diet dine dish lien link sail skit thin
20 diet dine dish lien link sail skit thin tile

Sentences

1 See, he is ill; his skin is thin; he feels faint. 10
2 The ill thief listened and slid his knife inside. 20
3 Enlist that inside aid that he shall indeed need. 30
4 I dislike that snide kid. He thinks it is a fad. 40

5 She is a skilled athlete and likes little detail. 10
6 The kitten is an infant and is a little lifeless. 20
7 The kid thinks I had the idea that he did finish. 30
8 He did ski that hill. That is indeed a sad test. 40

Required Activity

Session 56
Document 1
Filename:
056xxx01

Full sheet;
5 spaces
between
columns;
double-space
body.

Center
horizontally
and vertically.

DATA PROCESSING TERMINOLOGY

Relative	Printer	Magnetic
File	Disk	Terminal
Blocking	Address	Tape
Computer	Access	Data
Program	Symbolic	Random
Source	Object	Software
Read	Write	Sequential
Density	Flowcharting	Laser

Optional Activity

Session 56
Document 2
Filename:
056xxx02

Full sheet;
6 spaces
between
columns; double-space body.

Center
horizontally
and vertically.

CITIES WITH OVER 100,000 TELEPHONES

Akron	Albuquerque	Amarillo	Atlanta
Austin	Baltimore	Boston	Calgary
Canton	Charlotte	Chicago	Cleveland
Dallas	Dayton	Detroit	El Paso
Flint	Gary	Halifax	Houston
Indianapolis	Las Vegas	London	New York
Omaha	St. Louis	Seattle	Tampa

SESSION 57 TABLES

WARM-UP

Lines 1–5 once
Lines 1–5 again

1 The grim golfers merged on the driving range by the lagoon.

2 The large gray barge surges and swings against the bridges.

3 Green grapes and grapefruit grow in the good, grassy grove.

4 That guard is anguished as he argues with a fatigued guest.

5 Gail likes the technology of biology, geology, and ecology.

Lines 6 and 7 once
Lines 6 and 7 again

6 902 and 903 and 904 and 905 and 906 and 907 and 908 and 909

7 1929 30306 45317 79,320 134,332 134.76 95.35 87,369 1,370 8

1 2 3 4 5 6 7 8 9 10 11 12

INTRODUCTION TO THE QUESTION MARK

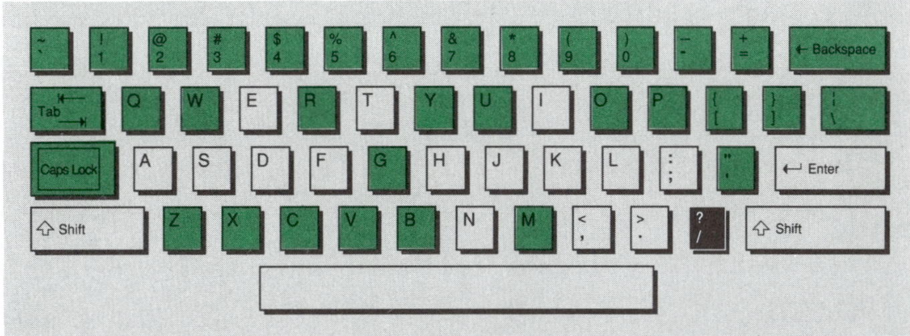

Home-row *semi* finger moves down and to the right to the *question mark* (*?*) key. Since the *question mark* is located at the top of the key, you must depress the *left shift* key before striking the *question mark*. Place both hands on the home row and practice the move from *semi* to *question mark*. Look at your hands and watch you finger make the motion. Do this several times; then look away and try the same motion.

Important: Tap *space bar* TWICE after question mark at end of sentence. (Note: If a question mark ends a line, return immediately—there is no need to tap the *space bar*.)

Line 1 once

1 `asdf jkl; ;? ;? ;? ;;; ;? ;? ;?; ?; ?; ;? ;? ;?;?`

Lines 2 and 3 once
Lines 2 and 3 again

2 `Is Jennie ahead?  Is Dennis safe?  Is Allen late?`

3 `Did Jake fall?  Did Leslie fail?  Did Jan tattle?`

Lines 4–7 once
Lines 4–7 again

4 `Is Ken late?  Is Dale fit?  Is Neil in his teens?`

5 `Did she dine?  Did the leaf fall?  Did Jane flee?`

6 `Has he landed?  Has the thief left?  Has she hit?`

7 `If Al faints, shall I still slide in the infield?`

Take two 5-minute timings on the following material. Determine your words-a-
minute rate. (Divide total words keyed by 5.)

S.I. 1.49

```
An unprecedented boom in the purchasing of house plants has been    14
taking place over the past decade.  The varieties that are prized for   28
their foliage rather than flowers have gained as favorites.  A quaint   42
vine, the familiar philodendron, was the basis of the plant boom.  It   56
was imported from the West Indies and gradually became the number one   70
house plant.  The little plants were readily available at a low cost,   84
causing a quick response from the public.  Plant lovers have expanded   98
their quest to include many varieties of rare and exotic plants.  Not  112
only are the potted ferns and palms popular, but many different kinds  126
of tropical plants are now available for home use.                     136

     Not all foliage plants are green.  Many have beautiful purple or  150
reddish leaves, while others have yellow or white markings.  Distinct  164
patterns and color combinations can be found in large numbers.  There  178
is one common trait of all foliage plants--attractive leaves.  Lavish  192
flowering plants last only a short time; foliage plants give pleasure  206
all year.  The elegant foliage plants thrive better in the houses and  220
buildings of today due to the low humidity and light levels.           232

     Plants, by tradition, have been displayed in windows.  Many more  246
creative ways range from indoor trees to handy hanging baskets.  Much  260
enjoyment will come from the greenery, but in some cases plants offer  274
ideal solutions to simple problems in home decor.  The straight lines  288
and drab contours can be softened.  Groupings of different species or  302
mass arrangements make effective displays.  It is a good idea to keep  316
sizes and shapes of individual plants in mind when choosing any plant  330
or container.  The primary focus must be on the very plant itself and  344
not on the container.  The safest selection of container is one which  358
has natural, simple lines and is neutral in color.                     368

     Plants can be identified by many methods.  Unique leaf shapes or  382
the arrangement of leaves on stems are all characteristics which help  396
identify plant types.  The leaf texture is another clue; not all leaf  410
surfaces are glossy and shiny.  Observe the texture of the leaf while  416
```

| 1 | 2 | 3 | 4 | 5 | 6 | 7 | 8 | 9 | 10 | 11 | 12 | 13 | 14 |

 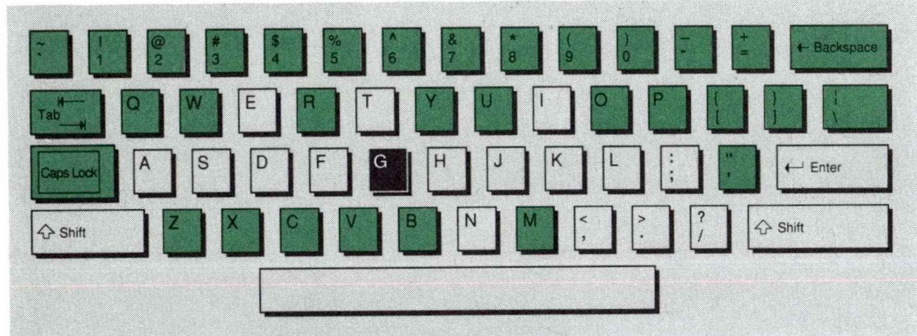

Home-row *f* finger moves to the right to the *g* key. Place both hands on the home row and practice the move from *f* to *g*. Look at your hands and watch your finger make the motion. Do this several times; then look away and try the same motion.

Line 1 once

1 f ff fg fg ff gf gf fg fgf fgf ff gg fg fg fgfgfg

Lines 2–5 once
Lines 2–5 again

2 fg gal gal gas gas get get sag sag egg egg gal fg

3 fg keg keg leg leg nag nag jig jig tag tag keg fg

4 fg gang gang gain gain Gale Gale gift gift gag fg

5 fg glad glad gate gate Gene Gene high high gas fg

Lines 6–10 once—speed
Lines 6–10 again—control

6 sign sign sing sing sang sang shag shag hang hang

7 fight fight eight eight light light tag tag night

8 again again sting sting hinge hinge egg egg glass

9 angle angle fling fling ledge ledge get get tight

10 Giant Giggle Glide Gentle Gene Gain Gift Glad Get

LOCATIONAL REINFORCEMENT

Key each line once. At end of each line, press *Enter* quickly and begin next line immediately. Then do again.

1 sag sag

2 high high

3 giant giant

4 taking taking

5 against against

6 delegate delegate

7 delighted delighted

8 flashlight flashlight

9 sightseeing sightseeing

Session 55
Document 2
Filename:
055xxx02

Half sheet;
10 spaces
between
columns;
double-space
body.

Center
horizontally
and vertically.

```
         COST OF MAINTAINING AN OFFICE

         Rent of Space                 $2,400

         Lighting                         210

         Heat                             240

         Water                             28

         Janitorial Service               900
```

SESSION 56 — TABLES

WARM-UP

Lines 1–5 once
Lines 1–5 again

1 The principal ship is equipped with a skipper on this trip.

2 A retired admiral inspired the pair with spirit and desire.

3 In spite of the waiver, Jill will win the elite quiz prize.

4 Fix the sixty mixtures and affix the prefixes to sixty-six.

5 As the pizza sizzles, the organized quiz will be continued.

Lines 6 and 7 once
Lines 6 and 7 again

6 802 and 803 and 804 and 805 and 806 and 807 and 808 and 809

7 23270 45524 89.10 5,739 91,524 7853 854.26 1,927 52,938 403

1   2   3   4   5   6   7   8   9   10   11   12

Timed Short Drills

Turn to pages TSD 1–8 (timed short-drill material) and complete the following:

1. Three 30-second timings for speed
2. Three 30-second timings for control/accuracy
3. Three 1-minute timings for speed
4. Three 1-minute timings for control/accuracy

Number Timings

Take two 30-second timings on Line 7 above.

Sentences

1 Dennis and Gene nailed a lath in the fallen gate. 10
2 The infant giggles in delight as the sled glides. 20
3 Helen had seen the elegant sign shining at night. 30
4 The endless agenda had eight legal details added. 40
5 The kitten tangled that tinsel. She disliked it. 50

□□□□1□□□□2□□□□3□□□□4□□□□5□□□□6□□□□7□□□□8□□□□9□□□1 0

6 Kale and Allan ate a salad and a fig and a steak. 10
7 Gina, the gentle giant, giggled at Tina, the elf. 20
8 Dad needs a light flashlight if he skis at night. 30
9 Leslie sang a jingle as she dashed ahead in glee. 40
10 Al tested his stiff ankle. He gnashed his teeth. 50

□□□□1□□□□2□□□□3□□□□4□□□□5□□□□6□□□□7□□□□8□□□□9□□□1 0

WHAT IS A KEYBOARDING ERROR?

A keyboarding error is an error that affects the document being keyboarded. The error need not affect the reading of the document and may be very minor in nature. On the other hand, a keyboarding error *can* have a drastic effect on the document. Consider the result of transposing two numbers (keying $19 instead of $91). Below is a listing of common keyboarding errors. Your instructor may point out additional errors or tell you to disregard items he/she does not consider as errors.

COMMON KEYBOARDING ERRORS

- Misspelling words
- Transposing numbers
- Placing two spaces between words or numbers
- Placing a space before a punctuation mark
- Failing to capitalize a proper noun or the first word of a sentence
- Capitalizing a word in a sentence that should not be capitalized
- Placing too many spaces after a punctuation mark or between paragraphs
- Using improper left, right, top or bottom margins
- Failing to indent properly
- Failing to be consistent in vertical spacing
- Using incorrect punctuation

MASTERY SOFTWARE

If you are using the software that accompanies this text, you should key all *paragraph* material using "wordwrap." Do not press Enter at the end of a line. Continue keying the next line. The software will control the length of each line by "wrapping" complete words to a new line.

3. Also note the location of the first character of the second column—this will be the tab setting for that column.

4. Delete the centered line. Then set the left margin and tab stop(s) as noted in Steps 2 and 3 and begin keying the first line of the tabulated information.

MASTERY SOFTWARE

When keying tables that are checked by the software, follow these steps:

1. Use the *F6* automatic centering feature to center headings and subheadings.

2. Use the Alternate Procedure for horizontal centering above to set your left margin and tab stops.

   Example:

   - Key *LTD Landau123456Continental*.

   - Press *F6* to center this line.

   - Note the location of the first character in the centered line (*L*). This will be the left margin setting for the table.

   - Note the location of the first character of the second column (*C*). This will be the tab setting for that column.

   - Press *Home* to return the cursor to the left margin. Press the *Delete* key to delete the centered line. Make sure that all spaces and characters have been deleted.

   - Press *F7* and set your new left margin and tab stop. Make sure all old tab settings have been deleted.

   - Key the first column of the table (*Chevelle*) at your new left margin.

   - Press the *Tab* key to move to the second column (*Prelude*).

CAPITALS OF SELECTED STATES   (all caps)

(ts)

Montana	Helena
Arizona	Phoenix
South Dakota	Pierre
Kansas	Topeka
New Mexico	Santa Fe
Minnesota	St. Paul
Wisconsin	Madison
Tennessee	Nashville
Pennsylvania	Harrisburg
Hawaii	Honolulu

(ds)

(10 spaces between columns)

Timings

Key once at controlled rate.

Take a 1-min. timing. Take another 1-min. timing.

If you finish before time is up, start over.

Key once at controlled rate.

Take a 1-min. timing. Take another 1-min. timing.

1 An idle lad finishes last. He is shiftless as he   10
sits and tells his tales. He needs an insight in   20
the elegant things in life.   25

2 Allan is attaining a skill in legal defense. The   10
giant task is thankless. He insists that all the   20
details heighten his thinking.   26

SESSION 6 — REINFORCEMENT SESSIONS 1–5

Push for SPEED

or

Drive for ACCURACY

The purpose of this session is for you the student to practice your keyboarding skills. You should approach this session with a desire to determine where you are in the skill development process and with a willingness to work to improve your speed and accuracy.

The material below has been word counted for 20-, 15-, and 10-second drills (look to the right of the lines). After determining which length timing you will be taking, go down that column of figures and select the rate that you think you can "average" a minute. Then key the line to the left of that figure. If you complete the line before time is up, it means that you averaged *at least* that many words a minute. Then go to the next line—which is longer—and attempt to complete it before time is up. Repeat the procedure until it is impossible for you to complete the line before time is up.

Remember: Be sure that you are looking at the correct time column.

Follow this procedure:

1. For *speed,* let your fingers fly and really "push" to finish the line before time is up. Don't worry about errors.

2. For *accuracy,* attempt to finish the line and have no more than one error before proceeding to the next longer line.

Speed Push

Lines 1–8 once

	20	15	10
1 A lank ant ate.	9	12	18
2 The sail is stained.	12	16	24
3 Dale ate that stale fish.	15	20	30
4 Dan and Jane hid in that shed.	18	24	36
5 That Ted is a tease and a sad fake.	21	28	42
6 Ski the hills and skate at the fine lake.	24	32	48
7 The sleet sent Jane and Sean in the tall tent.	27	36	54
8 The tank seat fit as if it had a snag in the side.	30	40	60

the left margin and tab stops(s) should be set. Refer to Session 33.

After determining the vertical placement of a table, center the title heading in all capital letters and triple-space below. You are now ready to determine where the left margin and tab stop must be set for horizontal placement. Assume you are going to key the following table:

MAJOR AUTOMOBILES

Chevelle	Prelude
Nova	Mustang
Firebird	Sunbird
Seville	Continental
Integra	Camaro
Probe	Celica
LTD Landau	Impala
Civic	Accord
Taurus	Audi Fox
Maxima	Cavalier

To determine placement of the left margin and tab stop:

1. Select the *guideline* in each column. The guideline is the longest entry in the column. In the example above, the guidelines would be:

   LTD Landau   Continental

2. Determine the number of blank spaces to leave between columns. (*Remember:* It is usually best to leave between 5 and 10 blank spaces). In this example, use 6.

   LTD Landau   Continental
             [123456]

3. Tab over to the center point of the paper. Remove the existing tab stop at the center—you do not need it any longer.

4. Using the guidelines and 6 blank spaces, backspace *once* for every *two* characters and spaces in the material.

   LT D La nd au 12 34 56 Co nt in en ta X

5. Set the left margin at this point.

6. To set the tab stop in the proper location, space forward *once* for each character and space in the first column and the blank spaces between columns.

   LTD Landau123456

7. Depress the *tab set* key.

8. Return to the left margin and begin keying the first line.

Alternate Procedure

If you are using a computer and your software package features automatic centering, you could follow these steps to determine the left margin and tab stops for keying tabulated information.

1. Key the guidelines for all columns, including the spaces between columns, as one centered line.

2. Note the location of the first character in the centered line—this will be the left margin setting for the table.

Accuracy Drive

<table>
<tr><td>Lines 1–8 once</td><td></td><td></td></tr>
</table>

1 Design the jig.   9 12 18

2 A dentist hesitated.   12 16 24

3 The gaslight is settling.   15 20 30

4 Essential thinking is gallant.   18 24 36

5 The legal delegate shall legislate.   21 28 42

6 The shifting seedling shed is settling.   24 32 48

7 His flashlight is hanging in the jet infield.   27 36 54

8 That dashing defendant enlisted in the nineteenth.   30 40 60

□□□□1□□□□2□□□□3□□□□4□□□□5□□□□6□□□□7□□□□8□□□□9□□□1 0

Check Your Skill

That gallant knight led the detail. A tall, thin 10
lad assisted at the flank. The knight failed the 20
task and feels the defeat. A sadness sifts in as 30
his shield falls.   33

□□□□1□□□□2□□□□3□□□□4□□□□5□□□□6□□□□7□□□□8□□□□9□□□1 0

Assessing your Skills

Determine the number of words and number of errors for each timing taken on the previous paragraph. The material provided on this page and the following two pages is to be used for additional practice on the keys that you have learned. There are no instructions in the left margins. Use the drills as follows:

1. If you have mastered the keys and do not hesitate when keying any letter, and you did not have an excessive number of errors (your instructor will tell you the maximum number of errors for an acceptable timing), you may proceed to the next session on page 22.

2. If you have not mastered the reach to a key(s) (you hesitate before striking the key), key the lines identified as
   a. balanced-hand words
   b. letter combinations

3. If you made an excessive number of errors, key the lines identified as
   a. double-letter words
   b. longer words

4. If you are not able to key as rapidly as you would like, key the lines identified as balanced-hand words.

After determining what you need to work on, continue building speed or accuracy.

Key once at controlled rate.

Take a 1-min. timing.

If you finish before time is up, start over.

Take another 1-min. timing.

MORE PRACTICE

HESITATE?

TOO MANY ERRORS?

NOT FAST ENOUGH?

1. Tables may be single-, double-, or triple-spaced.
2. A simple table consists of a heading(s) and two or more columns of material.
3. There is a triple space between the title heading and the body.
4. There are usually 5 to 10 blank spaces between columns.

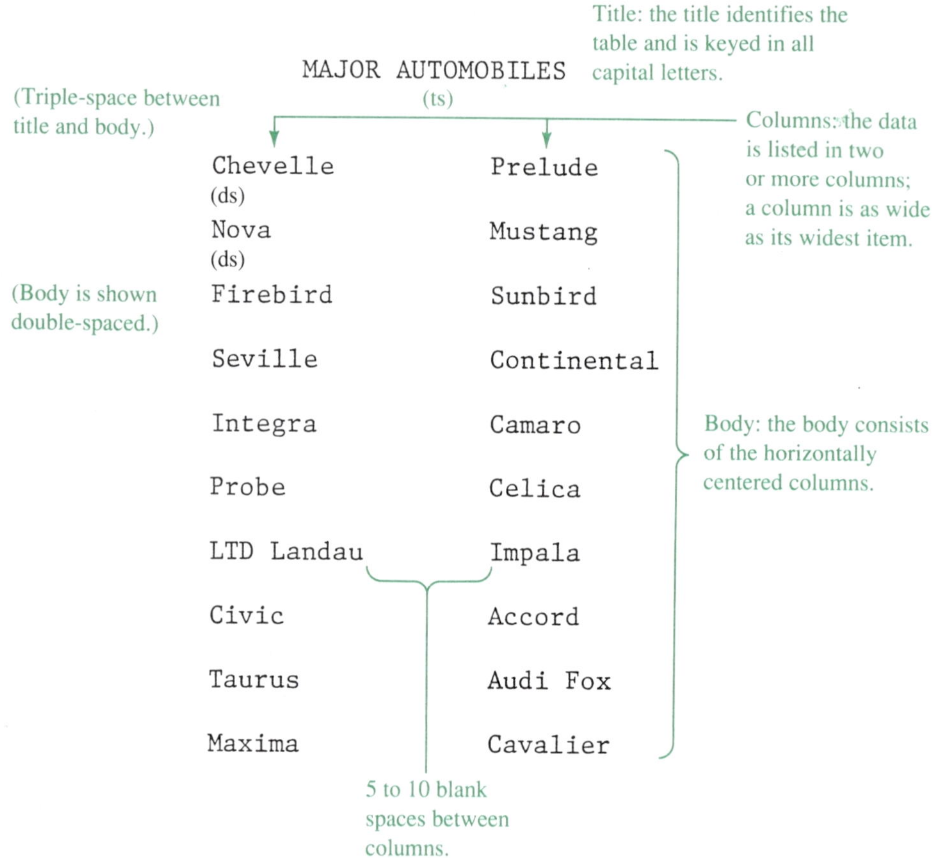

Title: the title identifies the table and is keyed in all capital letters.

(Triple-space between title and body.)

(Body is shown double-spaced.)

Columns: the data is listed in two or more columns; a column is as wide as its widest item.

Body: the body consists of the horizontally centered columns.

5 to 10 blank spaces between columns.

Machine Preparation—Typewriters

To prepare the machine for keying a table:

1. Set the paper guide at 0.
2. Move the left margin to the left as far as it will go.
3. Move the right margin to the right as far as it will go.
4. Clear all tab stops.
5. Set a tab stop at the middle of the page (12-pitch: 50; 10-pitch: 42).
6. Insert a piece of paper so that the top edge is at the line of writing.

Vertical Centering

The counting method of vertical centering that you learned earlier is to be used. Refer to Session 35 if you need to review.

Horizontal Centering

Many software packages allow the keyboarder to key tabulated information quickly, since the program can calculate and set tabs to align columns of information. However, it is always good to know how to determine horizontal placement without using automatic features. On the electric typewriter, the keyboarder must determine horizontal placement manually. Study the following to determine where

Balanced-Hand Words

1 and the ant sit ale elf end hen she end sigh sign
2 aid fit sit did tie die dig fig and the hang then
3 halt than hand lens lake lane then than sign fish
4 idle lens lane sigh then dish disk sign half lake
5 shake snake title aisle angle fight handle island
6 angle sight digit gland eight slant height sleigh
7 signal giant tight an he if it and elf the and he

Double-Letter Words

1 see glee needs indeed feeling needless teens seed
2 egg sell sniff haggle falling eggshell stall eggs
3 eel keen sheen needle fiddles seedling sleek deed
4 add kiss stiff assist endless lifeless still hill

5 fee need sheet seeing dissent likeness steed heel
6 add fell skill allied skilled settling shell tell
7 see feel teeth indeed gallant sledding sleet knee
8 all hall shall little install knitting stall tall

9 Sadness is a feeling I assess as an alleged need.
10 Assist the skiing attendant and lessen all falls.
11 Did the sleek kitten flee the illegal attendants?
12 Haggling is a senseless dissent that is needless.
13 Flatten the stiff fiddle and install the tassels.

Longer Words

1 endless athlete flatten inflated install disliked
2 lenient distant delighted heading inkling digital
3 A lenient athlete has inflated the flattened keg.

4 hesitating likeness indefinite alkaline initiated
5 heightened stealing gaslight lengthened delegates
6 The hesitating delegate is stealing the gaslight.

7 landslide skinflint stateside essential legislate
8 negligent lightness sightless delighted attendant
9 tasteless steadfast defendant thankless seashells
10 Seashells in the landslide delighted a skinflint.

Take one 3-minute timing on the following material. Determine your words-a-minute rate. (Divide total words keyed by 3.)

S.I. 1.49

```
      Groups of waterfowl fly thousands of miles north every spring to   14
the same breeding ground.  During the autumn, as all of their species    28
have done, they fly southward to winter in woody, hot marshes.  Is it     42
instinct, habit, or some other unknown mechanism in their brains that     56
forces their flight southward?  Whatever the cause, a large number of     70
species do follow the same flight pattern each year during migration.     84
The birds make the exact same stopovers, nesting areas, and winter in     98
warm marshes exactly as did their parent group.  This distinct flight    112
pattern can be observed year after year.                                 120

      Routine behavior by birds is actually predictable and does cause   134
some observers to wonder if all birds do have an instinct or merely a    148
habit.  Canadian Geese have long-established nesting colonies in many    162
places where they have not nested for years or decades.  Perhaps, the    176
changes in nesting areas are chiefly due to the fact that humans have    190
altered and changed nesting grounds to such an extent that many birds    204
are too frightened to return to the familiar grounds.                    215
```
□□□□1□□□□2□□□□3□□□□4□□□□5□□□□6□□□□7□□□□8□□□□9□□□10□□□11□□□12□□□13□□□14

PRODUCTION

A large amount of the information processed in business consists of numerical data. Because of the very nature of this type of data, it is often difficult and impractical to present it in sentence and paragraph form. Most readers prefer numerical data presented in *table* form. A table is a combination of centering and tabulation. An attractive and readable table is usually centered vertically as well as horizontally on either a full or half sheet of paper.

Letter Combinations

1 de den dead deal desk denial dense deft dental de
2 di dig dish dial digest dislike dine dike disk di
3 I dislike the heat dial that fits the dental fan.

4 fi fish final fine finish fight find fig field fi
5 ga gal gas gag gale gait gallant gasket gadget ga
6 Gal, finish the gasket that the gas gadget needs.

7 ha hate hassle halt hall half hash hang handle ha
8 ki kite kiss kindle kilt kiln king kink kitten ki
9 That hanging kite tail hassles the halted kitten.

10 le lest left lead lend ledge least leaf lessen le
11 li lid lie lied lien link linking linkage like li
12 At least link the left lid and lessen the length.

13 sa sad sat safe sake sale said sang Sal saline sa
14 si sit site sitting signal sighted sill silken si
15 Sad Sal sang a signal as she sighted a safe site.

16 st stead still steal steadiness stateside stag st
17 ta tag talk take tall tale taste task tan tall ta
18 Steadfast Stell still talks and tells tall tales.

19 te tea test tenth tell tend teen tennis tenant te
20 th then that than thing this theft thin thesis th
21 Then that teen tenant, Ted, did a tenth tea test.

Check Your Skill

Now that you have had many opportunities to work on building your skills, go back
to "Check Your Skill" on page 19 and take two 1-minute timings. Compare the rate
you just keyed with your very first attempt. Has your speed improved? Do you
have fewer errors? If you need additional practice, repeat the appropriate lines to
build speed or accuracy.

WARM-UP

Lines 1–5 once
Lines 1–5 again

1 To enact that epic opera, one is required to erect scenery.

2 Erase the errors and enter the correct equity in the entry.

3 A reunion banquet may reunite Beulah with her feuding sons.

4 A few extra blazers are needed to stop the freezing breeze.

5 That shrewd boxer exhaled deeply; are his eyes glazed, too?

Lines 6 and 7 once
Lines 6 and 7 again

6 702 and 703 and 704 and 705 and 706 and 707 and 708 and 709

7 11201 1316 14037 22304 3405 4506 34607 5703 78092 1415 6817

Timed Short Drills

Turn to pages TSD 1–8 (timed short-drill material) and complete the following:

1. Three 30-second timings for speed
2. Three 30-second timings for control/accuracy
3. Three 1-minute timings for speed
4. Three 1-minute timings for control/accuracy

Number Timings

Take two 30-second timings on Line 7 above.

Straight-Copy Timings

Take two 1-minute timings on the following material.

S.I. 1.47

The hard times and severe economic problems which were a part of   14
the early thirties affected all circuses. More circuses had to close   28
their doors than ever before. The yearning and the need for exciting   42
entertainment, however, still lingered in the hearts and minds of the   56
people. It is true that the modern circus is usually held in a large   70
arena or building and some of the old atmosphere is missing. But, an   84
element of excitement and fun lives on. The music, the cotton candy,   98
the animals, and the performers carry on a fine tradition.   110

WARM-UP

Lines 1–3 once
Lines 1–3 again

1 fi fish final fine finish fight find fig field fi

2 At least link the left lid and lessen the length.

3 th then that than thing this theft thin thesis th

INTRODUCTION TO P

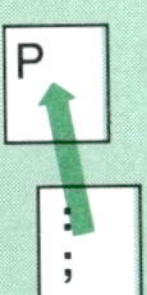

Home-row *semi* finger moves up and to the left to the *p* key. Place both hands on the home row and practice the move from *semi* to *p*. Look at your hands and watch your finger make the motion. Do this several times; then look away and try the same motion.

Line 1 once—speed

1 ; ;; ;p ;p ;p ;; p; p; p; ;p; ;p; ;; pp ;p ;P;P;P

Lines 2–5 once—speed
Lines 2–5 again—speed

2 ;p pan pat pea peg pen pep pet pie pig pin pit ;p

3 ;p ape apt dip gap hip lap nap pad sap tap tip ;p

4 ;p deep flap gape help jeep keep leap page lip ;p

5 ;p ship tape pink skip slap taps gaps pest sap ;p

Lines 6–10 once—speed
Lines 6–10 again—speed

6 pail pill pain pine pale pest past page plan pile

7 plight paddle peddle pellet planet pet pie peddle

8 depend splash splint elapse happen pen nip staple

9 napkin pledge appeal please dispel peg nap plight

10 Peasant Pennant Pitfall Patient Pheasant Pleasant

LOCATIONAL REINFORCEMENT

Key each line once. At end of each line, press Enter quickly and begin next line immediately. Then do again.

1 gasp gasp

2 leap leap peak peak

3 snap snap tape tape pile pile

4 spank spank spike spike aspen aspen

5 depend depend splint splint dispel dispel

6 splash splash happen happen sapling sapling

Session 54
Document 1
Filename:
054xxx01

Key as bound
multiple-page
manuscript with
headings.

Note: Page break
is for Mastery
Software users.

(ALL CAPS)

Office MANUALS

Purpose. (ts)

More and more offices are preparing and utilizing office manusals. (ds) There are many reasons why a firm would develop office manuals. (sh)

Information. (ts)

The manual usually is developed to share pertinent facts and basic information with all employees. (ds) Valuable supervisory time is saved because initial instructions to new employees need not be repeated. The new worker can read the manual carefully and refer back to it if necessary.

The printed manual is available to all employees at any time. This allows the employees to know exactly the areas of his or her responsibilities and duties.

Advantages and Disadvantages. (ts)

As with any printed information, the use of office manuals has both advantages and disadvantages. (ds)

Advantages (ts)

Publicizing the advantages of an office manual will make it much easier for employee acceptance. (ds)

Saves money. Using a printed office manual saves money because supervisory time is not taken up with endless repetitions of instructions. // (page break)

Eliminates errors. If an employee has a question about prcedure and the supervisor isn't available, he or she can refer to the manual promptly before a costly error is made.

Disadvantages (ts) Costly to produce. (ds) In some cases, the manual can be quite costly to produce. There will have to be time spent in the development of the manual, and employee time is a financial cost. The cost of printing and binding the manual must also be considered.

Lines 1–10 once—speed
Lines 1–10 again—control

1 Is that dashing pink paint in the shapeless pail? 10

2 Please appease that helpless, pleading plaintiff. 20

3 A sheep passed the pines and plants in the sleet. 30

4 A tall, split, peeling aspen sapling is diseased. 40

5 His pastel napkin keeps dipping in his apple pie. 50

□□□□ 1 □□□□ 2 □□□□ 3 □□□□ 4 □□□□ 5 □□□□ 6 □□□□ 7 □□□□ 8 □□□□ 9 □□□ 1 0

6 Did Jake pass that fast jeep in his pastel sedan? 10

7 Pat speaks and pleads and defends the plaintiffs. 20

8 The patient is in pain; his left thigh is gashed. 30

9 Did Jane tape that splint and dispense the pills? 40

10 The spaniel has fleas and needs his skilled help. 50

□□□□ 1 □□□□ 2 □□□□ 3 □□□□ 4 □□□□ 5 □□□□ 6 □□□□ 7 □□□□ 8 □□□□ 9 □□□ 1 0

ADDING AN *-ed* OR *-ing* ENDING

GENERAL GUIDELINES

There are exceptions to every general guideline. If you are in doubt, consult a recent dictionary.

Remember: The vowels are ***a, e, i, o u*** (and sometimes ***y***). All other letters are consonants.

1. Words ending in a silent ***e***: drop the ***e*** and add the ending.
   Example: tape—taping, taped

2. Words ending in a consonant with ***one*** vowel before the final consonant: double the final consonant and add the ending.
   Example: tap—tapped, tapping

3. Words ending in a consonant with ***two*** vowels before the final consonant: simply add the ending.
   Example: dream—dreamed, dreaming

4. Words ending in two or more consonants: simply add the ending.
   Example: rest—rested, resting

DRILL

Key each word and add an ***-ed*** and an ***-ing*** to it.

lean	fake
pet	pass
dip	fade
date	hate

Take one 3-minute timing on the following material. Determine your words-a-minute rate. (Divide total words keyed by 3.)

S.I. 1.49

```
        Reclining in the cabin of a luxurious airliner gives most people   14
one of the finest experiences in life.  Flying is the quickest way to       28
travel a long distance from one location to another.  In two or three       42
hours you can travel a distance by air that would require fourteen or        56
more hours of driving via car.  You can fly from the Pacific Coast to        70
the Atlantic Coast in a little over five hours.  The exact, same trip        84
by car would take you days of exhaustive driving.  If your goal is to        98
enjoy the varying scenery that stretches between the coasts, you will       112
definitely want to drive.                                                   117

        If you have never had the opportunity to glide through the skies    131
at a very high rate of speed, you might be somewhat nervous or appre-       145
hensive about your very first flight.  Rest assured--flying is always       159
safer than driving your own vehicle from your garage to school, work,       173
or on a shopping trip.                                                      177

        Traveling via the fantastic jet airplane is the fastest and most    191
economical way to travel for a person--if the distance traveled is at       205
least two hundred miles.  If two or more individuals will be covering       219
less than five hundred miles, travel by car will be considerably more       233
economical.  If the distance is over one thousand miles, traveling by       247
jet airplane is the fastest way to go and is usually considered to be       261
more economical.                                                            264
```
▢▢▢▢1▢▢▢▢2▢▢▢▢3▢▢▢▢4▢▢▢5▢▢▢▢6▢▢▢▢7▢▢▢▢8▢▢▢▢9▢▢▢10▢▢▢11▢▢▢12▢▢▢13▢▢▢14

PRODUCTION

Progress Check

You have now completed the activities related to manuscripts for the Basic-Level Productivity Module. It is time to determine how quickly you can key the production document task.

Key the following document as quickly as possible, correcting all errors. You want the document to be "mailable." In other words, when you finish the document, it will be completely correct—containing no errors.

Home-row *f* finger moves up and to the left to the *r* key. Place both hands on the home row and practice the move from *f* to *r*. Look at your hands and watch your finger make the motion. Do this several times; then look away and try the same motion.

R

Line 1 once—speed

1 f ff fr fr fr ff rf rf fr frf frf ff rr fr fr frf

Lines 2–5 once—speed
Lines 2–5 again—speed

2 fr red rag rid ran rig rip are ear rat sir her fr

3 fr air per era ire jar far par ark fir tar rap fr

4 fr rain rare real rink rake rage rear ripe rip fr

5 fr trap prep near girl pair dare rate rail sir fr

Lines 6–10 once—speed
Lines 6–10 again—speed

6 trip rest tree ring hire fire hard earn dirt fair

7 reign range raise ridge rinse risks art jar right

8 stare there their after pride tired far her press

9 green greed dress large heart after ran fir eager

10 Refrain Repress Release Retreat Resident Register

INTRODUCTION TO TAB KEY

The first line of a paragraph is usually indented five spaces. As explained below, set a tab stop for the indention.

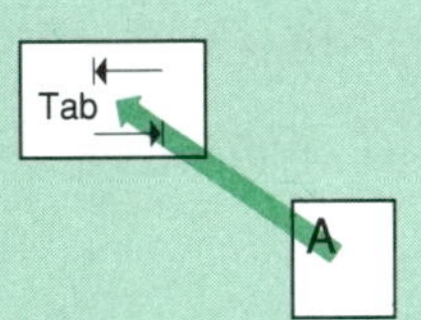

Home row *a* finger moves up and to the left to the *tab* key. Place both hands on the home row and practice the move from *a* to *tab*. Look at your hand and watch your finger make the motion. Do this several times; then look away and try the same motion.

On the Microcomputer

Each software package has its own set of instructions for setting tab stops. See your instructor for directions on your specific package.

MASTERY SOFTWARE

If you are using the software that accompanies this text, the tab settings are preset for you by the software for Sessions 1–30.

WARM-UP

Lines 1–5 once
Lines 1–5 again

1 He enlarged the unlisted analysis of the enlisted men only.

2 The agent insisted that none of the nouns need be censored.

3 A nurse insisted that a ransom note was inserted in a menu.

4 The frenzied inventor unwisely unpacked the bronzed handle.

5 The convicts invaded and conquered a convoy and ran onward.

Lines 6 and 7 once
Lines 6 and 7 again

6 602 and 603 and 604 and 605 and 606 and 607 and 608 and 609

7 416941 83201933 516386143 5113818 8542201 33790 1 2368791 2

　□□□□1□□□□2□□□□3□□□□4□□□□5□□□□6□□□□7□□□□8□□□□9□□□10□□□11□□□12

Timed Short Drills

Turn to pages TSD 1–8 (timed short-drill material) and complete the following:

1. Three 30-second timings for speed
2. Three 30-second timings for control/accuracy
3. Three 1-minute timings for speed
4. Three 1-minute timings for control/accuracy

Number Timings

Take two 30-second timings on Line 7 above.

Straight-Copy Timings

Take one 1-minute timing on the following material.

S.I. 1.46

Planning flower displays is a time-consuming but rewarding task.　14

For example, a mass of brilliant colors and textures could brighten a　28

dark corner or highlight darker foliage and shrubs. Some annuals are　42

better suited for border planting or edging. Others which grow quite　56

tall can be used for unique backgrounds or screening. There are many　70

annuals that make gorgeous bouquets of cut flowers. The gardener can　84

enjoy the fruits of his or her labor with vases of beautiful blossoms　98

placed all around the house.　104

　□□□□1□□□□2□□□□3□□□□4□□□□5□□□□6□□□□7□□□□8□□□□9□□□10□□□11□□□12□□□13□□□14

On the Electronic Keyboard

Depending on the keyboard, it may be necessary for you to obtain specific directions from your instructor. Some electronic keyboards have a function key that allows you to set the paragraph indention. Any tab function that follows will have to be set individually.

With the help of your instructor, determine the capabilities of your keyboard, and practice the procedure until you are proficient.

On the Electric Typewriter

To move the element to a particular position automatically, locate on your machine:
1. The *tab* key
2. The *tab clear* and *set* keys

To Clear Existing Tab Stops
1. Return the element to the left margin.
2. Depress *tab* key.
3. If the element stops before reaching the end of the line scale, there is a tab stop already set in the machine. To remove, push *tab clear* key. Continue this procedure until you have removed all existing tab stops.

To Set Tab Stops
1. Return the element to the left margin.
2. Move the element to desired point on line scale.
3. Push *tab set* key. Continue this procedure until you have set all required tab stops across your sheet of paper.
4. Return the element to left margin; depress *tab* key. The element should move to desired stopping point.

Timings

1   Jane prepares legal papers and letters. She prefers reading ledgers and graphs. It is tiring and drains her.   23

2   If Dan falters at the start, he is risking a defeat. The stern referee sees the sprinters and stresses fairness and praises spirit.   27

3   Print the paragraph in large letters. Raise the title and delete the diagraphs. Insert three fresh phrases at the end.   25

4   It is all right if Dane repairs that rattle. It is a danger and a threat. Perhaps the gear is sheared. He repairs tenders and engines.   28

Session 53
Document 2
Filename:
053xxx02

Following the instructions given here, key this table of contents for a bound manuscript with a 1 to 1-1/2-inch left margin.

MASTERY SOFTWARE

Use margins of 6 and 66.

Set tabs to align divisions. Refer to page 230.

(Space once after the last letter; determine if you are ready to key on an even- or odd-numbered space; begin all other "leader" lines on the same kind of numbered space. Note that the "leaders" are aligned vertically.)

TABLE OF CONTENTS   (Key on line 13; line 7 with Mastery Software.)

(Begin at left margin.)   (ts)

Acknowledgments iv

                                        (Key at right margin.)

List of Tables v

Chapter   (Can also be identified as "Section.")   Page

    I.   Introduction 1

        A.   Importance of American History 1

        B.   Settlers Move West 3

        C.   American Society 4

   II.   Review of Literature 6

        A.   1776 – 1876 6

        B.   1876 – 1956 8

        C.   1956 – 1988 10

  III.   Findings 13

   IV.   Summary and Recommendations 19

            (Note that roman numerals are right-justified.)

        A.   Summary 19

        B.   Recommendations 21

Bibliography 23

(Leaders help the reader's eyes move to the right to page number.)

READING ABILITY / By / Raymond Shepek / L.E. 690, Section 07 / Improvement of Reading / M/W/F/, 7:00 p.m. / Mrs. B. Leslman / Current Date

Session 53
Document 3
Filename:
053xxx03

Key as a title page.

<table><tr><td>THINKING DRILL</td><td>Adding an -ed or -ing ending</td></tr></table>

Remember the guidelines. If you have forgotten them, refer to page 23, or consult a dictionary if in doubt.

Remember: The vowels are *a, e, i, o, u* (and sometimes *y*). All other letters are consonants.

Key each word and add an *-ed* and an *-ing* to it.

sail	sip	relate
nap	seat	arrest
line	pin	resign
nip	dash	retire
peel	sprint	parade

WARM-UP

Lines 1–3 once
Lines 1–3 again

1 `asdf jkl; de fr ft fg jn jh ki k, l. ;p ;: ;? AJ:`

2 `and the and the and then and that and then and s;`

3 `I ran fast; I ran the sideline; he ran past fast;`

INTRODUCTION TO M

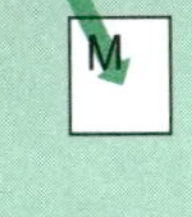

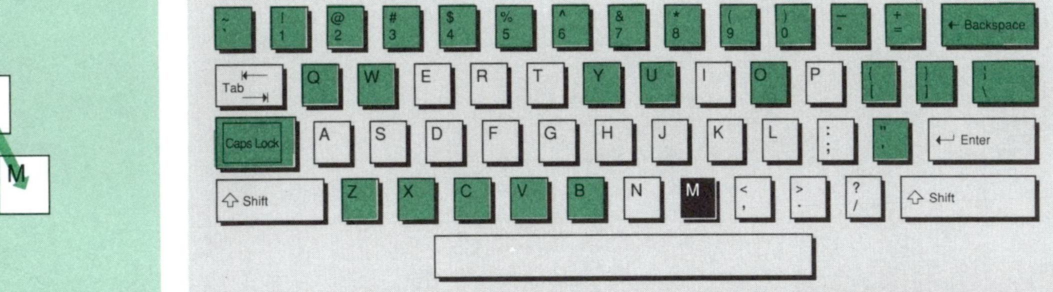

Home-row *j* finger moves down and to the right to the *m* key. Place both hands on the home row and practice the move from *j* to *m*. Look at your hands and watch your finger make the motion. Do this several times; then look away and try the same motion.

M

Line 1 once—speed

Lines 2–5 once—speed
Lines 2–5 again—speed

1 `j j jm jm jmj jmj jm mj jm mj jj mm jm mm jm jmjm`

2 `jm me me dim dim elm elm aim aim arm arm am am jm`

3 `jm am am him him man man mad mad jam jam me me jm`

4 `jm farm farm time time mean mean mail mail him jm`

5 `jm make make same same them them meet meet dim jm`

Session 53
Document 1
Filename:
053xxx01

Title Page

Using the
guides given
here for line
placement, key
this title page.
Be careful to
center each line
horizontally for
a bound manu-
script with a
1-1/2-inch left
margin.

**MASTERY
SOFTWARE**

Use margins of
6 and 66.

(Key on line 12; line 6 if you are using the Mastery Software.)

```
                    OFFICE MANUALS
```

(Key on line 32; line 26 Mastery Software.)

```
                          By
```

(Key on line 34; line 28 Mastery Software.)

```
                      John Smith
```

(Key on line 54; line 48 Mastery Software.)

```
          O.A. 417, Section 01
          Administrative Management
              T/Th, 2 o'clock
               Dr. Johnson
```

(Key on line 58; line 52 Mastery Software.)

```
               Current Date
```

6 seem seem miss miss made made game game mate mate
7 might might metal metal dream dream ram ram small
8 admit admit smile smile limit limit mad mad smash
9 theme theme remit remit stamp stamp gem gem ample
10 Mashed Mean Mailed Minted Melted Makes Melt Might

LOCATIONAL REINFORCEMENT

Key each line once. At end of each line, press *Enter* quickly and begin next line immediately. Then do again.

1 I see him.
2 He made me miss.
3 His name is Mr. Marris.
4 That farmer is smart this time.
5 She might feel this is a familiar item.

Key lines 6–10 once. At end of each line, press *Enter* quickly and begin next line immediately. Then do again.

6 I see her.
7 She made me miss.
8 Her name is Mrs. Harris.
9 That stamp is minted this time.
10 She might mail this theme if desired.

Sentences

Lines 1–10 once—speed
Lines 1–10 again—control

1 Mike is making a frame; he needs ample sandpaper. 10
2 The meat manager made a simple remark and smiled. 20
3 Did Mamie transmit the message after amending it? 30
4 Sandman, the fine farm animal, had a marked limp. 40
5 Pam had made a malt that had milk and mint in it. 50

6 Add ample stamps and mail the letter at midnight. 10
7 The fireman attempted an immense task and missed. 20
8 Did Sammie eliminate all mistakes in the message? 30
9 Jim, is that smashed metal mass a damaged helmet? 40
10 Minne missed the main message as her mind dimmed. 50

Take one 5-minute timing on the following material. Determine your words-a-minute rate. (Divide total words keyed by 5.)

S.I. 1.46

One of the finest fruits on the market today is the mango, which 14
is a fruit from the tropics. Mangos are becoming more and more popu- 28
lar all over the land. The papaya is also a very good tropical fruit 42
that has lots of vitamins and is good to eat. A carambola is quite a 56
strange looking fruit. It has a waxy appearance and contains a solid 70
meat. The cherimoya, or custard apple, is shaped like a large straw- 84
berry and is green in color and oval in shape. The fruit is not very 98
attractive, but has a delicious and delicate flavor. Kiwi fruit, the 112
Chinese gooseberry, is grown in New Zealand; thus the name "Kiwi" has 126
been given to this fruit in honor of the native kiwi bird. The taste 140
is mild and quite enjoyable. 146

The celery root has an ugly appearance. The outside of the root 160
is deceiving; inside the ugly wrapping lies a great surprising flavor 174
treat for vegetable lovers. Fine Jerusalem artichokes, also known as 188
sunchokes, have lots of uses. The crispy, crunchy food has a nutlike 202
flavor and makes a great finger food. A jicama is sometimes known as 216
a Mexican or Chinese potato. The brownish vegetable looks like a raw 230
turnip. The crispy and crunchy taste treat is quite good when served 244
with a dip of some sort. 249

Although all of us seem to be creatures of habit, there is a new 263
world of eating delights right in the produce bins, waiting for us to 277
discover new taste treats. All it takes is some searching and a very 291
sincere desire to try something new. Maybe a recipe or two would add 305
to the variety of these exotic vegetables and fruits. Many cookbooks 319
contain delightful recipes with which to vary our menus. 330

1   2   3   4   5   6   7   8   9   10   11   12   13   14

PRODUCTION

SUPPORTING PARTS OF THE MANUSCRIPT

Supporting parts, or pages, of a formal manuscript include a title page and a table of contents. Methods for preparing supportive parts vary; a popular method is shown on the following page. Illustrations of each and instructions for preparing them follow.

Take a 1-min. timing on each paragraph. Your instructor may ask you to take additional timings.

Remember to set a tab stop for a five-space paragraph indent.

Unless instructed otherwise, key at a controlled rate if you are making three or more errors a minute.

If you finish before time is up, start over.

1. The minimal marks alarmed Mae. She had made 10 three simple, mental mistakes in the math test; a 20 small, grim smile masked the dismal mental image. 30 She had failed the semester. 36

2. Marna smelled the simmering meat. The steam 10 permeated the air. She managed a small taste and 20 smiled. The meat and milk might help that little 30 girl and ease her pain. 35

3. As he firmed the damp earth at the tree, the 10 miser imagined he heard a small sigh. Mirages in 20 the misted marsh alarmed him. Grim fears emerged 30 as his mindless tramping faltered. 37

4. Make that simple diagram first. Then send a 10 message in the mail. Tell that salesman that his 20 latest remarks made the manager mad. The meeting 30 impaired the imminent merger. 36

Timed Short Drills

Turn to pages TSD 1–8 (timed short-drill material) and complete the following:

1. Three 30-second timings for speed
2. Three 30-second timings for control/accuracy
3. Three 1-minute timings for speed
4. Three 1-minute timings for control/accuracy

Number Timings

Take two 30-second timings on Line 7 on the previous page.

Straight-Copy Timings

Take one 3-minute timing on the following material. Determine your words-a-minute rate. (Divide total words keyed by 3.)

S.I. 1.49

When guests visit our homes, most of us enjoy the experience. A 14
preparation period preceding a visit is not so enjoyable. Usually, a 28
thorough cleaning and polishing is in order, along with planning good 42
meals for the guests. The entire family labors to prepare their home 56
for the expected guests. Excitement mounts as the magic time for the 70
arrival of the guests draws nearer. Sometimes, the waiting will seem 84
like an eternity. After the guests have arrived, there is usually an 98
excited hustle and bustle as the unpacking chores are done. Everyone 112
can then settle down for a friendly chat to catch up on all events at 126
a leisurely pace. A welcome guest is one who tries not to intrude in 140
established family routines. Guests might assist, whenever possible, 154
with the burden of routine chores such as cooking, cleaning, or other 168
duties. If a visit is lengthy, it is traditional to send a gift or a 182
small token of thanks to the host family after the visit is over. An 196
accompanying personal note is needed to thank the host family. 208

1   2   3   4   5   6   7   8   9   10   11   12   13   14

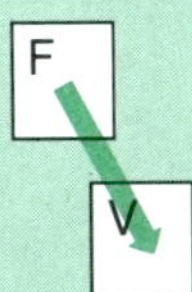

Home-row *f* finger moves down and to the right to the *v* key. Place both hands on the home row and practice the move from *f* to *v*. Look at your hands and watch your finger make the motion. Do this several times; then look away and try the same motion.

Line 1 once—speed

Lines 2–5 once—speed
Lines 2–5 again—speed

Lines 6–10 once—speed
Lines 6–10 again—speed

```
1   f f fv fv fvf fvf fv vf fv vf ff vv fv ff fv fvfv
2   fv van van vat vat vie vie via via vim vim van fv
3   fv dive dive five five give give grieve grieve fv
4   fv even even gave gave have have travel travel fv
5   fv leave leave seven seven alive alive seventh fv
6   saving saving eleven eleven selves selves divided
7   shelve shelve invite invite savage savage adverse
8   private private deliver deliver veteran even even
9   prevail prevail seventh seventh arrival vane vane
10  Negative Negative Seventeen Seventeen Advertising
```

THINKING DRILL	Double Letters

Each of the following words is spelled incorrectly. Each should have a double letter. Key each word, inserting the needed letter.

arest	stemed
pasing	smeled
maner	meting
imense	midle
hamer	dimer

3. The first line of a bibliographical entry is keyed at the left margin. All other
    lines of that entry are indented five spaces (hanging indention).

4. The title "Bibliography" is centered on line 13. Triple space after the title.

<table>
<tr><td>**DRILL E**</td><td>Key the following bibliography.</td></tr>
</table>

BIBLIOGRAPHY (line 13)

(ts)

Armes, Jane, E. J. James, and Betty Jane Onis. <u>Secretarial</u>
     <u>Systems</u>. Cincinnati, Ohio: Poston, Inc., 1989.

(ds)

Dane, Deborah. "The Rising Cost of Record Storage." <u>Management and</u>
     <u>Money</u>. April, 1989, p. 52.

Holbreck, Judy L. and Vincent T. Marcus. <u>Problems in Record</u>
     <u>Storage</u>. Dayton, Ohio: Western Publishing Company, 1989.

Onis, George. <u>Control in the Office</u>. Chicago, Illinois: A-Z
     Publishing Company, 1989.

Prentis, Richard A. and James E. Johnson. <u>Clerical Systems</u>.
     Dallas, Texas: Weston Publishers, 1986.

"Speed and Quality in Handling Workflow." <u>Office Systems</u>. Vol. 29,
     No. 3, January, 1983, p. 4.

Wilson, James. <u>Using Your Skills</u>. New York: Creative Enterprises,
     1989.

White, Ben and Vera Riles. <u>Filing, Retrieving, and Safekeeping</u>.
     Denver, Colorado: Mountain Air Printing Company, 1989.

WARM-UP

Lines 1–5 once
Lines 1–5 again

1 The champion jumper complained as he stomped from the camp.

2 Cam camped among the remnants of an old chimney for months.

3 The warmth and teamwork of the comrades might make enemies.

4 The smug musician was immune to the muttering and mumbling.

5 That whimsical hamster is amusing as it munches many meals.

Lines 6 and 7 once
Lines 6 and 7 again

6 502 and 503 and 504 and 505 and 506 and 507 and 508 and 509

7 6401 7483 9456 3529 5934 2635 4705 8932 6485 1956 2 9871 88

   □□□□1□□□□2□□□□3□□□□4□□□□5□□□□6□□□□7□□□□8□□□□9□□□10□□□11□□□12

Key each line once. At end of each line, press *Enter* quickly and begin next line immediately. Then do again.

1 save saved saving
2 rave raved raving
3 serve served serving
4 shave shaved shaving
5 vanish vanished vanishing
6 travel traveled traveling
7 prevail prevailed prevailing
8 varnish varnished varnishing
9 preserve preserved preserving
10 validate validated validating
11 ventilate ventilated ventilating
12 aggravate aggravated aggravating

Sentences

Lines 1–10 once—speed
Lines 1–10 again—control

1 That traveler arrived in a lavish, private plane. 10
2 Seven silver vases vanished at the evening event. 20
3 Did Van ever deliver the varnish and the shelves? 30
4 Vinnie lives in the villa; it has a vast veranda. 40
5 It is evident; the vital lever reverses the vent. 50

6 The rival divers tried varied dives in the river. 10
7 Val, deliver that vast velvet divan this evening. 20
8 Marvia served vanilla malts at the private event. 30
9 The driver has a grave fever; give him a vitamin. 40
10 The starved vandal evaded five vigilant servants. 50

Timings

Take a 1-min. timing on each paragraph. Your instructor may ask you to take additional timings.

Unless instructed otherwise, key at a controlled rate if you are making three or more errors a minute.

If you finish before time is up, start over.

1   Traveling in this vast native land is a near 10
marvel. The savage rivers and varied paved miles 20
are impressive. Vivid sights revive the mind and 30
lift spirits. Villages reveal veiled vestiges; a 40
dividend is derived. 44

Prepared Guide Sheet

1. Insert paper into machine; count down to line 48. Key the number 12 three spaces from the left edge of the paper.

2. Single-space and key the number 11; continue this procedure, keying down to the number 1. When completed, your guide sheet should look like the one illustrated here:

3. When ready to begin keying your manuscript, place the guide sheet under a clean sheet of paper and insert both into the machine. After completing approximately two-thirds of the page, begin to watch for the numbers appearing through the paper in the left margin. *Remember:* You want to allow three blank lines for *each* footnote, plus an additional blank for the divider line.

BIBLIOGRAPHY

1. A bibliography is a formalized listing of all the books, magazines, and other sources used in your report. The listing is placed at the end of the paper. The information given in a bibliographical entry contains the same facts as the footnote but it is arranged somewhat differently. The rules for the endnote bibliography are the same as for the footnote bibliography with the exception of the addition of page numbers.

```
Joynter, Louise R. Living Values.  Denver, Colorado:  Marchant
     Press, 1983.
```

Note: Author's last name is listed first.
Second line is indented normal paragraph indention (so the author's name is very apparent to the reader).
Parentheses are not used to enclose the facts of publication.
Page numbers are not included in the footnote bibliographical entry unless the publication is part of a larger work, such as a magazine or newspaper article.

The format for bibliographical entries that is used in this book is one of the more common styles. Other authors, institutions, and individuals may require a slightly different format. Consult your instructor or a style reference manual for further details.

2. Entries in the bibliography are listed alphabetically, according to the author's last name. If there is no author information (such as for a magazine article or newspaper article), key as indicated below:

```
"Time Marches On."  The Los Angeles Flyer.  March 10, 1983.
```

Use the word *Time* in alphabetizing.

2   Even if Gavin is vain, she has avid fans and 10
attentive friends. Her singing is sensitive; she 20
reveals her vast talent. She deserves lavish and 30
vivid praise. Her versatile verses are a massive 40
advantage and elevate her fevered fans. 48

□□□□1□□□□2□□□□3□□□□4□□□□5□□□□6□□□□7□□□□8□□□□9□□□1 0

3   Navigate the even trail in life. Derive all 10
things that are pleasant and reap the advantages. 20
Preserve the vital past and evade vile evils. An 30
avid, aggressive striving is needed in all lives. 40
A varied and diverse path prevents grief. 48

□□□□1□□□□2□□□□3□□□□4□□□□5□□□□6□□□□7□□□□8□□□□9□□□1 0

4   The vessel vanished in the savage river. An 10
adept diver salvaged several parts. Seven native 20
men assisted him. The added strength gave him an 30
advantage. He saved the silver investment. 39

□□□□1□□□□2□□□□3□□□□4□□□□5□□□□6□□□□7□□□□8□□□□9□□□1 0

THINKING DRILL	
LOOK	Look at these words: *shave village sea vase alive evening*
SELECT	Now—select the word that best answers each of the following statements. Read each statement, look at the words, and quickly key your selection.
KEY	1. What many men do each morning 2. Opposite of morning 3. Opposite of land 4. Opposite of dead 5. Another name for a small town

2. As you are keying the body of the text and come to material that will require a footnote, roll the paper up until you come to the warning pencil mark. Roll the paper back down three single spaces and make another mark. Then roll the paper back to your last line and resume keying. Follow this procedure for each reference you key that must be footnoted.

3. When you come to the last pencil mark that you made (the first one you will come to), stop keying, single-space, insert a divider line, double-space and indent, and begin keying the first line of the first footnote.

OUR PAPER HIGHWAY

Records

The storing of valuable documents and records has had a place in history almost from the beginning of time. Even then, early man sought to find a way to preserve and keep important records of his existence. As buying and selling evolved, the need to keep important records of business transactions also grew. Throughout history, records storage and retrieval has become an exciting and rather new career field.

Importance of Records Storage

Because of added productivity and correspondence of businesses of today, the sheer volume of paperwork has increased beyond one's wildest imagination. Business records take up more space than any other single item and more money is paid out for salaries and equipment than for any other single item.[1] Not only has the need for additional space become critical, but the cost of maintaining the records system has risen.

One expert indicated that if trends continue, the cost of filing just one document could rise to ten cents.[2] The problems increase, since one file drawer can hold only a certain number of items. Not only do the records take up precious space, but the need for higher salaries and equipment soars. Quite obviously, any time or effort spent by office

---

[1] Judy L. Holbreck and Vincent T. Marcus, Problems in Record Storage (Dayton, Ohio: Western Publishing Company, 1984), p.2.

[2] Deborah Dane, "The Rising Cost of Record Storage," Management and Money (April, 1983), p. 52.

WARM-UP

Lines 1–3 once
Lines 1–3 again

1 asdf jkl; de fr ft fg fv jn jm ki ;p ;? ;: fv fvf

2 eleven even save give travel leave five sensitive

3 The eleven travelers arrived at the lavish haven.

Lines 4–6 once
Lines 4–6 again

4 Negative Negative Seventeen Seventeen Advertising

5 Vinnie lives in the villa; it has a vast veranda.

6 The starved vandal evaded five vigilant servants.

INTRODUCTION TO O

Home-row *l* finger moves up and to the left to the *o* key. Place both hands on the home row and practice the move from *l* to *o*. Look at your hands and watch your finger make the motion. Do this several times; then look away and try the same motion.

Line 1 once—speed

1 l l lo lo lol lol lo ol lo lo ll oo lo ll lo lolo

Lines 2–5 once—speed
Lines 2–5 again—speed

2 lo do for hop log one old not off pot son golf lo

3 lo go too one oil ego odd top sod ton rot horn lo

4 lo no host moan more good roll hope joke floor lo

5 lo of loan knot post love from done vote stood lo

Lines 6–10 once—speed
Lines 6–10 again—speed

6 order prove among noise loose store flavor inform

7 along avoid drove prior other toast option oppose

8 stove movie shove floor front stole region reform

9 polite proper report remove lesson shovel opinion

10 Endorse Diamond Another Visitor Develop Insertion

Planning for Footnotes

When keying the final copy of your manuscript, you must determine when to stop keying the body of the text on a particular page in order to allow enough room to include the divider line and the footnotes required for that page. Follow this general rule: leave three blank lines for each footnote and one additional blank for the divider line.

To key a divider line, single-space after the last line of the body.

```
xxxxxxxxxxxxxxxxxxxxxxxxxx
__________________
```

The divider line is 18 spaces long for 12-pitch (elite), 15 for 10-pitch (pica) (1-1/2"); use the *underscore key*.

```
1
 xxxxxxxxxxxxxxxxxxxx
xxxxxxxxxxxxxxxxxxx.

2
 xxxxxxxxxxxxxxxxxxx
xxxxxxxxxxxxx.
```

Footnote Placement—Microcomputers

Many software packages have the capability of allowing the user to key the footnote at the time the superscript is keyed in the text. Consult your user manual to determine the procedures if your software package has this capability. You also need to determine which keys are to be used to tell the computer that the footnote number should be a superscript.

If you are using a software package that does not provide for footnote placement, you should refer to the line count display to estimate where to end the page of text. It is relatively easy to move lines of text to the next page to allow room for footnotes if you have not estimated correctly.

Footnote Placement—Typewriters

If you are using a typewriter, you should consider two common methods used for judging footnote placement on a page: (1) use of pencil marks in the margin, and (2) use of a prepared guide sheet.

Pencil-Mark Method

1. Before inserting paper, place a small, light pencil mark in the left margin approximately six lines (1 inch) from the bottom of the page.

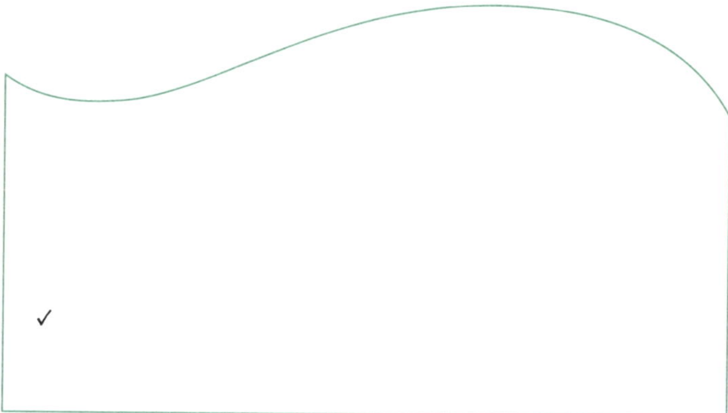

LOCATIONAL REINFORCEMENT

1 Deliver
2 Deliver melons
3 Deliver melons and
4 Deliver melons and onions
5 Deliver melons and onions to
6 Deliver melons and onions to the
7 Deliver melons and onions to the renovated
8 Deliver melons and onions to the renovated hotel.

Sentences

Lines 1–10 once—speed
Lines 1–10 again—control

1 He does not fool me; he is not an honest senator. 10
2 Ora ordered the onions and olives from the store. 20
3 That old man stooped among the roses and groaned. 30
4 The golden moon shone on the old prison rooftops. 40
5 The soft fog floated aloft over the lone trooper. 50

6 Someone noted the stolen passport photos at noon. 10
7 The senior pilot spotted an airport in the gloom. 20
8 Jo dropped the looped rope at the rodeo and lost. 30
9 A violent storm moved along the remote oak grove. 40
10 Did the florist remove the thorns from the roses? 50

Timings

Take a 1-min. timing on
each paragraph. Your
instructor may ask you to
take additional timings.

Unless instructed other-
wise, key at a controlled
rate if you are making
three or more errors a
minute.

If you finish before time
is up, start over.

1   It is good to have honest goals. Nothing is 10
gained if one goes forth in pointless roaming. A 20
major effort is needed to prosper. Isolate those 30
foolish errors and avoid them. Hold to a strong, 40
firm hope and move along. 45

DRILL C

Key each of the following footnote examples. Concentrate on inserting the quotation marks, superior numbers, and other punctuation marks in the proper position.

Book
(one author)

[1]Arthur J. Strage, <u>Healthy Dogs</u> (Dallas, Texas: Marston Printing Company, 1989), p. 110.

Book
(two authors)

[2]Marvel E. Star and Ann Smith, <u>Grooming Your Dog</u> (Denver, Colorado: Allison Publishers, 1989), p. 86.

Magazine Article
(author named)

[3]Olive T. Hearthic, "The Shame of Our Dog Population," <u>Dogs Today</u> (March 1988), p. 267.

Magazine Article
(no author named)

[4]"Trends in Dog Management," <u>Dog World</u> (January 1989), pp. 267-72.

Report

[5]Raymond R. Zich, <u>The Problems of Our Canine Society Today</u> (Madison, Wisconsin: Dane County Veterinarian Society, 1989), p. 39.

Interview

[6]Interview with Dr. Claude Davis, Veterinarian, Nelson, Nebraska, February 28, 1988.

Editor of
Collection

[7]Hiram P. Quick, ed., <u>Dogs and Cats</u> (New York: Marshall and Hines Publishing Company, 1989), p. 123.

Newspaper
Article

[8]Janell R. Dart, "The World Is Not Going to the Dogs," <u>Otis Flyer</u> (May 9, 1989), p. 4, col. 2.

Personal
Correspondence

[9]Dr. Phillip McKenzie, March 3, 1989, personal correspondence.

DRILL D

From the following information, key a correct footnote for each item.

1. Twenty-Nine Ways to Please Customers--Barker Review (magazine) by Ms. Gladys Fox. Appeared in the March, 1983 issue on page 29.

2. Book--Exciting Sales Techniques by J. R. Scott. Published by Winston Royal Pub. Co. in Havertown, New Jersey in 1984. Taken from page 14.

3. Interviewed Dr. Allie Joy in May, 1983 at her home in Denver, Colorado.

4. Book by Joanne Dowl and Kenneth Eden. Title: Will Friday Never Come? Published in 1983 by the Fridley Pub. Co. in Dallas, Texas. Quoted information on pp. 196-200.

5. Quoted from the Sept. 19, 1983, issue of the San Jose Independent newspaper, page 17, column 3.

2   Floss shook in terror as the tornado stormed 10
along the shore. The radio droned on foretelling 20
doom and gloom. The phone popped in her ear as a 30
torrent of rain fell. Alone in the lone mansion, 40
her fear overtook her for a moment. 47

░ ░ ░ ░ 1 ░ ░ ░ ░ 2 ░ ░ ░ ░ 3 ░ ░ ░ ░ 4 ░ ░ ░ ░ 5 ░ ░ ░ ░ 6 ░ ░ ░ ░ 7 ░ ░ ░ ░ 8 ░ ░ ░ ░ 9 ░ ░ ░ 1 0

3   Ron is fond of opera. The golden tones of a 10
violin smooth his tense nerves. Visions arise in 20
his mind as the viola responds to the mood. Soft 30
tones float in the air as the piano renders notes 40
of dimension and diversion. 45

░ ░ ░ ░ 1 ░ ░ ░ ░ 2 ░ ░ ░ ░ 3 ░ ░ ░ ░ 4 ░ ░ ░ ░ 5 ░ ░ ░ ░ 6 ░ ░ ░ ░ 7 ░ ░ ░ ░ 8 ░ ░ ░ ░ 9 ░ ░ ░ 1 0

4   Oatmeal is often a good food to eat. Add an 10
orange, hot toast, and milk to a morning meal for 20
digestion. It is important to eat in the morning 30
to avoid tension. Restore vim and vigor at noon; 40
do not overeat. 43

░ ░ ░ ░ 1 ░ ░ ░ ░ 2 ░ ░ ░ ░ 3 ░ ░ ░ ░ 4 ░ ░ ░ ░ 5 ░ ░ ░ ░ 6 ░ ░ ░ ░ 7 ░ ░ ░ ░ 8 ░ ░ ░ ░ 9 ░ ░ ░ 1 0

THINKING DRILL	
LOOK	Look at these words:
	Senator envelope sirloin opened editor airport
SELECT	Now—key each sentence below, using one of the words to fill in the blank.
KEY	1. The __________ of the paper resigned.
	2. __________ James remained in the state to vote.
	3. Fold the letter and insert it in the __________.
	4. The __________ ramp is not long or large.
	5. Lots of people like __________ steak.
	6. Rain pelted into the __________ door.

3. Interviewed Dr. Allie Joy in May, 1983 at her home in
    Denver, Colorado.

4. Book by Joanne Dowl and Kenneth Eden. Title: Will Friday
    Never Come? Published in 1983 by the Fridley Pub. Co. in
    Dallas, Texas. Quoted information on pp. 196-200.

5. Quoted from the Sept. 19, 1983, issue of the San Jose
    Independent newspaper, page 17, column 3.

6. Office Equipment (book)--edited by Mark Nelson, published by
    Ralsten Publishers, Inc., in 1983--location, Des Moines, Iowa.
    Material quoted from p. 397.

7. Used quote from p. 86 in March issue of Times & Trends maga-
    zine in article entitled Dynamic Decorating--no author given.

8. Report by Jane Green, Office Issues & Trends, put out by
    New York Office Managers Association, New York City, in 1983,
    page 46.

9. Letter received from Mayme Goldstein dated 8-16-84.

The Footnote System

1. Footnotes are used to tell your reader the exact source of your quoted material
   and where additional information can be found.

2. The formats for keying footnotes can differ slightly, depending on which
   reference book is used. Choose one method and be consistent throughout the
   entire manuscript. One of the most accepted formats is used in this text. Generally, a footnote must include the following:

   Author, title, facts of publication (place, publisher, date), page on which you
   found the information.

   Example:

   [1]James L. Johnson, <u>All You Wanted to Know About the Moon</u>
   (Tucson, Arizona: Minute Publishing Company, 1989), p. 117.

3. Footnotes are numbered in order to prevent confusion about sources. Notice that
   the number is raised from the rest of the line. (This is known as a ***superior*** or
   superscript number.) Many software packages have both superscript and
   subscript capabilities.

   To key this raised number when using a typewriter:

   a. Move the *line finder* toward you and roll the cylinder toward you slightly
      (about one-half line).

   b. Key the number.

   c. Push the *line finder* back and return the cylinder to its original line.

4. ***Remember:*** Titles of poems, short stories, chapters, essays, and articles in
   magazines are enclosed in quotation marks. Titles of books, newspapers, and
   magazines are underscored or keyed in all capitals.

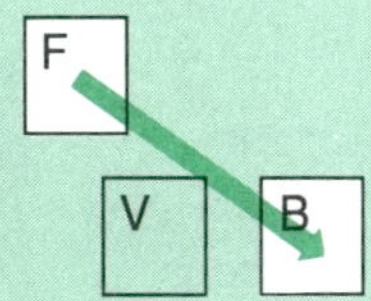

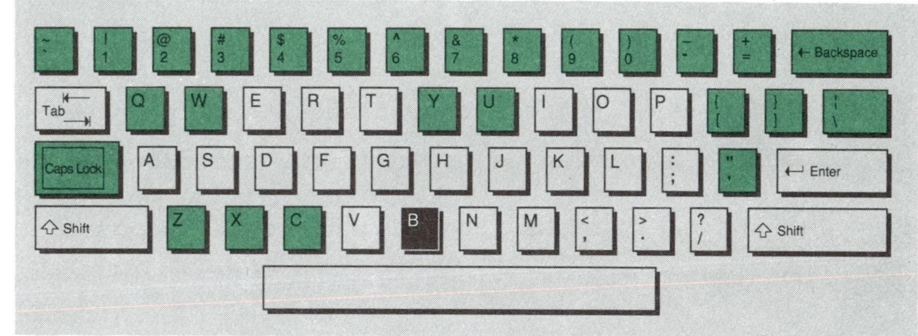

Home-row *f* finger moves down and to the right to the *b* key. Place both hands on the home row and practice the move from *f* to *b*. Look at your hands and watch your finger make the motion. Do this several times; then look away and try the same motion.

Line 1 once—speed

1 f f fb fb fbf fbf fb bf fb fb ff bb fb ff fb fbfb

Lines 2–5 once—speed
Lines 2–5 again—speed

2 fb bad bag ban bar bat bed bee beg Ben bet bid fb

3 fb be bid big bit Bob bop dab mob lob job limb fb

4 fb bank barb lamb best bake bank bear bite rob fb

5 fb bald best bias herb book bend able brag rib fb

Lines 6–10 once—speed
Lines 6–10 again—speed

6 libel fiber broil amber begin labor label algebra

7 bread bingo label brave alibi blast debit vibrate

8 barter member harbor banker ballot border benefit

9 verbal emblem better before absorb absent tremble

10 Alphabet Basement Neighbor Remember Remarkable Be

LOCATIONAL REINFORCEMENT

Key lines 1–6 once. At end of each line, press *Enter* quickly and begin next line immediately. Then do again.

1 bad bag bat

2 bail bait bake

3 badge barge baste

4 banish banker basket

5 bandage bailiff barrage

6 baseball bailment barefoot

Key lines 7–12 once. At end of each line, press *Enter* quickly and begin next line immediately. Then do again.

7 beg bed bet

8 beat belt beef

9 beast berth beard

10 behalf bedlam behave

11 believe belated bearing

12 befriend bearable behavior

> Dr. Davis has emphasized the importance of early training of the young puppy. . . .
>
> It is clear that there continues to be an overwhelming need for control of our animal population, according to recent sources.
>
> The <u>Otis Flyer</u> has reported that only 20 percent of the animal population is really neglected.
>
> "Although you may find this strange to believe, there are no cures for the deadly bacteria found in dogs' ears during the month of August."

The Endnote System

The endnote system for referencing notes places the complete source information in a bibliography at the back of the paper. The abbreviated note that is placed in the text refers the reader to the bibliography if more information is desired. This system is easy to key. *Remember:* Before keying a paper, always determine which style of referencing will be required.

Use the following procedure to key the endnote method of referencing:

1. Space once following the quoted material and key the author's last name, date of publication, and page number enclosed in parentheses.

   Example:

   ```
   . . . and equipment" (Holbreck:1989:2).
   ```

2. Do not put any source note information at the bottom of the page; continue keying the text material down to the point where there are 6 to 9 blank lines at the bottom of the page (1 to 1-1/2-inch margin).

3. If you should have more than one publication by the same author(s) with the same publication date, use *a, b, c,* and so on, to let the reader know which publication in the bibliography is being referenced.

   Example:

   ```
   (Holbreck and Marcus:1989a:2)     (listed first in bibliography)
   (Holbreck and Marcus:1989b:16)    (listed second in bibliography)
   (Holbreck and Marcus:1989c:118)   (listed third in bibliography)
   ```

4. If a publication has no author, use the title instead for the endnote reference and bibliography.

DRILL B

From the following information, key a correct endnote entry for each item.

1. Twenty-Nine Ways to Please Customers--Barker Review (magazine) by Ms. Gladys Fox. Appeared in the March, 1988 issue on page 29.

2. Book--Exciting Sales Techniques by J. R. Scott. Published by Winston Royal Pub. Co. in Havertown, New Jersey in 1989. Taken from page 14.

(continued on next page)

Sentences

1 Bev gobbled broiled beef, bread, and baked beans. 10
2 A nimble rabbit nibbles bean blossoms and blinks. 20
3 Debbi observed a brash bandit robbing a big bank. 30
4 I grabbed a dab of bread and biked to the harbor. 40
5 The bears bathed beneath the bridge in the brook. 50

6 Babe is baffled; the beverage bottles are broken. 10
7 The dark banjo is broken; he is bitter and bleak. 20
8 The big battered barrels bent the riverbed barge. 30
9 Barb babbles to her bored brother; she is a snob. 40
10 Barni, the beagle, barks and begs for a big bone. 50

Timings

1 Labor to do a noble job. Bosses like brains 10
and ambition. A blend of both brings a desirable 20
habit that boosts a beginner. A babbling boaster 30
absorbs a bore. The absent laborer blemishes his 40
possible bankroll boost. 45

2 Bif booked a berth on the battered boat. As 10
he bragged to his somber brother, the boom of the 20
harbor bells vibrated. Beneath the boasting, Bif 30
began to babble. A belated bolt of disbelief and 40
brooding stabbed at him. 45

3 Barbi is able to make edible spareribs. She 10
blends the best herbs and parboils the ribs. The 20
ribs are broiled and basted. She adds vegetables 30
and bread to the elaborate meal. The first bites 40
are a believable treat. 45

Quotations—Direct or Paraphrased

1. ***Direct Quotation***   Use quotation marks to enclose the exact words or ideas of another person whom you are quoting directly. *Note:* The source note information in the following examples is shown in the endnote format.

   Examples:

   ```
   Dane stated, "If current trends continue, the cost of filing just
   one document could rise to twenty cents" (Dane:1989:57).
   ```

   ```
   "If current trends continue," stated Dane, "the cost of filing
   just one document could rise to twenty cents" (Dane:1989:57).
   ```

2. ***Paraphrased Quotation***   In formal writing, material that has been directly quoted is enclosed in quotation marks as shown above. If you were to paraphrase (not to quote the words exactly), you would not need the quotation marks, but you must still give credit for the idea by using a source note. *Note:* The source note information in the following example is shown in the footnote format. A superior number is placed after the quote in the text of your written report; this same number is also placed at the beginning of the corresponding footnote at the bottom of the page.

   Example:

   ```
   One expert indicated that if trends continue, the cost of storing
   just one document could rise to twenty cents.¹
   ```

3. ***Quote within a Quote***   In some situations, you may have a quote within a quote. It should be keyed as follows:

   Example:

   ```
   Dane stated, "The cost of filing a document could go 'out of
   sight' if trends continue" (Dane:1989:57).
   ```

4. ***Ellipsis***   In some printed materials, you will notice a series of three evenly spaced periods (. . .), called an *ellipsis*. The ellipsis indicates that some words have been omitted from quoted material. When an ellipsis appears at the end of a statement, four periods are used.

D R I L L   A

MASTERY SOFTWARE

Key Drills A–E on the Drill Screen provided in the software.

Note: Drills can be completed in Freeform as an option.

Key each of the following statements. Concentrate on keying the quotation marks and other punctuation marks in the proper position.

```
In his latest book, Strage states, "Dogs should never be given

more food than they can eat in one sitting."

Star and Smith have said, "The healthy coat of a dog should be

shining and glowing at all times."

Hearthic has stated clearly, "There is no excuse for an unhealthy

dog in this day and age."

According to the latest information, the one leading cause of

animal neglect is human indifference.

Zich has declared that, "Nine million dogs are suffering each day

in our country."
```

(continued on next page)

4   Bo is indebted to Ben, the able banker. The 10
liberal loan is to brighten a drab sailboat. Big 20
debts are a problem to Ben, the banker. Sensible 30
debtors absolve all debts. Bo might have a habit 40
of breaking his verbal bindings. 46

□□□□1□□□□2□□□□3□□□□4□□□□5□□□□6□□□□7□□□□8□□□□9□□□1 0

THINKING DRILL

LOOK
THINK
KEY

Key as many words as you can think of that begin with:

bo   bl

bi   br

INTRODUCTION TO W

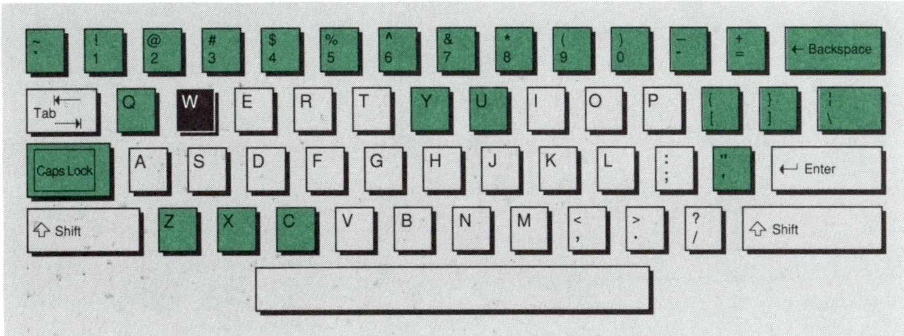

Home-row *s* finger moves up and to the left to the *w* key. Place both hands on the home row and practice the move from *s* to *w*. Look at your hands and watch your finger make the motion. Do this several times; then look away and try the same motion.

Line 1 once—speed

1 s s sw sw sws sws sw ws sw sw ss ww sw ss sw swsw

Lines 2–5 once—speed
Lines 2–5 again—speed

2 sw jaw wag raw two war wet saw hew how new sew sw

3 sw wig won few awe law wit win now owl wan web sw

4 sw down draw news town walk when twig wish dew sw

5 sw word plow west twin with swim week know now sw

Lines 6–10 once—speed
Lines 6–10 again—speed

6 white grown waist drown waken swamp elbow welfare

7 brown water twine where swell write frown awkward

8 review warmer bowler wiring inward wisdom preview

9 window follow waiver jigsaw within warmth lawless

10 Hardware Workable Followed Weakness Endowment Two

Source Note Style—Endnotes or Footnotes?

Some reference style manuals use the words *endnote* and *footnote* interchangeably. Some sources also refer to "text notes" when the note is inserted within the body of the paper. This book will use "footnote" to refer to the traditional style of using a superior (raised above the line) number in the text and the full reference listed at the bottom of the same page; "endnote" will refer to an abbreviated notation in the text and the reference listed in a bibliography at the back of the paper. Because there are several acceptable formats for footnotes and endnotes, you should determine which style is preferred by your institution and be consistent throughout your paper.

In the following examples of the sample manuscript "Our Paper Highway," the writer is quoting material from an article written by Deborah Danc entitled "The Rising Cost of Record Storage" from the April, 1989 edition of the magazine *Management and Money,* page 52; and from a book written by Judy L. Holbreck and Vincent T. Marcus, *Problems in Record Storage,* published in Dayton, Ohio, by the Western Publishing Company in 1989. Example 1 shows the endnote style of formatting research source notes. Example 2 shows the traditional footnote style.

Simplified Format (Endnote Style)

OUR PAPER HIGHWAY

The storing of valuable documents and records has had a place in history almost from the beginning of time. Even then, people tried to find a way to preserve and keep important records of their existence. As buying and selling evolved, the need to keep important records of major business transactions also grew. Throughout history, records storage and retrieval has always been an exciting and interesting career field.

Importance of Records Storage

Because of added productivity and correspondence of businesses of today, the sheer volume of paperwork has increased beyond human expectations or imagination. Business records, in spite of computerized data storage, take up more space than any other single item (Holbreck and Marcus:1989:2). Not only has the need for additional space become critical, but the added expenses of maintaining the records storage has also risen.

One expert indicated that if trends continue, the cost of storing just one document could rise to twenty cents (Dane:1989:57). The storage problem will continue to increase, as one file drawer can hold only a certain number of items. Not only do the records take up precious space, but the need for higher salaries and equipment soars. Quite obviously, any time or effort spent by office workers or any money spent by a business firm is totally wasted if the records are not really needed, or if those records cannot be easily located and retrieved

Example 1

Traditional Format (Footnote Style)

OUR PAPER HIGHWAY

The storing of valuable documents and records has had a place in history almost from the beginning of time. Even then, people tried to find a way to preserve and keep important records of their existence. As buying and selling evolved, the need to keep important records of major business transactions also grew. Throughout history, records storage and retrieval has always been an exciting and interesting career field.

Importance of Records Storage

Because of added productivity and correspondence of businesses of today, the sheer volume of paperwork has increased beyond human expectations or imagination. Business records, in spite of computerized data storage, take up more space than any other single item.[1] Not only has the need for additional space become critical, but the added expenses of maintaining the records storage has also risen.

One expert indicated that if trends continue, the cost of storing just one document could rise to twenty cents.[2] The storage problem will continue to increase, as one file drawer can hold only a certain amount of items. Not only do the records take up precious space, but the need for higher salaries and equipment soars. Quite obviously, any time or

____

[1]Judy L. Holbreck and Vincent T. Marcus, Problems in Record Storage, (Dayton, Ohio: Western Publishing Company, 1989), p. 2.

[2]Deborah Dane, "The Rising Cost of Record Storage," Management and Money, (April, 1989), p. 52.

Example 2

TAB DRILL

I	like	to	feel	good.
When	one	feels	good,	one
will	attempt	to	feel	good
at	all	times.	Shall	we
all	attempt	to	feel	good?

Sentences

1 Will Marlow wash that wool sweater in warm water? 10
2 Their nephew was a fellow bowler with the winner. 20
3 Wear a warm gown if it snows; the weather is raw. 30
4 The new lawn will grow when watered well at dawn. 40
5 Warren wiped the jeweled bowl with a white towel. 50

6 Is Win wasting water if he washes the new window? 10
7 It is wise to wire the news to the waiting woman. 20
8 The wealth of the world will not wield wiser men. 30
9 He saw few minnows swimming in the shallow water. 40
10 Widen the wooden window and rewire the two bells. 50

Timings

1   We will await the word of warning in the new 10
tower. The wise stalwart leader wants to preview 20
the writings of men of worth. He frowns on wrong 30
narrow views. We will follow wise wishes and win 40
a wearisome war and bestow a renewed foothold.   49

2   Will reviewed the written words. He did not 10
wish to show that witless newsman how shallow his 20
words were. However, he wanted to warn the world 30
of the wasted wealth in the wages of the man. He 40
showed the network the handwriting on the wall.   49

Take one 3-minute timing on the following material. Determine your words-a-minute rate. (Divide total words keyed by 3.)

S.I. 1.49

```
Many beautiful and stately elm trees which have covered our huge      14
nation for several decades are in trouble.  Spreading chestnut trees, 28
common a few years ago, no longer populate the forests of our nation. 42
The magnificent species are the victims of fungal parasites that have 56
invaded our lands.  At first, halting the diseases seemed to be quite 70
impossible, but now the prospects are excellent that the ravaging and 84
destructive blight can be arrested.  The future of both species seems 98
to look very much brighter.                                          103

    The bark disease, or chestnut blight, was first discovered on an 117
eastern site in the early nineteen hundreds.  Within but a few years, 131
the parasites had spread throughout the entire eastern coastal states 145
and damaged trees.  The Dutch Elm disease was brought into our nation 159
in the nineteen thirties.  Within a period of forty-five years, great 173
numbers of mature elm trees have been destroyed throughout the entire 187
nation.  Although the two blights are quite similar, there is a major 201
difference.  The chestnut disease can be spread by airborne spores; a 215
bird, insect, or animal can also carry the parasite.  The elm disease 229
is spread by spores also but is only carried by a species of beetle.  243

    A major hope for both types of trees remains in chemical preven-  257
tion and biological strains.  On test plots, the use of chemicals has 271
been quite successful; however, when tested in the major forest areas 285
of our land, it has not been so successful.  At this time, control of 299
the diseases seems to offer the best answer to the problem.          311
```

1□□□□2□□□□3□□□□4□□□□5□□□□6□□□□7□□□□8□□□□9□□□10□□□11□□□12□□□13□□□14

PRODUCTION

RESEARCH SOURCE NOTE PREPARATION

If you use someone else's exact words or ideas in your written manuscript, you must give that person credit for his or her ideas. To not give credit for others' ideas is called *plagiarism,* which in some cases is against the law, and in all cases is unethical. You *must* give credit to another author if you use his/her ideas.

If you quote directly or indirectly from another source, you can identify the quote by using source notes in the form of endnotes or footnotes. Footnotes are usually numbered, and both styles are prepared according to specific guidelines. In any case, you must include enough information for the reader to identify the source of the quoted material (author's name, publication data, and page numbers).

```
3        Barlow, a shrewd fellow, winked as he waited    10
in the shadows.  A whistle warned him of the slow     20
walk of his fellow worker.  As he wallowed in the     30
warmth of that workshop, Will worked in the wild,     40
blowing wind.  Barlow was worthless.                  47
```

THINKING DRILL

LOOK
SELECT
KEY

Look at the words listed below. Select a word from each list to make up a compound word. There may be more than one right answer.

ward	lash	*Example*
whip	horse	wardrobe
wind	robe	
home	down	
saw	work	
snow	mill	
team	grown	
mark	storm	
soft	ware	

Push for SPEED

or

Drive for ACCURACY

The purpose of this session is for you the student to practice your keyboarding skills. You should approach this session with a desire to determine where you are in the skill development process and with a willingness to work to improve your speed and accuracy.

The material below has been word counted for 20-, 15-, and 10-second drills (look to the right of the lines). After determining which length timing you will be taking, go down that column of figures and select the rate that you think you can "average" a minute. Then key the line to the left of that figure. If you complete the line before time is up, it means that you averaged **at least** that many words a minute. Then go to the next line—which is longer—and attempt to complete it before time is up. Repeat the procedure until it is impossible for you to complete the line before time is up.

Remember: Be sure that you are looking at the correct time column.

Follow this procedure:

1. For *speed*, let your fingers fly and really "push" to finish the line before time is up. Don't worry about errors.

2. For *accuracy*, attempt to finish the line and have no more than one error before proceeding to the next longer line.

Lines 1–5 once
Lines 1–5 again

WARM-UP

1 A dozen zesty spices are drizzling and oozing from a pizza.

2 Liza seized the magazine and zipped to the zillion zinnias.

3 The dazed czar gazed at the zillions of lizards and zebras.

4 The zodiac puzzle makes the dazzled wizard dizzy and woozy.

5 Lazy Fritz is woozy and dizzy from that crazy, zany puzzle.

Lines 6 and 7 once
Lines 6 and 7 again

6 402 and 403 and 404 and 405 and 406 and 407 and 408 and 409

7 27 821 59361 40352 89434 92035 65019 9356 693 958 3177 6071

Timed Short Drills

Turn to pages TSD 1–8 (timed short-drill material) and complete the following:

1. Five 15-second timings for speed
2. Five 30-second timings for speed
3. Five 30-second timings for control/accuracy

Number Timings

Take two 30-second timings on Line 7 above.

Speed Push

		20	15	10
1	I will see her.	9	12	18
2	There goes his fish.	12	16	24
3	Sam is a good man to see.	15	20	30
4	Babe went to town to the bank.	18	24	36
5	John does not fool me; he is there.	21	28	42
6	A big dark bear bit Ron on the left arm.	24	32	48
7	The rain and an old storm moved to the shore.	27	36	54
8	The pilot saw the bad fog float to the small town.	30	40	60

Accuracy Drive

		20	15	10
1	Repair a graph.	9	12	18
2	Deliver the diagram.	12	16	24
3	Print the dark paragraph.	15	20	30
4	The salesman made the man mad.	18	24	36
5	Mamie managed to fail the semester.	21	28	42
6	It is important that we respond to Ned.	24	32	48
7	Traveling a savage river has some advantages.	27	36	54
8	Perhaps the farmer is avoiding a terrible tornado.	30	40	60

Check Your Skill

Key once at controlled rate.

Take a 1-min. timing. Take another 1-min. timing.

If you finish before time is up, start over.

> When the winter snow thaws, warm rain washes 10
> the world. Wild flowers begin to weave in a slow 20
> swing with the wind. Whiffs of a meadow awakened 30
> swirl down at the dawn. The dew is a rainbow and 40
> twinkles as a jewel. Winter has blown onward. 49

Assessing Your Skills

MORE PRACTICE

Determine the number of words and number of errors for each timing taken on the previous paragraph. The material provided on the following two pages is to be used for additional practice on the keys that you have learned. There are no instructions in the left margins. Use the drills as follows:

1. If you have mastered the keys and do not hesitate when keying any letter, and you did not have an excessive number of errors, omit this section and proceed to Session 11.

HESITATE?

2. If you have not mastered the reach to a key(s) (you hesitate before striking the key), key the lines identified as
   a. speed push (review)
   b. speed push (balanced-hand words)
   c. speed push

2

<u>Change in Employees</u>

There also has been a dramatic change in the characteristics of office personnel throughout the years.

<u>Retiring workers</u>. Many employers feel that there just aren't enough employees to replace older, experienced workers who have retired. New workers are costly to train and sometimes just can't do the job.

<u>Lack of skills</u>. Until a few years ago, office workers could usually obtain employment directly from high school. Many office positions, however, now require more specialized training.

<u>Automated equipment</u>. Because of the development of highly automated equipment, many offices require employees with a background in electronic office systems. The new employee must be skilled in software-driven electronic systems and thoroughly understand the impact of office automation and telecommunications.

<u>Career as Office Systems Manager</u>

Because of the changes that have taken place, there is a definite need for offices to use modern techniques and scientific methods. This in turn increases the need for efficient office systems managers. The area of office management as a career can be profitable and productive. Training is available at most post-secondary schools that offer specialized courses in "office systems management."

3. If you made an excessive number of errors, key the lines identified as
   a. accuracy drive (double-letter words)
   b. accuracy drive (longer words)

4. If you are not able to key as rapidly as you would like, key the lines identified as
   a. speed push (balanced-hand words)
   b. speed push

After determining what you need to work on, continue building speed or accuracy.

Speed Push (Review)

HELPS BUILD
YOUR SPEED

```
1 asdf jkl; ;p; frf jmj fvf lol fbf sws pr mv db wm
2 p pad pan peg pen pin pit pie plan phase pledge p
3 r rap ran red rip rent rests real repels refers r
4 m ham hem men him mate mind mesh manage mandate m
5 v vat vim vet vise vent vane vigil valid veneer v
6 o oh or odd old one oaf opens omit ogle oval of o
7 b bad beg bid bop brag blend board brake better b
8 w was wed who win woe were when went where with w
9 Janell Kenneth Morris William Shanon Olan Bronson
```

Speed Push (Balanced-Hand Words)

STOPS HESITATION

```
 1 lamb blend bland blame amble emblem problem bible
 2 lap nap pen paid pane flap span pale spent dispel
 3 air pan sir risks lair heir pair hair flair widow
 4 map maid mane melt sham lame mend firm make flame
 5 vie via pair vivid pelvis disown pens laps disown
 6 fog sod oak rod foam fork form foam odor soak rod
 7 bow wig wow vow down gown wisp with wish when wit
 8 Did the lame lamb amble down to the big pale oak?
 9 The pale widow paid for the vivid gown and a wig.
10 When did Vivian mend the pair of problem emblems?
```

Accuracy Drive (Double-Letter Words)

HELPS ELIMINATE
ERRORS

```
1 slipping sipping happen flipping appease shipping
2 terriers irritates terrains follow all narratives
3 dimmer dinners hammering manners immense immerges
4 moon roof pool hood hook loot took mood root door
5 gobble rabble hobble babble pebble nibbles rabbit
6 Janell slipped the irritated terrier in the door.
7 That immense rabbit emerged and nibbled a bottle.
8 She will be shipping the poor winter winner soon.
```

Session 51
Document 2
Filename:
051xxx02

Key as bound
multiple-page
manuscript with
headings.

THE OFFICE SYSTEMS MANAGER

Need

The office scene has changed considerably over the past few years. Business has grown, more transactions are taking place, and certain incidents have occurred that require most offices of today to hire a new type of employee--the office systems manager. His or her duties mainly are to see that the office is run as efficiently as possible.

Changes

There are many exciting and new changes that have taken place in the world of offices today. Some of them are inevitable and others have been developed to replace older methods.

Financial Costs

Many businesses have tended to view the cost of operating an office as a necessary, but unproductive, evil. Executives have seen the cost of operating an office rise rapidly.

Increased paperwork. One reason costs have increased is the fact that paperwork in an office has increased dramatically. Unless the flow of paperwork is carefully controlled, costs will skyrocket.

Inflationary times. During the past ten years, the pattern of constantly rising costs has been consistent. Many businesses are forced to cut costs in every conceivable manner. The office systems manager is directly responsible for cost analysis and efficient production.

(continued on next page)

Accuracy Drive (Longer Words)

1 elephant dependent safekeeping plaintiff pipeline
2 standard registrar parenthesis telegrams resident
3 That resident registrar sends standard telegrams.

4 familiar eliminate sentimental dependent estimate
5 retrieve primitive advertising privilege negative
6 Eliminate that sentimental, familiar advertising.

7 rational tradition imagination negotiate renovate
8 ambition elaborate observation establish possible
9 stalwart knowledge handwriting wholesale whenever
10 Establish rational imagination whenever possible.

Speed Push

1 pe peg pen pest peeps peddles pellet pets peep pe
2 pi pin pie piles pills pitfall pipes pink pine pi
3 That pill peddler peddled piles of pinkish pills.

4 ra ran rap ranks rake rates raised range rapid ra
5 ri rid rip rises ripe right ridges rigid rinse ri
6 Rapid Red ran to the raised ridges on that range.

7 ma man mat math make mail marsh manager margin ma
8 mi mid mild mind mint midst might misting mire mi
9 The manager might mail the mild mints to the man.

10 va van vat vane vases vast valid varied vanish va
11 vi vie vim vise vile vine visits vital vintage vi
12 The vital vintage vases vanished from a vast van.

13 oa oak oats oath oatmeal load toad roast float oa
14 of off offers offends offset offense offensive of
15 Those offensive oats floated off of that oatmeal.

16 ba bad bag bail balk bath badge barks bandages ba
17 bl blade bleak blast blank blight blind blinks bl
18 The babe blinked at a baboon blinded in bandages.

19 wa was war wag wade wait wane wash waste waves wa
20 wi win wit wig wide wipe will wise wield wiper wi
21 Winna washed and wiped her wig; she wasted water.

2

<u>Procedure</u>
(ds)

The technique involves setting aside one cup of flour and then mixing the yeast directly into the remaining dry ingredients. Then the dry ingredients are combined with the liquid and fat heated to 125 to 130 degrees and kneaded with the remaining flour, according to literature provided by the companies.

Both firms say the fast-rising yeasts also may be rehydrated like regular yeast by dissolving them directly in water heated to 105 to 115 degrees before mixing with the remaining ingredients.
(ts)

<u>Characteristics</u>
(ds)

There are several differences between regular yeast and the fast-rising varieties.
(ds)
<u>Odor</u>. The fast-rising product gives off more yeasty odor while proofing or rising.
(ds)
<u>Foam</u>. Unlike regular yeast, the fast-rising product will not foam while proofing or rehydrating in warm water unless a little sugar is added.
(ds)
<u>Rising time</u>. Fast-rising yeast rises more quickly in warmer temperatures but also is more sensitive to temperature extremes.
(ds)
<u>Texture</u>. Breads made with fast-rising yeast have a slightly more open texture than that made with regular yeast. The resulting breads and rolls, however, don't appear to be significantly different from those made with regular yeast.

Check Your Skill

Now that you have had many opportunities to work on building your skills, go back to "Check Your Skill" on page 40 and take two 1-minute timings. Compare the rate you just keyed with your very first attempt. Has your speed improved? Do you have fewer errors? If you need additional practice, repeat the appropriate lines to build speed or accuracy.

SESSION 11	U, Z, C

WARM-UP

Lines 1–3 once
Lines 1–3 again

1 asdf jkl; sw de fr ft fg fv fb jh jn jm ki lo ;p;

2 as ask asked saw seen seem sent dare darn door is

3 and the when where this there their those gone at

Lines 4–6 once
Lines 4–6 again

4 When did Vivian mend the pair of problem emblems?

5 That immense rabbit emerged and nibbled a bottle.

6 She will be shipping the poor winter winner soon.

INTRODUCTION TO U

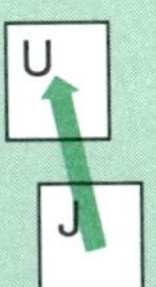

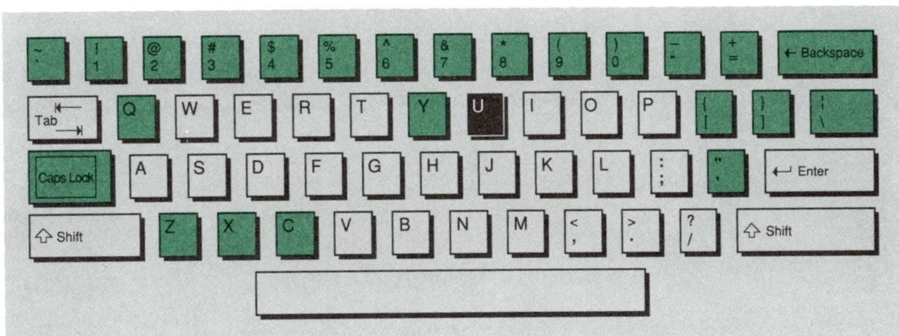

Home-row *j* finger moves up and to the left to the *u* key. Place both hands on the home row and practice the move from *j* to *u*. Look at your hands and watch your finger make the motion. Do this several times; then look away and try the same motion.

Line 1 once—speed

1 j ju ju jj ju uj jj uu juj juj ju ju juj juj juju

Lines 2–5 once—speed
Lines 2–5 again—speed

2 ju up up us us due due out out use use rub rub ju

3 ju put put sun sun fun fun mud mud gum gum sum ju

4 ju just just jump jump junk junk jug jug judge ju

5 ju rust rust sure sure turn turn pull pull but ju

Session 51
Document 1
Filename:
051xxx01

Key as bound
multiple-page
manuscript with
headings.

RISING TO THE OCCASION

Major title: center all
caps, triple-space after

(ts)

Yeast Breads

First level (major subheading): center,
capitalize major words, triple-space before
and double-space after

(ds)

Most people bake breads for the process as much as for the product. Mixing the ingredients, kneading the warm dough by the centuries-old rhythm of push-and-pull, fold-and-press, and watching it rise in a warm oven almost gives one the feeling of creating a living thing more than making something to eat.

Nearly one-third of all people who cook bake yeast breads. Of those people, nearly half are women who work outside the home, according to Syndicated Research Data. And most of that baking takes place on weekdays.

(ts)

Second level (side headings): flush left,
capitalize major words, underscore,
triple-space before and double-space after

<u>Saving Time</u>

(ds)

The nation's leading yeast producers say there's one aspect of the breadbaking process that home cooks would rather do without. That's the time it takes to let yeast dough rise. Most recipes require at least one rising of an hour or longer, and many recipes require a second rising.

Both the major yeast companies, Fleischmann's and Red Star, have come out with fast-rising yeasts that can cut in half the amount of time a home cook spends waiting for breads to rise.

The fast-rising yeasts have a finer grain than regular dry yeast. The firms say the finer grain adapts well to a quick-mixing technique that allows cooks to save additional time. // (page break)

(continued on next page)

6 duel shut gulf fund dump bulb hunt must rude true
7 build fault under usual until awful insure budget
8 vault audit rumor truth about nurse sprung refund
9 adjust endure refuge manual fourth versus publish
10 Fusion Lawful Nature Urgent Plural Module Suppose

LOCATIONAL REINFORCEMENT

Key lines 1–4 once. At end of each line, press *Enter* quickly and begin next line immediately. Then do again.

1 Sue rubbed
2 Sue rubbed the
3 Sue rubbed the furred
4 Sue rubbed the furred pup.

Key lines 5–9 once. At end of each line, press *Enter* quickly and begin next line immediately. Then do again.

5 Bud tugged
6 Bud tugged and
7 Bud tugged and lugged
8 Bud tugged and lugged the
9 Bud tugged and lugged the rug.

Sentences

Lines 1–10 once—speed
Lines 1–10 again—control

1 The guest menu featured halibut and autumn fruit. 10
2 Louis hunts for sunken ruins and hauls treasures. 20
3 Sue slumps and sulks as she slurps the sour soup. 30
4 Just be sure to return that blouse to the bureau. 40
5 That auto bumper is a hunk of junk; it is ruined. 50
    1   2   3   4   5   6   7   8   9   10

6 Buff found a huge bug on the shrub in the puddle. 10
7 A stout runner shouted and slumped to the ground. 20
8 The group hummed a rousing tune during the stunt. 30
9 Susan put tuna on a bun and built a super supper. 40
10 The pup dug around in the mud and found a peanut. 50
    1   2   3   4   5   6   7   8   9   10

PRODUCTION

MANUSCRIPT HEADINGS

Manuscripts may be prepared in numerous formats. The main purpose of headings is to call the reader's attention to the important ideas and portions of the manuscript. Companies, institutions, and individuals usually use a specific format designed for their unique use. Regardless of the format, you must be careful to be consistent throughout the document. Give careful attention to the punctuation and spacing in your report.

Traditional Format

Major title: Key on line 13 (line 7 with Mastery Software) on first page; center; capitalize all letters; triple-space after (leaving two blank lines between title and body).

First-level heading: Center; capitalize first letter of each major word; triple-space before and double-space after.

Second-level heading: Flush with left margin on separate line; capitalize first letter of each major word; underscore; triple-space before and double-space after.

Third-level heading: Indent with paragraph; capitalize only first letter or first word followed by a period; underscore; double-space before.

```
                  PROPER TELEPHONE TECHNIQUES

                             (ts)

                      The Business Image
                             (ds)
     It is widely accepted that proper use of the telephone as a

business tool is one important quality of an outstanding employee.

Most office workers spend two or more hours each day in telephone

contact with clients and customers.

          (ts)

Caller's Response
          (ds)
     A prompt answer.  Answering the telephone promptly will give

the caller
```

Major Title — (margin label)
First Level — (margin label)
Second Level — (margin label)
Third Level — (margin label)

Note: In a formal report that requires chapter headings, the format would differ slightly. Consult a reliable reference book for further details.

Simplified Format (Using Word Processing Application Programs on Computers)

The manuscript is keyed using double spacing throughout, except for the bibliography and footnote references.

Take a 1-min. timing on each paragraph. Your instructor may ask you to take additional timings.

Unless instructed otherwise, key at a controlled rate if you are making three or more errors a minute.

If you finish before time is up, start over.

1   The blunt auditor suggested to Duke that the 10
business returns were a fraud. The usual routine 20
of minimum turnovers of funds had been sound, but 30
that fortune of thousands paid to a juror had not 40
been inserted in the annual input. Duke presumed 50
he was ruined and flushed with guilt. 57

2   Ruth sulked as her aunt poured a dose of the 10
awful blue fluid. The sour stuff was supposed to 20
be used for fatigue from the flu. She paused for 30
a minute and gulped it down. Her aunt found four 40
lumps of sugar for a bonus. Sullen disgust would 50
turn into a laugh as a result. 56

3   Muffin is a genuine bulldog. Although he is 10
a plump pup, he bounds about with a flourish. It 20
is fun to see him plunge around, indulging in the 30
pure pleasure of running. He huffs and puffs and 40
slumps to the ground. No doubt, he will jump and 50
lunge again after a pause and find trouble. 59

4   Thomas bought a used auto from a true fraud. 10
Although the bumper and the trunk were ruined, he 20
assumed that it would run. If he would flush the 30
rust from the lumbering hulk of junk, he might be 40
able to use it. His woeful anguish spurred a new 50
thought; perhaps it was useless. 56

Take one 5-minute timing on the following material. Determine your words-a-minute rate. (Divide total words keyed by 5.)

S.I. 1.42

Wise managers of money seem to have the ability or the foresight   14
to make their money stretch a long way. Others spend haphazardly and   28
always seem to be short of money long before the next salary check is   42
due. What factors do the wise managers follow?   52

Food buying takes a large part of the salary check. In the area   66
of buying groceries, one can save a large amount of money by wise and   80
careful buying. There are many fine guides that a shopper can follow   94
to economize and save money.   100

Probably the one best rule to attempt, at the outset, is to plan   114
ahead. Plan all your meals in detail for a certain period--a week, a   128
month--but never day by day. After making the complete plan for your   142
groceries, you are then ready to prepare your shopping list. Be cer-   156
tain that you have included all items necessary for cooking the meals   170
to come. Many people forget to include the small items such as salt,   184
pepper, and needed condiments. Once you have made a list, additional   198
guides are very useful and helpful.   205

After making the major shopping list, you should compare prices.   219
You should look at all the local advertisements in newspapers. Quite   233
often, you will save considerable amounts of your money by comparison   247
shopping. One caution--do not waste time or money for gas by driving   261
your car from store to store. If you do this, you are defeating your   275
purpose. After deciding where to do your shopping, your next step is   289
that of doing the actual shopping.   296

1   2   3   4   5   6   7   8   9   10   11   12   13   14

INTRODUCTION TO Z

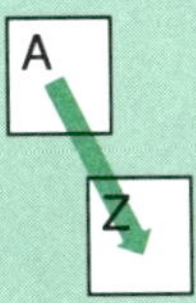

Home-row *a* finger moves down and to the right to the *z* key. Place both hands on the home row and practice the move from *a* to *z*. Look at your hands and watch your finger make the motion. Do this several times; then look away and try the same motion.

Line 1 once—speed

1 a aa az az zz za aza aza az aza az az zz aza azaz

Lines 2–5 once—speed
Lines 2–5 again—speed

2 az zig zig zip zip zoo zoo buzz buzz daze daze az

3 az fizz fizz fuzz fuzz gaze gaze haze haze zoo az

4 az jazz jazz maze maze doze doze raze raze zip az

5 az size size whiz whiz zeal zeal zest zest zig az

Lines 6–10 once—speed
Lines 6–10 again—speed

6 zing zone zoom zero blaze gauze glaze graze prize

7 seize breeze amaze razor pizza hazel zombi wizard

8 bronze wheeze frozen nozzle zipper fizzle seizing

9 freeze bazaar hazard puzzle zealot zinnia sneezed

10 Trapeze Zealous Pretzel Drizzle Horizon Embezzler

Sentences

Lines 1–8 once—speed
Lines 1–8 again—control

1 Liz seized that sizzling pizza and ate with zeal. 10

2 Hazel embezzled a zillion and has been penalized. 20

3 He authorized Zeb to organize the bronze nozzles. 30

4 The zinnias were glazed in that freezing drizzle. 40

    1   2   3   4   5   6   7   8   9   10

5 Minimize the hazard and stabilize that bulldozer. 10

6 Dozens of zealous buzzards whizzed over the zone. 20

7 Buzz gazed with amazement as Hazel won the prize. 30

8 Zeb baked a dozen pretzels in the sizzling blaze. 40

    1   2   3   4   5   6   7   8   9   10

Turn to pages TSD 1–8 (timed short-drill material) and complete the following:

1. Five 15-second timings for speed
2. Five 30-second timings for speed
3. Five 30-second timings for control/accuracy

Number Timings

Take two 30-second timings on Line 7 on the previous page.

Straight-Copy Timings

Take one 3-minute timing on the following material. Determine your words-a-minute rate. (Divide total words keyed by 3.)

S.I. 1.48

```
        Plants that have been started can also be purchased at all local    14
nursery or garden shops in the spring.  Usually, these flowers are in      28
full bloom at the period when they are offered for sale; the gardener      42
can then select the colors and kinds of plants that will look best in      56
the specific garden sites and areas.  After the flower garden bed has      70
been prepared, the gardener can simply place the fine blooming plants      84
in the earth and will have an instant garden.                             93

        Planning flower displays is a time-consuming but rewarding task.  107
For example, a mass of brilliant colors and textures could brighten a    121
dark corner or highlight darker foliage and shrubs.  Some annuals are    135
better suited for border planting or edging.  Others which grow quite    149
tall can be used for unique backgrounds or screening.  There are many    163
annuals that make gorgeous bouquets of cut flowers.  The gardener can    177
enjoy the fruits of his or her labor with vases of beautiful blossoms    191
placed all around the house.                                             197

        Growing annuals in containers has become very popular.  Creative 211
gardeners will move containers from one place to another to highlight    225
the most beautiful plants in bloom.  A movable or mobile green garden    239
allows for the maximum use of color.                                     246
```

□□□□1□□□□2□□□□3□□□□4□□□□5□□□□6□□□□7□□□□8□□□□9□□□10□□□11□□□12□□□13□□□14

Take a 1-min. timing on each paragraph. Your instructor may ask you to take additional timings.

Unless instructed otherwise, key at a controlled rate if you are making three or more errors a minute.

If you finish before time is up, start over.

1   Zeb zipped to that zoo with zest and nuzzled 10
the zebras. He sneezed in the breeze and went to 20
see the lizards. He wants to be a zoologist when 30
he gets older. He knows a zillion things and his 40
dazed and puzzled parents are amazed.   47

    1   2   3   4   5   6   7   8   9   10

2   Zelda gazed in amazement as Zip, the wizard, 10
seized a wand. It was ablaze with a maze of fire 20
and lights. He did dozens of hazardous feats and 30
puzzled all at the bazaar. He also was a trapeze 40
whiz and dazzled folks.   45

    1   2   3   4   5   6   7   8   9   10

THINKING DRILL

Set two tabs 15 spaces apart. Review general guidelines on pages 24–25 for setting tabs and on page 23 for word endings. Key the word, tab over, and key the word with an **-ed** ending; tab again and key the word with an **-ing** ending.

Remember: The vowels are **a, e, i, o, u,** (and sometimes **y**). All other letters are consonants.

	-ed	-ing
doze	*dozed*	*dozing*
graze		
waltz		
zoom		
seize		
amaze		
sneeze		
zip		

LOOK
THINK
KEY

Required Activity

Session 50
Document 1
Filename:
050xxx01

Key as bound manuscript.

Note: For Mastery Software, use default margins.

A NEW TRAVEL ADVENTURE / There is a way to travel that doesn't cost much money and uses very little energy. The only thing needed is time, a place to relax, and an imagination. This method of travel is commonly called "armchair" travel. People have been sitting at home and transporting their minds and imaginations all over the world and sometimes even into outer space simply by reading. / (Para.) / The simplest method of "armchair" travel is to sit back and relax and do a bit of daydreaming. From the age of a few years to a very old age, all of us indulge in daydreams at one time or another. Picture yourself in the one place in the world you would like to visit. What does it look like? The pictures in your mind are providing you with some armchair traveling. / (Para.) / Another method of armchair traveling is provided through reading. You can travel along many roads by reading what others have written. It can be pure fiction or a factual atlas describing the scenery. Soaring away into far-off lands using your imagination can be one of the greatest thrills ever experienced. The vivid words used to describe a unique spot on the earth can transport you beyond your wildest dreams.

Optional Activity

Session 50
Document 2
Filename:
050xxx02

Key as bound manuscript with 1-1/2-inch left margin.

EVALUATING WHAT YOU READ / Many persons have the one basic fault of believing anything that is printed. How many times have you heard someone say, "I know it is true because I read it in black and white." This someone is telling you that he or she lacks the skill to evaluate and compare what he or she is reading. / (Para.) / It is important that you make it a practice to read one or several newspapers each day. In addition, to be an effective person, you will want to read current periodicals, books, and so on. This is a "must" if you want to become an intelligent citizen. Read a variety of material and views. Too many people make the mistake of reading articles that conform only to their own view and simply ignore any other view. As you read the current information, you must try to understand what the writer is attempting to tell you. This is called comprehension. / (Para.) / After you have comprehended or understood what the writer is trying to say, the next step is to evaluate the information. Is it backed up by facts or is it merely the writer's opinion? Is the writer a respected expert on the subject? / (Para.) / The last step after comprehension and evaluation is to compare the information you have just read to other types of information. This is basic to becoming an efficient citizen in matters of politics and consumer problems and just simply becoming a knowledgeable person.

SESSION 51	MANUSCRIPT HEADINGS

WARM-UP

Lines 1–5 once
Lines 1–5 again

1 The yardarm on the royal yacht is gaudy; boycott the entry.

2 The cyclist will buy a motorcycle or bicycle on the voyage.

3 Yesterday Candy daydreamed about skydiving and hydroplanes.

4 Yes, buy the layers of yellow nylon for the sunny skylight.

5 The style of yellow nylon and vinyl is certainly very ugly.

Lines 6 and 7 once
Lines 6 and 7 again

6 302 and 303 and 304 and 305 and 306 and 307 and 308 and 309

7 21,468 38,107 48,243 1,509 5,114 15,816 6,184,377 9,608 761

1 2 3 4 5 6 7 8 9 10 11 12

INTRODUCTION TO C

Home-row *d* finger moves down and to the right to the *c* key. Place both hands on the home row and practice the move from *d* to *c*. Look at your hands and watch your finger make the motion. Do this several times; then look away and try the same motion.

Line 1 once—speed

1 d dd dc dc dc dd cc dcd dcd cd cd dcd dc dc ddccd

Lines 2–5 once—speed
Lines 2–5 again—speed

2 dc cod cat car cap can cab cut cow cup cop cue dc

3 dc card came care cast calm cask call cash cur dc

4 dc calk cane case calf camp carp cave cede cad dc

5 dc coke cord come coin coil cool corn cook ace dc

Lines 6–10 once—speed
Lines 6–10 again—speed

6 chain notch chute touch cheap since chase ancient

7 career public credit police carpet income decease

8 camera notice commit impact circle decide attract

9 compute deceive collate finance climate placement

10 Compare Produce Consult Service Council Enclosure

LOCATIONAL REINFORCEMENT

Key lines 1–5 once. At end of each line, press *Enter* quickly and begin next line immediately. Then do again.

1 The

2 The consulting

3 The consulting service

4 The consulting service produced

5 The consulting service produced income.

Key lines 6–11 once. At end of each line, press *Enter* quickly and begin next line immediately. Then do again.

6 Notice

7 Notice how

8 Notice how the

9 Notice how the camera

10 Notice how the camera attracted

11 Notice how the camera attracted attention?

PRODUCTION

Bound Manuscripts

1. A bound manuscript normally is a longer manuscript (more than three pages). It is usually placed in some type of cover or folder or stapled along the left side.

2. Because additional space is needed to allow for the left edge "binding," a minimum of 1-1/2-inch left margin and 1-inch right margin is used.

3. Because the left margin is 1/2 inch wider than the right margin, it is necessary to move the center point of the paper to the right so that it is centered within your margin settings.

4. Today, electronic printing is so exact that bound manuscripts are often printed with 1-inch margins on the left and right. New binding methods do not necessarily require the extra 1/2 inch in the left margin.

MASTERY SOFTWARE

If you key a bound manuscript with a 1-1/2-inch left margin, use a 60-space line (6 and 66) and a horizontal center point of 35 instead of 33. If the directions do not specify a 1-1/2-inch left margin, use the default margins of 1 and 66 to key bound manuscripts.

WHERE TO BUY

Most cities have several stores which carry similar, or identical types of merchandise. The people of a particular city, therefore, have a choice of stores in which to buy certain products. Several factors which may influence their decision about where to purchase are quality, style, cost and location. If two items are of the same quality and the same style, people will usually buy the item which costs less; that is, if they know which store is selling the item for less.

Most consumers depend upon advertising for information about sales and bargains. Although pricing is an important consideration, in far too many instances it becomes the only factor in a decision. The consumer forgets that there are two additional factors which must be considered along with price. These two factors are the amount of traveling time required to get to the store and the cost involved in the travel. Most people fail to recognize these added factors.

If a consumer must spend quite a bit of time traveling to the store which has the merchandise for the lowest price, travel time becomes a major consideration. How much is time worth? Each individual must answer that particular question.

The cost of travel, whether by private or public transportation, has continued to rise. Again, if the distance involved is quite far, the consumer may spend more on transportation than would be saved on a "bargain" purchase; thus he or she will not save any money.

2

The intelligent consumer must be aware of all factors involved with purchasing. Too many times the consumer considers difference in prices as only "cents" and not dollars. Yet, "cents" add up to dollars over the duration of a small period of time.

Bound Manuscript

Lines 1–10 once—speed
Lines 1–10 again—control

Sentences

1 Carlton, the cat, curled in comfort in the chair. 10
2 Can Carrie cure colds with tonic and citric acid? 20
3 A lack of ethics caused the doctor to face scorn. 30
4 Clarice recalled the basic facts of the accident. 40
5 Chris decided to purchase a record and a picture. 50

□□□□1□□□□2□□□□3□□□□4□□□□5□□□□6□□□□7□□□□8□□□□9□□□10

6 Cecelia consumed a rich chocolate ice cream cone. 10
7 The clever client could conceal crucial evidence. 20
8 Carol watched a cautious crow circle the cottage. 30
9 The wicked witch cackles as she concocts recipes. 40
10 Can Cam choose music as a classic school subject? 50

□□□□1□□□□2□□□□3□□□□4□□□□5□□□□6□□□□7□□□□8□□□□9□□□10

Timings

Take a 1-min. timing on each paragraph. Your instructor may ask you to take additional timings.

Unless instructed otherwise, key at a controlled rate if you are making three or more errors a minute.

If you finish before time is up, start over.

1   A cookout on the beach could include cheese, 10
carrots, meat sandwiches, and cold juice. If the 20
chill of the ocean is too much, hot chocolate and 30
hot coffee can chase the cold chills. The decent 40
lunch and a chat with chums can enrich affection. 50

□□□□1□□□□2□□□□3□□□□4□□□□5□□□□6□□□□7□□□□8□□□□9□□□10

2   An office clerk who lacks basic ethics could 10
become the subject of scorn. Those persisting in 20
cruel and careless attacks on certain new workers 30
can cause havoc. It is logical to follow strict, 40
concise rules concerning office tact. Choose the 50
right track and be sincere.   55

□□□□1□□□□2□□□□3□□□□4□□□□5□□□□6□□□□7□□□□8□□□□9□□□10

3   A career in science includes certain choices 10
to consider. One could choose to become a doctor 20
in a clinic or a teacher in a medical school. An 30
active search of a current college catalog should 40
indicate which courses to select. Contact campus 50
finance officers to check cost factors.   58

□□□□1□□□□2□□□□3□□□□4□□□□5□□□□6□□□□7□□□□8□□□□9□□□10

Take two 1-minute timings on the following material.

S.I. 1.45

```
To honor a deserving person in the community is a fine thing.  A    14
most interesting factor becomes apparent many times--in the ugly form   28
of jealousy for another's accomplishments.  Most people can take high   42
honor quite graciously--that is, if they were the ones to win.  Those   56
individuals who did not win may begin to hold a grudge against anyone   70
who was a winner.  When something like a community honor causes deep,   84
hard feelings on the part of some people, it becomes an empty prize--   98
the winner may be the loser.  The spirit of honors and awards must be   112
one of generous and living happiness.                                   119
```

☐☐☐☐1☐☐☐☐2☐☐☐☐3☐☐☐☐4☐☐☐☐5☐☐☐☐6☐☐☐☐7☐☐☐☐8☐☐☐☐9☐☐☐10☐☐☐11☐☐☐12☐☐☐13☐☐☐14

Take two 3-minute timings on the following material. Determine your words-a-minute rate. (Divide total words keyed by 3.)

S.I. 1.48

```
If you have never had the opportunity to glide through the skies    14
at a very high rate of speed, you might be somewhat nervous or appre-   28
hensive about your very first flight.  Rest assured--flying is always   42
safer than driving your own vehicle from your garage to school, work,   56
or on a shopping trip.                                                  60

Traveling via the fantastic jet airplane is the fastest and most   74
economical way to travel for a person--if the distance traveled is at   88
least two hundred miles.  If two or more individuals will be covering   102
less than five hundred miles, travel by car will be considerably more   116
economical.  If the distance is over one thousand miles, traveling by   130
jet airplane is the fastest way to go and is usually considered to be   144
more economical.  The time saved is valuable, especially if your time   158
is limited.                                                             160

Traveling across an entire ocean to another country can be quite   174
an enjoyable experience, especially if traveling in one of the newest   188
wide-bodied jet planes.  All seating is quite comfortable and all the   202
aisles are wide.  These jumbo jets have a staircase which leads to an   216
upper lounge for the first-class passengers to enjoy.  Some airplanes   230
now have a closed-circuit television screen which enables everyone to   244
observe the take-off and landing and the cockpit gauges and controls.   258
On longer flights, you might enjoy a full-length movie in addition to   272
delicious meals and snacks.                                             277
```

☐☐☐☐1☐☐☐☐2☐☐☐☐3☐☐☐☐4☐☐☐☐5☐☐☐☐6☐☐☐☐7☐☐☐☐8☐☐☐☐9☐☐☐10☐☐☐11☐☐☐12☐☐☐13☐☐☐14

4   Mack, a black Scottie, is a champion canine. 10
A constant companion is the chocolate colored cat 20
called Chicco. Crowds chuckle as Mack and Chicco 30
do their tricks to music. Mack can count objects 40
and prance on a bench. Clever Chicco climbs upon 50
Mack, adding a certain clownish touch to the act. 60

□□□□1□□□□2□□□□3□□□□4□□□□5□□□□6□□□□7□□□□8□□□□9□□□1 0

THINKING DRILL

Set two tabs 15 spaces apart. Review general guidelines on pages 24–25 for setting tabs and on page 23 for word endings. Key the word, tab over, and key the word with an *-ed* ending; tab again and key the word with an *-ing* ending.

Remember: The vowels are *a, e, i, o, u,* (and sometimes *y*). All other letters are consonants.

	-ed	-ing
cure	*cured*	*curing*
curl		
sack		
back		
tack		
pack		
face		
chop		
slap		
kick		

LOOK
THINK
KEY

SESSION 12   Y, X, Q

WARM-UP

Lines 1–3 once
Lines 1–3 again

1 asdf jkl; juj aza dcd a z a j u j d c d dcd cd dc
2 car clip curb bunch curve wreck place crowd scrap
3 The wrecked cars are in the ditch near the curve.

Lines 4–6 once
Lines 4–6 again

4 Compare Produce Consult Service Council Enclosure
5 Clarice recalled the basic facts of the accident.
6 Can Cam choose music as a classic school subject?

GETTING ALONG WITH FELLOW WORKERS / Although an employee may be highly skilled and talented in a chosen job, s/he may fail dismally at the task simply because s/he could not get along with fellow workers. The ability to get along with others is probably one of the greatest single assets a worker can possess. / (Para.) / One of the first rules in getting along with others is to be courteous to everyone. Although the world is moving at a very rapid rate, the old-fashioned art, as some would call it, of good manners is not out of date. Remembering to use words such as "please," "thank you," and "excuse me" will take you a long way in your quest in getting along with others. / (Para.) / Another rule is to be interested in the other person. This will take an effort, at times, on your part. Perhaps the other person is interested in something that you utterly cannot stand or that you know nothing about. But remembering a very common idea, that the other person is interested in oneself and what she or he does, will help you gain a friendly "footing" with that person. And, who knows—you may learn something about a new subject! / (Para.) / Being a good listener and caring about others follows naturally from being interested. Perhaps it will take an effort on your part not to talk so much and listen more. Most of us have the bad habit of talking and carrying on a conversation with others but never listening to what others say. Listening involves not only hearing words but comprehending the meaning of those words and responding to them.

SESSION 50   BOUND MANUSCRIPT

WARM-UP

Lines 1–5 once
Lines 1–5 again

1 Examine the exhaust on the taxi and fix that vexation soon.

2 An executive relaxed as the boxer executed mixed exercises.

3 That exhibitor exhorted the exhausted exercisers to exhale.

4 The sixteen extra oxygen mixtures exploded next to an exit.

5 The extra text on the extractions of textiles is extensive.

Lines 6 and 7 once
Lines 6 and 7 again

6 202 and 203 and 204 and 205 and 206 and 207 and 208 and 209

7 45,134 38,751 7,893 5,313 4,497 1,438 6,719 6,151 34,511 67

1 2 3 4 5 6 7 8 9 10 11 12

Timed Short Drills

Turn to pages TSD 1–8 (timed short-drill material) and complete the following:

1. Five 15-second timings for speed
2. Five 30-second timings for speed
3. Five 30-second timings for control/accuracy

Number Timings

Take two 30-second timings on Line 7 above.

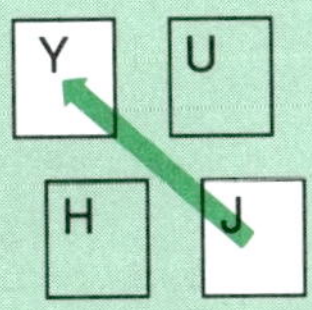

Home-row *j* finger moves up and to the left to the *y* key. Place both hands on the home row and practice the move from *j* to *y*. Look at your hands and watch your finger make the motion. Do this several times; then look away and try the same motion.

Y

Line 1 once—speed

1 j jj jy jy jy jj yy jyj jyj yj yj jyj jy jy jj yj

Lines 2–5 once—speed
Lines 2–5 again—speed

2 jy you yes yet yew yaw yea spy shy sky may key jy
3 jy yarn they yawn gray your type year stay lye jy
4 jy yard play yowl very yolk away yell lazy sly jy
5 jy stay only defy easy rely vary obey hazy pay jy

Lines 6–10 once—speed
Lines 6–10 again—speed

6 angry rhyme daily enjoy fancy happy leaky yowling
7 allay spray dairy entry foggy handy lucky staying
8 alley stray daisy essay fiery heavy loyal yawning
9 assay style dandy every fifty hasty lowly defying
10 Alloy Yearn Decay Empty Forty Hurry Lousy Playing

LOCATIONAL REINFORCEMENT

Key lines 1–6 once. At end of each line, press *Enter* quickly and begin next line immediately. Then do again.

1 The
2 The yowling
3 The yowling stray
4 The yowling stray enjoyed
5 The yowling stray enjoyed the
6 The yowling stray enjoyed the alley.

Key lines 7–11 once. At end of each line, press *Enter* quickly and begin next line immediately. Then do again.

7 Type
8 Type your
9 Type your essay
10 Type your essay every
11 Type your essay every day.

Medicare and Medical Assistance expenditures for home care have grown from $90 million in 1974 to nearly $2 billion in fiscal 1982. But that $2 billion is minor compared with the $50 billion spent for institutional care the same year.

Skyrocketing hospital costs and the continued graying of America will place stiffer demands on the health-care system and on the public and private agencies that help pay for that care. By the year 2050, more than 22 percent of our population is expected to be older than 65. The so-called Medicare Trust Fund could be bankrupt by then. Home care's cost effectiveness could help reduce this fiscal pressure.

During Home-Care Week, we should applaud the work of the thousands of nurses, doctors, therapists, and aides who make home care the thoughtful, humane, and effective program that it is. But we also should use this time to look to the future and address some of the needs on the horizon.

It will be up to us and to our elected officials to effect further reforms in the health-care system. Reforms must reduce costs and maintain quality care for citizens of all age groups and socioeconomic backgrounds and with varying needs. Home care is now and must continue to be an important part of that education and transformation.

Lines 1–10 once—speed
Lines 1–10 again—control

1 The sassy gray puppy plays daily in a sunny yard. 10
2 Why did that shy boy enjoy the truly scary story? 20
3 A nearby sentry eyed a hungry baby in the subway. 30
4 The hungry boy easily ate one cookie at the curb. 40
5 The kitty and the puppy may not enjoy happy play. 50

◻◻◻◻1◻◻◻◻2◻◻◻◻3◻◻◻◻4◻◻◻◻5◻◻◻◻6◻◻◻◻7◻◻◻◻8◻◻◻◻9◻◻◻1 0

6 It is only your duty to obey every law of safety. 10
7 An early yellow lily may defy a wintry windy day. 20
8 Silly Sally annoys that friendly young boy, Gary. 30
9 Billy is ready to carry the heavy load Wednesday. 40
10 Accuracy at a typewriter keyboard may imply zest. 50

◻◻◻◻1◻◻◻◻2◻◻◻◻3◻◻◻◻4◻◻◻◻5◻◻◻◻6◻◻◻◻7◻◻◻◻8◻◻◻◻9◻◻◻1 0

Timings

Take a 1-min. timing on each paragraph. Your instructor may ask you to take additional timings.

Unless instructed otherwise, key at a controlled rate if you are making three or more errors a minute.

If you finish before time is up, start over.

1　　Basically, employers like a loyal secretary. 10
Honesty and courtesy always pay off in any job or 20
duty. Apathy and sloppy typing are always likely 30
to be very costly to a company. Any employee who 40
displays a steady style will be properly rewarded 50
and enjoy a fairly large salary. 56

◻◻◻◻1◻◻◻◻2◻◻◻◻3◻◻◻◻4◻◻◻◻5◻◻◻◻6◻◻◻◻7◻◻◻◻8◻◻◻◻9◻◻◻1 0

2　　There is simply no key to easy money. A bad 10
agency may say that you are lucky and a legacy of 20
wealthy glory is yours. Yet, if you try fancy or 30
phony schemes, you will be mighty sorry. Steady, 40
weekly saving is the thrifty means to easy money. 50
Lay a penny away a day and be happy. 57

◻◻◻◻1◻◻◻◻2◻◻◻◻3◻◻◻◻4◻◻◻◻5◻◻◻◻6◻◻◻◻7◻◻◻◻8◻◻◻◻9◻◻◻1 0

1. An unbound manuscript is usually a very short one (three or fewer pages). If more than one page, the pages may be stapled in the upper left corner.

2. Use a minimum 1-inch side margin for unbound manuscripts.

If you are using the Mastery Software, use the default margins of 1 and 66 to key unbound manuscripts.

Required Activity

Session 49
Document 1
Filename:
049xxx01

Key as unbound manuscript.

(2" top margin)

(1" side margins)

(centered, all caps)

HOME-CARE IMPORTANCE GROWS

(Begin on line 13; line 7 for Mastery Software.)

(5-space paragraph indent)

(triple-space)

(double-space body)

National Home-Care Week has been set aside to pay tribute to the many care-givers who serve not only the elderly but also the sick, disabled, and terminally ill of all ages in the comfort and security of their own homes.

It is striking how few people are aware of home care. It has been around for more than 100 years. Millions of people are given necessary health-care services at home each year by thousands of dedicated individuals.

If given a choice, most of us would prefer to stay at home rather than go to a hospital or nursing home. Home offers us sanctuary and privacy. Being cared for at home keeps our families together. It preserves the dignity of the individual in need of care, be that person young, old, temporarily or permanently disabled, or even dying.

It also is less expensive than institutional care. The National Association for Home Care reports that in 1989 the average cost per Medicare beneficiary was about $1,819 for home care, $2,170 for nursing care, and $6,675 for hospital care.

Home care has grown in recent years. In 1986, there were about 2,275 home-health agencies meeting Medicare standards. Today there are more than 6,000. Only about a half million people were served by home-care programs ten years ago. The current figures exceed two million for the elderly alone.//

(page break)

(continued on next page)

3   A lazy bicycle ride in the country is surely   10
a healthy and worthy activity. A sunny sky and a   20
dry day is surely an omen to any type of cyclist.   30
Be wary of cloudy and windy days. A daily remedy   40
for a healthy and spry body is a ride on a cycle.   50
Energy is enjoyed by young and not so young.   59

☐☐☐☐1☐☐☐☐2☐☐☐☐3☐☐☐☐4☐☐☐☐5☐☐☐☐6☐☐☐☐7☐☐☐☐8☐☐☐☐9☐☐☐10

4   That overly busy lady is not tidy. She pays   10
dearly for her folly and hasty ways. A sloppy or   20
dirty habit will always imply a lazy personality.   30
In theory, a neatly and correctly done job hardly   40
portrays apathy. The lady is in a hurry and only   50
makes costly errors for her employer.   57

☐☐☐☐1☐☐☐☐2☐☐☐☐3☐☐☐☐4☐☐☐☐5☐☐☐☐6☐☐☐☐7☐☐☐☐8☐☐☐☐9☐☐☐10

THINKING DRILL

LOOK	Look at these words:
	jockey *guilty* *yellow* *bicycle* *empty* *birthday*
SELECT	Now—key each sentence below, using one of the words to fill in the blank.
KEY	1. The pail was full; now it is __________.
	2. My favorite color is __________.
	3. A horse is ridden by a __________.
	4. Someone stole my __________.
	5. If he is not innocent, he must be __________.
	6. Ted will have a party on his __________.

PRODUCTION

Educational papers are usually prepared as either *unbound* or *bound* manuscripts. As explained in the last session, the simplified format is becoming popular; however, the traditional format described below is still widely used.

MANUSCRIPT PRODUCTION (TRADITIONAL FORMAT)

1. Double space the body of the manuscript for ease of reading.

2. Use a 5-space paragraph indention for keying the documents that follow.

3. Center titles and key in all capital letters.

4. Triple-space after titles when using the traditional format.

5. Begin title on line 13 (line 7 for Mastery Software) on first page; place page number on second and succeeding pages on line 7 (line 1 for Mastery Software) at the right-hand margin; triple-space after the page number to the first line of copy.

6. Leave a 1 to 1-1/2-inch bottom margin.

WHERE TO BUY

Most cities have several stores which carry similar, or identical types of merchandise. The people of a particular city, therefore, have a choice of stores in which to buy certain products. Several factors which may influence their decision about where to purchase are quality, style, cost and location. If two items are of the same quality and the same style, people will usually buy the item which costs less; that is, if they know which store is selling the item for less.

Most consumers depend upon advertising for information about sales and bargains. Although pricing is an important consideration, in far too many instances it becomes the only factor in a decision. The consumer forgets that there are two additional factors which must be considered along with price. These two factors are the amount of traveling time required to get to the store and the cost involved in the travel. Most people fail to recognize these added factors.

If a consumer must spend quite a bit of time traveling to the store which has the merchandise for the lowest price, travel time becomes a major consideration. How much is time worth? Each individual must answer that particular question.

The cost of travel, whether by private or public transportation, has continued to rise. Again, if the distance involved is quite far, the consumer may spend more on transportation than would be saved on a "bargain" purchase; thus, he or she will not save any money.

Unbound Manuscript

2

The intelligent consumer must be aware of all factors involved with purchasing. Too many times the consumer considers difference in prices as only "cents" and not dollars. Yet, "cents" add up to dollars over the duration of a small period of time.

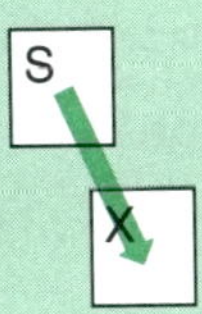

Home-row *s* finger moves down and to the right to the *x* key. Place both hands on the home row and practice the move from *s* to *x*. Look at your hands and watch your finger make the motion. Do this several times; then look away and try the same motion.

Line 1 once—speed

Lines 2–5 once—speed
Lines 2–5 again—speed

1 s ss sx sx sx ss xx sxs sxs xs xs sxs xs sx ssxxs
2 sx axe box fix fox lax mix six tax wax exhaust sx
3 sx axle next exam flex text hoax apex expedite sx
4 sx affix excel index toxic latex annex sixteen sx
5 sx fixed mixed boxer exist relax exact mixture sx

Lines 6–10 once—speed
Lines 6–10 again—speed

6 sixty extra sixth borax waxen vixen luxury export
7 deluxe excise expand export prefix excite example
8 oxygen reflex exotic expert boxing expire textile
9 explain extinct perplex mixture expense expecting
10 Explode Exhaust Toolbox Examine Anxiety Exporting

Sentences

Lines 1–10 once—speed
Lines 1–10 again—control

1 Maxine was exposed to smallpox; examine her next. 10
2 Six expert boxers were boxing in the extra annex. 20
3 Did excess oxygen explode during that experiment? 30
4 The textbook explained the new relaxing exercise. 40
5 Explain the context and expedite that experiment. 50

1 2 3 4 5 6 7 8 9 10

6 Did Baxter excuse the next six tax experts, then? 10
7 Maxim exchanged a box of textiles for a textbook. 20
8 Is the lynx an exotic pet or is it a vexing jinx? 30
9 Fix the exhaust and examine the axle of the taxi. 40
10 Did experts exclude the existence of an appendix? 50

1 2 3 4 5 6 7 8 9 10

Take two 1-minute timings on the following material.

S.I. 1.45

      A good typist soon learns how to proofread. Glaring errors will 14
mar the neatness and quality of a good report. Find all the mistakes 28
before you type the final copy. Learn to watch for correct spelling, 42
grammar, and typing. You might wish to examine your typewritten work 56
two or three times and make quite certain it is without mistakes. In 70
the long run, you will be pleased that you have carefully prepared an 84
excellent typewritten copy. The person who reads your copy will have 98
much respect for your ability as a typist. Learn to proofread. 111

    1   2   3   4   5   6   7   8   9   10   11   12   13   14

Take two 3-minute timings on the following material. Determine your words-a-minute rate. (Divide total words keyed by 3.)

S.I. 1.48

      During every moment of the day or night, all kinds of storms are 14
in the process of raging over land and sea. Over 1,800 thunderstorms 28
or blizzards pelt the earth with rain or snow. Somewhere over a high 42
sea, a hurricane with an awesome wind may be forming. In some areas, 56
the people may be looking at a cloudless sky, but not more than a few 70
hundred miles away other people are sheltering themselves from a wild 84
and furious snowstorm or a pelting rain. 92

      A storm is a disturbance of the upper atmosphere and contains an 106
added element of strong winds. During many storms, destructive winds 120
have been known to cause great damage. During a blizzard on the wide 134
open prairie, snowdrifts pile high and block roads. Ice storms cause 148
widespread damage to telephone and power lines. 157

      Distinctive forms of clouds and precipitation, as well as winds, 171
are common to storms. Precipitation is the weather bureau's name for 185
all forms of water falling from the sky. Clouds are the first signal 199
of an incoming storm. Signals of the hurricane, for example, move in 213
with little or no noise. An alert weatherperson is well aware of the 227
danger signals. First, the wispy, veil-like cirrus clouds appear and 241
dance on the horizon. 245

    1   2   3   4   5   6   7   8   9   10   11   12   13   14

Timings

1   Max expects to chop those six boxes with the 10
old ax. This excellent exercise helps flex those 20
lax muscles. He plans to exchange the boards for 30
deluxe mailboxes. His fixed expenses perplex him 40
and influence his expansion. 46

□ □ □ □ 1 □ □ □ □ 2 □ □ □ □ 3 □ □ □ □ 4 □ □ □ □ 5 □ □ □ □ 6 □ □ □ □ 7 □ □ □ □ 8 □ □ □ □ 9 □ □ □ 1 0

2   An extra exercise to help your mind relax is 10
inhaling and exhaling deeply. It extends all the 20
oxygen capacity before it is expelled. Choose an 30
exact time each day to expedite an extra relaxing 40
exertion. Your anxieties and vexations disappear 50
and you relax. Try this exciting experience. 59

□ □ □ □ 1 □ □ □ □ 2 □ □ □ □ 3 □ □ □ □ 4 □ □ □ □ 5 □ □ □ □ 6 □ □ □ □ 7 □ □ □ □ 8 □ □ □ □ 9 □ □ □ 1 0

3   Exercise an extreme caution before investing 10
in an old duplex. Have an expert examine all the 20
existing details and explain them to you. It may 30
be easier to buy a luxurious and deluxe apartment 40
house. An experienced land expert knows if it is 50
an expensive venture. 54

□ □ □ □ 1 □ □ □ □ 2 □ □ □ □ 3 □ □ □ □ 4 □ □ □ □ 5 □ □ □ □ 6 □ □ □ □ 7 □ □ □ □ 8 □ □ □ □ 9 □ □ □ 1 0

4   An excursion into an old cave excites expert 10
explorers. The expedition offers mixed anxieties 20
and an extreme joy. Excavating an old cave takes 30
dexterity and complex reflexes to examine ancient 40
examples of a past existence. Some old caves are 50
a hoax and are a pretext to extract extra cash. 60

□ □ □ □ 1 □ □ □ □ 2 □ □ □ □ 3 □ □ □ □ 4 □ □ □ □ 5 □ □ □ □ 6 □ □ □ □ 7 □ □ □ □ 8 □ □ □ □ 9 □ □ □ 1 0

Session 48
Document 2
Filename:
048xxx02

```
I.   NEED

     A.   Business grown considerably
     B.   New employee--the administrative manager

II.  CHANGES

     A.   Rising financial costs
          1.   Increased paperwork
          2.   Inflation
     B.   Employee change
          1.   Retiring workers
          2.   Lack of skills
          3.   Automated systems
     C.   Career options
          1.   Definite need
          2.   Post-secondary school programs
```

SESSION 49   UNBOUND MANUSCRIPT

WARM-UP

Lines 1–5 once
Lines 1–5 again

1 That rowdy crowd swarmed on the west freeway and went wild.

2 Wes was awarded with twelve weeks of rest as a wise reward.

3 Wendy and Will were weary of the unwelcome weekend showers.

4 Who wired the winch to that warship and prowled in the bow?

5 The scowling prowler scowled as the dog howled and growled.

Lines 6 and 7 once
Lines 6 and 7 again

6 102 and 103 and 104 and 105 and 106 and 107 and 108 and 109

7 23,265.08 186.84 4.23 .87 990.85 546.27 61.34 91,007.23 .46

Timed Short Drills

Turn to pages TSD 1–8 (timed short-drill material) and complete the following:

1. Five 15-second timings for speed
2. Five 30-second timings for speed
3. Five 30-second timings for control/accuracy

Number Timings

Take two 30-second timings on Line 7 above.

| <table><tr><td>LOOK
THINK
KEY</td></tr></table> | **THINKING DRILL**

Key each word below, inserting an appropriate letter. Use the letters *a, b, c, e, o, t,* or *x*. |

THINKING DRILL

LOOK
THINK
KEY

Key each word below, inserting an appropriate letter. Use the letters *a, b, c, e, o, t,* or *x.*

b__x	rel__x
ax__	six__een
ta__	to__lbox
si__th	text__ook
ex__use	dupl__x

INTRODUCTION TO Q

Home-row *a* finger moves up and to the left to the *q* key. Place both hands on the home row and practice the move from *a* to *q*. Look at your hands and watch your finger make the motion. Do this several times; then look away and try the same motion.

Line 1 once—speed

1 a aa aq aq aq aa qq aqa aqa qa qa aqa aq aq aaqqa

Lines 2–5 once—speed
Lines 2–5 again—speed

2 aq quid quip quit quiz quack quail quake quart aq

3 aq queen quell quest quick quill quire require aq

4 aq quote quire squid quiet squaw query qualify aq

5 aq equip equal squat squad queer quilt acquire aq

Lines 6–10 once—speed
Lines 6–10 again—speed

6 quartz acquit squash unique squeezing questioning

7 quench equate squeak equity squelching quarreling

8 squawk liquid squeal queasy inquiring acquainting

9 square opaque squint equate antiquated conquering

10 Squire Quarry Quaver Quorum Quartering Requesting

Key the following outline using the format instructions given in the left margin.

Document 1
Session 48
File 048xxx01

Format as follows:

1. Set side margins of 12 spaces for 12-pitch (elite) type and 10 spaces for 10-pitch (pica) type (1-inch margins).
2. Start heading on line 13 (2-inch top margin).
3. Center the main heading in all capital letters.
4. Capitalize all words in major divisions.
5. Capitalize only the first letter of the first word in second-, third-, fourth-, and fifth-level divisions.
6. Set tabs to align material within each division.
7. Allow two spaces after the period or parenthesis following numerals and letters when setting tabs.
8. Triple-space after the main heading. Double-space before and after a major division. Single-space before and after all other divisions.

```
                    OUR PAPER HIGHWAY


     I.    IMPORTANCE OF RECORDS STORAGE

           A.   Usage today
                1.   Productivity increase
                2.   Correspondence volume
           B.   Costs today
                1.   Higher salaries
                2.   Need for more equipment

    II.    METHODS OF STORAGE AND RETRIEVAL

           A.   Alphabetic filing
                1.   Characteristics
                2.   Specific uses
                     a.   Telephone books
                          (1)  Uniform information presentation
                          (2)  Easy-to-locate format
                     b.   Libraries
                          (1)  Combination records storage
                          (2)  Concise retrieval system
           B.   Computer storage
                1.   Tape
                2.   Disk

   III.    ADDITIONAL PROBLEMS IN RECORDS STORAGE

           A.   Faxed documents
           B.   Mistrust of computer data storage
```

Key lines 1–5 once. At end of each line, press *Enter* quickly and begin next line immediately. Then do again.

1 The guest
2 The guest acquired
3 The guest acquired a
4 The guest acquired a unique
5 The guest acquired a unique antique.

Key lines 6–9 once. At end of each line, press *Enter* quickly and begin next line immediately. Then do again.

6 The squatter
7 The squatter squandered
8 The squatter squandered a
9 The squatter squandered a quarter.

Sentences

Lines 1–10 once—speed
Lines 1–10 again—control

1 Go quickly; request the exquisite quartz antique. 10
2 Do that quotient; it is a frequent quiz question. 20
3 Does that quart of liquid quinine quiver quietly? 30
4 Did the squadron eat squab and squash frequently? 40
5 Put thick lacquer on the unique antique aquarium. 50

    1   2   3   4   5   6   7   8   9   1 0

6 Ducks squirmed and quacked in the squalid quarry. 10
7 Quarantine the queasy squirrel in the square box. 20
8 The quake left queer quagmires in the old square. 30
9 That squad had qualms about the frequent quizzes. 40
10 Does the quitter frequently squabble and quibble? 50

    1   2   3   4   5   6   7   8   9   1 0

Timings

Take a 1-min. timing on each paragraph. Your instructor may ask you to take additional timings.

Unless instructed otherwise, key at a controlled rate if you are making three or more errors a minute.

If you finish before time is up, start over.

1   The ability to key at a very rapid rate will 10
be a skill that you will never forget. Keying is 20
a useful skill almost all of the time if you work 30
with computers. It is an important skill even if 40
you end up using it only for your personal needs. 50

    1   2   3   4   5   6   7   8   9   1 0

The Outline

Although there are a number of acceptable outline formats, the one shown in Document 1 is used frequently. Read the following guidelines before keying Document 1 on page 231.

Major Points (divisions) and Minor Points (subdivisions):

```
      I.   MAJOR DIVISION OR POINT

           A.  Second-level division
               1.  Third-level division
                   a.  Fourth-level division
                       (1)  Fifth-level division

     II.   SECOND MAJOR DIVISION OR POINT

           A.  Second-level division

    III.   THIRD MAJOR DIVISION OR POINT
```

Note the alignment of division numbers or letters. The Roman numerals are aligned flush right.

```
                      I.
                     II.
                    III.
```

You will need to key in two spaces from the left margin before the I; key in one space before the II. Be sure to allow two spaces after each period or parenthesis when setting tab stops.

When keying outlines that are checked by the software, you must use the *tab* key after keying numerals and letters. For Document 1 on page 231, set tabs at 7, 11, 15, 19, and 24 before keying the outline. Use the default margins and space twice before keying I. Press the *tab* key after the I. to key IMPORTANCE OF RECORDS STORAGE.

2   The quick squad conquered the unique quintet   10
without question. The quarterback squelched most   20
questions about technique or quality of the team.   30
If they qualify for the trophy, will they quietly   40
squash the next team or will the coach require an   50
extra practice session?   55
□□□□ 1 □□□□ 2 □□□□ 3 □□□□ 4 □□□□ 5 □□□□ 6 □□□□ 7 □□□□ 8 □□□□ 9 □□□ 1 0

3   Angelique might request a price quotation on   10
an exquisite antique quilt. She acquired it from   20
a queen in a quaint town near the equator. Quiet   30
inquiries have arisen from qualified buyers. The   40
question is, should she keep the quality quilt or   50
sell it quickly as requested?   56
□□□□ 1 □□□□ 2 □□□□ 3 □□□□ 4 □□□□ 5 □□□□ 6 □□□□ 7 □□□□ 8 □□□□ 9 □□□ 1 0

4   The quaint quill is only a quarter. Is it a   10
unique antique? Inquire quickly and acquire that   20
exquisite pen. The tip makes queer squibbles and   30
squirts ink. It requires a queer technique for a   40
quality work. Quaint old squires always used the   50
antique quill pens in all inquiries.   57
□□□□ 1 □□□□ 2 □□□□ 3 □□□□ 4 □□□□ 5 □□□□ 6 □□□□ 7 □□□□ 8 □□□□ 9 □□□ 1 0

THINKING DRILL

LOOK	Look at these words:
	equator *quality* *Queen* *quarrel* *quarter* *quiet*
SELECT	Now—key each sentence below, inserting the appropriate word.
KEY	1. The King was on tour with the __________.
	2. Two dimes and a nickel equal one __________.
	3. It is very hot at the __________.
	4. Quantity is not as important as __________.
	5. You are too loud; please be __________.

(2 inch top margin)

(1-1/2 inch left margin)

(1 inch right margin)

OUR PAPER HIGHWAY

The storing of valuable documents and records has had a place in history almost from the beginning of time. Even then, people tried to find a way to preserve and keep important records of their existence. As buying and selling evolved, the need to keep important records of major business transactions also grew. Throughout history, records storage and retrieval has always been an exciting and interesting career field.

Importance of Records Storage

Because of added productivity and correspondence of businesses of today, the sheer volume of paperwork has increased beyond human expectations or imagination. Business records, in spite of computerized data storage, take up more space than any other single item (Holbreck and Marcus:1989:2). Not only has the need for additional space become critical, but the added expenses of maintaining the records storage has also risen.

One expert indicated that if trends continue, the cost of storing just one document could rise to twenty cents (Dane:1989:57). The storage problem will continue to increase, as one file drawer can hold only a certain number of items. Not only do the records take up precious space, but the need for higher salaries and equipment soars. Quite obviously, any time or effort spent by office workers or any money spent by a business firm is totally wasted if the records are not really needed, or if those records cannot be easily located and retrieved

endnote

endnote

(1 to 1-1/2 inch bottom margin)

Key each line once as quickly as you can. Your instructor may also have you complete some timings.

1 The patient is in pain; his left thigh is gashed. 10
2 Did John tape that splint and dispense the pills? 20
3 The sad person lingered in the stadium and cried. 30
4 The firemen attempted an immense task and failed. 40
5 Did Linda eliminate all of the mistakes required? 50

6 David missed the message that the teacher wanted. 10
7 The wealth of the world will not be obtained now. 20
8 The group sang a rousing tune during the matches. 30
9 He is a plump pup but will become a slim dog now. 40
10 Compute the monthly amount by dividing the total. 50

11 It is only your duty to complete the tasks today. 10
12 Accuracy at a keyboard is very important to them. 20
13 The dancers sang songs and mingled among dealers. 30
14 Mike might make more of the problem on the plane. 40
15 While I was doing this, where were the elephants? 50

1 2 3 4 5 6 7 8 9 1 0

SESSION 13 — REINFORCEMENT SESSIONS 1–12

The purpose of this session is for you the student to practice your keyboarding skills. You should approach this session with a desire to determine where you are in the skill development process and with a willingness to work to improve your speed and accuracy.

The material below has been word counted for 20-, 15-, and 10-second drills (look to the right of the lines). After determining which length timing you will be taking, go down that column of figures and select the rate that you think you can "average" a minute. Then key the line to the left of that figure. If you complete the line before time is up, it means that you averaged *at least* that many words a minute. Then go to the next line—which is longer—and attempt to complete it before time is up. Repeat the procedure until it is impossible for you to complete the line before time is up.

Remember: Be sure that you are looking at the correct time column.

Follow this procedure:

Push for SPEED

or

Slow down and key with CONTROL to improve accuracy.

1. For *speed,* let your fingers fly and really "push" to finish the line before time is up. Don't worry about errors.

2. For *accuracy,* attempt to finish the line and have no more than one error before proceeding to the next longer line.

PRODUCTION

EDUCATIONAL MANUSCRIPTS

A manuscript, in contrast to a business report, is usually prepared for publication purposes (such as magazine articles) or for research projects (class reports). The writer usually quotes ideas or words from authors who have researched the same topic. A formal educational manuscript often includes an outline, a title page, a table of contents, the basic report supplemented by reference sources in the form of footnotes or endnotes, and a bibliography. You will key all parts of an educational manuscript in the sessions that follow.

At the beginning of manuscript preparation, you will want to research (study) articles, books, and other sources to obtain more information about your topic. As you read and collect information, you will find it helpful to prepare notes on cards. You will also want to include all publishing data (author's name, book or magazine title, place and date of publication, and page number) on each note card in case you or your reader would like to research further.

From the note cards, a skeleton or basic design called an *outline* is then prepared. The outline lists only main points and subpoints to help you get your ideas in a logical order. You will key an outline in this session.

The *body* of the report is prepared according to specific guidelines usually unique to a company or educational institution. The report should be written in your own words, but you may want to quote a statement from another book or article to substantiate your report.

If you use someone else's words or ideas, you must prepare *research source notes* in the endnote or footnote format and give credit for those ideas that are not your own.

At the end of the paper, a *bibliography* is included; this is a list of all reference sources and includes author's name, book or magazine title, and publishing facts.

As mentioned, manuscripts are usually prepared using a specific format. The format must be consistent, with careful attention given to details such as spacing, punctuation, and order. An illustration of the first page of a manuscript follows. The reference source notes are formatted in the endnote style. The manuscript is shown in 12-pitch type with a 1-1/2-inch left margin and a 1-inch right margin for a bound report. The traditional format of line spacing (2 blank lines between the title and body of the report and between the sections of the manuscript) is still followed in some educational institutions. However, a simplified format (double spacing throughout, with the exception of the bibliography and footnote format) has evolved with the usage of word-processing application programs on the computer, making it easier and quicker to format. Another time-saving feature of many of the advanced software packages is the ability to develop an outline with the appropriate indentions automatically.

The simplified format shown in the illustration on the next page uses double spacing throughout. If you are keying a manuscript for a specific purpose, however, be sure to follow the guidelines given.

Speed Push

	20	15	10
1 Now is the time to study.	15	20	30
2 Move the computer to the room.	18	24	36
3 You should eat a healthy breakfast.	21	28	42
4 The grass needs to be mowed and watered.	24	32	48
5 Place those big tickets in the long envelope.	27	36	54

1 2 3 4 5 6 7 8 9 10

Accuracy Drive

	20	15	10
1 Create a spreadsheet.	13	17	25
2 Deliver the mailgram to her.	17	23	34
3 You will have to create a letter.	20	27	40
4 The computer will help improve accuracy.	24	32	48
5 Soon you will learn to use the word processor.	28	37	55

1 2 3 4 5 6 7 8 9 10

Check Your Skill

It is good to have honest goals. Nothing is 10
gained if one goes forth in pointless roaming. A 20
major effort is needed to prosper. Isolate those 30
foolish errors and avoid them. Hold to a strong, 40
firm hope and move along. 45

1 2 3 4 5 6 7 8 9 10

Assessing Your Skills

Determine the number of words and number of errors for each timing taken on the previous paragraph. The material provided on the following four pages is to be used for additional practice on the keys that you have learned. There are no instructions in the left margins. Use the drills as follows:

1. If you have mastered the keys and do not hesitate when keying any letter, and you did not have an excessive number of errors (your instructor will tell you the maximum number of errors for an acceptable timing), you may proceed to the next session on page 65.

2. If you made an excessive number of errors, key the lines identified as
   a. double-letter words
   b. longer words

3. If you have not mastered the reach to a key(s) (you hesitate before striking the key), key the lines identified as
   a. balanced-hand words
   b. letter combinations
   c. sentences with letter combinations

4. If you are not able to key as rapidly as you would like, key the lines identified as balanced-hand words.

After determining what you need to work on, continue building speed or accuracy.

Key lines 1–5 once to review keystrokes learned in previous sessions before taking timings.

Key lines 1–5 once before taking timings.

Key paragraph once at controlled rate.

Take a 1-min. timing. Take another 1-min. timing.

MORE PRACTICE

TOO MANY ERRORS?

HESITATE?

NOT FAST ENOUGH?

Take two 1-minute timings on the following material.

S.I. 1.45

```
        Recreation is becoming more and more popular among people of all   14
ages.  One particular sport which is growing rapidly is cross-country   28
skiing.  If a person makes an effort to get out of the house and puts   42
on a pair of skis, cross-country skiing can be a great enjoyment.  No   56
specialized skills are needed to learn to cross-country ski.  The few   70
basic beginning instructions are simple to master.  The excitement of   84
gliding over that snowy countryside, through the magnificent forests,   98
and over the hills is a thrill that no one should miss.                109
    1     2     3     4     5     6     7     8     9    10    11    12    13    14
```

Take two 3-minute timings on the following material. Determine your words-a-minute rate. (Divide total words keyed by 3.)

S.I. 1.47

```
        In the autumn, when the grass begins to turn brown and the trees   14
begin to lose their leaves, many persons turn their attentions to the   28
upcoming sports season.  Appearing high on the list of sports fans is   42
professional football.  Every weekend there are a variety of exciting   56
games to attend, watch, or listen to.  As the season progresses, much   70
excitement is evident; the excitement culminates in the last big game   84
of the year--in Canada, it's the Grey Cup--in the United States, it's   98
the Super Bowl Game.  The winning team in each country is declared to  112
be "the" football league champion.                                     119

        Other winter sports games draw the attention of many folks.  Ice  133
hockey has grown considerably as a professional sport during the past  147
few years.  The whizzing skaters, the delicate skills of the players,  161
and the element of competition will add to a winter spectator's joy.   175

        Basketball draws its share of attention during the long winters.  189
The game of basketball is played at a steady pace and usually is very  203
exciting.  As in other professional sports, the teams travel all over  217
the nation, giving the spectators one thrilling game after another.    231
    1     2     3     4     5     6     7     8     9    10    11    12    13    14
```

Balanced-Hand Words

1 sign and the sigh ant sit ale elf hen end she and
2 then hang the and fig dig die tie did sit fit aid
3 fish sign than then lane lake lens hand than halt
4 lake idle half lens lane sign dish sign then disk
5 aisle island handle fight angle title shake snake
6 gland sleigh height fight slant digit angle eight
7 he and the elf and it if he an tight giant signal
8 amble bible problem blame bland blend lamb emblem
9 gown wig bow wow vow down wit when wish with wisp
10 flap pane paid pale spent dispel lap nap pen paid
11 foam fork form foal odor soak rod fog sod oak rod
12 heir lair risks sir pan air widow flair hair pair
13 pelvis disown pens laps vie via pair vivid flames
14 map mane maid melt sham lame mend firm make disks
15 The pale maid paid for the vivid title and a wig.
16 Did the lank lamb amble down to the big dark pen?
17 When did Victor sign the pair of problem emblems?

Double-Letter Words

1 seed teens needless feeling indeed needs glee see
2 tall stall knitting install little shall hall all
3 heel steed likeness dissent seeing sheet need fee
4 see feel teeth indeed gallant sledding sleet knee
5 hill still lifeless endless assist stiff kiss add
6 eggs stall eggshell falling haggle sniff sell egg
7 tell shell settling skilled allied skill fell add
8 deed sleek seedling fiddles needle sheen keen eel
9 rabble rabbit gobble nibbles pebble babble hobble
10 narratives all follow terrains irritates terriers
11 door root mood took loot hook hood pool roof moon
12 immerges immense manners hammering dinners dimmer
13 shipping appease flipping happen sipping slipping
14 She will be stalling the nice contest winner now.
15 That immense rabbit emerged and nibbled a carrot.
16 Tu Wee slipped the irritated kitten in the house.

(Current date) / TO: Mr. John Kearney, Editorial Department / FROM: Frances Dalton, Administrative Secretary / SUBJECT: Information on Office Systems Seminar / Jack, here is a revised copy of our Office Systems Seminar outline to highlight the conversation that we had regarding the programs available through our department. ¶ Also attached is a revised copy of the letter that we will mail to potential participants. ¶ Thank you for the opportunity to share these thoughts with you and your staff. / your initials / attachments

SESSION 48   OUTLINE

WARM-UP

1 The evil virus invaded the valley of very lively villagers.

2 Elvis invited the evil visitor to see our village vineyard.

3 Is it valid if Van vetoes the valuable division of travels?

4 The silver velvet covering on that davenport is attractive.

5 A savory flavor is evoked in veal by serving anchovies too.

6 91 and 92 and 93 and 94 and 95 and 96 and 97 and 98 and 990

7 6,117.08 7.43 298 634,513.77 3,398.18 311,453,024 413.77 47

1 2 3 4 5 6 7 8 9 10 11 12

Timed Short Drills

Turn to pages TSD 1–8 (timed short-drill material) and complete the following:

1. Five 15-second timings for speed
2. Five 30-second timings for speed
3. Five 30-second timings for control/accuracy

Number Timings

Take two 30-second timings on Line 7 above.

Longer Words

1 negative retrieve primitive privilege advertising
2 estimate familiar eliminate dependent sentimental
3 Eliminate that sentimental, familiar advertising.
4 resident standard telegrams registrar parenthesis
5 pipeline elephant dependent plaintiff safekeeping
6 That resident registrar sends standard telegrams.
7 initiated hesitating alkaline likeness indefinite
8 delegates heightened lengthened stealing gaslight
9 The hesitating delegate is stealing the gaslight.
10 digital lenient distant inkling heading delighted
11 disliked endless athlete install flatten inflated
12 A lenient athlete has inflated the flattened keg.
13 whenever stalwart wholesale handwriting knowledge
14 renovate negotiate imagination tradition rational
15 possible establish observation elaborate ambition
16 Establish rational imagination whenever possible.
17 seashells tasteless steadfast thankless defendant
18 attendant delighted sightless lightness negligent
19 legislate essential stateside skinflint landslide
20 Seashells in the landslide delighted a skinflint.

Letter Combinations

1 ta tall tan task taste tale tall take talk tag ta
2 th thesis thin theft this think than that then th
3 te tenant tennis teen tend tell tenth test tea te
4 st stead still steal steadiness stateside stag st
5 sa sad saline Sal sang said sale sake safe sat sa
6 si since simple sinker sit single sift sip sin si
7 pe peep pets pellet peddles peeps pest pen peg pe
8 pi pine pink pipes pitfall pills piles pie pin pi
9 li like linkage linking link lien lied lie lid li
10 le lessen leaf least ledge lend lead left lest le
11 bl blade bleak blast blank blinds blind blight bl

Take two 3-minute timings on the following material. Determine your words-a-minute rate. (Divide total words keyed by 3.)

S.I. 1.46

```
Since the first moment in time when two people traveled beyond a      14
shouting distance of each other, humans have searched for a method of  28
talking over a long distance.  Earlier cultures tried drums and smoke  42
signals for messages.  Today, the traffic noises in most places would  56
cover the sounds of a drum; fire engines would arrive on the scene to  70
drown the fire.  People communicate easily today with our telephones.  84
Most of us don't realize how advanced the technology of phone service  98
has now become.  Old photos show endless miles of phone wires hung on  112
poles; today we would find the wire buried.  The switchboard operator  126
has been replaced by automatic dialing handled by a big computer with  140
the sound waves being relayed across the world by one satellite.  The  154
repair person has now been replaced by a trained service person.  The  168
changes that have taken place are numerous; however, the objective of  182
the service is still the same--allowing people to talk with the other  196
people.  The next time you have a chance, look for other changes; you  210
will be amazed with what you will find.                                218
```

□□□□1□□□□2□□□□3□□□□4□□□□5□□□□6□□□□7□□□□8□□□□9□□□10□□□11□□□12□□□13□□□14

PRODUCTION

Progress Check

You have now completed all the activities related to letters, envelopes, and memos for the Basic-Level Productivity Module. It is time to determine how quickly you can key these production tasks.

Key each of the following documents as quickly as possible, correcting all your errors. You want each document to be "mailable." In other words, when you finish each project, it could be "mailed" or sent without any other corrections.

Required Activity

Session 47
Document 1
Filename:
047xxx01

Block-letter style with mixed punctuation

Mr. Patrick Shields, 3228 Glenview Circle, Staten Island, NY 10302-1620/ Dear Mr. Shields: In accordance with your request, enclosed is an agreement which sets forth our relationship in assisting you in finding an appropriate business investment. Please sign one copy and return it to us for our files. / We appreciate this opportunity to be of assistance to you and hope that our efforts will be successful in achieving your objectives. / Any communications in this regard will be treated as strictly confidential. / Sincerely, Robert E. Truax, Senior Vice President

12 ba bandages barks badge bath balk bail bag bad ba
13 mi mire misting might midst mint mind mild mid mi
14 ma margin manager marsh mail make math mat man ma
15 oa float roast toad load oatmeal oath oats oak oa
16 of offensive offense offset offends offers off of
17 ri rinse rigid ridges right ripe rises rip rid ri
18 ra rapid range raised rates rake ranks rap ran ra
19 vi vintage vital visits vine vile vise vim vie vi
20 va vanish varied valid vast vases vane vat van va
21 wa waves waste wane wait wade wag war was wash wa
22 wi wiper wield wise will wipe wide wig wit win wi

Sentences with Letter Combinations

1 Janie washed and wiped her wig; she wasted water.
2 The babe blinked at a baboon blinded in bandages.
3 Those offensive oats floated off of that oatmeal.
4 The vital vintage vases vanished from a vast van.
5 The manager might mail the mild mints to the man.
6 Rapid Red ran to the raised ridges on that range.
7 That pill peddler peddled piles of pinkish pills.
8 Then that teen tenant, Ted, did a tenth tea test.
9 Steadfast Stell still talks and tells tall tales.
10 Sad Sal sang a signal as she sighted a safe date.
11 At least link the left lid and lessen the length.
12 That hanging kite tail hassles the halted kitten.
13 Gal, finish the gasket that the gas gadget needs.
14 I dislike the heat dial that fits the dental fan.

Check Your Skill

Now that you have had many opportunities to work on building your skills, go back to "Check Your Skill" on page 60 and take two 1-minute timings. Compare the rate you just keyed with your very first attempt. Has your speed improved? Do you have fewer errors? If you need additional practice, repeat the appropriate lines to build speed or accuracy.

WARM-UP

Lines 1–5 once
Lines 1–5 again

1 Put lettuce, cucumbers, and zucchini squash on the saucers.

2 Chuck is lucky; that subtle judge is too grouchy in public.

3 Good judgment should be included in any student's attitude.

4 The quiet guy is suffering as that ugly cough gets rougher.

5 I guess that tough guide has taught thousands about values.

Lines 6 and 7 once
Lines 6 and 7 again

6 81 and 82 and 83 and 84 and 85 and 86 and 87 and 88 and 890

7 1,676,352.17 3,131 2.24 436,342 101.31 166,891 543891 40005

□□□□1□□□□2□□□□3□□□□4□□□□5□□□□6□□□□7□□□□8□□□□9□□□10□□□11□□□12

Timed Short Drills

Turn to pages TSD 1–8 (timed short-drill material) and complete the following:

1. Five 15-second timings for speed
2. Five 30-second timings for speed
3. Five 30-second timings for control/accuracy

Number Timings

Take two 30-second timings on Line 7 above.

Straight-Copy Timings

Take two 1-minute timings on the following material.

S.I. 1.45

If you enjoy observing the many species of birds, there are many 14

ways of attracting them. A bird requires a shelter, food, and water. 28

Provide fresh, clean drinking and bathing water each day. Some fresh 42

seeds and fruit placed in accessible feeders are necessary. The bird 56

shelters should be quite durable and waterproof. All baths, feeders, 70

and shelters should be kept out of the reach of other animals. Those 84

birds need all the security and safety that you can provide for them. 98

Your new friends will appreciate your efforts. 107

□□□□1□□□□2□□□□3□□□□4□□□□5□□□□6□□□□7□□□□8□□□□9□□□10□□□11□□□12□□□13□□□14

NUMERIC KEYS

Numbers Are Important. Whether you are learning to keyboard for personal or vocational use, the numeric portion of the keyboard is certainly as important as the alphabetic one. Numbers used by people on a personal basis include social security, telephone, address/zip code/postal zone, age, weight, height, serial, and driver's license numbers, to name a few.

There are countless ways in which numbers are used in business documents. Some examples include current date, business address and telephone, price of goods and/or services, salaries, insurance policy number, and meeting and conference dates.

Numbers and the Keyboard. Look at your keyboard. Notice that the numbers are placed in numerical order on the top row. Numbers will be easier for you to learn than alphabetic characters because there are only 10 of them, as compared to 26 letters of the alphabet; and the numbers are in order, as compared to the letters, which are randomly placed on the keyboard.

Hands. Place your fingers on the home row (*a s d f   j k l ;*) of the keyboard as shown here.

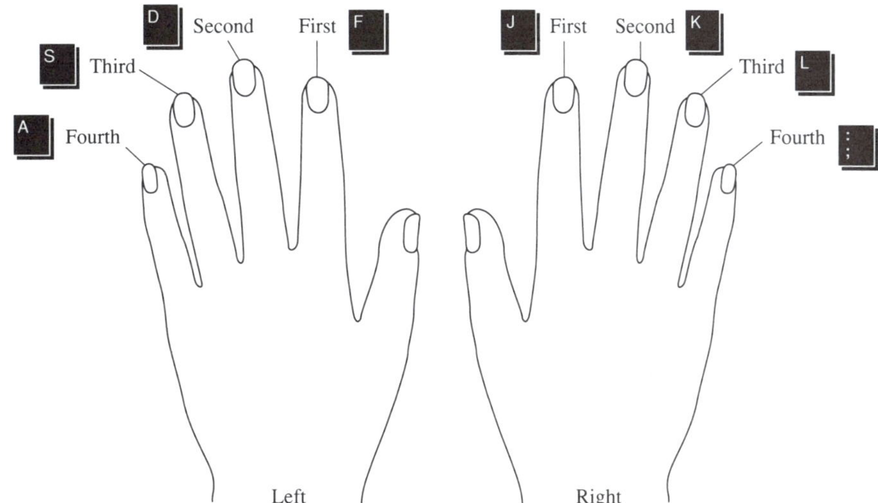

How to Key Numbers. Since numbers appear most frequently with alphabetic characters, you will learn the home-row method of keying numbers. You will work from the home row in developing locational security. To help you stay close to the

Session 46
Document 2
Filename:
046xxx02

Block-letter
style with mixed
punctuation

12411 Palm Drive
Santa Ana, CA 92650
Current Date

Mrs. Helen Ryan
California Trust Company
12 Warren Place
Santa Ana, CA 92654-1123

Dear Mrs. Ryan:

Please consider me for any clerical positions you may have available
for the summer months of June, July, and August. I am interested in
either full-time or part-time employment.

I am presently a full-time student at Santa Ana College where I am
completing a degree in administrative management with emphasis in
word processing.

Previous summer work has given me experience on electronic typewriters
as well as personal computers, in handling basic filing routines, answering the telephone, and other general clerical duties.

The experience gained working for your company would prove most valuable.
Your organization has a reputation for providing excellent, worthwhile
experience for part-time employees.

You may contact me at (714) 755-6832 before 7:30 a.m. and after 3:30 p.m.
on weekdays. I am available for a personal interview at your convenience.

Sincerely,

Betty Dawson

home-row keys, the letter *a* will be used as an anchor key for the left hand. Because
commas and decimals are used frequently with numbers, these keys will be
included. The reaches to the comma and decimal (period) keys will bring your right
hand back to the home-row position.

THE SPACE BAR AND THE LETTER A

Left fourth finger (home row) strokes the letter *a*. The right thumb strikes the
space bar.

Key each line twice.

1 a a a a aa aa aa a a a aa aa a a aa a aa aa a a a

2 aa aaa a a aa a aaa aa a aaa a a aa aa aaa a aa a

INTRODUCTION TO 1

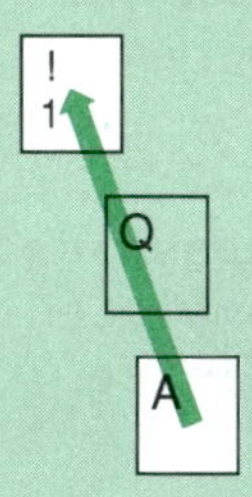

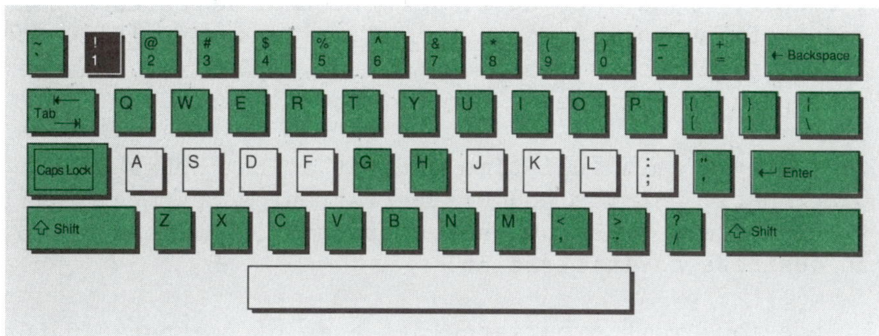

Home-row *a* finger moves up and to the left to the *1*. To key the number *1*, you
must strike the *1* key on the upper row. (Do not use the lowercase L key in the
home row to key the number 1.) Place both hands on the home row and practice the
move from *a* to *1*. Look at your hands and watch your finger make the motion. Do
this several times; then look away and try the same motion. Continue this procedure
until you can make the motion correctly without looking at the keyboard.

Developing Speed-Thinking of Numbers

As you key the number 1, think *one* to yourself. As you key 11, think *eleven*. As
you key 111, think *one eleven*. This procedure will help increase your keying speed
as you begin keying numbers in units of two and three digits.

   When letters and numbers are combined, use the following technique for reading
the copy. For the combination a1, think *ay-one*. For the combination a111, think
ay/one-eleven.

Key each line once.
Then repeat, for speed.

1 a1 1a1 a111 a1 a1 a11 a111 a1 11a11 a1 1a1 a11 a1

2 a11 a111 11a a1 1a1 a11 111a 111 11a 11 a1 11a 1a

An example of a "specialized" personal business letter is the letter of application.
You will want to prepare a letter of application and submit it whenever you apply
for a job. The documents you will be keying are letters for other people; however,
they should give you some ideas on how to prepare your own letter of application.
Read the letters before you start to key.

**Required
Activity**

Session 46
Document 1
Filename:
046xxx01

Block-letter
style with mixed
punctuation

```
Box 93
Cincinnati, OH 45227
Current Date


Mr. William Haggert
Paragon Laboratories, Inc.
19011 NE 36th Way
Redmond, WA 98073-9717

Dear Mr. Haggert:

I recently read your advertisement that appeared in the January 20
issue of The Wall Street Journal.  I was especially interested in the
summer internships that your company sponsors.  Please consider me as
an applicant for one of those internships.

Currently I am a full-time student at the Weber School of Business in
Cincinnati.  At the end of the current semester, I will have completed
two semesters of a four-semester curriculum leading to a certificate
in business administration.

My previous work experience has been of a general nature and includes
two to three months' (summer-time) work doing the following:  swimming
pool lifeguard; receptionist for a music store; delivery of newspapers;
and helping my father in his small business by waiting on customers.

The experience gained working for your company would prove most valuable.
Your organization has a reputation for providing excellent experiences
through your internships.

Because of the distance involved between Cincinnati and Redmond, it is
impossible for me to come for a personal interview.  However, I can be
contacted at (699) 347-9123 before 7:30 a.m. and after 3:30 p.m. on
weekdays.

Sincerely,


Ho Sung Lee
```

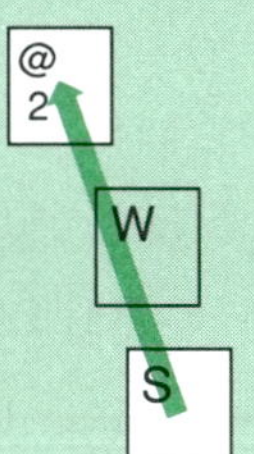

INTRODUCTION TO 2

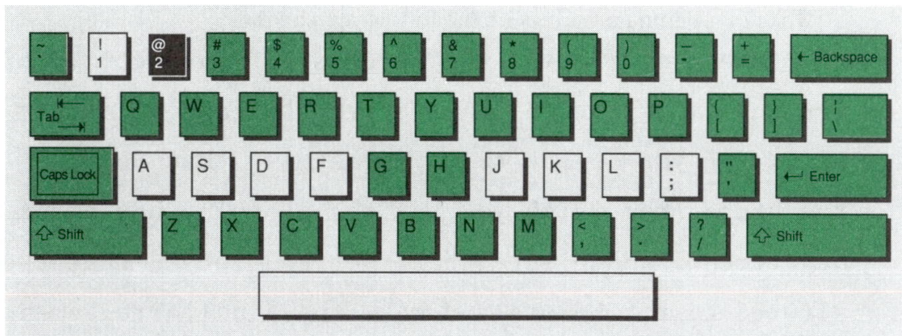

Home-row *s* finger moves up and to the left to the number *2.* Place both hands on the home row and practice the move from *s* to *2.* Look at your hands and watch your finger make the motion. Do this several times; then look away and try the same motion. Continue this procedure until you can make the motion correctly without looking at the keyboard.

1 2 2 22 22 222 222 2 2 22 222 222 2 222 22 222 222

2 1 2 1 21 221 122 121 221 2 1 212 112 1 12 21 21 2

3 a12 2a1 112a 12a12 21a1 122a a11 a2a 12a 1a2a 122

Note: Did you think of 221 as *two-twenty-one*? Did you think of 112a as *one-twelve/ay* ?

Keying Numbers with Four Digits

When working with groups of numbers having four digits and no natural break, think of the numbers as two pairs.

1 1221 1112 1221 1112 2112 2112 1122 1122 1221 2221

2 a1122 a1221 1112a 1212a a1112 a2112 a1212 a1221a2

Keying Numbers with Five or More Digits

When keying number groups that have more than four digits and no natural breaks such as spaces, commas, or decimals, use a 2-3-2 reading pattern. For the number 21221, think *twenty-one/two twenty-one.* For the number 2121221, think *twenty-one/two-twelve/twenty-one.*

1 21 221 21 221 21 221 a21 212a 12 11a 2121 a121 a2

2 21221 21121 21221 a21112 a12212 a12121 21212 a122

3 a2112121 22 1 21a 2122121 12221 a212a 1221a 12221

4 12 12 12 12 121 121 121 121 a2a a221 a221 2a211 1

5 212a1 121221a 12122a1 22221a 12212a 221221a 21a22

Remember: Keep your fingers on the home row unless you are keying a number or several numbers.

Key each line once.
Then repeat, for speed.

Key each line once.

Key each line once.

Repeat each line, pushing for speed.

Take two 1-minute timings on the following material.

S.I. 1.45

When considering the purchase of any article of clothing, do not 14
let any sales person convince you to take a garment that does not fit 28
well. If you decide to buy something that does not fit, be sure that 42
the store from which you buy the clothing has an excellent alteration 56
department. Make sure that they understand that the clothing must be 70
altered to fit before you make the final arrangements to purchase the 84
item. To be completely assured and satisfied, take a friend along to 98
give you another opinion on how you look. 106

| 1   2   3   4   5   6   7   8   9   10   11   12   13   14

Take two 3-minute timings on the following material. Determine your words-a-minute rate. (Divide total words keyed by 3.)

S.I. 1.45

New statistics show that every year twelve thousand persons will 14
lose their lives in home fires. Another thirty thousand could suffer 28
serious injuries because of fire. Experts agree that as many as half 42
of those lives might have been spared if each homeowner had taken one 56
simple safety measure. A simple device, the smoke detector, has been 70
in production for many years. In the past, the fire alarms have been 84
sold mostly to a few building contractors who installed them in homes 98
that were being built. Recently, the alarms have been advertised and 112
offered for sale to all consumers. Yet, very few homes have an alarm 126
system. Why aren't all homes equipped with these lifesaving devices? 140
The major reason seems to be much apathy and lack of awareness. Many 154
people feel that a fire just could not happen to them. Sadly enough, 168
records show that no one is safe from a dangerous fire. A good smoke 182
detector, which can be installed in minutes, is needed for each home. 196
A consumer should shop carefully for an alarm and compare the quality 210
and purchase price of several smoke detectors. 219

| 1   2   3   4   5   6   7   8   9   10   11   12   13   14

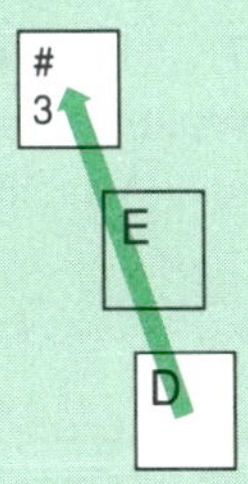

INTRODUCTION TO 3

Home-row *d* finger moves up and to the left to the *3*. Place both hands on the home row and practice the move from *d* to *3*. Look at your hands and watch your finger make the motion. Do this several times; then look away and try the same motion. Continue this procedure until you can make the motion correctly without looking at the keyboard.

Remember: Return your finger to the home-row position after striking a number.

Key each line once.

1 3 3 3 33 33 33 3 3 3 33 33 333 33 33 33 33 33 3 3

2 332 32 213 231 12 1321 231 32 231 2312 232 1213 3

3 a33 a3 a32 a321 a233 a3232 a132 13232 3223212 a23

4 a323 a3212321 a1323la al 231a al23 232 32 332 al3

5 3 233 13 231 23 233 323321 33212 13 321 3323 1231

6 323132112 231132a 22312a 2a 2331 a21321 a22132213

Timings

How many "words" of numbers can you key in 30 seconds? The material below is marked as "words" (see the end of each line). A "word" is made up of five letters, digits, and/or spaces.

Take two 30-second timings on line 1. If you finish the line before time is up, repeat it. Since you keyed for only 30 seconds, double your rate to compute your words-a-minute rate. Repeat the drill on lines 2, 3, and 4.

1 1233 1223 3221 3222 1312 3122 2311 3321 1232 3112 10

2 12 31131 221312 12131 32 233 121 123 2231 3231 23 10

3 21 1132 132 32 3112 321233 123 133132 123212 3123 10

4 311132 1223 12 1122331 23222123 3 12 33312 321 32 10

    1   2   3   4   5   6   7   8   9   1 0

Note: If you have not covered the Alphabetic Keys, omit the sentences and paragraph timings. Proceed to Session 15.

Sentences (Speed)

Lines 1–4 once
Lines 1–4 again

1 Jean shall sell the seashells, saddle, and jeans. 10

2 Taste the lean tea; handle the kettle that leaks. 20

3 The athlete tensed a knee as she dashed and fell. 30

4 The fat hen left the lake. She landed at a nest. 40

    1   2   3   4   5   6   7   8   9   1 0

(Current date) / TO: Ms. Pat Ganser, Editorial Department / From: Amos Grant, Research Director / Subject: Abstracts of Office Research Studies / The National Business Educator's Association (NBEA) is calling for abstracts of research studies that were completed in office systems during the past calendar year. If you are interested in submitting your abstract, note the attached directions from Oscar Byrnside, Executive Director of NBEA. / All abstracts must reach NBEA headquarters within the next 30 days. / your initials / Attachments

(current date) / TO: David Mattes, Director / Computer Center / From: Maureen Burns, Research / Subject: Computer Reports on Seminar Registration / Dave, since we don't have a microfilm reader, please send us hard copies of the following reports on a regular basis: / 1. Quarterly seminar size report, / 2. Preliminary seminar registration report (listing), / 3. Final seminar registration report (listing). / your initials

SESSION 46	LETTER OF APPLICATION

WARM-UP

1 Do not use a whiskbroom on the workbooks or the blackboard.

2 Evelyn welcomed the clerical classes in the balcony alcove.

3 The meal of omelets and melons was welcomed by the farmers.

4 The singers sang songs and mingled among the hungry diners.

5 An oldtimer scolds the troops only once, then moves onward.

6 123 and 456 and 789 and 890 and 321 and 654 and 987 and 090

7 1,234 5,678 9,012 10,234 20,456 30,987 40,567 56,789 23,908

    1   2   3   4   5   6   7   8   9   10   11   12

Timed Short Drills

Turn to pages TSD 1–8 (timed short-drill material) and complete the following:

1. Five 15-second timings for speed
2. Five 30-second timings for speed
3. Five 30-second timings for control/accuracy

Number Timings

Take two 30-second timings on Line 7 above.

5 Send the dated lease and halt the endless hassle. 10
6 A talented athlete eats steak and salad at least. 20
7 A flannel hat fell as Allen defended a keen lead. 30
8 The sad attendant halted a theft. He felt tense. 40

□□□□1□□□□2□□□□3□□□□4□□□□5□□□□6□□□□7□□□□8□□□□9□□□1 0

Sentences (Accuracy)

1 See, he is ill; his skin is thin; he feels faint. 10
2 The ill thief listened and slid his knife inside. 20
3 Enlist that inside aid that he shall indeed need. 30
4 I dislike that snide kid. He thinks it is a fad. 40

□□□□1□□□□2□□□□3□□□□4□□□□5□□□□6□□□□7□□□□8□□□□9□□□1 0

5 She is a skilled athlete and likes little detail. 10
6 The kitten is an infant and is a little lifeless. 20
7 The kid thinks I had the idea that he did finish. 30
8 He did ski that hill. That is indeed a sad test. 40

□□□□1□□□□2□□□□3□□□□4□□□□5□□□□6□□□□7□□□□8□□□□9□□□1 0

Timings

1   Jane prepares legal papers and letters. She 10
prefers reading ledgers and graphs. It is tiring 20
and drains her. 23

□□□□1□□□□2□□□□3□□□□4□□□□5□□□□6□□□□7□□□□8□□□□9□□□1 0

2   If Dan falters at the start, he is risking a 10
defeat. The stern referee sees the sprinters and 20
stresses fairness and praises spirit. 27

□□□□1□□□□2□□□□3□□□□4□□□□5□□□□6□□□□7□□□□8□□□□9□□□1 0

3   The blunt auditor suggested to Duke that the 10
business returns were a fraud. The usual routine 20
of minimum turnovers of funds had been sound, but 30
that fortune of thousands paid to a juror had not 40
been inserted in the annual input. Duke presumed 50
he was ruined and flushed with guilt. 57

□□□□1□□□□2□□□□3□□□□4□□□□5□□□□6□□□□7□□□□8□□□□9□□□1 0

Traditional
memo format

Use default tabs
to key heading.

**ITG
PROGRAM
BUREAU**

MEMORANDUM

DATE: Current Date   (Begin 3 lines below the letterhead or line 7 for blank paper.)
                              (ds)
TO: Ron Decker, Editorial Department
                              (ds)
FROM: Bill Walczak, Educational Consultant
                              (ds)
SUBJECT: SEMINAR OUTLINE

                              (ts)

Ron, attached is the revised seminar outline for the program on
Organizational Communication.
                              (ds)
Ned Ostenso, Bill Sleep, Randy Smith and I collaborated on this
revision. Please note that we changed the name of the program.
We feel that this is really a better description of the content
of the seminar.
                              (ds)
Please let us know when you are ready to review the program.
                              (ds)
your initials
                              (ds)
Attachment
                              (ds)
c: Mark Mitchell
    Ned Ostenso
    Bill Sleep
    Randy Smith

**MASTERY
SOFTWARE**

Space 4 times
before keying
additional
names in copy
notation.

Key each line twice.

WARM-UP

Concentrate on keeping your eyes on the copy. Read numbers in groups.

1 1233 1213 1223 1223 1133 3311 2211 2211 1132 2211

2 112 31131 231321 211312 112132 32233 1121 123 233

3 1233 1222 1333 1221 1331 3331 2222 2221 1112 1113

INTRODUCTION TO 4

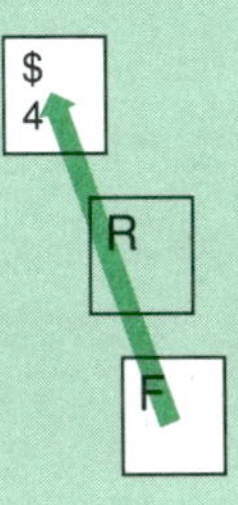

Home-row *f* finger moves up and to the left to the number *4*. Place both hands on the home row and practice the move from *f* to *4*. Look at your hands and watch your finger make the motion. Do this several times; then look away and try the same motion. Continue this procedure until you can make the motion correctly without looking at the keyboard.

Be sure to concentrate on the number combinations as you key.

Key each line once.

1 4 4 44 44 444 444 4 4 44 4444 4 44 44 44 444 44 44

2 14 134 1431 2343 343123 43 334 3 3421 23214 432442

3 a14 a4231 24 4a24 1432a 34 a4321 a4323 a431 a342 a

4 4 43 344 343 4321 3422 23423 3443 22343 343 44 334

5 4343213413 34343213311 4323412341 3431233 44342 43

Timings

Take a 1-minute timing on the following material.

> **MASTERY SOFTWARE**

Press *Enter* at the end of each line.

Unless instructed otherwise, key at a controlled rate if you are making three or more errors a minute.

If you finish before time is up, start over.

1 333 333 333 444 444 444 333 333 444 444 222 222 22 10

2 333 333 333 444 444 444 333 333 444 444 222 222 22 20

3 12221 12221 13331 13331 14441 14441 12221 12221 13 30

4 12221 12221 13331 13331 14441 14441 12221 12221 13 40

▢▢▢▢ 1 ▢▢▢▢ 2 ▢▢▢▢ 3 ▢▢▢▢ 4 ▢▢▢▢ 5 ▢▢▢▢ 6 ▢▢▢▢ 7 ▢▢▢▢ 8 ▢▢▢▢ 9 ▢▢▢ 1 0

4. *Subject Line.* The subject line identifies the purpose of the memo. On preprinted forms, you will find a variety of designations for this section of the memo; *SUBJECT, SUBJ., REGARDING,* and *RE* are some examples. If you are using blank or letterhead paper, you can use one of these designations and then key the appropriate information. The designation *SUBJECT* can be eliminated to save time and the information representing the subject keyed in all capital letters as illustrated in the Simplified Memo Format on page 217. Triple-space after the subject line.

   Note: The order and the placement of the introductory parts to a memorandum are not standardized. In some organizations, the order used has the subject or recipient listed first. In terms of format, you will find some cases where the recipient and sender names are on the left, with the date and subject on the right. To be sure of the appropriate order and format, it is a good idea to check an organization's procedures manual.

5. *Body.* The body, or message of the memo, is single-spaced, with double spacing between paragraphs. Double-space before keying reference initials.

6. *Reference Initials.* Reference initials identify the person who keyed the memorandum.

7. *Enclosure/Attachment.* The word *Enclosure* or *Attachment* is added to the memorandum if something is to accompany the message.

8. *Copy Notation.* The letter *c* followed by one or more names listed alphabetically in a column tells the recipient of the memo who else has received a copy. Space twice after the c: before keying the first name.

Note that there is no place for a signature on a memo. The person who prepared the message simply writes his or her initials following the name in the *FROM* line of the memo.

Review carefully the formatted memo with supporting instructions that follows. Be sure to note the various sections of the memo. Remember to use the tab key to align the heading. Then key Documents 1 and 2 on page 219.

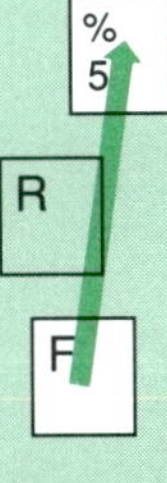

INTRODUCTION TO 5

Home-row *f* finger moves up and to the right to the number *5*. Place both hands on the home row and practice the move from *f* to *5*. Look at your hands and watch your finger make the motion. Do this several times; then look away and try the same motion. Continue this procedure until you can make the motion correctly without looking at the keyboard.

Remember to read the number combinations correctly.

Key each line once.
Then do again.

1 5 5 55 55 55 5 5 5 15 15 15 51 15 55 51 55 51 151

2 11 55 a55 11 55 a55 11 55 55 11 51 a51 15 15 15 5

3 55 44 a45 54 14 15 24 25 34 35 53 43 52 42 51 41a

4 15115 15115 55151 55151 15 51511 151 155 15115 51

5 15115 15115 a55151 a55151 15 5151 151 a155 a51151

6 15115 15115 a21515 a21515 a321 a321 a15a a15a 123

Timings

Use the following lines for speed practice. Use the same procedure that you did earlier. Take two 30-second timings on line 1. If you finish before time is up, begin again. Since you keyed for only 30 seconds, double your rate to compute your words-a-minute rate. Repeat the drill on lines 2, 3, and 4.

1 25 35 345 34 45 15 251 2342 235 325 325 1451 5141 10

2 4241 4521 31442 51431 51431 4251 4251 5421 5421 2 10

3 12 41 41 31 31 31 155 55 15 51 4544 3344 2233 112 10

4 12 51 31 21 31 31 55 55 51 15 455 344 233 1231 15 10

☐☐☐☐1☐☐☐☐☐2☐☐☐☐☐3☐☐☐☐☐4☐☐☐☐☐5☐☐☐☐☐6☐☐☐☐☐7☐☐☐☐☐8☐☐☐☐☐9☐☐☐10

Parts of Memorandum

1. ***Date Line.*** The date line contains the current date. If you are using a preprinted memo form, the word **DATE** is printed with sufficient space provided to fill in the information. If you are using blank or letterhead paper, you can key the word **DATE** in all capitals, followed by a colon; and then key the month, day of the month, and year. Set a tab stop 10 spaces from the left margin and key each heading line at that setting. With the Mastery Software, use the default tab settings to align text keyed after the guide words. To reduce the time required to prepare a memo, you can eliminate keying the word **DATE** as illustrated in the Simplified Memo Format shown below. Double-space after the date line.

Traditional Memo Format

WALCZAK CONSULTING CO.
MEMORANDUM

```
date:   February 9, 19--

  to:   Ron Decker, Editorial Department

from:   Bill Walczak, Educational Consultant

subject:   SEMINAR OUTLINE


Ron, attached is the revised seminar outline for the program on
Organizational Communication.

Ned Ostenso, Bill Sleep, Randy Smith and I collaborated on this
revision.  Please note that we changed the name of the program.
We feel that this is really a better description of the content
of the seminar.

Please let us know when you are ready to review the program.

kw

Attachment

c:  Mark Mitchell
    Ned Ostenso
    Bill Sleep
    Randy Smith
```

Simplified Memo Format

```
February 9, 19--

TO:  Ron Decker, Editorial Department

Bill Walczak, Educational Consultant

SEMINAR OUTLINE


Ron, attached is the revised seminar outline for the program on
Organizational Communication.

Ned Ostenso, Bill Sleep, Randy Smith and I collaborated on this
revision.  Please note that we changed the name of the program.
We feel that this is really a better description of the content
of the seminar.

Please let us know when you are ready to review the program.

kw

Attachment

c:  Mark Mitchell
    Ned Ostenso
    Bill Sleep
    Randy Smith
```

2. ***Recipient.*** The recipient is the person or persons who will receive the memo. On preprinted forms, the word **TO** is included. If you use blank or letterhead paper, key the word **TO**, followed by a colon, and then add the name of the individual(s) receiving the memo. Double-space after the recipient line(s).

3. ***Sender.*** The sender is the person who prepared the message. On preprinted forms, this line is labeled with the word **FROM**, with space to fill in the data. On blank or letterhead paper, key the word **FROM**, followed by a colon and then the name of the sender. In order to conserve time in preparing the document, the word **FROM** can be eliminated as illustrated in the Simplified Memo Format shown above. When this is done, the name of the sender starts at the left margin. Double-space after the send line.

INTRODUCTION TO 6

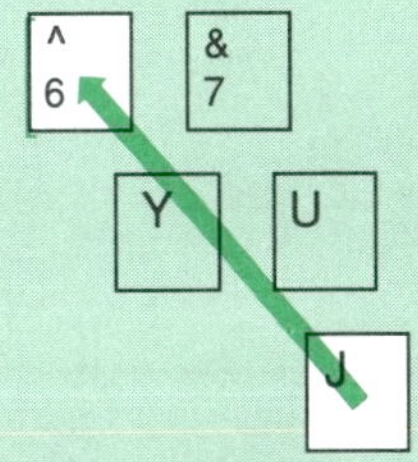

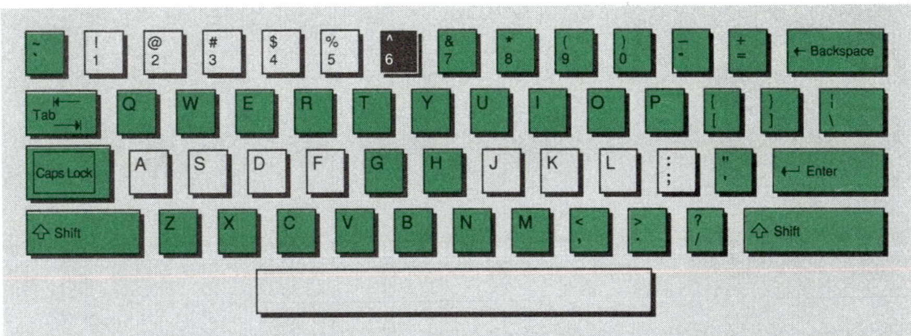

Home-row *j* finger moves up and to the left to the number *6*. Place both hands on the home row and practice the move from *j* to *6*. Look at your hands and watch your finger make the motion. Do this several times; then look away and try the same motion. Continue this procedure until you can make the motion correctly without looking at the keyboard.

Key each line once.
Then do again.

1 6 6 6 66 66 66 66 6 6 6 6 66 666 61 61 61 61 61 6

2 ll a66 ll 66 ll 66 ll 66 ll 66 a66 ll 66 ll 66 61

3 166 166 a661 661 161 161 a611 661 661 116 ll a666

4 11666 16661 61 66 66 111 666 661 1166 16661 61 61

Timings

Take a 1-minute timing on the following material.

MASTERY SOFTWARE

Press *Enter* at the end of each line.

1 26 35 346 34 45 46 251 2346 235 325 625 463 51616   10

2 6242 4621 31446 51432 51431 4265 4261 5431 5421 6   10

3 16 61 61 31 31 31 3655 66 16 61 5661 6546 665 566   10

4 16 661 626 365 4466 1263 4565 16 15 1615 26 62 54   10

    1   2   3   4   5   6   7   8   9   10

Sentences

If you finish before time is up, start over.

1 Dennis and Gene nailed a lath in the fallen gate.   10

2 The infant giggles in delight as the sled glides.   20

3 Helen had seen the elegant sign shining at night.   30

4 The endless agenda had eight legal details added.   40

5 The kitten tangled that tinsel. She disliked it.   50

    1   2   3   4   5   6   7   8   9   10

Lines 1–10 once—speed
Lines 1–10 again—control

Reminder: Omit the sentences and paragraph timings if you have not covered the Alphabetic Keys.

6 Kale and Allan ate a salad and a fig and a steak.   10

7 Gina, the gentle giant, giggled at Tina, the elf.   20

8 Dad needs a light flashlight if he skis at night.   30

9 Leslie sang a jingle as she dashed ahead in glee.   40

10 Al tested his stiff ankle. He gnashed his teeth.   50

    1   2   3   4   5   6   7   8   9   10

WALCZAK CONSULTING CO.
MEMORANDUM

date:

to:

from:

subject:

DATE:

TO:

FROM:

SUBJECT:

Horizontal Placement

The information on a memorandum is to be centered horizontally. Some preprinted forms are set up so that the length of the writing line is predetermined. If you are using blank or letterhead paper, the margins are the same width as those for a letter: 12–18 spaces (1 to 1-1/2 inches) for left and right margins for 12-pitch (elite) type and 10–15 spaces for 10-pitch (pica) type.

WALCZAK CONSULTING CO.
MEMORANDUM

date: February 9, 19--

to: Ron Decker, Editorial Department

from: Bill Walczak, Educational Consultant

subject: SEMINAR OUTLINE

Ron, attached is the revised seminar outline for the program on
Organizational Communication.

Ned Ostenso, Bill Sleep, Randy Smith and I collaborated on this
revision. Please note that we changed the name of the program.
We feel that this is really a better description of the content
of the seminar.

Please let us know when you are ready to review the program.

kw

Attachment

c: Mark Mitchell
    Ned Ostenso
    Bill Sleep
    Randy Smith

DATE: February 9, 19--

TO: Ron Decker, Editorial Department

FROM: Bill Walczak, Educational Consultant

SUBJECT: SEMINAR OUTLINE

Ron, attached is the revised seminar outline for the program on
Organizational Communication.

Ned Ostenso, Bill Sleep, Randy Smith and I collaborated on this
revision. Please note that we changed the name of the program.
We feel that this is really a better description of the content
of the seminar.

Please let us know when you are ready to review the program.

kw

Attachment

c: Mark Mitchell
    Ned Ostenso
    Bill Sleep
    Randy Smith

11 Is that dashing pink paint in the shapeless pail? 10
12 Please appease that helpless, pleading plaintiff. 20
13 A sheep passed the pines and plants in the sleet. 30
14 A tall, split, peeling aspen sapling is diseased. 40
15 His pastel napkin keeps dipping in his apple pie. 50

□□□□ 1 □□□□ 2 □□□□ 3 □□□□ 4 □□□□ 5 □□□□ 6 □□□□ 7 □□□□ 8 □□□□ 9 □□□ 1 0

16 Did Jake pass that fast jeep in his pastel sedan? 10
17 Pat speaks and pleads and defends the plaintiffs. 20
18 The patient is in pain; his left thigh is gashed. 30
19 Did Jane tape that splint and dispense the pills? 40
20 The spaniel has fleas and needs his skilled help. 50

□□□□ 1 □□□□ 2 □□□□ 3 □□□□ 4 □□□□ 5 □□□□ 6 □□□□ 7 □□□□ 8 □□□□ 9 □□□ 1 0

Timings

Take a 1-min. timing on each paragraph. Your instructor may ask you to take additional timings.

Unless instructed otherwise, key at a controlled rate if you are making three or more errors a minute.

If you finish before time is up, start over.

1   Print the paragraph in large letters. Raise 10
the title and delete the diagraphs. Insert three 20
fresh phrases at the end.   25

□□□□ 1 □□□□ 2 □□□□ 3 □□□□ 4 □□□□ 5 □□□□ 6 □□□□ 7 □□□□ 8 □□□□ 9 □□□ 1 0

2   It is all right if Dane repairs that rattle. 10
It is a danger and a threat. Perhaps the gear is 20
sheared. He repairs tenders and engines.   28

□□□□ 1 □□□□ 2 □□□□ 3 □□□□ 4 □□□□ 5 □□□□ 6 □□□□ 7 □□□□ 8 □□□□ 9 □□□ 1 0

3   Muffin is a genuine bulldog. Although he is 10
a plump pup, he bounds about with a flourish. It 20
is fun to see him plunge around, indulging in the 30
pure pleasure of running. He huffs and puffs and 40
slumps to the ground. No doubt, he will jump and 50
lunge again after a pause and find trouble.   59

□□□□ 1 □□□□ 2 □□□□ 3 □□□□ 4 □□□□ 5 □□□□ 6 □□□□ 7 □□□□ 8 □□□□ 9 □□□ 1 0

4   Thomas bought a used auto from a true fraud. 10
Although the bumper and the trunk were ruined, he 20
assumed that it would run. If he would flush the 30
rust from the lumbering hulk of junk, he might be 40
able to use it. His woeful anguish spurred a new 50
thought; perhaps it was useless.   56

□□□□ 1 □□□□ 2 □□□□ 3 □□□□ 4 □□□□ 5 □□□□ 6 □□□□ 7 □□□□ 8 □□□□ 9 □□□ 1 0

PRODUCTION

Memorandums are the most frequently produced type of correspondence in the office today. Read the following information relating to memorandums before keying the required activities.

MEMORANDUMS

The memorandum (or memo for short) is a means of communication used within an organization. The majority of information keyed in offices is distributed internally, and memos are the most common form of document used. It has many of the same characteristics of a letter, but it also has some unique features.

Style/Format

Some organizations have preprinted memo forms so that the person preparing the document has no decisions to make regarding vertical and horizontal placement, what information to include in the heading, and where to place the body or message of the memo.

Memorandums are usually prepared in block style, with all parts starting at the left margin.

When guide words in the heading are aligned on the left, set a tab stop two spaces after the colon in the longest line as a margin for the heading information. Align the left margin for the body of the memo with the guide words. (See Example 1 below.)

When guide words are aligned on the right, set the left margin two spaces after the colon to key the material in the heading and body. (See Example 2 below.)

Example 1

WALCZAK CONSULTING CO.
MEMORANDUM

```
date:     February 9, 19--

to:       Ron Decker, Editorial Department

from:     Bill Walczak, Educational Consultant

subject:  SEMINAR OUTLINE


Ron, attached is the revised seminar outline for the program on
Organizational Communication.

Ned Ostenso, Bill Sleep, Randy Smith and I collaborated on this
revision.  Please note that we changed the name of the program.
We feel that this is really a better description of the content
of the seminar.

Please let us know when you are ready to review the program.

kw

Attachment

c:  Mark Mitchell
    Ned Ostenso
    Bill Sleep
    Randy Smith
```

Example 2

WALCZAK CONSULTING CO.
MEMORANDUM

```
   date:  February 9, 19--

     to:  Ron Decker, Editorial Department

   from:  Bill Walczak, Educational Consultant

subject:  SEMINAR OUTLINE


          Ron, attached is the revised seminar outline for the
          program on Organizational Communication.

          Ned Ostenso, Bill Sleep, Randy Smith and I collaborated
          on this revision.  Please note that we changed the name
          of the program.  We feel that this is really a better
          description of the content of the seminar.

          Please let us know when you are ready to review the
          program.

          kw

          Attachment

          c:  Mark Mitchell
              Ned Ostenso
              Bill Sleep
              Randy Smith
```

Vertical Placement

Unlike the letter, the memorandum is not centered vertically on the page. Whether you are using a preprinted memo form, blank paper, or letterhead paper, the parts of a memo begin at the top of the page; no attempt is made to center the message vertically. If you are using letterhead paper, start the memo 3 lines below the last line of the letterhead. If you are using a blank sheet of paper to prepare a memo, the top margin should be 6–9 lines (1–1-1/2 inches). Double-space between each part of the memorandum heading and triple-space after the subject line.

WARM-UP

Lines 1–3 once
Lines 1–3 again

1 112 223 334 445 556 645 645 432 432 132 132 12345

2 6645 3342 1134 2245 6632 6161 2525 3456 4321 3165

3 165432 234516 465321 2243 4423 5364 14356 432 432

INTRODUCTION TO 7

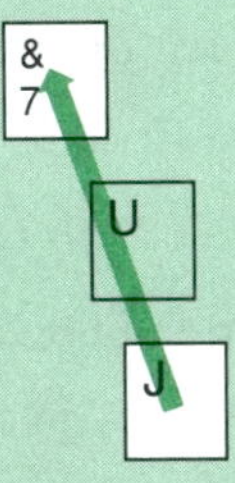

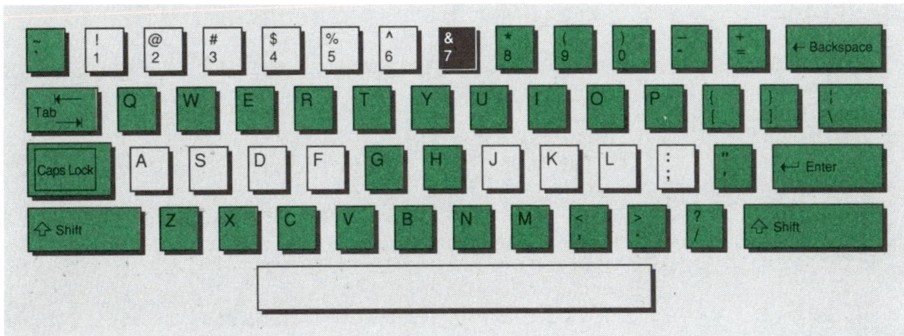

Home-row *j* finger moves up and to the left to the number *7*. Notice the difference between the reaches to the number *6* and the number *7*. Place both hands on the home row and practice the move from *j* to *7*. Look at your hands and watch your finger make the motion. Do this several times; then look away and try the same motion. Continue this procedure until you can make the motion correctly without looking at the keyboard.

Key each line once.
Then do again.

1 7 7 7 77 77 7 7 7 77 7 7 77 77 7 77 7 7 77 77 777

2 7 77 777 7777 7 7 77 77 777 777 7777 7777 7 77 77

3 76 76 67 77 66 776 776 77 777 6776 76 76 67 66 77

4 75 75 a55 77 66 76 57 57 a76 77 777 677 a555 76 6

5 a755a a755a 767 767 5767 5757 a576 7675a 7675a 77

6 777 666 555 a756a a576a 76a5a 6675a 6675 5667 777

Number Concentration Drill

See how quickly you can complete the following:

1. Key the numbers 1 through 7 three times. Space once after each number.

2. Key the number 1 through 7 three times. Space twice after each number.

3. Reverse the order; key from 7 down to 1. Space once after each number.

4. Key from 7 down to 1. Space twice after each number.

Take one 3-minute timing on the following material. Determine your words-a-minute rate. (Divide total words keyed by 3.)

S.I. 1.42

```
Each spring thousands of gardeners declare war on one bothersome      14
weed that seems to plague everyone.  This weed is the lowly dandelion   28
plant.  In earlier times, people savored all the virtues of this many  42
faceted plant.  Rather than referring to it as a weed, folks utilized  56
the very fine herbal qualities.  Some broths and tonics were made and  70
utilized to restore health to persons who were ill.  Even now, modern  84
pharmacies continue to use extracts of this springtime plant in quite  98
a number of medicines on the market for our use.                      108

    As a food, the dandelion is a big source of nutritious, healthy,  122
and delicious food.  It is quite rich in proteins, calcium, and iron.  136
The plant contains more Vitamin A than spinach or green peppers.  The  150
durable leaves, which may be used in many delicious salads, should be  164
picked before the first blossoms appear.  The tender leaves, although  178
tangy in taste, are very nutritious.  If you carefully dry the leaves  192
and boil them correctly, you can make delicious teas.  You might wish  206
to consume the new blossoms and make wines, salad garnishes, and some  220
blossoms which have been surrounded by a very tasty batter.           232
```

□□□□1□□□□2□□□□3□□□□4□□□□5□□□□6□□□□7□□□□8□□□□9□□□10□□□11□□□12□□□13□□□14

PREPARING THE FINAL COPY—STAGE 4

1. *Key the final copy.*

   a. Use white paper of good quality.
   b. Key on one side only.
   c. Double-space between lines of text.
   d. Indent the first line of paragraphs.
   e. Set margins for a 60-space line.
   f. Center the title.

2. *Proofread the final copy.*

   a. Proofread the copy carefully.
   b. Check for mechanics, spelling, and keyboarding errors.
   c. Read slowly.

DRILL

MASTERY SOFTWARE

Key your final copy on the Drill Screen provided in the software.

Key the final copy of the rough draft you revised in Session 43. Be sure to proofread it before you take it out of the machine or before you print the hard copy if you are using an electronic device.

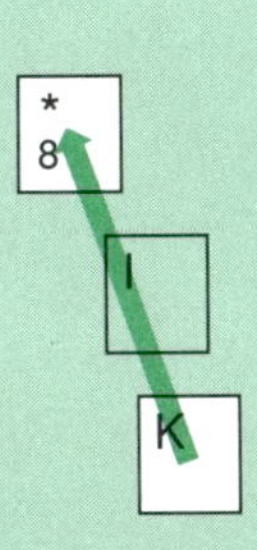

Key each line once.
Then do again.

Timings

How many "words" a minute can you key now that the numbers 6 and 7 have been added? Take two 30-second timings on line 1. If you finish before time is up, begin again. Because you keyed for only 30 seconds, double your rate to compute your words-a-minute rate. Repeat the drill on lines 2, 3, and 4.

1 71234 5671 62345 56712 3457 461234 3467 1234 4651 10

2 6771 4323 1612 5661 6675 31267 5672 4216 5437 243 10

3 5734273 5743216 11276516 225123 67 7113 6711 6 67 10

4 5421 4375 16 2367 5 672 51 61742 6611317 16 767 5 10

INTRODUCTION TO 8

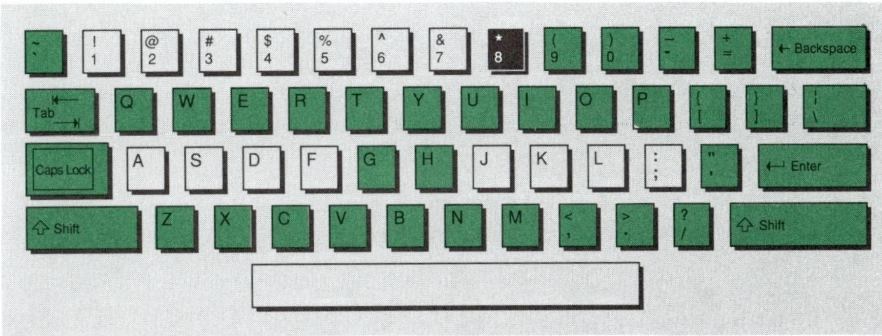

Home-row **k** finger moves up and to the left to the number **8**. Place both hands on the home row and practice the move from **k** to **8**. Look at your hands and watch your finger make the motion. Do this several times; then look away and try the same motion. Continue this procedure until you can make the motion correctly without looking at the keyboard.

1 8 8 8 88 88 88 8 8 8 88 88 888 888 88 88 88 88 88

2 87 18 6876 287 2248 836 872 347 2883 6788 8 82678

3 411 88 11 588 11 88 11 88 11 88 11 688 11 88 11 8

4 83 83 38 733 88 81 88 88 283 83 38 33 388 81 4188

5 8823 1482 8182 81828 2845 6817 71882 6818 2238 88

6 888 288 388 8283 38482 78681 11812 8823 28 28 888

Number Concentration Drill

See how quickly you can complete the following:

1. Key the numbers 1 through 8 as many times as you can in 30 seconds. Space once between numbers.

2. Reverse the order; key from 8 back to 1 as many times as you can in 30 seconds. Space once between numbers.

WARM-UP

Lines 1–5 once
Lines 1–5 again

1 Scratch that scene in the script and schedule the newscast.

2 Browse in that immense museum and observe the bird section.

3 The flashy salesroom she visited was a disgraceful mistake.

4 The publisher is shrewdly dishonest and shoddy in his work.

5 Silas considers that offensive noise as a passing nuisance.

Lines 6 and 7 once
Lines 6 and 7 again

6 61 and 62 and 63 and 64 and 65 and 66 and 67 and 68 and 690

7 2,361,731 231,464 55,565,577 39,918,867 9,586,713 341 89721

Timed Short Drills

Turn to pages TSD 1–8 (timed short-drill material) and complete the following:

1. Five 15-second timings for speed
2. Five 30-second timings for speed
3. Five 30-second timings for control/accuracy

Number Timings

Take two 30-second timings on Line 7 above.

Straight-Copy Timings

Take two 1-minute timings on the following material.

S.I. 1.45

To use your spare time effectively, you must have a plan. Every 14

successful person knows how to utilize spare hours. Plans with goals 28

are a must to enjoying leisure time. Many folks waste precious hours 42

trying to decide what to do for recreation. By the time they decide, 56

the leisure time has vanished. You must plan ahead for activities or 70

relaxing times. Forget your own problems while you focus on enjoying 84

those games, books, and vacations. 91

Timings

Take a 1-minute timing on the following material.

MASTERY SOFTWARE

Press *Enter* at the end of each line.

1 81 85 823 8466 8877 7868 58 45 238 845 866 8143 8 10

2 81234 5671 82345 3458 8612348 3467 1238 886 81387 10

3 5834278 58743218 11386518 2251386 87 88 8811318 8 10

4 5481 8375 18 2368 8 7628 81 61842 8811318 18 8788 10

☐☐☐☐ **1** ☐☐☐☐ **2** ☐☐☐☐ **3** ☐☐☐☐ **4** ☐☐☐☐ **5** ☐☐☐☐ **6** ☐☐☐☐ **7** ☐☐☐☐ **8** ☐☐☐☐ **9** ☐☐☐ **1 0**

INTRODUCTION TO 9

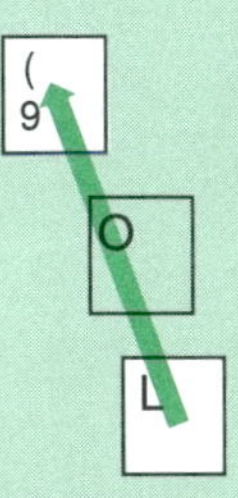

Home-row *l* finger moves up and to the left to the number *9*. Place both hands on the home row and practice the move from *l* to *9*. Look at your hands and watch your finger make the motion. Do this several times; then look away and try the same motion. Continue this procedure until you can make the motion correctly without looking at the keyboard.

1 99 9 999 9 99 91 91 91 99 99 99 9 999 9 99 999 91

2 989 8489 19891 1919 1891 9981 19867 183218 189 19

3 698 98 99 88 589 998 998 888 991 999 498 98 99 88

4 94 32989 2923 1989 2239 39823 59891 123 698 92919

Number Concentration Drill

1. Key the numbers 1 through 9 as many times as you can in 30 seconds. Space once between numbers.

2. Reverse the order; key from 9 back to 1 as many times as you can in 30 seconds. Space once between numbers.

Timings

Take a 1-minute timing on the following material.

1 91 95 923 8466 9977 7898 69 45 239 945 966 9143 9 10

2 91234 5671 92345 3458 9612349 3467 1239 996 81389 10

3 5934278 59743219 11386519 2251396 97 99 9911319 9 10

4 5491 9375 19 2368 9 7629 94 61942 99111319 19 979 10

☐☐☐☐ **1** ☐☐☐☐ **2** ☐☐☐☐ **3** ☐☐☐☐ **4** ☐☐☐☐ **5** ☐☐☐☐ **6** ☐☐☐☐ **7** ☐☐☐☐ **8** ☐☐☐☐ **9** ☐☐☐ **1 0**

**ITG
PROGRAM
BUREAU**

3609 EAST MARSHALL STREET • CHICAGO, ILLINOIS 60602-1598 • (312) 495-6134

Current Date

Mr. Timothy Palmer
Wagoner Consultants Corporation
2091 Front Avenue
Rochester, MN 55904-8493

Dear Mr. Palmer:

SUBJECT: Contract for Ms. Margaret Lloyd

Enclosed is a contract for the above person. Please sign all four
copies of the contract and return them addressed to my attention.
We will mail you one copy of the fully-executed contract for your
records.

Also enclosed is the Requisition for Advertising Materials. Please
fill in the information requested and return the completed form as
soon as possible.

We appreciate your prompt attention to these matters and urge you
to write or telephone if we may be of any further assistance.

Sincerely yours,

Pedro Garcia
Advertising Director

your initials

Enclosures

c: Margaret Lloyd

INTRODUCTION TO 0

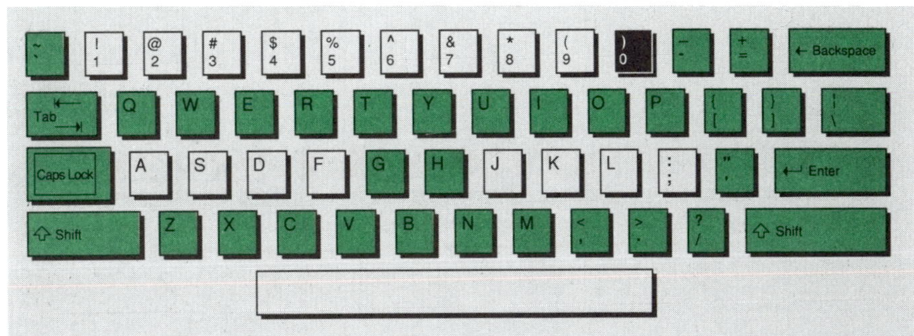

Home-row *semi* finger moves up and to the left to the number *0*. Place both hands on the home row and practice the move from *semi* to *0*. Look at your hands and watch your finger make the motion. Do this several times; then look away and try the same motion. Continue this procedure until you can make the motion correctly without looking at the keyboard.

Note: Be sure to use the *zero* key, not the capital *O*.

1 0 00 0 000 0 000 0 00 0 0 00 0 000 00 0 00 000 00

2 10 20 30 40 50 60 70 80 90 a10 a20 a30 240 250 10

Number Concentration Drill I

1. Key the numbers from 1 on as far as you can in 30 seconds. Space once after each number.

2. Key the numbers from 2 on increasing by two's (2, 4, 6, 8, 10, 12, etc.), as far as you can in 30 seconds. Space once after each number.

Number Concentration Drill II

Concentrate on keeping your eyes on the copy as you key the material below.

1 11201 1316 14037 22304 3405 4506 35607 6708 78092

2 1415 6816 62317 73218 2219 32206 8782 19222 90234

3 1929 30306 45317 7932 34332 13476 9535 87369 1370

4 1743 37744 7645 2674 65647 1674 84859 34750 25151

5 23270 45524 8910 5739 91524 7853 85426 1927 52938

Timings

Take two 1-minute timings on lines 1 through 3. If you finish all three lines before the time is up, begin again on line 1. Then take two 1-minute timings on lines 4 through 6. If you finish all three lines, begin again on line 4.

1 27 821 59361 40352 89734 92035 64019 9356 693 958 10

2 3177 50 6512 96 8742 56034 56832 85923 780 847 91 10

3 6409 7483 9467 3520 5945 2635 5705 8932 6485 1956 10

4 23670 81251800 165 908125635 69312 9871 6017340 2 10

5 716941 83201933 516386143 5113818 8542001 88490 1 10

6 236115432 11621618 1123419051 33991668 45441 4091 10

□□□□1□□□□2□□□□3□□□□4□□□□5□□□□6□□□□7□□□□8□□□□9□□□10

Key each line once.
Then do again.

Key each line once.

Push for SPEED

or

Concentrate for ACCURACY

**Required
Activity**

Session 44
Document 1
Filename: 044xxx01

Letter with enumeration
and attention line

Refer to page 180 for
more information on
keying the attention line.

Block style with mixed
punctuation

TRUAX–VEHLOW INVESTMENT SERVICES

10 KEARNEY DRIVE ■ KEARNEY, NE 68847-2817   (402) 554-6314

Current Date

Birnamwood Law School
733 Main
New York, NY 10032-4963
                                        (ds)
Attention: Dean of the Law School
                                        (ds)
Dear Ladies and Gentlemen:

We have received from the transfer agent the 100-share certificate
of Essex Industries common stock which was donated to your institution by Mr. and Mrs. William M. Larson.

You have indicated that you would like to sell the shares. We
will be in a position to proceed with the sale as soon as we
receive the following:
                                        (ds)
1. A resolution stipulating who is authorized to act in such
    matters for your institution.
                                        (ds)
2. A stock power signed by the authorized person.

Sincerely,

Robert T. Shaw
Senior Consultant

your initials

MASTERY SOFTWARE

You must use the *F4*
Indent feature to key the
enumerations.

THE COMMA AND THE DECIMAL

You have now mastered all ten digits and are ready to move into other areas of the keyboard. There are two symbols used frequently with numbers—the **comma** and the **decimal point**.

Home-row **k** finger moves down and to the right to the **comma**. Place both hands on the home row and practice the move from **k** to **comma**. Look at your hands and watch your finger make the motion. Do this several times; then look away and try the same motion. Continue this procedure until you can make the motion correctly without looking at the keyboard.

When numbers are separated by commas, decimals, spaces, letters, or other symbols, use these division points to read numbers. For example, 5,134 would be read **five/comma/one thirty-four**.

Key each line once.
Then do again.

1 45,134 38,751 7,893 5,313 4,497 1,438 6,719 6,151

2 7,361 1,368 1,434 9,860 5,167 34,511 76,924 6,331

3 21,468 38,107 48,243 1,509 5,114 15,816 6,184,336

4 98,165,225 4,408,452 251,145 12,259 1,259 159 467

5 987,587,462 467 254,241 48,204 96,285,341 1,284 5

6 49,285 49,285 285,495,496 465,284,261 504,261 284

Home-row **l** finger moves down and to the right to the **decimal** (**period**). Place both hands on the home row and practice the move from **l** to **decimal**. Look at your hands and watch your finger make the motion. Do this several times; then look away and try the same motion. Continue this procedure until you can make the motion correctly without looking at the keyboard.

Key each line once.
Then do again.

1 41,345.51 15,378.78 31,428.27 89,261,500.68 59.63

2 61.34 91,007.23 851,267.18 109.01 13.17 8.43 4.40

3 596.27 990.85 67,349.34 23,265.08 186.84 4.23 .87

4 8,582 284,496 162,285,796 2,268,241 1,285 3,285 5

5 4,285 5,285 4,296 6,289 4,279,201 830,287 494,294

6 798 280 184,495 420 1,280 492,850,294 465,240 496

Straight-Copy Timings

Take two 1-minute timings on the following material.

S.I. 1.45

    You are a consumer. Without you and millions of other consumers   14
in the nation, businesses would have to close. There would be nobody   28
to buy those goods and services which businesses produce. The impact   42
of ceasing all operations would quickly affect every person. Workers   56
would have no jobs and would have no money to continue living. There   70
would be no hustle and bustle of daily life. Every family would have   84
to supply all the necessities in life for themselves. Each family or   98
group would have to grow food, produce clothing, and provide shelter.   112

　　　1　　　2　　　3　　　4　　　5　　　6　　　7　　　8　　　9　　10　　11　　12　　13　　14

Take two 3-minute timings on the following material. Determine your words-a-
minute rate. (Divide total words keyed by 3.)

S.I. 1.42

    To avoid consumer problems, some decisions should be made before   14
buying a product. The first major point is to decide if you and your   28
family really need that new product or new service. If the answer is   42
yes, then the next step is to shop around and compare prices. A good   56
library will have publications which give helpful comparisons between   70
similar products. Check on the firm with which you are dealing--call   84
the Better Business Bureau for more information. Make certain that a   98
guarantee is in writing. Before you sign a contract, read it to make   112
sure that you understand it fully. If you have any doubts at all, it   126
would be wise to wait and think about the purchase a little longer.   140

    When you buy a product or a service, be sure that you understand   154
the method of payment if it is to be a credit purchase. Know exactly   168
when each payment is due, how much interest is being charged, and how   182
many months the payments are to be made. Read all tags and labels to   196
learn all about the product before you use it.   205

    If you have any problems with the product or service, speak with   219
the seller first. If you find that a seller does not give the proper   233
satisfaction to a problem, there are many consumer protection groups,   247
or agencies, for you to contact.   254

　　　1　　　2　　　3　　　4　　　5　　　6　　　7　　　8　　　9　　10　　11　　12　　13　　14

Sentences

1 Rip, the ranger, fell and sprained his left knee. 10

2 An irate diner startled the frightened girl here. 20

3 Dirk did the drill first and drank the tea later. 30

4 Fresh, green grapes are great as a dessert treat. 40

5 Al related the entire tale in the strange letter. 50

6 Spread the lard in the skillet and grill a treat. 10

7 He risks great danger if he departs after dinner. 20

8 The eastern ship at sea held pearls and trinkets. 30

9 The sad intern lingered in the garden and rested. 40

10 The raging giraffe splintered that ringside seat. 50

11 Mike is making a frame; he needs ample sandpaper. 10

12 The meat manager made a simple remark and smiled. 20

13 Did Mamie transmit the message after amending it? 30

14 Sandman, the fine farm animal, had a marked limp. 40

15 Pam had made a malt that had milk and mint in it. 50

16 Add ample stamps and mail the letter at midnight. 10

17 The fireman attempted an immense task and missed. 20

18 Did Sammie eliminate all mistakes in the message? 30

19 Jim, is that smashed metal mass a damaged helmet? 40

20 Minne missed the main message as her mind dimmed. 50

Timings

1   Zeb zipped to that zoo with zest and nuzzled 10
the zebras. He sneezed in the breeze and went to 20
see the lizards. He wants to be a zoologist when 30
he gets older. He knows a zillion things and his 40
dazed and puzzled parents are amazed. 47

(Current date) / Mr. Gary Wenner / Business Publications / 510 Third Avenue / TORONTO, ON / CANADA / M2H 2S6 / Mr. Wenner, your letter regarding the proposal by Mrs. Darlene Jones arrived while I was on vacation. I've reviewed the proposal carefully and here are my observations. / 1. The sequence for the proposed textbook is oriented to one job occupation, namely the secretarial profession. However, this may be what you are shooting for. / 2. Textbooks are not included in the following areas: / a. Data Processing / b. Office Systems, Layout, and Design / c. Office Management / 3. The business communications text that was recommended does not include anything about oral communications. / 4. In the secretarial procedures textbook, the emphasis is devoted to legal secretary and medical secretary work. However, a large number of secretaries today are working in manufacturing and government firms. It would seem that simulation programs in these areas would be more appropriate. / 5. I would include the following items in one textbook: office automation, machine transcription, and administrative support. / 6. In the filing and records management text, nothing was mentioned about electronic filing systems or the cost of maintaining and disposing of recorded information. I believe this should be added. / 7. The textbook that Mrs. Jones recommends on adding and calculating machines is purely traditional. I would refer to ten-key electronic calculation using electronic terminals. / 8. As far as the principles of accounting text, it doesn't seem to go far enough. No mention is made of managerial accounting. / 9. The duplicating processes text doesn't cover laser printers. Also, it seems that there should be more emphasis on how to prepare material for these machines rather than on how to operate them. / 10. As far as the keyboarding text is concerned, I believe it should include materials for in-basket exercises. / I hope that these comments will help in your decision to publish in the office education area. I certainly would promote this venture and would be happy to help you in any way possible. If you have any questions, please write or call me. My telephone number is (312) 864-5622. / Lorraine Misslingham / Editor / your initials

<table><tr><td>SESSION 44</td><td>ATTENTION/SUBJECT LINES</td></tr></table>

WARM-UP

1 Catch that tall, thin teen and tell her to watch the store.

2 The wretched witch tended to foretell fortunes in tea cups.

3 The stern reporter noticed the courteous tennis team often.

4 Tim writes creative articles and practices dramatic acting.

5 The gentle cattle are too thin; the earth's thaw is timely.

6 71 and 72 and 73 and 74 and 75 and 76 and 77 and 78 and 790

7 2,361 67,201403 336 932,341,176 700,318173 57,318,923 77551

☐☐☐☐1☐☐☐☐2☐☐☐☐3☐☐☐☐4☐☐☐☐5☐☐☐☐6☐☐☐☐7☐☐☐☐8☐☐☐☐9☐☐☐10☐☐☐11☐☐☐12

Timed Short Drills

Turn to pages TSD 1–8 (timed short-drill material) and complete the following:

1. Five 15-second timings for speed
2. Five 30-second timings for speed
3. Five 30-second timings for control/accuracy

Number Timings

Take two 30-second timings on Line 7 above.

2   Zelda gazed in amazement as Zip, the wizard, 10
seized a wand. It was ablaze with a maze of fire 20
and lights. He did dozens of hazardous feats and 30
puzzled all at the bazaar. He also was a trapeze 40
whiz and dazzled folks.   45

□□□□1□□□□2□□□□3□□□□4□□□□5□□□□6□□□□7□□□□8□□□□9□□□1 0

3   A cookout on the beach could include cheese, 10
carrots, meat sandwiches, and cold juice. If the 20
chill of the ocean is too much, hot chocolate and 30
hot coffee can chase the cold chills. The decent 40
lunch and a chat with chums can enrich affection. 50

□□□□1□□□□2□□□□3□□□□4□□□□5□□□□6□□□□7□□□□8□□□□9□□□1 0

4   An office clerk who lacks basic ethics could 10
become the subject of scorn. Those persisting in 20
cruel and careless attacks on certain new workers 30
can cause havoc. It is logical to follow strict, 40
concise rules concerning office tact. Choose the 50
right track and be sincere.   55

□□□□1□□□□2□□□□3□□□□4□□□□5□□□□6□□□□7□□□□8□□□□9□□□1 0

SESSION 17 — NUMBER PATTERNS

Remember, when numbers are grouped naturally by commas, spaces, and decimals,
read the number by divisions. For example 1,676,352.17 is read *one/comma/six/
seventy-six/comma/three fifty-two/decimal/seventeen.*

Key each line once.
Then do again.

1 1,676,352.17 3,131 2.24 436,342 101.31 166,891 89 10
2 236,731 831,643 534.67 4,091,867 3,587.13 501,316 10
3 61,301.04 .36 89,341.76 31,700.73 151,317 416,319 10
4 6,117.08 7.43 298 634,513.77 3,397.13 811,543,024 10
5 76,244.83 7.43 98 634,413.77 5,397.13 1,815.43 21 10

□□□□1□□□□2□□□□3□□□□4□□□□5□□□□6□□□□7□□□□8□□□□9□□□1 0

Mr. Thomas Quaker, Jr.   Line 7 (1-inch) top margin
Page 2   (Line 1 of Mastery Software)
Current Date

                                      (triple-space)

The exact terms of the underwriting will be set forth in an underwriting agreement to be entered into by Quaker Business Machines and Truax-Vehlow Investment Services. The underwriting discounts and commissions will not exceed 10 percent of the public offering price.

Truax-Vehlow is a hyphenated company name. Do not drop the hyphen.

Except for any reimbursement provided for in this letter, Truax-Vehlow Investment Services will pay its own expenses and the expenses of its attorney. The underwriters will also pay the expenses of running the customary advertisements in various publications following the offering.

Quaker Business Machines will pay the fees and expenses of its legal counsel; all printing charges relating to the registration statement, prospectus, and underwriting agreements; postage; SEC, state, and federal filing fees; and the reasonable costs of a due diligence meeting.

Following conclusion of the public offering, Quaker Business Machines agrees to furnish quarterly unaudited financial statements to its shareholders and the underwriters with audited reports to be issued annually.

We look forward to working with you and your associates on the proposed public offering. This letter is accepted by Quaker Business Machines and Truax-Vehlow Investment Services as a statement of mutual intent to carry out the proposed transactions, but it does not constitute a firm commitment on the part of either the Company or the underwriters.

If this letter correctly sets forth your understanding of our arrangement, please contact us.

Sincerely,

Robert E. Truax   (4 line spaces down)
Senior Vice President

                             (ds)

your initials

                             (ds)

c: Accounting Department

Tabulation Drill

Set four tab stops at 10-space intervals across the page. Refer to page 24 for Tab Key instructions.

1 4901	8702	3303	3904	7205
2 6106	8307	9408	2709	3710
3 1511	5712	2613	9114	1515
4 5716	9117	5618	6619	3820
5 2621	3122	4523	2324	3125
6 6726	3528	8528	3529	4130
7 7731	6932	8533	7434	9935
8 8836	2337	6138	1639	5840

Number Drill I

Remember to read numbers in 2-3-2 combinations. However, if the number group is separated by a letter, space, comma, decimal, or some other symbol, use those points as divisions for reading.

Take one 30-sec. timing on each line.

If you finish before time is up, start over.

1 7371130 91368840 1534986003 51673455189 963310931 10
2 45134157 386005138 789 5133459 1 38886190 34141 2 10
3 21468159 515113 6873931 438761 223026501 89340013 10
4 6135910 619822385 3676 1090101 3948131 1788434341 10
5 161,761 36,017 18,131 2,924 361,342 101,431 2,699 10
6 2,361,731 231,464 55,565,577 39,913,867 9,586,713 10
7 61,201,304 336 932,341,176 700,318,173 57,318,923 10
8 63,116 10.81 5.87 34,238 4.98 11,151 69,138 15.38 10
9 76,924 40.83 78,431 .98 63,485 13,667 59.39 4,131 10

□□□□1□□□□2□□□□3□□□□4□□□□5□□□□6□□□□7□□□□8□□□□9□□□1 0

Number Drill II

Take one 30-sec. timing on each line.

If you finish before time is up, start over.

1 161176 36017 38131 2924 361.42 101431 166,810 895 10
2 236,731 831464 55565577 3,013.67 4586713 50131672 10
3 51201304 436 892341176 31,700.73 151,837 415531 1 10
4 631171081 587 34238 10989115 15 5,148.01 538.32 7 10
5 6,924,083 7.34 98 634,413.77 69397413 81145438571 10
6 7361130 9,368.40 153,986.03 51673455189 9655151 5 10
7 45134145 387005138 .89 5313459 14,887.09 53151557 10
8 2146859 381076 48,331.90 41133590 1518614 1610720 10
9 413451 51513 6783931 529761 22,026.01 89376003183 10

□□□□1□□□□2□□□□3□□□□4□□□□5□□□□6□□□□7□□□□8□□□□9□□□1 0

Two-page business letter

Block style with mixed punctuation

Be careful where you stop keying at the bottom of a page.

General Rule: If a full paragraph will not fit and part of it must be carried over to next page, leave *at least* two lines of paragraph at bottom of page and always carry *at least* two lines to next page.

TRUAX–VEHLOW INVESTMENT SERVICES

10 KEARNEY DRIVE ■ KEARNEY, NE 68847-2817　　　　(402) 554-6314

Current Date

(Begin 2–3 lines below letterhead or on line 13; line 7 of Mastery Software)

Mr. Thomas Quaker, Jr.　　　　(4 line spaces down)
President
Quaker Business Machines
2401 Lincoln Boulevard
New York, NY 10037-6847

(ds)

Dear Mr. Quaker:

(ds)

This is to record the mutual intention of Quaker Business Machines and Truax-Vehlow Investment Services to undertake a public offering of common stock of Quaker Business Machines (the "Company").

(ds)

It is our intention to form an underwriting syndicate to purchase up to 250,000 shares of new common stock from Quaker Business Machines and to reoffer the shares to the public at a price mutually agreed upon. This agreement is subject to the following:

(ds)

1.　The assurance that no materially adverse change in the affairs of the Company and its prospects occurs which appears sufficient, in our opinion, to threaten the success of our effort;

2.　The market conditions at the time of the offering;

3.　The filing of a prospectus with the Securities and Exchange Commission and its subsequent notification of effectiveness.

We will not be bound to receive and pay for your shares until the completion of the following procedures:

1.　Blue Sky qualifications have been met in a reasonable number of states of our mutual selection,

2.　A final underwriting agreement satisfactory to each of us is executed. // (page break)

Note: The // (page break) direction is for the Mastery Software user.

6–9 lines (1–1-1/2 inches) bottom margin

MASTERY SOFTWARE

You must start a new page when you see the page-break symbol (//).

(continued on next page)

Number Drill III

```
1  2634 10485 10.90 a64781 2.89 11,584,609 449345125   10
2  656.98 11,067 14 48067015 28 842 550.18 56,679 23    10
3  12 4954 50,874 280 796,416.83 92645 15,041 550914     10
4  4 284 96175 2.95 59,602.88 15281 23 741 681104 47      10
5  99 84.22 903 571.28 67,832,523.15 82 904 56451089     10
6  80 106 29.15 61700 281,401,282.00 67414451 510 15     10
7  224 50 4605141 489,753 4.86 21 8674005 71.26 4559     10
8  667101 8.26 5,410 49724301 9,454.89 556 78911 531     10
9  46 82 96.48 4457004 33216 5436 434215 61780 2,466     10
```

☐ ☐ ☐ ☐ **1** ☐ ☐ ☐ ☐ **2** ☐ ☐ ☐ ☐ **3** ☐ ☐ ☐ ☐ **4** ☐ ☐ ☐ ☐ **5** ☐ ☐ ☐ ☐ **6** ☐ ☐ ☐ ☐ **7** ☐ ☐ ☐ ☐ **8** ☐ ☐ ☐ ☐ **9** ☐ ☐ ☐ **1 0**

NUMBERS

GENERAL GUIDELINES

GENERAL

Authorities do not agree on absolute rules about when to spell out numbers and when to use figures. The guidelines illustrated here are those that are generally acceptable. For more detailed information, consult a style reference manual.

1. Spell out numbers one through ten; use figures for numbers 11 and above.

```
There are six boys enrolled in shorthand.
There are 40 boys in beginning typewriting.
```

2. If most of the numbers in a series are ten and below, spell them out.

```
We have six Apple computers, eight IBM Personal
Computers, and twenty IBM "Selectric" typewriters.
```

However, if most of the numbers in a series are above ten, use figures.

```
We have 16 Apple computers, 14 IBM Personal
Computers, and 8 IBM "Selectric" typewriters.
```

3. When a sentence begins with a number, spell it out.

```
Three hundred students are majoring in business.
```

DATES

4. If the day precedes the month, express it either in words or figures.

```
We will meet on the 6th of December.
We will meet on the sixth of December.
```

5. If the day follows the month, express it in figures.

```
We will meet on December 6 at the restaurant.
```

6. If in the form of month, day, and year, express the day and year in figures.
Note: Always follow the year with a comma.

```
We will meet on December 6, 19--, at
    the restaurant.
```

REVISING THE ROUGH DRAFT—STAGE 3

1. *Evaluate the material carefully.* Read the composition several times. Examine every word and sentence. Sometimes it helps if you read it aloud; you will be amazed at how errors and offending phrases come to light. Mark any changes you wish to make.

2. *Every sentence should pertain to the topic.* In a short composition, there is no room for irrelevant sentences.

3. *Checklist for revision:*

   a. Is the introductory paragraph interesting and useful?

   b. Are the sentences and paragraphs coherent and clear?

   c. Is there a smooth transition from sentence to sentence, paragraph to paragraph?

   d. Is the sequence a logical one?

   e. Do your sentences provide some variety?

   f. Are the word choices precise and descriptive?

   g. Is every comma justified?

   h. Do the verb tenses correspond to each other properly?

   i. Is every word spelled correctly?

   j. Are words capitalized correctly?

   k. Are there any misplaced modifiers?

DRILL

Using the revision checklist above, carefully evaluate the rough draft that you composed during the last session. Mark the necessary corrections on your rough draft using the proofreader's marks on page 174. If you are in doubt about something, consult a reference book.

PRODUCTION

MASTERY SOFTWARE

If you are using the Mastery Software, you must adhere to the page breaks (//) as indicated in multiple-page documents to enable the software to check your work correctly. Hard returns, keyed by pressing the *Enter* key, must be inserted after the last line of text on the first page to force a page break; an automatic page break is inserted after line 54. It is recommended that you use the Mastery Software default margins of 1 and 66.

Enumerations, as shown in Document 1 on page 207, must be keyed using the Indent (*F4*) function of the Mastery Software. To use this feature, follow this procedure:

1. Set a tab at column 5.
2. Key the number and period (i.e., 1.).
3. Depress the *F4* function key and key the enumeration.
4. Depress the *Enter* key at the end of the enumeration (i.e., effort;).
5. Repeat Steps 2–4 for each enumeration.

| **MONEY** | 7. When keying exact or approximate amounts of money, use figures. *Note:* Do not add zeros to whole dollar amounts. |

```
The repair bill will be $200.
The carbon ribbon sells for $2; the cloth one
    for $1.55.
```

8. When keying amounts less than a dollar, use figures. *Note:* Always use the word *cents* unless it is a series containing amounts of $1 and more.

```
We felt a 35-cent reduction in price was appropriate.
The items cost $1.17, $.45, and $2.10.
```

MEASUREMENT

9. Use figures when keying measurements except when the measurement lacks technical significance.

```
This machine weighs approximately 7 pounds.
This will be approximately three times as much.
```

10. Temperature, size, and dimension are always in figures.

```
It was 23 degrees below 0 last night.
Her glove size is 3.
The mobile home measures 8 x 32 feet.
```

DECIMAL/PERCENT

11. Use figures to express a whole number with a decimal (mixed number).

```
1.5   or   1.45
```

12. Key percentages in figures. *Note:* Spell out the word *percent.* Also, if a range, the word *percent* follows the last figure only.

```
10 percent        10 to 20 percent
```

AGE

13. Age is spelled out.

```
He was twenty years old.
```

TIME

14. Periods of time are spelled out.

```
sixteen hours        twelve months
```

15. Use figures to express time.

```
4:30 a.m.        2:20 p.m.
```

Except when using "on the hour" without a.m. or p.m.

```
His plane will be arriving about ten tonight.
```

ADDRESSES

16. Key house numbers in figures.

```
His address is 3103 Eddy Lane.
```

17. Spell out street, avenue, and boulevard names that carry numbers ten or below; above ten, express their names in figures.

```
The store is located on First Avenue.
My address is 3103 14th Street.
```

Take two 1-minute timings on the following material.

S.I. 1.45

A very common job today is the home worker. Many people are very   14
happy working at home. They will be more productive doing their tasks   28
at home. It will give them a chance to care for the children and also   42
provide them the opportunity to earn an income. Computer programming,   56
among other occupations, is a typical type of work completed while the   70
worker remains in the home. As more and more of the workers earn more   84
of their income at home, many seem to believe that social problems are   98
going to evolve. Many believe that people have to work in the offices   112
if they are to have the right social surroundings.   122

□□□□1□□□□2□□□□3□□□□4□□□□5□□□□6□□□□7□□□□8□□□□9□□□10□□□11□□□12□□□13□□□14

Take one 3-minute timing on the following material. Determine your words-a-minute rate. (Divide total words keyed by 3.)

S.I. 1.39

Many people are growing herb gardens. The herb plants provide a   14
variety of new seasonings, fragrances, and flavorings. Growing herbs   28
is quite similar to growing a vegetable garden. You should select an   42
area for your herb garden that is sunny, as herbs demand an abundance   56
of sunlight to make them sweet and flavorful. To supply enough herbs   70
for a family of four, you would need a garden space about ten to fif-   84
teen feet square. If you do not have enough room, it is very easy to   98
grow an abundance of herbs in an ordinary window box or in small clay   112
flower pots. If grown inside, the herbs should be placed in a window   126
which receives full sunlight at least one half of the day. In a case   140
where sunlight is not available, a fluorescent-light garden will give   154
you an abundant harvest of herbs. To promote a compact growth, it is   168
a good idea to snip the plants back on a regular basis. Herbs placed   182
with other plants add charm and grace with the rich foliage. Freshly   196
picked herbs can either be dried or frozen for future use. Many good   210
cookbooks will give directions for using a variety of herbs.   222

□□□□1□□□□2□□□□3□□□□4□□□□5□□□□6□□□□7□□□□8□□□□9□□□10□□□11□□□12□□□13□□□14

Sentences

1 That traveler arrived in a lavish, private plane. 10
2 Seven silver vases vanished at the evening event. 20
3 Did Van ever deliver the varnish and the shelves? 30
4 Vinnie lives in the villa; it has a vast veranda. 40
5 It is evident; the vital lever reverses the vent. 50

6 The rival divers tried varied dives in the river. 10
7 Val, deliver that vast velvet divan this evening. 20
8 Marvia served vanilla malts at the private event. 30
9 The driver has a grave fever; give him a vitamin. 40
10 The starved vandal evaded five vigilant servants. 50

11 He does not fool me; he is not an honest senator. 10
12 Ora ordered the onions and olives from the store. 20
13 That old man stooped among the roses and groaned. 30
14 The golden moon shone on the old prison rooftops. 40
15 The soft fog floated aloft over the lone trooper. 50

16 Someone noted the stolen passport photos at noon. 10
17 The senior pilot spotted an airport in the gloom. 20
18 Jo dropped the looped rope at the rodeo and lost. 30
19 A violent storm moved along the remote oak grove. 40
20 Did the florist remove the thorns from the roses? 50

Timings

1   The minimal marks alarmed Mae. She had made 10
three simple, mental mistakes in the math test; a 20
small, grim smile masked the dismal mental image. 30
She had failed the semester. 36

Mr. John Gardner, Kresge Laboratories, 3611 51st Avenue, San Diego, CA 92101-7211 Dear Mr. Gardner: Attached is your form memorandum which has been completed to show the audio-visual equipment needs for our program at the Biological Research Association Conventin to be held in San Diego on June 22. The equipment may be picked up for return immediately following the program. Our first preference for seating arrangements would be theater style, with calssroom seating as our second choice. You are to be highly commended for your thorough convention preparations. This certainly will ehlp assure a smooth-rinning porogram. Paul Ganser, Executive Director Attachment

---

SESSION 43 TWO-PAGE BUSINESS LETTER

WARM-UP

Lines 1–5 once
Lines 1–5 again

1 The queen questioned the unique request for that equipment.

2 Quentin acquired the liquid lacquer for the quaint antique.

3 The squad questioned and quizzed the quiet delinquent lads.

4 The squadron ate squab and squash after the quick conquest.

5 The quick quakes brought queasy quiverings to the squadron.

Lines 6 and 7 once
Lines 6 and 7 again

6 51 and 52 and 53 and 54 and 55 and 56 and 57 and 58 and 490

7 45134157 386005138 789 5133459 1 38886190 034141 89023 1889

Timed Short Drills

Turn to pages TSD 1–8 (timed short-drill material) and complete the following:

1. Five 15-second timings for speed
2. Five 30-second timings for speed
3. Five 30-second timings for control/accuracy

Number Timings

Take two 30-second timings on Line 7 above.

2   Marna smelled the simmering meat. The steam 10
permeated the air. She managed a small taste and 20
smiled. The meat and milk might help that little 30
girl and ease her pain.   35

3   A career in science includes certain choices 10
to consider. One could choose to become a doctor 20
in a clinic or a teacher in a medical school. An 30
active search of a current college catalog should 40
indicate which courses to select. Contact campus 50
finance officers to check cost factors.   58

4   Mack, a black Scottie, is a champion canine. 10
A constant companion is the chocolate colored cat 20
called Chicco. Crowds chuckle as Mack and Chicco 30
do their tricks to music. Mack can count objects 40
and prance on a bench. Clever Chicco climbs upon 50
Mack, adding a certain clownish touch to the act. 60

Session 42
Document 1
Filename:
042xxx01

Business letter

Block style
with enclosure
or attachment
and open
punctuation

Current Date   (Begin on line 13 or 14.)

Mr. Ronald A. Christner   (5 line spaces down)
Chief Administrator
Lincolnwood Manor
4762 W. Touhy Avenue
Lincolnwood, IL 60646-5121
                                     (ds: double-space)
Dear Mr. Christner
                                     (ds)
Attached are the resumes, pictures and outline for the Time
Management Seminar to be held in January at the Hilton Hotel.
                                     (ds)
The program will be geared to the needs of nursing home
administrators. If you have questions about the program,
please give me a call.
                                     (ds)
Dr. John Schillak of the University of Illinois and I will
present the program.
                                     (ds)
Sincerely yours

L. Ferrari

Sandra Ferrari   (4 line spaces down)
Division Chairman
                                     (ds)
your initials
                                     (ds)
Attachments

10-KEY NUMERIC KEYBOARD

Generally, microcomputers and display terminals have a 10-key numeric keyboard located to the right of the alphabetic keyboard. The numeric keyboard allows the operator to enter numeric data. This keyboard may be used instead of the numeric row on the alphabetic keyboard. With a minimum amount of practice, you can enter numeric data at a rate of well over 100 digits per minute. Industry standards usually identify a rate of 250 digits per minute as "average" on the 10-key keyboard.

The illustrations below show the general arrangement of most 10-key numeric keyboards. The top row contains the 7, 8 and 9. The middle row contains the 4, 5, and 6. This row is identified as the *home row*. The bottom row of keys contains the 1, 2, and 3. The 0 (zero) key is at the very bottom.

TYPICAL 10-KEY KEYBOARD CONFIGURATION

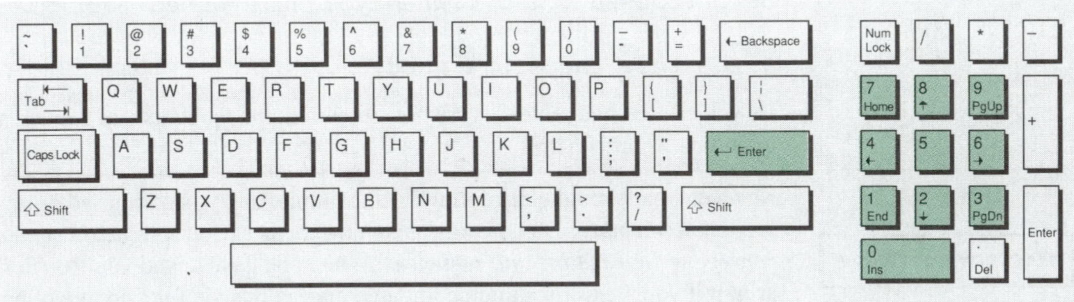

The *Enter* key is used to enter information after keying the data.

On a microcomputer the num lock key must be "on" in order to use the 10-key numeric keyboard.

ALTERNATE 10-KEY KEYBOARD CONFIGURATIONS

Several alternate 10-key keyboards are being used today by various computer manufacturers. The alternate keyboards provide additional keys in conjunction with the 10-key pad. The most common keys next to the number keys are the *plus* (+), the *minus* (–), the *comma* (,), and the *decimal* (.). You will generally find that it is more efficient to use the keys next to the 10-key pad.

Two alternate 10-key keyboards are shown below:

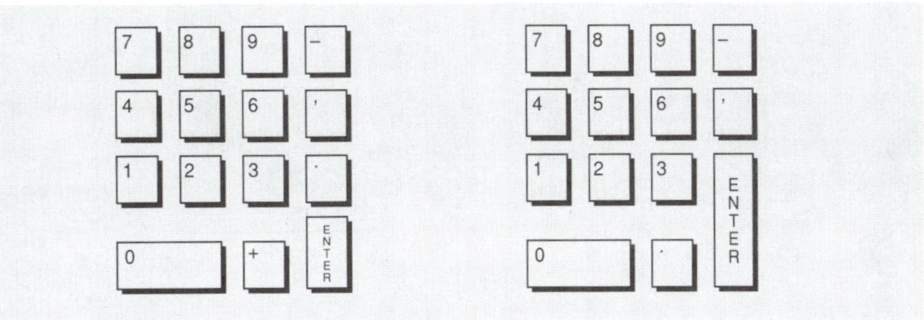

COMPOSING THE ROUGH DRAFT—STAGE 2

1. *Compose or key quickly.* Put your thoughts on paper from your outline.

2. *Concentrate on content.* At this point, don't worry about grammar, punctuation, or mechanics. Let the thoughts flow. Concentrate entirely on converting the outline to sentences and paragraphs. Occasionally you may find that you have failed to include an important point in the outline. If this happens, by all means add it to the composition.

3. *Keep potential readers in mind.* As you key, try to visualize your reader(s) and keep the level of language geared to them.

   Example:

TACOS

```
     Tacos are a lot of fun to make and eat.  They are easy to

make at home and do not take a lot of work.  The tortillas can

be purchased . . . . When you have eaten your first taco, you will

agree that tacos are good.
```

As you can see, the sentences are not structured; the thoughts and content are more important in a rough draft.

<table>
<tr>
<td>

MASTERY SOFTWARE

Key your rough draft on the Drill Screen provided in the software.

</td>
<td>

Key a one-page rough draft following the outline that you composed during the last session. **Remember:** Do not worry about mechanics. Concentrate on *content and converting your outline into sentences.* When you have keyed your rough draft, print it if you are using a microcomputer, and set it aside for a couple of days.

</td>
</tr>
</table>

The 10-key keyboard also appears in other formats on certain computer keyboards used for word and data processing. Even though these keyboards are uncommon, you should realize that in some offices you might encounter the numeric keyboard in these formats:

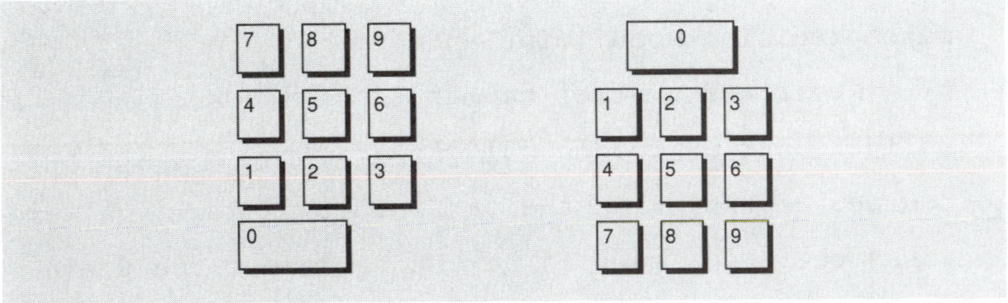

After a few hours of drill, you should be able to operate the keyboard without looking at the keys that you are touching. As you learn the key location and build your confidence, try to keep your eyes on the copy.

Locate the illustration that best fits the configuration of your machine and become familiar with the arrangement of the keys.

THE HOME ROW

To operate the 10-key keyboard, float your right hand from the location on the alphabetic keyboard to the home-row position on the 10-key keyboard. Your first finger should be placed on the *4* key, the second finger on the *5* key, and the third finger on the *6* key. Note: if you are right-handed, you may find it more efficient to operate the 10-key numeric keyboard with your left hand. This leaves your right hand free to write notes. The instructions in this text, however, assume you are using your right hand to operate the 10-key numeric keyboard.

Strike each key with a firm, quick motion. Practice striking each home-row key several times. When completed, continue on to the drill material below. Use your left thumb on the *space bar*. Press *Enter* at the end of each line.

Review the material on pages 66 and 67 on reading numbers as combinations. This will help to increase your speed.

Key each line once.
Then do again.

1	456	456	456	456	456	456	456	456	456	456	456	456	45	10
2	444	444	555	555	555	666	666	555	444	444	555	666	45	20
3	456	456	456	654	654	564	564	654	564	565	564	456	46	30
4	456	456	456	654	654	555	444	666	456	654	456	456	64	10
5	654	654	654	456	456	666	444	555	546	546	546	456	46	20
6	555	666	444	555	654	555	456	456	654	645	645	645	45	30
7	654	654	456	456	456	456	456	655	556	556	664	664	56	10
8	456	546	546	546	645	456	546	566	566	664	665	444	44	20
9	544	544	566	544	644	644	554	555	444	655	444	555	44	30

□ □ □ □ 1 □ □ □ □ 2 □ □ □ □ 3 □ □ □ □ 4 □ □ □ □ 5 □ □ □ □ 6 □ □ □ □ 7 □ □ □ □ 8 □ □ □ □ 9 □ □ □ 1 0

Take one 3-minute timing on the following material. Determine your words-a-minute rate. (Divide total words keyed by 3.)

S.I. 1.39

A wood chisel may be used to remove extra wood when another tool 14
will not do the job efficiently. The wood chisel can also be used to 28
make precision wood joint cuts. 34

Never use a steel hammer to strike a chisel. Utilize either the 48
solid rubber or wooden mallet. You can use the palm of your hand, of 62
course, depending on the particular project. A mallet can be used in 76
cases where the edge to be cut is across the grain. If, however, the 90
cutting edge is with the grain, a mallet could easily split the wood. 104
Remember to angle the chisel slightly when starting a cut. The angle 118
makes smooth or pared cuts easier to do. Cutting on the angle leaves 132
the piece of wood much smoother when cutting either with or against a 146
grain. To make a vertical cut against the grain, tilt the chisel off 160
to one side to initiate a sliding action to the flat cutting edge. A 174
surface which is wider than the chisel is easier to cut if the chisel 188
is pressed against the cut-out portion. The procedure will provide a 202
guide for that portion of the chisel when cutting out the new portion 216
or edge. Always remember to cut with the grain so that any excess or 230
extra wood will split away in a straight line and not cause a further 244
problem to the woodcutter. 249

1 2 3 4 5 6 7 8 9 10 11 12 13 14

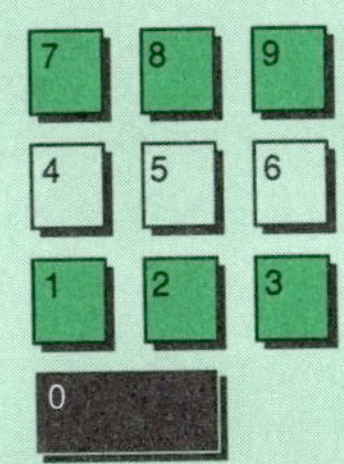

Key each line once.
Then do again.

INTRODUCTION TO 0

The *0* key is usually a large key and can be easily hit with the thumb on the right hand. Place your fingers on the *4*, *5*, and *6* keys. Look at your hand and watch as you make the reach to strike *0* with your thumb. Do this several times; then look away and try the same motion.

```
1  0 00 000 000 000 000 50 50 50 50 50 50 60 60 40 40   10
2  400 400 400 400 500 500 600 600 500 400 400 500 60    20
3  405 504 506 605 440 400 550 660 660 550 440 456 60    30

4  440 500 450 450 560 4560 4560 4560 6540 6540 56000    10
5  550 600 540 540 650 6540 6440 4560 6540 6054 56605    20
6  500 600 400 545 545 6545 4505 5460 5440 5540 50404    30

7  644 654 4560 4560 4560 4560 6540 6540 6540 450 406    10
8  556 654 6540 5460 5046 0564 0546 5040 5000 605 404    20
9  600 500 4000 4005 5004 6005 5004 6005 0665 044 606    30
```

Lines 1–10 once—speed
Lines 1–10 again—control

Reminder: Omit the sentences and paragraph timings if you have not covered the Alphabetic Keys.

Sentences

```
1   Bev gobbled broiled beef, bread, and baked beans.   10
2   A nimble rabbit nibbles bean blossoms and blinks.   20
3   Debbi observed a brash bandit robbing a big bank.   30
4   I grabbed a dab of bread and biked to the harbor.   40
5   The bears bathed beneath the bridge in the brook.   50

6   Babe is baffled; the beverage bottles are broken.   10
7   The dark banjo is broken; he is bitter and bleak.   20
8   The big battered barrels bent the riverbed barge.   30
9   Barb babbles to her bored brother; she is a snob.   40
10  Barni, the beagle, barks and begs for a big bone.   50
```

Lines 11–15 once—speed
Lines 11–15 again—control

```
11  Will Marlow wash that wool sweater in warm water?   10
12  Their nephew was a fellow bowler with the winner.   20
13  Wear a warm gown if it snows; the weather is raw.   30
14  The new lawn will grow when watered well at dawn.   40
15  Warren wiped the jeweled bowl with a white towel.   50
```

WARM-UP

Lines 1–5 once
Lines 1–5 again

1 Peg's helpful nephew peered into the topcoat for a red pen.

2 Phyllis can spare a cupful of soap and a pail if Pa phones.

3 His nephew won a trophy for the photograph of the elephant.

4 Peter spoke with poise as the spring prom plans progressed.

5 Place the splendid duplicate on the plain plywood platform.

Lines 6 and 7 once
Lines 6 and 7 again

6 41 and 42 and 43 and 44 and 45 and 46 and 47 and 48 and 490

7 63,116 10.81 5.87 34,238 4.98 11,151 69,138 15.38 15473 .01

Timed Short Drills

Turn to pages TSD 1–8 (timed short-drill material) and complete the following:

1. Five 15-second timings for speed
2. Five 30-second timings for speed
3. Five 30-second timings for control/accuracy

Number Timings

Take two 30-second timings on Line 7 above.

Straight-Copy Timings

Take two 1-minute timings on the following material.

S.I. 1.45

When considering the purchase of any article of clothing, do not 14

let any sales person convince you to take a garment that does not fit 28

well. If you decide to buy something that does not fit, be sure that 42

the store from which you buy the clothing has an excellent alteration 56

department. Make sure that they understand that the clothing must be 70

altered to fit before you make the final arrangements to purchase the 84

item. To be completely assured and satisfied, take a friend along to 98

give you another opinion on how you look. 106

16 Is Win wasting water if he washes the new window? 10
17 It is wise to wire the news to the waiting woman. 20
18 The wealth of the world will not wield wiser men. 30
19 He saw few minnows swimming in the shallow water. 40
20 Widen the wooden window and rewire the two bells. 50

☐☐☐☐ 1 ☐☐☐☐ 2 ☐☐☐☐ 3 ☐☐☐☐ 4 ☐☐☐☐ 5 ☐☐☐☐ 6 ☐☐☐☐ 7 ☐☐☐☐ 8 ☐☐☐☐ 9 ☐☐☐ 1 0

Timings

1   As he firmed the damp earth at the tree, the 10
miser imagined he heard a small sigh. Mirages in 20
the misted marsh alarmed him. Grim fears emerged 30
as his mindless tramping faltered. 37

☐☐☐☐ 1 ☐☐☐☐ 2 ☐☐☐☐ 3 ☐☐☐☐ 4 ☐☐☐☐ 5 ☐☐☐☐ 6 ☐☐☐☐ 7 ☐☐☐☐ 8 ☐☐☐☐ 9 ☐☐☐ 1 0

2   Make that simple diagram first. Then send a 10
message in the mail. Tell that salesman that his 20
latest remarks made the manager mad. The meeting 30
impaired the imminent merger. 36

☐☐☐☐ 1 ☐☐☐☐ 2 ☐☐☐☐ 3 ☐☐☐☐ 4 ☐☐☐☐ 5 ☐☐☐☐ 6 ☐☐☐☐ 7 ☐☐☐☐ 8 ☐☐☐☐ 9 ☐☐☐ 1 0

3   Basically, employers like a loyal secretary. 10
Honesty and courtesy always pay off in any job or 20
duty. Apathy and sloppy typing are always likely 30
to be very costly to a company. Any employee who 40
displayed a steady style will be properly awarded 50
and enjoy a fairly large salary. 56

☐☐☐☐ 1 ☐☐☐☐ 2 ☐☐☐☐ 3 ☐☐☐☐ 4 ☐☐☐☐ 5 ☐☐☐☐ 6 ☐☐☐☐ 7 ☐☐☐☐ 8 ☐☐☐☐ 9 ☐☐☐ 1 0

4   There is simply no key to easy money. A bad 10
agency may say that you are lucky and a legacy of 20
wealthy glory is yours. Yet, if you try fancy or 30
phony schemes, you will be mighty sorry. Steady, 40
weekly saving is the thrifty means to easy money. 50
Lay a penny away a day and be happy. 57

☐☐☐☐ 1 ☐☐☐☐ 2 ☐☐☐☐ 3 ☐☐☐☐ 4 ☐☐☐☐ 5 ☐☐☐☐ 6 ☐☐☐☐ 7 ☐☐☐☐ 8 ☐☐☐☐ 9 ☐☐☐ 1 0

Required Activity

Session 41
Document 1
Filename:
041xxx01

Business letter

Block style with mixed punctuation

Key the following letter. Proofread carefully and correct any errors before removing it from your machine or before saving your document.

Mr. Howard Young / West, Young & Stern / 4200 Exchange Building / new york, NY 10014-3728 / Dear Mr. Young: On November 18, a non-qualified stock option was issued to Mr. Ann Stewart for 2,500 shares of Life Devices, Inc. common stock. You have informed us that these shares, when issued, bear a two-year restrictive legend. ¶Life Devices, Inc., engaged in the manufacture and sale of implantable neurological pain-relieving devices, has been in business less than five years and has a limited sales and earnings history. The company's common stock is currently traded on the national over-the-counter market. On November 18, the stock closed at 14 5/8 bid and 15 1/8 asked. ¶Based on the two-year restriction as well as the speculative nature of the company, it is our opinion that the fair market value, for the purpose of the stock option described above, would be a 50 percent discount from the market price. The mean between the bid and asked prices on November 18 was $14.875, resulting in our valuation of $7.44 per share. Sincerely, Robert E. Truax, Senior Vice President

Optional Activity

Session 41
Document 2
Filename:
041xxx02

Business letter

Block style with mixed punctuation

Key the following letter. Proofread carefully and correct any errors.

(Current date) / Dr. Carolyn Bonner / Department of Business Education / University of Southern Mississippi / Southern Station, Box 83 / Hattiesburg, MS 39401-2117 / Dear Dr. Bonner: / Dr. Livingston indicated that you would be serving as coordinator for the workshop that Dr. Ed Wanzer and I will be presenting in Hattiesburg in July. ¶ Could you please make arrangements to have the following equipment available for our presentations: (1) an overhead projector, (2) a 16mm projector, and (3) a 35mm carousel slide projector. ¶ I will send you an outline of the program that we will be presenting. Also, we will be sending you materials to duplicate for distribution to the participants of the workshop. ¶ If there is anything else that you need from us, please drop me a line or give me a call at (505) 332-6944. / Sincerely yours, / Dennis Czeslaw / President / Your initials / c: Janet Livingston / c: Ed Wanzer

WARM-UP

Lines 1–3 once
Lines 1–3 again

1 456 405 406 506 504 645 645 4650 5050 4060 504 56

2 4050 5060 5060 5064 4645 5065 45645 64645 5064 56

3 44056 55064 55645 55645 64465 46050 40645 54605 5

INTRODUCTION TO 7

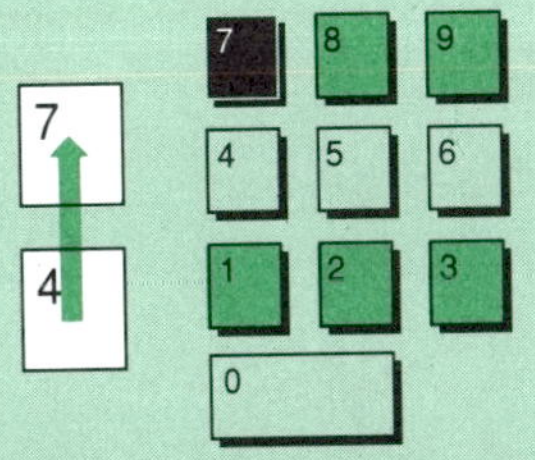

Key each line once.
Then do again.

Home-row *4* finger moves up to the number *7*. Place your hand on the home row
and practice the move from *4* to *7*. Look at your hand and watch your finger make
the motion. Do this several times; then look away and try the same motion.

1 444 47 47 47 47 47 47 47 74 74 74 74 74 74 74 74 4 10

2 555 57 57 57 57 57 57 57 75 75 75 75 75 75 75 75 5 20

3 666 67 67 67 67 67 67 76 76 76 76 67 76 76 76 67 6 30

4 777 74 75 76 74 74 567 567 567 567 567 4567 4567 7 10

5 456 45 67 67 65 64 675 456 456 456 456 4567 4567 6 20

6 777 765 7567 5560 57670 56660 5670 45670 45670 567 30

7 765 657 654 475 476 457 45776 4576 45577 45567 467 10

8 576 475 777 777 667 666 65777 7445 57774 77745 774 20

9 707 706 706 704 705 700 70650 7055 65005 00456 007 30

□□□□ 1 □□□□ 2 □□□□ 3 □□□□ 4 □□□□ 5 □□□□ 6 □□□□ 7 □□□□ 8 □□□□ 9 □□□ 1 0

INTRODUCTION TO 8

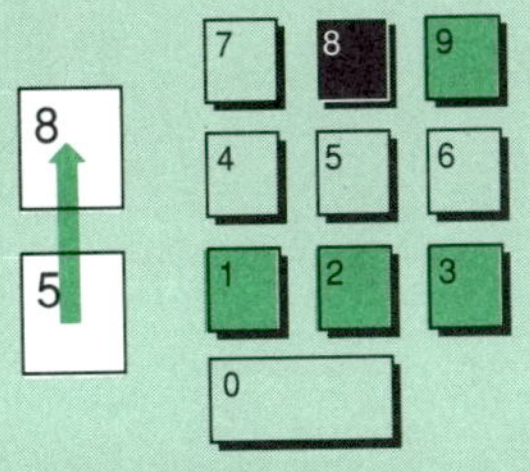

Key each line once.
Then do again.

Home-row *5* finger moves up to the number *8*. Place your hand on the home row
and practice the move from *5* to *8*. Look at your hand and watch your finger make
the motion. Do this several times; then look away and try the same motion.

1 555 58 58 58 58 58 58 58 58 85 85 85 85 85 85 58 5 10

2 888 58 68 68 68 48 48 48 48 58 78 78 78 78 58 58 6 20

3 777 78 78 68 86 86 86 84 88 88 88 80 80 80 80 88 7 30

4 800 800 800 800 807 807 806 805 508 508 408 804 88 10

5 876 568 678 468 780 786 807 876 558 558 558 778 78 20

6 888 888 787 787 686 865 585 858 484 848 808 878 80 30

7 45678 87654 80765 876 8888 7787 7877 6778 5678 458 10

8 85868 58566 88458 800 8008 6758 5858 6868 7887 848 20

9 80000 87778 88585 848 5858 8585 5857 5857 8575 885 30

□□□□ 1 □□□□ 2 □□□□ 3 □□□□ 4 □□□□ 5 □□□□ 6 □□□□ 7 □□□□ 8 □□□□ 9 □□□ 1 0

SHORT COMPOSITION AND INFORMAL WRITING

When preparing short compositions or informal writing, you must pay careful attention to grammar, punctuation, spelling, and overall construction. You must also be concerned with organizing your material so that it is presented in a logical manner. The four major stages involved in the process of writing a short composition are preparing to write, composing the rough draft, revising the rough draft, and preparing the final copy.

PREPARING TO WRITE—STAGE 1

1. *Choose a subject that is familiar to you.* Most beginning writers find that it is easier to write about familiar things. Search your experiences for interesting subjects, look through newspapers for ideas, or look around you for an interesting topic.

2. *Organize your thoughts by making an informal outline.*

    Example:

```
                          TACOS


          I.   Ingredients needed:
               A.  Tortillas
               B.  Meat
               C.  Cheese
               D.  Lettuce and tomatoes
               E.  Onions
               F.  Sauce


         II.   Procedure for making:
               A.  Cook and season meat
               B.  Chop other ingredients
               C.  Fill tortillas
               D.  Heat tacos
               E.  Add other ingredients


        III.   How to eat:
               A.  Atmosphere
               B.  No utensils
```


Choose a subject about which you would like to write, drawing from your own experiences and knowledge. Some possibilities include hobbies, pets, vacations, interesting buildings, peculiar customs, superstitions, or any other topic that interests you.

You will learn formal outline formatting techniques in Session 48. For this drill, prepare and key a one-page informal outline on the subject you have chosen. Save the outline; you will need it in the following sessions.

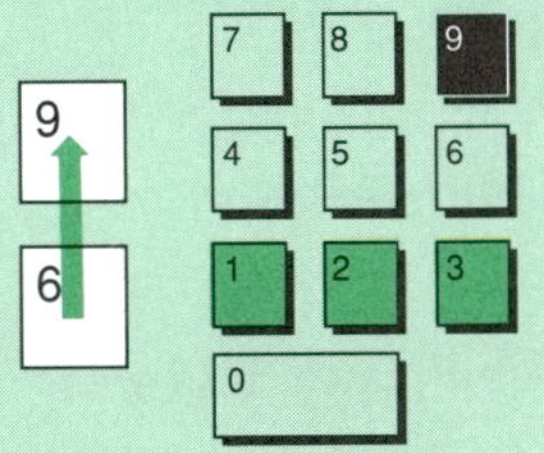

Key each line once.
Then do again.

INTRODUCTION TO 9

Home-row finger **6** moves up to the number **9**. Place your hand on the home row and practice the move from **6** to **9**. Look at your hand and watch your finger make the motion. Do this several times; then look away and try the same motion.

1 69 69 69 69 99 99 99 66 66 66 69 69 69 69 69 66 66 10

2 99 89 89 89 79 79 79 66 69 69 59 59 59 49 49 49 99 20

3 90 90 90 90 98 98 98 97 79 79 89 89 69 69 96 96 96 30

4 789 789 456 456 475 678 789 908 908 970 970 987 09 10

5 890 890 690 690 906 960 978 589 479 690 978 890 89 20

6 900 909 909 969 969 696 898 797 690 578 589 987 95 30

7 6989 6989 6979 6979 69879 69879 69857 96857 456789 10

8 9678 9687 8985 9678 96745 45678 56789 98765 987654 20

9 9889 8899 9999 7999 69969 69969 94569 49566 594695 30

Lines 1–10 once—speed
Lines 1–10 again—control

Reminder: Omit the sentences and paragraph timings if you have not covered the Alphabetic Keys.

Sentences

1 The guest menu featured halibut and autumn fruit. 10

2 Louis hunts for sunken ruins and hauls treasures. 20

3 Sue slumps and sulks as she slurps the sour soup. 30

4 Just be sure to return that blouse to the bureau. 40

5 That auto bumper is a hunk of junk; it is ruined. 50

6 Buff found a huge bug on the shrub in the puddle. 10

7 A stout runner shouted and slumped to the ground. 20

8 The group hummed a rousing tune during the stunt. 30

9 Susan put tuna on a bun and built a super supper. 40

10 The pup dug around in the mud and found a peanut. 50

Lines 11–14 once—speed
Lines 11–14 again—control

11 Liz seized that sizzling pizza and ate with zeal. 10

12 Hazel embezzled a zillion and has been penalized. 20

13 He authorized Zeb to organize the bronze nozzles. 30

14 The zinnias were glazed in that freezing drizzle. 40

Take two 1-minute timings on the following material.

S.I. 1.45

```
        To honor a deserving person in the community is a fine thing.  A     14
most interesting factor becomes apparent many times--in the ugly form        28
of jealousy for another's accomplishments.  Most people can take high        42
honor quite graciously--that is, if they were the ones to win.  Those        56
individuals who did not win may begin to hold a grudge against anyone         70
who was a winner.  When something like a community honor causes deep,         84
hard feelings on the part of some people, it becomes an empty prize--         98
the winner may be the loser.  The spirit of honors and awards must be        112
one of generous and living happiness.                                        119
```

□□□□1□□□□2□□□□3□□□□4□□□□5□□□□6□□□□7□□□□8□□□□9□□□10□□□11□□□12□□□13□□□14

Take one 3-minute timing on the following material. Determine your words-a-minute rate. (Divide total words keyed by 3.)

S.I. 1.38

```
        Rain is quite welcome when the land is dry.  The earth's surface      14
holds quite a bit of water but in times of very dry weather it always         28
seems to be in the wrong place--or it is of the type that it can't be         42
used.  Normally, the U.S. receives adequate amounts of rain; however,         56
there are particular periods when clouds don't release their moisture         70
for long amounts of time.  Most clouds usually move from west to east         84
across the nation.  If there should be a high pressure system holding         98
near the West Coast, it will divert the clouds and moisture northward        112
into Canada.  Many experts feel that the climate over the whole earth        126
is becoming warmer and drier.  These experts state that the supply of        140
water we now have in the nation will not be enough for us to continue        154
wasting our water in the future as we have done in the past.  To most        168
people, the warning might go unheeded; some will help to conserve our        182
water supply.  New ways of obtaining water will have to be developed;        196
we cannot afford to depend entirely on rain for all our water source.        210
```

□□□□1□□□□2□□□□3□□□□4□□□□5□□□□6□□□□7□□□□8□□□□9□□□10□□□11□□□12□□□13□□□14

Lines 15–18 once—speed
Lines 15–18 again—control

15 Minimize the hazard and stabilize that bulldozer. 10
16 Dozens of zealous buzzards whizzed over the zone. 20
17 Buzz gazed with amazement as Hazel won the prize. 30
18 Zeb baked a dozen pretzels in the sizzling blaze. 40

☐☐☐☐1☐☐☐☐2☐☐☐☐3☐☐☐☐4☐☐☐☐5☐☐☐☐6☐☐☐☐7☐☐☐☐8☐☐☐☐9☐☐☐10

Timings

Take a 1-min. timing on each paragraph. Your instructor may ask you to take additional timings.

Unless instructed otherwise, key at a controlled rate if you are making three or more errors a minute.

If you finish before time is up, start over.

1   Traveling in this vast native land is a near 10
marvel. The savage rivers and varied paved miles 20
are impressive. Vivid sights revive the mind and 30
lift spirits. Villages reveal veiled vestiges; a 40
dividend is derived. 44

☐☐☐☐1☐☐☐☐2☐☐☐☐3☐☐☐☐4☐☐☐☐5☐☐☐☐6☐☐☐☐7☐☐☐☐8☐☐☐☐9☐☐☐10

2   Even if Gavin is vain, she has avid fans and 10
attentive friends. Her singing is sensitive; she 20
reveals her vast talent. She deserves lavish and 30
vivid praise. Her versatile verses are a massive 40
advantage and elevate her fevered fans. 48

☐☐☐☐1☐☐☐☐2☐☐☐☐3☐☐☐☐4☐☐☐☐5☐☐☐☐6☐☐☐☐7☐☐☐☐8☐☐☐☐9☐☐☐10

3   A lazy bicycle ride in the country is surely 10
a healthy and worthy activity. A sunny sky and a 20
dry day is surely an omen to any type of cyclist. 30
Be wary of cloudy and windy days. A daily remedy 40
for a healthy and spry body is a ride on a cycle. 50
Energy is enjoyed by young and not so young. 59

☐☐☐☐1☐☐☐☐2☐☐☐☐3☐☐☐☐4☐☐☐☐5☐☐☐☐6☐☐☐☐7☐☐☐☐8☐☐☐☐9☐☐☐10

4   That overly busy lady is not tidy. She pays 10
dearly for her folly and hasty ways. A sloppy or 20
dirty habit will always imply a lazy personality. 30
In theory, a neatly and correctly done job hardly 40
portrays apathy. The lady is in a hurry and only 50
makes costly errors for her employer. 57

☐☐☐☐1☐☐☐☐2☐☐☐☐3☐☐☐☐4☐☐☐☐5☐☐☐☐6☐☐☐☐7☐☐☐☐8☐☐☐☐9☐☐☐10

Dr. James Moline, Metropolitan Professional Building, 5991 Madison Drive, New York, NY 10055-9110. Dear Dr. Moline: ~~It was a pleasure to visit with you on the phone this morning.~~ Truax-Vehlow Investment Services has been in the brokerage and investment banking business for over 25 years and specializes in new growth companies. We firmly believe that such companies represent the greatest profit potential for individual investors. In recent years, we have devoted considerable attention to the medical industry through our research and investment banking activities. We have played an important role in the early stages of several recently emerging medical firms in the city of New York. Please give me a call whenever it is convenient, and I will be pleased to set up an appointment to discuss a mutually satisfying business relationship. Sincerely, Roberta E. Thomas, Investment Consultant

---

SESSION 41 — BUSINESS LETTER

WARM-UP

Lines 1–5 once
Lines 1–5 again

1 Token office offenses often evoke spoken and pointed words.
2 Oil that boiler at all points to avoid noises and moisture.
3 Take the textbooks and workbooks from that broken bookcase.
4 Omit the olives and onions from the omelet and let it cool.
5 An oldtimer scolds the troops only once, then moves onward.

Lines 6 and 7 once
Lines 6 and 7 again

6 31 and 32 and 33 and 34 and 35 and 36 and 37 and 38 and 390
7 7371130 91368840 1534986003 51673455189 963310931 4,131 134

☐☐☐☐1☐☐☐☐2☐☐☐☐3☐☐☐☐4☐☐☐☐5☐☐☐☐6☐☐☐☐7☐☐☐☐8☐☐☐☐9☐☐☐10☐☐☐11☐☐☐12

Timed Short Drills

Turn to pages TSD 1–8 (timed short-drill material) and complete the following:

1. Five 15-second timings for speed
2. Five 30-second timings for speed
3. Five 30-second timings for control/accuracy

Number Timings

Take two 30-second timings on Line 7 above.

Lines 1–3 once
Lines 1–3 again

WARM-UP

1 456 45 67 67 65 64 675 456 456 456 456 4567 4567 6

2 876 568 678 468 780 786 807 876 558 558 558 778 78

3 890 890 690 690 906 960 978 589 479 690 978 890 89

INTRODUCTION TO 1

Home-row finger **4** moves down to the number **1**. Place your hand on the home row and practice the move from **4** to **1**. Look at your hand and watch your finger make the motion. Do this several times; then look away and try the same motion.

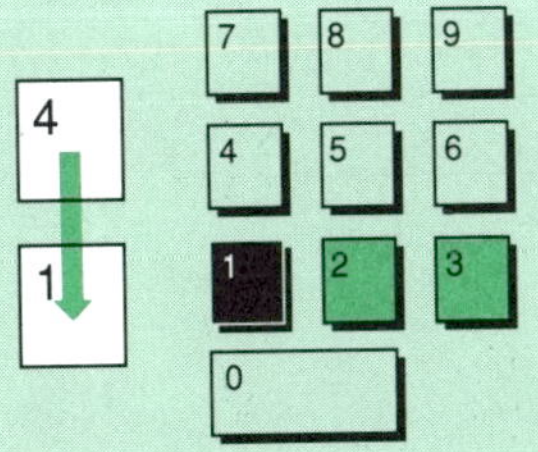

Key each line once.
Then do again.

1 41 14 41 41 41 14 14 14 451 415 514 614 614 716 41   10

2 41 41 51 61 71 81 91 11 141 141 141 141 145 146 14   20

3 61 61 61 51 71 81 91 17 171 171 187 187 191 151 19   30

4 100 100 100 140 140 140 145 146 147 148 149 101 11   10

5 168 187 187 186 175 177 109 186 101 186 186 196 19   20

6 145 156 195 157 145 198 966 919 818 717 616 515 41   30

7 1467 1458 1469 1908 1097 16788 16587 169789 196979   10

8 1474 4010 4561 4561 4710 46678 15851 979711 987919   20

9 4111 1444 4568 1787 1679 88981 98871 019091 001001   30

□□□□ 1 □□□□□ 2 □□□□□ 3 □□□□ 4 □□□□ 5 □□□□ 6 □□□□ 7 □□□□ 8 □□□□ 9 □□□ 1 0

INTRODUCTION TO 2

Home-row finger **5** moves down to the number **2**. Place your hand on the home row and practice the move from **5** to **2**. Look at your hand and watch your finger make the motion. Do this several times; then look away and try the same motion.

Key each line once.
Then do again.

1 52 52 52 52 52 52 25 25 25 25 25 24 24 42 62 72 82   10

2 24 56 25 58 47 71 89 80 20 20 20 50 50 20 70 45 86   20

3 52 25 62 72 82 92 02 42 52 27 85 58 85 95 96 90 88   30

4 456 789 125 125 127 124 126 129 125 128 982 982 12   10

5 242 252 252 262 852 258 158 148 284 282 272 958 94   20

6 222 224 225 226 227 228 228 822 922 202 202 212 21   30

7 2456 2789 2010 2456 2678 2525 24567 27890 12456 12   10

8 9876 9876 9090 8080 7028 7262 27287 26524 21919 52   20

9 2222 2525 2582 2582 9792 2728 26267 88771 07862 72   30

□□□□ 1 □□□□□ 2 □□□□ 3 □□□□ 4 □□□□ 5 □□□□ 6 □□□□ 7 □□□□ 8 □□□ 9 □□□ 1 0

THE ASLOW COMPANY

1448 QUIMBY LANE • KELLY, LOUISIANA 71441-6290 • (318) 716-9200

Current Date

(Since this is a short letter,
begin on line 15; Mastery Software
users begin on line 9.)

Ms. Madeline Serro   (6 line spaces down)
Office Systems Publishing Company
280 Fulton Avenue
Hempstead, NY 11550-1624

(ds: double-space)

Dear Ms. Serro:

(ds)

Our department administrative assistant, Cynthia Brummond,
has talked with you on two occasions about your instructional
cassettes and slides for office inservice programs that were
sent to us.

(ds)

I previewed these materials myself and felt that they were
not the calibre we had in mind. In fact, some of the slides
are quite out of date.

(ds)

These materials were returned to you more than 45 days ago.

(ds)

Sincerely yours,

Barbara Caserza
Research Assistant   (4 line spaces down)

(ds)

your initials

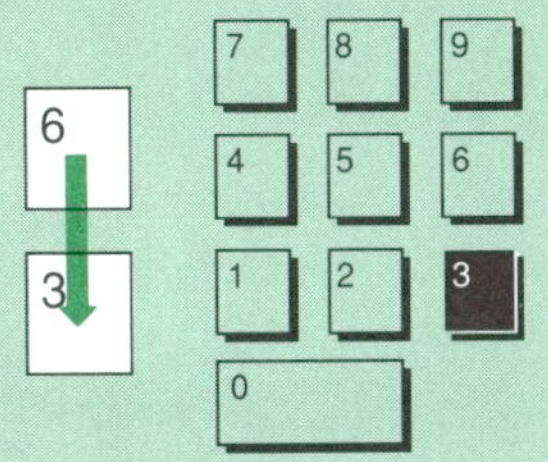

Key each line once.
Then do again.

INTRODUCTION TO 3

Home-row finger *6* moves down to the number *3*. Place your hand on the home row and practice the move from *6* to *3*. Look at your hand and watch your finger make the motion. Do this several times; then look away and try the same motion.

1	63 63 63 63 63 36 36 36 36 36 93 39 39 39 69 69 63	10
2	34 35 36 73 73 93 83 23 13 30 54 65 63 36 83 49 34	20
3	30 39 38 37 36 35 34 32 31 33 34 35 33 32 36 63 45	30
4	345 636 663 663 663 336 393 393 993 993 339 936 93	10
5	234 354 345 456 383 838 938 736 373 369 936 963 33	20
6	568 936 947 373 464 585 484 737 363 922 291 302 30	30
7	3748 3833 9374 0585 0392 0458 0382 0483 3230 30339	10
8	4435 4344 3345 3443 2343 2334 4873 4848 3929 26282	20
9	4844 6673 8733 5663 5543 3323 6788 6733 2343 23343	30

Sentences

Lines 1–10 once—speed
Lines 1–10 again—control

Reminder: Omit the sentences and paragraphs if you have not covered the Alphabetic Keys.

1	Carlton, the cat, curled in comfort in the chair.	10
2	Can Carrie cure colds with tonic and citric acid?	20
3	A lack of ethics caused the doctor to face scorn.	30
4	Clarice recalled the basic facts of the accident.	40
5	Chris decided to purchase a record and a picture.	50

6	Cecelia consumed a rich chocolate ice cream cone.	10
7	The clever client could conceal crucial evidence.	20
8	Carol watched a cautious crow circle the cottage.	30
9	The wicked witch cackles as she concocts recipes.	40
10	Can Cam choose music as a classic school subject?	50

Lines 11–15 once—speed
Lines 11–15 again—control

11	The sassy gray puppy plays daily in a sunny yard.	10
12	Why did that shy boy enjoy the truly scary story?	20
13	A nearby sentry eyed a hungry baby in the subway.	30
14	The hungry boy easily ate one cookie at the curb.	40
15	The kitty and the puppy may not enjoy happy play.	50

PRODUCTION

One of the most efficient business letter styles is the *block* style. Review the letter to Ms. Dettman below. Then key Document 1 on page 195 to Ms. Serro, following the vertical spacing instructions shown to the right of the letter.

Block style:
All lines begin
at left margin.

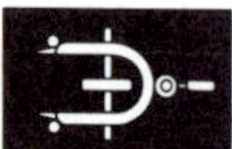

February 3, 19--

Ms. Mary Dettman
12411 Pine Street
Garden Grove, CA 92640

Dear Ms. Dettman:

We are pleased to learn that you are interested in serving as a
member of the panel discussion group meeting at the WBEA Convention. As you know, the convention will be held in Calgary on
April 3.

Please notify me as soon as possible regarding the audio visual
equipment you will need. If you are going to distribute some
written information, I will be most happy to have it duplicated.
You will need to get the information to me by March 15. Please
indicate the number of copies you will need.

We look forward to having a most exciting convention. Also, I
look forward to finally meeting you in person.

Sincerely,

William Walczak

William Walczak
Educational Consultant

kam

Lines 16–20 once—speed
Lines 16–20 again—control

16 It is only your duty to obey every law of safety. 10
17 An early yellow lily may defy a wintry windy day. 20
18 Silly Sally annoys that friendly young boy, Gary. 30
19 Billy is ready to carry the heavy load Wednesday. 40
20 Accuracy at a typewriter keyboard may imply zest. 50

1 2 3 4 5 6 7 8 9 10

Timings

Take a 1-min. timing on each paragraph. Your instructor may ask you to take additional timings.

Unless instructed otherwise, key at a controlled rate if you are making three or more errors a minute.

If you finish before time is up, start over.

1   Navigate the even trail in life. Derive all 10
things that are pleasant and reap the advantages. 20
Preserve the vital past and evade vile evils. An 30
avid, aggressive striving is needed in all lives. 40
A varied and diverse path prevents grief. 48

1 2 3 4 5 6 7 8 9 10

2   The vessel vanished in the savage river. An 10
adept diver salvaged several parts. Seven native 20
men assisted him. The added strength gave him an 30
advantage. He saved the silver investment. 39

1 2 3 4 5 6 7 8 9 10

3   Max expects to chop those six boxes with the 10
old ax. This excellent exercise helps flex those 20
lax muscles. He plans to exchange the boards for 30
deluxe mailboxes. His fixed expenses perplex him 40
and influence his expansion. 46

1 2 3 4 5 6 7 8 9 10

4   An extra exercise to help your mind relax is 10
inhaling and exhaling deeply. It extends all the 20
oxygen capacity before it is expelled. Choose an 30
exact time each day to expedite an extra relaxing 40
exertion. Your anxieties and vexations disappear 50
and you relax. Try this exciting experience. 59

1 2 3 4 5 6 7 8 9 10

Take two 3-minute timings on the following material. Determine your words-a-minute rate. (Divide total words keyed by 3.)

S.I. 1.37

Many of the metal articles in everyday use are made of brass. A 14
bookend or candlestick made of brass is quite common. But no one has 28
ever heard of brass mines, because there are none. Brass is a blend, 42
or mixture, of metals. Copper and zinc are usually mixed when making 56
brass. These two metals are heated to their melting points, at which 70
time they are joined together. After the mixture cools, it begins to 84
harden. The copper and zinc have blended and formed a new metal with 98
which one can make many creations. 105

There are quite a few other alloys. In fact, almost none of the 119
metal items we have are made of a single pure metal. By far the most 133
common alloy is steel. Steel is chiefly iron. Since iron is not the 147
strongest metal in the world, it must be combined with just the right 161
amount of carbon for strength. The steel is then used to construct a 175
number of objects such as cars, bridges, skyscrapers, and rails. The 189
iron is also mixed with chromium and nickel to form stainless steel. 203

Bronze is another common alloy. Bronze is made from the mixture 217
of copper and tin. We call our pennies copper, but actually they are 231
made of bronze. Another alloy called pewter is made of tin. 243

1   2   3   4   5   6   7   8   9   10   11   12   13   14

COMPOSITION: PARAGRAPH RESPONSE

Review the guidelines on page 162 for composing paragraphs.

Compose a paragraph in response to one or more of the following questions.

1. Do you believe that everyone is ready to vote at the age of 18?

2. Do you believe that every car owner should be required to have a driver's license?

3. Do you believe in saving money? Why or why not?

4. Do you believe that there is too much violence shown on television? Why or why not?

5. If you had the opportunity to serve as a teacher next year, what courses would you teach? Why?

Lines 1–3 once—speed
Lines 1–3 again—control

Alphabetic Sentences

1 It seems that I missed the road; it makes me mad.

2 Those wrecked cars are in the ditch at the curve.

3 Endure the thousand, routine, suspended problems.

Top-Row Numbers

Lines 4–9 once—speed
Lines 4–9 again—control

4 1323 2131 3123 3143 3311 1133 1122 2211 1121 2211

5 52 53 545 43 45 51 152 3243 235 542 421 3143 4523

6 554 32k 876 6k4 572 936 392k 5594 7976 432k 87654

7 a498a a498a 8852 76410 5805 a495k8 591 8505 795ka

8 495 4302 480k8 a08406 8432 8430 88405 080k 80a08k

9 497 7920 8209 k08a97 79k86 8825a0 7920 792 682 55

10-Key Numeric Keyboard

Lines 10–15 once—speed
Lines 10–15 again—control

10 654 54 76 56 46 767 46 654 6054 567 7655 6054 456

11 687 577 575 876 754 796 697 757 885 855 644 54 66

12 78 81 8687 782 8422 789 987 432 8282 6732 321 989

13 08 080 797 580 680 4986 7984 47782 78853 88795 85

14 19105 05084 88 384 18 682 9764 7976 8828 55130 56

15 66938 88282 775 993 5549 7970 2810 82 879 8322 87

Sentences

Lines 1–10 once—speed
Lines 1–10 again—control

1 Russel was exposed to smallpox; look at her next. 10

2 Explain the context and expedite the experiments. 20

3 Did excess oxygen explode during the experiments? 30

4 Did Rodney excuse the next six tax experts, then? 40

5 Is the lynx an exotic pet or is it a vexing jinx? 50

    1   2   3   4   5   6   7   8   9   1 0

6 Did experts exclude the existence of an appendix? 10

7 Two expert boxers were boxing in the daily annex. 20

8 Maxim exchanged a box of textiles for a textbook. 30

9 Fix the exhaust and examine the axle of the taxi. 40

10 The textbook explained the new complex exercises. 50

    1   2   3   4   5   6   7   8   9   1 0

WARM-UP

Lines 1–5 once
Lines 1–5 again

1 Nancy and Andy concur; nail the fence to the round benches.

2 Amanda and Randy defended the landfill amendment on Monday.

3 The conference on infectious invasions was confusing to me.

4 The singers sang songs and mingled among the hungry diners.

5 Cranky Nina's nice pink banjo is nicked; she plans revenge.

Lines 6 and 7 once
Lines 6 and 7 again

6 21 and 22 and 23 and 24 and 25 and 26 and 27 and 28 and 290

7 413451 51513 6783931 5297618 226,892 89376003183 22,0267.10

Timed Short Drills

Turn to pages TSD 1–8 (timed short-drill material) and complete the following:

1. Five 15-second timings for speed
2. Five 30-second timings for speed
3. Five 30-second timings for control/accuracy

Number Timings

Take two 30-second timings on Line 7 above.

Straight-Copy Timings

Take two 1-minute timings on the following material.

S.I. 1.43

Roller skating can provide hours of exciting fun. If there is a   14
nearby rink, the rest is simple. A pair of roller skates is the only   28
equipment needed. Most modern roller skating rinks are equipped with   42
rental skates at a nominal price. Skating requires lots of energy or   56
zest to keep skating for a long period of time. The beginning skater   70
should only skate for a short time and not get too tired. After some   84
time has passed, the skater should be able to skate for hours without   98
ever getting tired.   102

Timings

1
      Glenn shook in terror as the tornado stormed 10
along the shore. The radio droned on foretelling 20
doom and gloom. The radio popped in his ear as a 30
torrent of snow fell. Alone in the dark mansion, 40
his fear overtook him for a moment. 47

▢▢▢▢1▢▢▢▢2▢▢▢▢3▢▢▢▢4▢▢▢▢5▢▢▢▢6▢▢▢▢7▢▢▢▢8▢▢▢▢9▢▢▢1 0

2
      Eve is fond of opera. The golden tones of a 10
violin smooth her tense nerves. Visions arise in 20
her mind as the viola responds to the mood. Soft 30
tones float in the air as the piano renders notes 40
of dimension and diversion. 45

▢▢▢▢1▢▢▢▢2▢▢▢▢3▢▢▢▢4▢▢▢▢5▢▢▢▢6▢▢▢▢7▢▢▢▢8▢▢▢▢9▢▢▢1 0

3
      Oatmeal is often a good food to eat. Add an 10
orange, hot toast, and milk to a morning meal for 20
digestion. It is important to eat in the morning 30
to avoid tension. Restore vim and vigor at noon; 40
do not overeat. 43

▢▢▢▢1▢▢▢▢2▢▢▢▢3▢▢▢▢4▢▢▢▢5▢▢▢▢6▢▢▢▢7▢▢▢▢8▢▢▢▢9▢▢▢1 0

TOP-ROW NUMBERS

Number Review I

Remember to read numbers in 2-3-2 combinations. However, if the number group is separated by a letter, space, comma, decimal, or some other symbol, use those points as divisions for reading.

1 3711730 19368804 1358966003 15764355198 693301139 10
2 54143751 830061583 987 1533549 9 83881690 43142 6 20
3 12641896 151513 8684831 438616 220372061 98430031 30
4 1695190 168922835 6376 1001011 9384313 8178893262 40
5 611,761 63,107 81,311 2,942 361,432 101,341 2,996 50
6 2,631,871 312,646 55,565,775 93,319,868 9,865,713 60
7 16,102,403 633 239,143,671 700,183,731 65,813,329 70
8 36,611 10.18 7.85 43,832 8.94 11,511 96,831 15.63 80
9 67,429 40.38 87,413 .89 36,584 31,766 95.93 4,313 90

▢▢▢▢1▢▢▢▢2▢▢▢▢3▢▢▢▢4▢▢▢▢5▢▢▢▢6▢▢▢▢7▢▢▢▢8▢▢▢▢9▢▢▢1 0

Session 39
Document 2
Filename:
039xxx02

(Letter originating in Canada)

1 MR KENNETH Y WATANABE
   IBM CORPORATION
   OFFICE PRODUCTS DIVISION
   PARSONS POND DRIVE
   FRANKLIN LAKES NJ 07417-3478
   USA

(Letter originating in Canada)

2 DR CAROLYN BONNER
   DEPARTMENT OF BUSINESS EDUCATION
   UNIVERSITY OF SOUTHERN MISSISSIPPI
   SOUTHERN STATION BOX 83
   HATTIESBURG MS 39401-2117
   USA

3 MR A R BRADFORD
   CREDIT MANAGER
   OFFICE ADMINISTRATION BOOK COMPANY
   24 CONRAD ROAD
   WATERFORD CT 06385-1834

(Letter originating in the U.S.)

4 Dr. Ethel Hunter, Dean
   Red Deer College
   Box 2005
   RED DEER, AB
   CANADA   T4N 5H5

5 DR WILLIAM ANDREA
   STANFORD UNIVERSITY
   PALO ALTO CA 94305-5567

6 Ms. Sheila Graham
   Midwest Learning Center
   1308 South Wabash Avenue
   Chicago, IL 60605-5621

7 DR MARCELLA REICHERTER
   DIVISION OF BUSINESS AND
     BUSINESS EDUCATION
   EMPORIA STATE COLLEGE
   1200 COMMERCIAL
   EMPORIA KS 66801-8390

8 MR ROBERT CARLSON
   AMERICAN RIVER COLLEGE
   4700 COLLEGE OAK DRIVE
   SACRAMENTO CA 95841-4439

9 MS ROBERTA MELROSE
   LOS ANGELES CITY COLLEGE
   855 NORTH VERMONT AVENUE
   LOS ANGELES CA 90029-4571

10 Mr. Steven Ainsworth
   Anchor Inc.
   Software Development Division
   75 Normandale Drive
   Bloomington, IL 60601-1829

Number Review II

Take one 30-sec. timing on each line.

If you finish before time is up, start over.

1 611176 63071 83311 9243 631.24 101341 661,018 598 10
2 623,371 384116 766656677 3,103.67 5468731 5013167 20
3 51021403 634 9832141176 13,700.37 511,738 41553 7 30
4 367110118 785 43438 90198115 61 5,418 835.32 7117 40
5 9,642,192 8.47 98 436,314.77 96937314 11854638574 50
6 3761103 9,863.04 541,896.30 61574355198 6955158 3 60
7 54314541 837005318 .98 3513498 41,788.90 36115989 70
8 1264859 831086 84,331.09 11433950 518614 51107200 80
9 143541 15315 7683931 269761 22,620.01 89376001835 90

□□□□ 1 □□□□ 2 □□□□ 3 □□□□ 4 □□□□ 5 □□□□ 6 □□□□ 7 □□□□ 8 □□□□ 9 □□□ 1 0

Number Review III

Take one 30-sec. timing on each line.

If you finish before time is up, start over.

1 6243 01785 10.09 16478189.21 11,854,096 449541234 10
2 656.89 11,860 41 8406101 32 823 550.18 65,976 230 20
3 21 9445 50,784 820 967,146.83 92545.10 46,9087132 30
4 4 248 69157 2.59 95,602.88 51218 32 471 681104 47 40
5 99 48.22 309 751.82 76,832,523.51 28 409 65541098 50
6 80 601 92.16 16700 821,041,822.00 76416651 510 15 60
7 422 50 6401541 894,735 8.46 12 6847005 17.26 3511 70
8 661017 8.62 4,510 94723301 9,545,988 655 78912 12 80
9 64 28 69.84 5447004 41336 5463 34215 61870 21,466 90

□□□□ 1 □□□□ 2 □□□□ 3 □□□□ 4 □□□□ 5 □□□□ 6 □□□□ 7 □□□□ 8 □□□□ 9 □□□ 1 0

10-KEY NUMERIC KEYBOARD

DRILL

Key each line once as quickly as you can. Your instructor may also have you complete some timings.

1 12 34 56 78 90 123 456 789 987 654 321 4321 8765 9 10
2 98 76 54 32 10 321 654 897 978 456 123 1234 5678 1 20
3 76 89 32 12 01 789 564 987 654 545 231 2413 7568 3 30
4 54 12 12 34 28 897 546 978 123 466 132 1432 6785 2 40
5 32 54 78 56 58 978 645 789 101 654 213 2431 5867 9 50

Note: The decimal point will be keyed with either the third finger or the fourth finger of your right hand, depending on the 10-key keyboard configuration.

6 1.3 12.9 14.87 123.456 1.456 14.567 56.21 156.02 4 10
7 7.8 67.8 67.21 478.231 2.789 27.879 87.90 879.08 5 20
8 6.9 42.7 32.56 978.123 3.462 34.620 62.08 620.81 8 30
9 4.8 21.6 41.72 687.452 4.872 48.729 72.94 729.45 2 40
10 5.2 52.5 98.12 187.243 9.678 96.786 78.69 687.89 2 50

□□□□ 1 □□□□ 2 □□□□ 3 □□□□ 4 □□□□ 5 □□□□ 6 □□□□ 7 □□□□ 8 □□□□ 9 □□□ 1 0

For window envelopes:

1. Place the letter on the desk in the normal reading position.
2. Turn the letter over, with letterhead closest to you.
3. Fold the top third of the letter (furthest away from you) toward you and crease.
4. Fold the bottom of the letter up so that the inside address will be on the outside.
5. Insert the letter into a window envelope with the address facing the front. Check to make sure the complete address shows in the window.

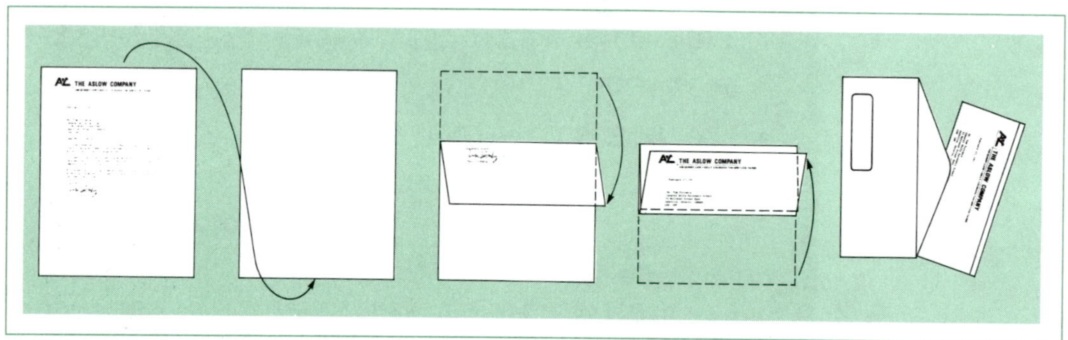

Key a business size (large) envelope for each of the following addresses. *Note:* If you do not have envelopes, it will be necessary that you cut paper to simulate them.

If you are using the Mastery Software, key the addresses at the left margin; double-space between addresses.

1 MS LORETTA BAGLEY CHAIRWOMAN
DEPARTMENT OF OFFICE EDUCATION
CHICAGO VOCATIONAL HIGH SCHOOL
8700 SOUTH STONY ISLAND AVENUE
CHICAGO IL 60617-1043

2 Ms. Bobbi Ray, Director
Personal Development Division
Office Systems Publishing Corporation
3839 White Plains Drive
Bronx, NY 10467-1910

3 MS JOYCE VEROS
INDIANA VOCATIONAL TECHNICAL CENTER
P O BOX 1776
INDIANAPOLIS IN 46206-2971

4 MR JOHN L SCHWARTZ
GENERAL MANAGER
NORTHERN STATES POWER COMPANY
EAU CLAIRE WI 54701-1611

5 Mr. Philip Ruehl
Center for Vocational Technical
  & Adult Education
Department of Public Instruction
Springfield, IL 62302-6240

6 MS MADELINE SERRO
OFFICE SYSTEMS PUBLISHING COMPANY
280 FULTON AVENUE
HEMPSTEAD NY 11550-1624

7 MRS DOROTHY M SOBOTA
COLLECTION-BOOK DEPARTMENT
OFFICE SYSTEMS PUBLISHING COMPANY
280 FULTON AVENUE
HEMPSTEAD NY 11550-1624

8 BOSSHART STOPWATCHES
PREMIER DIVISION
RIVER VALE NJ 07675-5333

(Letter originating in the U.S.)

9 Mrs. Jean Mills-Lord
Bank of Nova Scotia
166 Bedford Highway
HALIFAX, NS   CANADA
B3M 2J6

(Letter originating in Canada)

10 Mr. Robert Strang
Shaw-Smith Limited
1822 Blanshard Street
VICTORIA, BC
CANADA   V8T 4J1

SESSION 22 · **HYPHEN, DASH, UNDERSCORE**

WARM-UP

Lines 1–3 once
Lines 1–3 again

```
1 abide absorb slab babbly jab act actor react bacon

2 bag bar bat ban bake back batch battle urban debar

3 chew chat chief change choice ache much each ditch
```

Certain punctuation marks may be used to set apart or to distinguish a word or words. Because of the varying rules regarding the use of these marks, they are presented here as a separate section.

INTRODUCTION TO THE HYPHEN

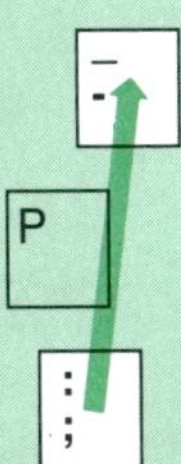

Unless instructed otherwise, use the following margin settings for the entire Specialized Punctuation-Mark section:

12-pitch: 25 and 75
10-pitch: 17 and 67

Home-row *semi* finger moves up and to the right to the *hyphen* (–) key. Place both hands on the home row and practice the move from *semi* to *hyphen*. Look at your hands and watch your finger make the motion. Do this several times; then look away and try the same motion.

Lines 1 and 2 once—speed

Line 2 again

Line 3 and the following partial line once

```
1 ;- ;- ;- ;-; ;-; -;-; ;- ;- ;-;- ;-; ;-; ;-; ;-;-

2 two-thirds, high-level, soft-spoken, high-ability

3 Dan said that the paper had at least fifteen mis-
  takes in it.
```

WORD DIVISION

GENERAL GUIDELINES

A hyphen is a mark of punctuation used to divide words that must be carried over to the next line. Care must be taken to divide words correctly. Listed on the following page are some of the more common rules. There is an exception to every rule—if in doubt, consult a dictionary. (Numerous word divisions in a manuscript should be avoided.)

On the Microcomputer

Some software packages offer automatic hyphenation. The same rules should be followed whether automatic or manual hyphenation is used. When using a software package with automatic word wraparound (word wrap), it will sometimes be necessary to key a hyphen and to press the *Enter* key to divide a long word in order to avoid an uneven right margin.

9. With electronic equipment, you may be able to store several addresses and then print them on envelopes one at a time. Some systems allow the keyboarder to do a screen print. A screen print allows you to insert an envelope into the printer, key the address on the screen in an appropriate location, and print it quickly.

A letter should be inserted into an envelope so that when it is removed and unfolded it will be in a normal reading position.

For the large (business) envelope:

1. Place the letter on the desk in the normal reading position.
2. Fold a little less than a third of the letter up from the bottom and crease.
3. Fold upward again to within 1/2 inch of the top and crease.
4. Insert the last fold into the envelope first. The top of the sheet of paper will be at the top of the envelope.

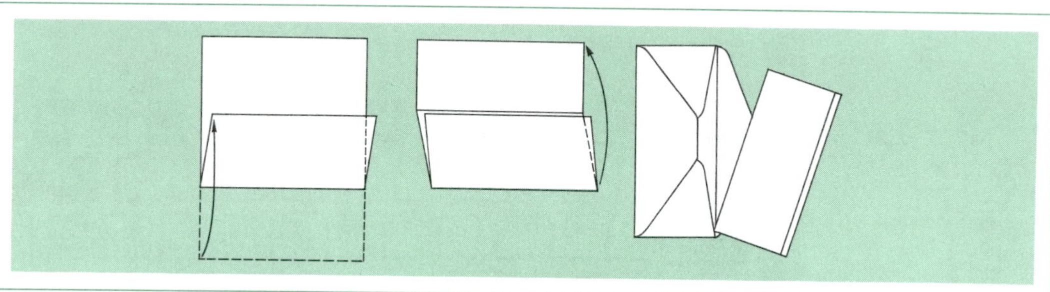

For the small (personal) envelope:

1. Place the letter on the desk in the normal reading position.
2. Fold from the bottom up to 1/2 inch from the top.
3. Fold a little less than the right third over to the left.
4. Fold the left third over to 1/2 inch beyond the last crease.
5. Insert last-creased edge into the envelope first.

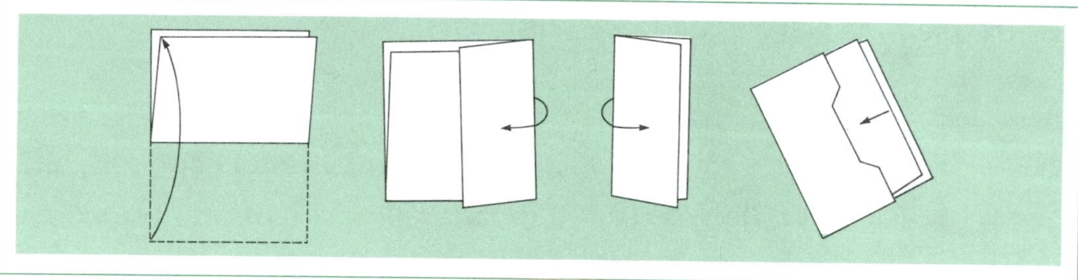

Common Rules

1. Leave at least three letters of a word at the end of a line and carry over at least three letters to the next line. Note: Some software packages leave or carry over only two letters of a word.

2. Never divide a word that is the last word of a paragraph or a page.

3. Between syllables according to pronunciation	provoke	*may be divided*	pro-voke
4. Between two consonants *unless* a root word would be destroyed	napkin billing	*may be divided* *may be divided*	nap-kin bill-ing (not bil-ling)
5. Between two vowels that are pronounced separately	continuation	*may be divided*	continu-ation
6. *After* a one-syllable vowel rather than *before* (preferable) *unless* the vowel is a part of a suffix	benefactor acceptable	*may be divided* *may be divided*	bene-factor accept-able
7. Between two parts of a compound word	salesperson	*may be divided*	sales-person

8. Do not key more than two consecutive lines ending with hyphens. Note: Some software packages allow three lines with automatic hyphenation.

Do not divide:

9. Words of one syllable	which storm	*never* *never*	wh-ich sto-rm
10. If one or two letters in a word are to be separated	along enough almost	*not* *not* *not*	a-long e-nough al-most
11. A syllable with a silent vowel sound	yelled strained	*never* *never*	yel-led strain-ed
12. Proper nouns, abbreviations, contractions, or number combinations	Barbara PSI couldn't 31 Oak Lane March 14	*not* *not* *not* *not* *not*	Bar-bara P-SI could-n't 3-1 Oak Lane March 1-4

2. Also acceptable is the traditional format shown below. Key the address single-spaced, in capital letters and lower case letters with normal punctuation; it should be in block form in the **read zone.**

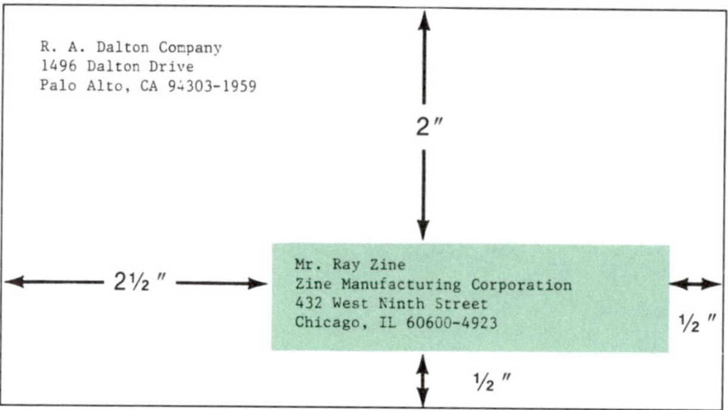

Small Envelope

3. For United States addresses, key the two-letter state abbreviation in capital letters with no periods. Space once and then key the nine-digit zip code (ZIP + 4).

4. For Canadian addresses, after keying the city in all capital letters followed by a comma and a space, key the two-letter province abbreviation in capital letters with no periods. The six-character Canadian postal code appears on the last line of the address. The first three characters (consisting of letter, number, letter) are followed by a space and then the last three characters (consisting of number, letter, number).

5. A letter mailed from Canada to the United States includes the initials *USA* as the last line of the address. Letters originating in the United States and mailed to Canada include the word *Canada* in all capital letters two spaces after the province, or it may be keyed on the line with the Canadian postal code number. The word *Canada* would come first, followed by two spaces and then the Canadian postal zone.

6. Notations such as *confidential* are keyed in all capital letters three or four lines below the return address.

7. Special mailing instructions such as *registered* and *special delivery* are keyed in all capitals in the upper right-hand corner, below the postage area.

8. Business envelopes usually have the return address printed on the envelope. If not, key it in the upper left-hand corner, block style, single-spaced, approximately two lines down from the top and three spaces in from the left edge.

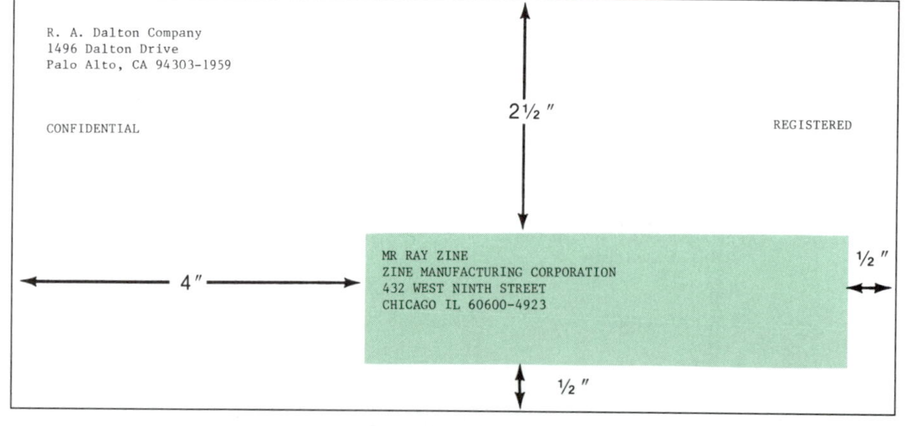

Large Envelope

After keying each word below, tab over and rekey it, showing how it should be divided.

Set a tab stop as follows:

12-pitch: 50
10-pitch: 42

```
 1 letter              let-ter
 2 March               March
 3 compose
 4 enough
 5 anyplace
 6 perpetrator
 7 wouldn't
 8 walked
 9 homerun
10 important
11 Delaware
12 almost
13 stenographer
14 technique
15 introduce
```

COMPOUND WORDS AND NUMBERS

GENERAL
GUIDELINES

A hyphen is used to separate some compound words; it is also used in spelled-out numbers.

1. A hyphen is used as a "combining" mark. Not all authorities agree on which combinations should or should not be hyphenated. If in doubt, consult a reference book or dictionary.

   a. As a general rule, use a hyphen between two or more word combinations used as a unit *before* a noun.

   ```
   a fifteen-story building
   the still-active volcano
   a hard-working person
   ```

   b. If the word combinations used as a unit appear *after* a noun, do not hyphenate.

   ```
   a building fifteen stories high
   the volcano that is still active
   a person who is hard working
   ```

   c. Words beginning with *ex*, *self*, and *vice* are usually hyphenated.

   ```
   ex-roommate
   self-taught
   vice-principal
   ```

PRODUCTION

You are now ready to prepare envelopes. First, read the instructions. Then key the addresses that follow.

Envelopes

There are two popular envelope sizes for letters:

1. The smaller size is approximately 3-1/2 inches wide and 6-1/2 inches long; it is known as a "personal-use" or "small" envelope.

2. The larger size is approximately 4-1/4 inches wide and 9-1/2 inches long; it is known as a "business" or "large" envelope.

The upper left-hand corner of an envelope is reserved for the return address (address of the sender). The address of the person or firm to receive the contents of the envelope is keyed in the lower right section.

The postal service uses a high-speed optical character reader to scan mail electronically. Mail that is not properly addressed is rejected by the machine and set aside until it can be read manually.

To avoid delays in the delivery of mail, you should follow these guidelines:

1. The Postal Service recommends keying the address single-spaced, in all capital letters, omitting all punctuation; it should be in block form in the *read zone* (shaded area shown on the envelope below). The address should be in three or four lines and the same as the inside address.

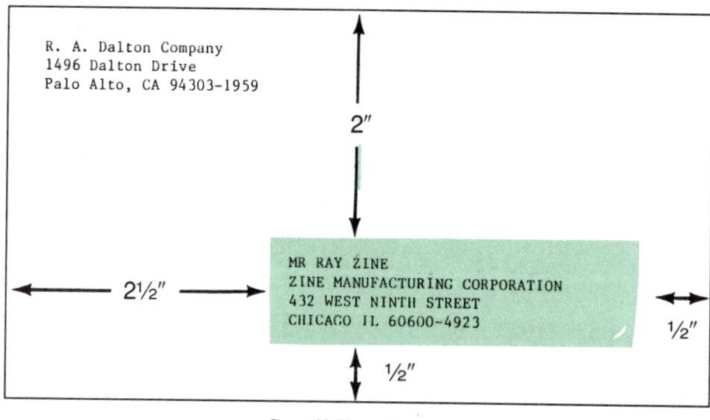

Small Envelope

2. Hyphenate *spelled-out* fractions and hyphenate numbers between 21 and 99 if they stand alone or if they are used with numbers over 100. Never hyphenate digits.

```
one and one-third
sixty-six
one hundred sixty-six
```

DRILL

Key the statements below, inserting hyphens where appropriate.

```
 1 eight cylinder engine

 2 an engine that has eight cylinders

 3 an effort at the last minute

 4 a last minute effort

 5 the man was self employed

 6 a self employed man

 7 twenty six

 8 thirty four

 9 one hundred

10 one hundred fifty six
```

THE DASH

GENERAL GUIDELINES

A dash is formed by keying two hyphens with no space before, between, or after them. The dash is often used (1) in place of quotation marks or parentheses, (2) to avoid the confusion of too many commas, and (3) for special emphasis.

```
There is a flaw in the plan--a fatal one.
All books--fiction, poetry, and drama--are on sale.
I cooked the meal--but they got the credit for it.
I said once--and I will say it again--I disagree.
```

DRILL

Key each sentence below, inserting dash(es) where appropriate.

```
 1 Send that order to the fourth floor not the third.

 2 Next year, Mary with the help of her mother, her
   father, and her uncle will be able to make a trip
   to Europe.

 3 Dawn ordered chili not tomato soup.

 4 Send that order today not tomorrow.

 5 Whenever he gets that look on his face look out.
```

WARM-UP

Lines 1–5 once
Lines 1–5 again

1 The bamboo limbs were climbing and rambling over the tombs.

2 He made amends for smashing the melons and making the mess.

3 The meal of omelets and melons was welcomed by the farmers.

4 Please move the model and the motor to the armory tomorrow.

5 Mike might mope more if the campus merger is in the autumn.

Lines 6 and 7 once
Lines 6 and 7 again

6 11 and 12 and 13 and 14 and 15 and 16 and 17 and 18 and 190

7 45134145 387001838 .89 5313499 14,887.09 53151557 431189601

Timed Short Drills

Turn to pages TSD 1–8 (timed short-drill material) and complete the following:

1. Five 15-second timings for speed
2. Five 30-second timings for speed
3. Five 30-second timings for control/accuracy

Number Timings

Take two 30-second timings on Line 7 above.

Straight-Copy Timings

Take two 1-minute timings on the following material.

S.I. 1.42

The ceiling fixtures which were standard equipment in many older   14

homes do nothing more than flood the rooms with a harsh, unflattering   28

light. The glaring effect can be greatly softened by bringing lights   42

down to the areas in which they will be used. The direction and also   56

the intensity of the lights can be controlled. The older fixture can   70

be replaced with a newer style such as a hanging swag lamp or a floor   84

lamp. Table lamps can be purchased in a wide variety of sizes, style   98

choices, and colors which blend and harmonize with any decor.   110

COMPOSITION: PARAGRAPH RESPONSE

DRILL

MASTERY SOFTWARE

Key your paragraph response on the Drill Screen provided in the software.

Compose a paragraph consisting of three or more sentences for one or more of the situations given below.

1. Look at the person next to you. Describe him or her.

2. Describe what you do not like about your home.

3. Describe what you like about your home.

4. If you were elected mayor of your city or town, what would be the first thing you would attempt to change after taking office?

5. What do you want to do for an occupation?

On the Microcomputer

Word processing packages generally include a preprogrammed key that must be depressed immediately before and after the underscored text. To underscore, depress the designated underscore key, key in the text to be underscored, and again depress the underscore key to turn off the underscoring mechanism.

> **MASTERY SOFTWARE**

The F8 function key located at the top or to the left of your keyboard activates the automatic underscore feature of the mastery software. Automatic underscoring will not be used during this session.

On the Typewriter

Newer electronic typewriters have a function key similar to that found on microcomputers using word processing packages. However, on traditional typewriters, the text and underscore must be keyed separately. First key in the text to be underscored, then backspace to the beginning of the text to be underscored, and key in the underscore.

Should you underscore the spaces between words?

Although this is an individual decision, there is a growing preference for continuous underscoring because of the procedures used with electronic typewriters and microcomputers.

INTRODUCTION TO THE UNDERSCORE

The **underscore** (__) is the shift of the **hyphen** key. Home-row *semi* finger moves up and to the right to the **underscore** key. Be sure to depress the *left shift* key. Place both hands on the home row and practice the move from *semi* to **underscore**. Look at your hands and watch your finger make the motion. Do this several times; then look away and try the same motion.

Lines 1–3 once—speed

Lines 2 and 3 again—speed

1 ; ;- ;- ;_ ;_ ;_; _;_ ;; __ ;_ ;_ _;_ _;_ ;- ;-;_

2 Look at this. The book title is, Slow Down Soon.

3 I read Changing Times, American Home, and Sports.

Session 38
Document 2
Filename:
038xxx02

Personal
business letter

Block style
with mixed
punctuation

1964 Showgate Way
Denver, CO 80219
Current Date

Mr. Tom Torrence
General Wolfe Secondary School
55 McCraney Street East
OAKVILLE, ON CANADA
L6H 1H9

Dear Mr. Torrence:

For the presentation in Toronto on March 8 I would like to
have the following equipment: an overhead projector, a 35mm
carrousel slide projector, and a large screen.

You need not worry about sending an advance for the cost of
airfare as I will put the ticket on my credit card. It takes
approximately 30 days for the bill to catch up.

By the way, would you give me an idea of the approximate
number attending the workshop. I want to have sufficient
materials to hand each participant.

Sincerely yours,

Paula Goldberg

THE UNDERSCORE

Some words are italicized in typeset printed material; italics are indicated in keyboarded materials—and on electronic printers—by underlining the words. Follow these guidelines for italicizing (underscoring).

1. Underscore titles of books, magazines, and newspapers.

   <u>Gone with the Wind</u>   <u>Harper's Bazaar</u>   <u>New York Times</u>

2. Underscore the names (not makes or models) of ships, trains, and aircraft.

   the ocean liner <u>Queen Mary</u>
   the train <u>Chicago Sun Streak</u>
   the aircraft <u>Silver Eagle One</u>

3. Underscore technical words that are not part of our normal language.

   The coast redwood, or <u>Sequoia sempervirens</u>

4. Underscore for special emphasis of a word or words in a sentence.

   He said there were <u>many</u> problems involved in the contract agreement.

DRILL

Note: Use the underscore key.

Key each of the statements below, concentrating on the use of the underscore.

1 <u>Quality of Roses</u> by Juan L. Cordoba--a book

2 <u>He Ran Alone</u> by Barbara Whitter--a book

3 <u>San Francisco Examiner</u>--a newspaper

4 <u>Popular Mechanics</u>--a magazine

5 <u>Chicago Zephyr</u>--a train

6 the <u>Nautilus</u>--a ship

7 <u>Air Force One</u>--a jet

8 <u>panettone</u>--an Italian bread

Speed and Accuracy Development

It is again time for you to concentrate on further developing your straight-copy speed and accuracy. Key the material below following the instructions shown in the left margin.

Lines 1–5 once—speed
Lines 1–5 again—speed

1 sign sign sing sing sang sang shag shag hang hang

2 fight fight eight eight light light tag tag night

3 again again sting sting hinge hinge egg egg glass

4 angle angle fling fling ledge ledge get get tight

5 ing seeing taking dealing finding landing talking

Take two 15-sec. timings on lines 6–10.

Then take two 30-sec. timings.

6 Kale and Allan ate a salad and a fig and a steak.

7 Gina, the gentle giant, giggled at Tina, the elf.

8 Dad needs a light flashlight if he skis at night.

9 Leslie sang a jingle as she dashed ahead in glee.

10 Dan tested his stiff ankle and gnashed his teeth.

Session 38
Document 1
Filename:
038xxx01

Personal
business letter

Block style
with mixed
punctuation

Margins:
Left and right
margins should
be approximately
1 to 1-1/2 inches.

MASTERY
SOFTWARE

Use the
default margins
of 1 and 66.

3103 Eddy Lane
Eau Claire, WI 54701
Current Date

(Begin first line of return address on line 13.
This will vary from letter to letter, depending
on length.)

Note: The Mastery Software has a 1-inch
(6 lines) top default margin; begin on line 7
of the editor.

(4 line spaces down: this will also vary,
depending on length.)

Ms. Bobbi Ray, Director
Personal Development Division
Office Systems Publishing Corporation
3839 White Plains Drive
Bronx, NY 10467-1910

(ds: double-space)

Dear Ms. Ray:

(ds)

Thank you for the brochures describing programs that are
available through Office Systems Publishing Corporation.

(ds)

Please send me, on a ten-day free inspection basis, the
following programs. The first is Series 8--"How to Face
an Audience with Poise" (Cat. No. 14-2.1.8), and the second
is "The Employment Interview" (Cat. No. 14-5.4).

(ds)

These programs will be viewed for possible use in workshops
and seminars for business and office education.

(ds)

Sincerely yours,

Kathy Aarons

Kathy Aarons

(4 line spaces down)

1 pail pill pain pine pale pest past page plan pile 10
2 plight paddle peddle pellet planed pet pie peddle 20
3 depend splash splint elapse happen pen nip staple 30
4 napkin pledge appeal please dispel peg nap plight 40
5 peasant pennant pitfall patient pheasant pleasant 50

6 Did Jake pass that fast jeep in his sedate sedan? 10
7 Pat speaks and pleads and defends the plaintiffs. 20
8 The patient is in pain; his left thigh is gashed. 30
9 Did Jane tape that splint and dispense the pills? 40
10 The spaniel has fleas and needs his skilled help. 50

Timings

1   Print the paragraph in large letters. Raise 10
the title and delete the diagraphs. Insert three 20
fresh phrases at the end. 25

2   It is all right if Dane repairs that rattle. 10
It is a danger and a threat. Perhaps the gear is 20
sheared. He repairs brakes and engines. 28

3   Russel bought a used auto from a true fraud. 10
Although the bumper and the trunk were ruined, he 20
assumed that it would run. If he would flush the 30
rust from the lumbering hunk of junk, he might be 40
able to use it. His woeful anguish spurred a new 50
thought--perhaps it was useless. 56

The personal business letter is keyed on plain paper. It is necessary that you include your return address as shown in this model.

Block style with mixed punctuation

Note: No reference initials are necessary since you prepared (composed) and keyed the letter yourself.

```
2350 Catalina Drive
Denver, CO 80219
February 12, 19--


Mr. Barth Trimble, Manager
Creative Printing Service
4950 Heights Drive Circle
Denver, CO 80219-1698

Dear Mr. Trimble:

Our communications class is planning a series of intense studies
on various aspects of office automation.  As part of this series,
we would like to visit a printing firm that is known for modern
and innovative practices.

Our class meets every day from 8:30 a.m. to 11:30 a.m.  Would
it be possible for our class to visit your firm sometime during
the month of April?  If so, please contact me at 777-9462 any day
after 3:30 p.m.

Sincerely yours,



Margo Hillman, Chairman
Communications Series 1190
```

WARM-UP

Lines 1–3 once
Lines 1–3 again

```
1 Add ample stamps and mail the letter at midnight.
2 The fireman attempted an immense task and missed.
3 The senior pilot spotted an airport in the gloom.
```

Lines 4 and 5 once
Lines 4 and 5 again

```
4 One-half of the high-level men were high-ability.
5 All songs--rock, country, and symphony--are fine.
```

INTRODUCTION TO THE APOSTROPHE

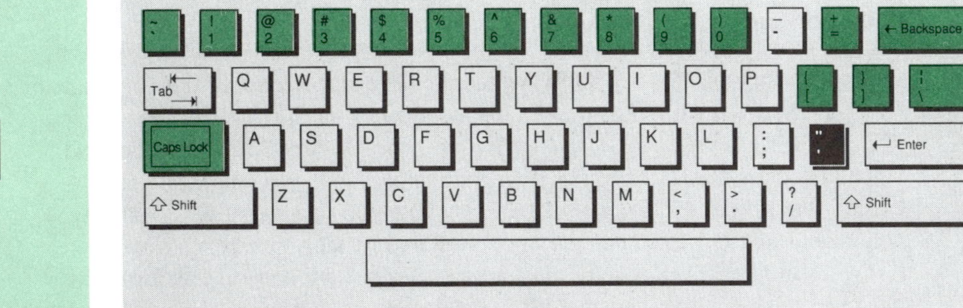

The *apostrophe* (') is located next to the *semi* key. Home-row *semi* finger moves to the right to the *apostrophe* key. Place both hands on the home row and practice the correct motion. Look at your hands and watch your finger make the motion. Do this several times; then look away and try the same motion.

Lines 1 and 2 once—speed

Line 2 again—speed

Lines 3 and 4 once—speed

```
1 ;' ;' ;' ;'; ;'; ';'; ;' ;' ;';' ;'; ;'; ;'; ;';'
2 Al's Dad's Ted's Allen's Jane's Jan's Ken's Len's
3 Alfie's neat sedan hasn't had a dent; he's tense.
4 Dale's latest theft hadn't shaken Jeanne's faith.
```

THE APOSTROPHE

GENERAL GUIDELINES

1. An apostrophe is used in a contraction (shortened spelling of a word, substituting an apostrophe for the missing letters).

```
cannot                    can't
could not                 couldn't
```

2. An apostrophe can be used to show possession by adding an *'s*.

```
a hat belonging to John      John's hat
the voices of the people     people's voices
the guess of anybody         anybody's guess
```

If a noun ends in *s*, add the apostrophe only.

```
the sonnets of Keats         Keats' sonnets
the clothes of the girls     girls' clothes
```

Filenames

Each document is identified by a filename (e.g. 038xxx01). If you are using a typewriter, key the filename one double space below the last item on the document.

Filenames are assigned to identify each document. Positions 1, 2, and 3 are numeric and represent the session number. Positions 4, 5, and 6 are alphabetic and represent your initials. These are shown as "xxx" in the text. You should replace the "xxx" with your initials when creating a filename. If you do not have a middle initial, use an "N" in position 5 to represent "none." Positions 7 and 8 are numeric and represent the document number.

Example:

038pta01   Identifies the session as 38, the initials of the keyboarder as pta, and the document number as 1.

MASTERY SOFTWARE

If you are using the Mastery Software, the filenames for *Required Activities* that are checked (graded by the software) will be assigned by the software and cannot be changed. After keying a *Required Activity* with the Mastery Software, proofread and edit your document. Select CHECK only after you have completed your editing. Your score will be recorded the first time you select CHECK. You may continue to edit, but your score will not be altered by the software. *Optional Activities* and *Required Activities* that are not checked are done in Freeform and must be keyed with the filenames when the document is created. The Freeform option of the Mastery Software is accessed from the Main Menu. After selecting the Freeform option, you will be asked to enter a filename before keying the document. The function key prompts that appear at the bottom of the editor screen are further explained on the Help Screens, which are accessed by depressing the *F3* function key; these also appear in the front section of the text. You should review these functions before beginning your production work.

Key production documents using wordwrap. Drop any hyphen at the end of a line except where noted.

Required Activity

Review the example of a personal business letter to Mr. Trimble on the following page. Then key Document 1 to Ms. Ray on page 184 following the vertical spacing instructions shown to the right of the letter.

Remember: It will be your responsibility to watch for—and correct—any intentional errors in spelling, spacing, or arrangement that appear in the documents. This will help you become a *thinking* keyboarder.

3. An apostrophe can also be used as a symbol for feet.

```
100 feet        100'
255 feet        255'
```

Note: Some individuals have trouble determining if a word is a personal pronoun or a contraction.

Example: `their      they're`

Remember: THE APOSTROPHE INDICATES A MISSING LETTER.
Therefore, *they're* has to indicate *they are*.

Additional examples:

```
They're taking their own sleeping bags.
```

not

```
They're taking they're (they are) own sleeping bags.

It's a treat to give the dog its bone.
```

not

```
It's a treat to give the dog it's (it is) bone.
```


Key each entry in the left column. Tab over and key the same phrase, but show possession, dimension, or contraction, as appropriate.

```
1   boat belonging to Don          Don's boat
2   lawyer for the ladies          ladies' lawyer
3   the house Billy lives in
4   car belonging to Mavis
5   a luncheon of managers
6   it is
7   are not
8   he is
9   we are
10  do not
11  does not
12  100 feet
13  396 feet
```

WARM-UP

Lines 1–5 once
Lines 1–5 again

1 Lay the toolbox by the mailbox and latch the balcony doors.

2 Evelyn welcomed the clerical classes in the balcony alcove.

3 Leaves engulfed that golfer's cleats; his lead is building.

4 Aldo pleaded with the child to leave the calf in the field.

5 Lil is willing to duplicate the list of disciplined drills.

Lines 6 and 7 once
Lines 6 and 7 again

6 10 and 20 and 30 and 40 and 50 and 60 and 70 and 80 and 900

7 77.315.634 793,313.815 105,613.89341 632,731,244.314634 100

Timed Short Drills

Turn to pages TSD 1–8 (timed short-drill material) and complete the following:

1. Five 15-second timings for speed
2. Five 30-second timings for speed
3. Five 30-second timings for control/accuracy

Number Timings

Take two 30-second timings on Line 7 above.

Straight-Copy Timings

Take two 1-minute timings on the following material.

S.I. 1.40

A good typist soon learns how to proofread. Glaring errors will 14
mar the neatness and quality of a good report. Find all the mistakes 28
before you type the final copy. Learn to watch for correct spelling, 42
grammar, and typing. You might wish to examine your typewritten work 56
two or three times and make quite certain it is without mistakes. In 70
the long run, you will be pleased that you have carefully prepared an 84
excellent typewritten copy. The person who reads your copy will have 98
much respect for your ability as a typist. Learn to proofread. 111

PRODUCTION

You are now ready to learn how to prepare letters, memos, manuscripts, and tables. Each of the following sessions will have two types of Activities—*Required* and *Optional*. You must complete the *Required Activity*. You should complete the *Optional Activity* if you feel you have not mastered the *Required Activity*. If you do not need to do the *Optional Activity*, then go to the next session.

The first production documents you will prepare will be personal business and business letters. You will be using the *block* style, although a variety of different format styles may be used in letters. Examples of the various styles are shown in the *Reference Summary*.

Key each of the following sentences, inserting the correct word. **Remember:** *An apostrophe stands for a missing letter.*

```
its      it's    1. _____ clear that the dog buried
                     _____ bone.
they're  their   2. There are twenty-one dents in
                     _____ car.
whose    who's   3. _____ coat is that?
whose    who's   4. _____ going to the picnic next week?
your     you're  5. _____ going to regret _____
                     rash action.
```

INTRODUCTION TO THE QUOTATION MARK

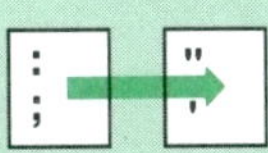

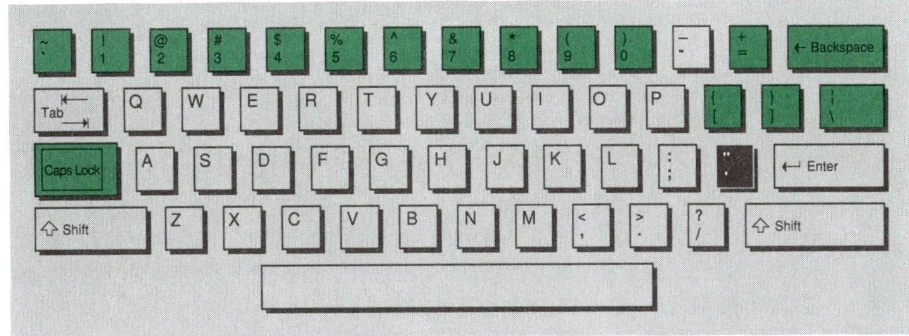

The **quotation-mark** (") is the shift of the **apostrophe** key. Home-row **semi** finger moves to the right to the **quote** key. Be sure to depress the *left shift* key. Place both hands on the home row and practice the move from **semi** to **quote**. Look at your hands and watch your finger make the motion. Do this several times; then look away and try the same motion.

Lines 1–4 once—speed
Lines 1–4 again—control

```
1 ;' ;" ;" ;" ;"; ;"; ;"; ;" ;" ;" ;"; ;";" ;" ;";"

2 "hello" "Help" "gasp" "Fiddle" "Ha" "Hi" "splash"

3 "At last," said Sal, "is that lad's knee healed?"

4 "At least," said Al, "Jake ate the jelled salad."
```

QUOTATION MARKS (WRITTEN CONVERSATION)

GENERAL GUIDELINES

1. Quotation marks are used to indicate written conversation to avoid difficulty in reading. When each new speaker says something, the material begins on a new line and is indented.

```
      "The weather is really nasty," said Nancy.

      Relaxed, Jan yawned and said, "Oh, I really
hadn't noticed."

      "That's because you have been sleeping all
morning," murmured Nancy with a slight sneer in
her voice.
```

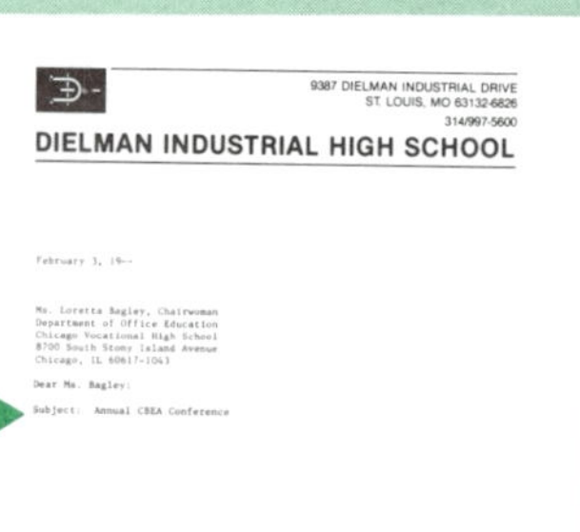

2. *Miscellaneous.* There are other types of lines that may be included in particular letters.

   a. *Attention Line.* There are instances when correspondence is addressed to an organization rather than to a specific individual or division of the organization. If the name of the individual or division that is to receive the correspondence is known, an attention line can be used. The attention line is keyed at the left margin, a double space below the last line of the inside address; double-space again after the attention line. There are various styles for keying the attention line:

   ```
   Attention Accounting Department
   Attention:   Accounting Department
   Attention:   Accounting Department
   ATTENTION:   ACCOUNTING DEPARTMENT
   ```

   b. *Subject Line.* A subject line is used to draw the reader's attention to something of importance. The subject line is keyed a double space below the greeting; it can begin at the left margin or be centered. Double-space again after the subject line. The subject line can be keyed in the same styles used for an attention line.

THINKING DRILL

This drill will help you think at the keyboard as you test your knowledge of the parts of a business letter. Key the word or words that best answer the following statements. Look up your answer, if necessary, from the preceding material.

1. Stationery with preprinted headings is called ________.

2. The month, day, and year of the letter are included in the ________.

3. The address of the person to whom you are writing is the ________.

4. Zip codes for all addresses in this text are ________ numbers long.

5. The greeting in a letter is known as the ________.

6. The message of the letter makes up the ________.

7. The farewell at the end of a letter is known as the ________.

8. The blank space between the closing and the title line is called the ________.

9. The initials of the preparer are the ________.

10. When something is included in a letter it is known as a(n) ________.

11. If the item is attached to the letter it is known as a(n) ________.

12. If a copy has been prepared, the letter should contain a(n) ________.

13. The reader's attention is drawn with a(n) ________ line.

2. The comma and period are customarily placed inside the quotation marks. See the examples above.

3. The question mark can be placed either inside or outside the end quotation mark, depending on the sentence logic.

   a. Place outside if the entire sentence is a question.

   ```
   When did he say, "I shall not return"?

   Did he say, "I saw ten paintings at the exhibit"?
   ```

   b. Place inside if the quotation *only* is a question.

   ```
   The owner shouted, "Why don't you just leave?"

   She asked, "Do you know if the train is late?"
   ```

4. The semicolon and colon *always* go outside the end quotation mark.

   ```
   Last week she announced, "Recreation time will be
   lengthened"; however, we have not experienced it yet.
   ```

DRILL

Key each of the following sentences, inserting quotation marks where appropriate.

```
1 The typewriter is old, stated Mr. Barlow, and must be
  replaced.

2 Why did the pilot say, We'll be thirty minutes late?

3 Catherine sleepily said, Why don't you just be quiet?
```

Key the following three sentences as conversation.

```
4 We will be landing thirty minutes late, announced the
  pilot.  Deanna muttered, I suppose that means we miss
  dinner.  The flight attendant smiled and said, Perhaps
  we'll be on time after all.

5 The pilot announced, Due to fog, we will be forced to
  land in Omaha instead of Minneapolis.  Deanna's fears
  were confirmed, Omaha? she blurted.  Yes, it's a
  wonderful city.  I vacation there often, replied the
  flight attendant.  The pilot was heard again, We may
  not be able to leave Omaha for 36 hours.  Be prepared
  to spend the night in the airport.  An unexpected
  treat! exclaimed the smiling flight attendant.
```

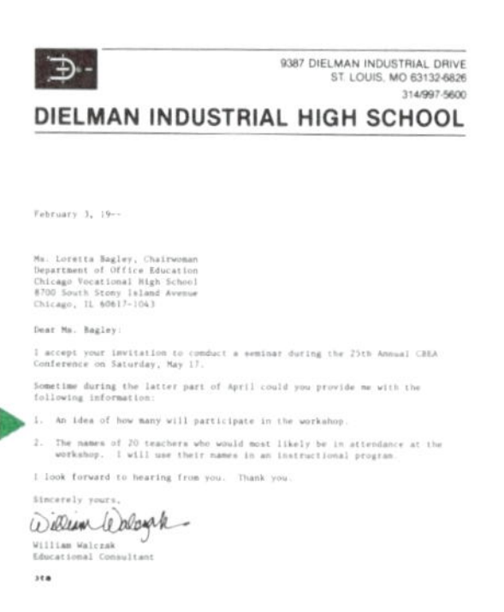

9. ***Reference Initials.*** Reference initials are the initials of the person who has prepared the communication. There are many different styles of keying these. The most popular style does not show the initials of the person who created the correspondence but simply shows the initials of the person who keyed the copy in lowercase letters: ***pta***

10. ***Two-Page Letters.*** If a letter exceeds one or more pages, start the second and succeeding pages on line 7 (Mastery Software, line 1). Key the name of the person receiving the letter at the left-hand margin; single-space; underneath the name, key the page number; single-space; then, under the page number, key the date. Triple-space to the continuation of the body of the letter. Carry at least two lines of a paragraph over to a new page.

Common Letter Notations

There are a number of other notations that might appear if they are appropriate to a particular letter. They would be keyed after the reference initials. As each is presented, refer to the letters in the left-hand margin.

1. ***Enclosure/Attachment.*** The word ***Enclosure*** or ***Attachment*** at the bottom of a letter tells the reader that something has been included with the letter itself. (In some cases, there may be more than one enclosure. In this instance, it is appropriate to include the word ***Enclosures*** or ***Attachments***; you may list the title of each item underneath.)

2. ***Copy Notation.*** In some cases, individuals other than the person whose name appears on the inside address will receive copies of a letter. Traditionally, you will find the initials ***cc***, representing ***carbon copy***, at the bottom of the letter. This will be followed by the name or names of the individuals to receive copies. Today copies of letters are made so frequently on copying machines that ***carbon copy*** may not be an appropriate reference. In this text, you will find the letter ***c*** used (representing ***copy***) to indicate that more than one person is to receive a copy of the letter.

   When two or more people are to receive copies of the correspondence, there may be a problem in determining whose name should be written first. It may not always be clear by job title which person is the highest ranking official. To eliminate this problem, list all persons receiving copies of the correspondence in alphabetical order.

Special Letter Notations

1. ***Enumerated Items.*** In some letters, a list or section of enumerated items is included. The items can be keyed at the left margin or indented five spaces. The second and additional lines of an item begin under the first word of the numbered line. The items are keyed single-spaced for each number and double-spaced between the items.

GENERAL GUIDELINES

1. Quotation marks are used to enclose titles of works such as poems; short stories; chapters, essays, or articles in magazines and other larger works; radio and television programs; and short musical works.

```
"The Midnight Ride of Paul Revere" is a good poem.

The last episode of "Star Trek" was really
interesting.

The plot of "Last Rays of Daylight" was dull for
a short story.

Did the band perform "Stardust" last evening?

I read the article "Thirty Ways to Avoid Work" in
the magazine.
```

2. Quotation marks may be used within a sentence to give a word or words special emphasis; for example, a technical word used in a nontechnical sentence, slang expressions, humorous expressions, or defined words. (In typeset printed material, defined words are usually set in italics.) Be careful not to overuse the quotation mark in this manner.

```
The "aglaonema" is commonly called the Chinese
Evergreen.

Marvin thought the concert was "far out" and
enjoyable.

Their idea of "fast" service is serving one customer
at a time.

According to Webster's dictionary, a wren is a
"brown singing bird."
```

DRILL

Key each of the following sentences, inserting quotation marks to enclose titles or special words of emphasis.

```
1 That story was a real corker.

2 The gemot was used largely in early English
  government.

3 With friends like you, who needs enemies?

4 A narrow path or ledge is sometimes called a berm.

5 The poem entitled Barney's Revenge is not very long.

6 At midnight, Joan saw The Night of Laughter on
  television.

7 The author's last short story, Bars on the Doors, was
  a mystery.

8 Her favorite song is Thunder Serenade by Marlo Zahn.
```

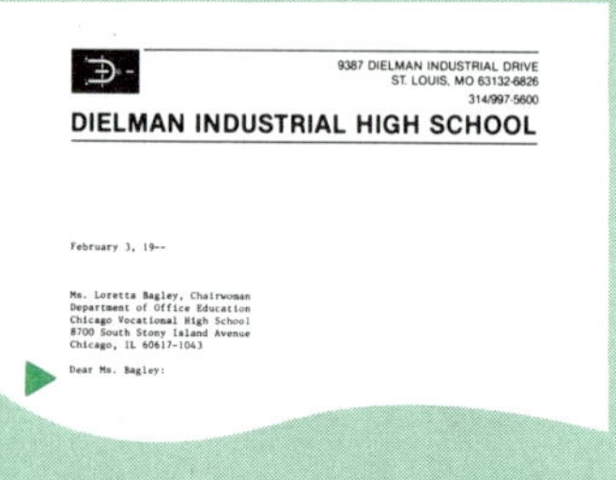

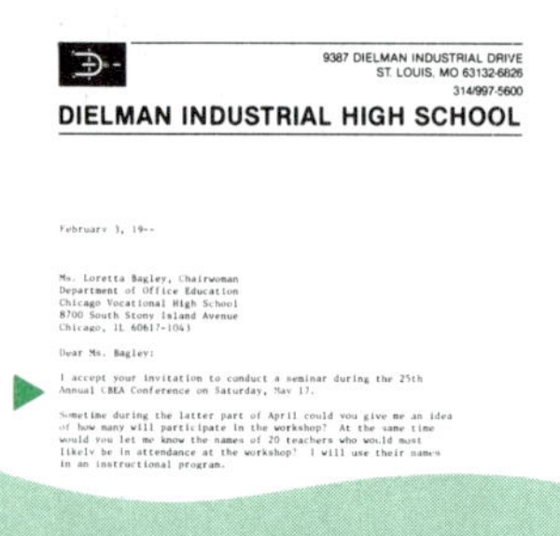

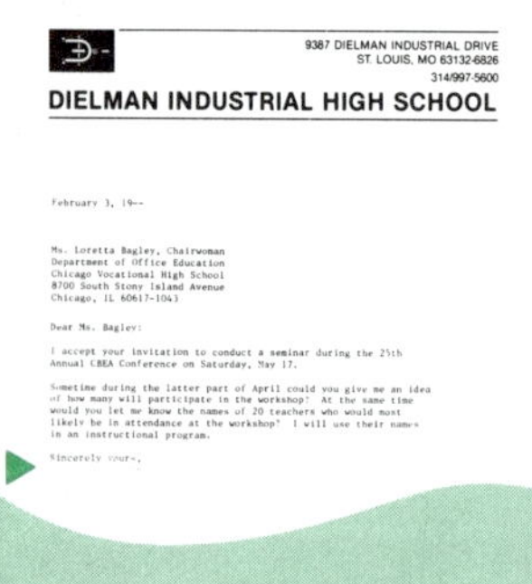

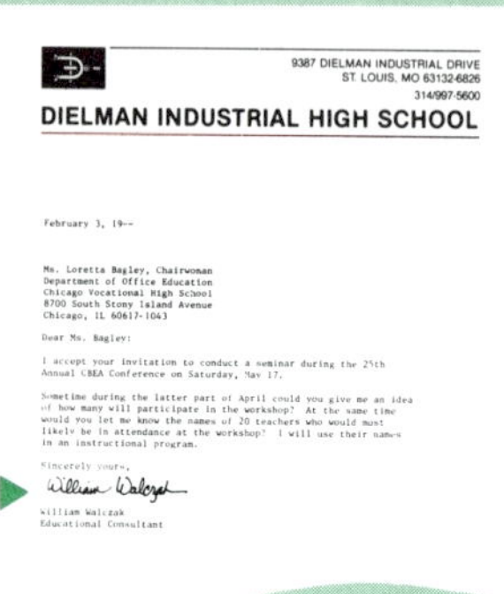

45   indicates the delivery station

27   indicates the delivery sector (may be several blocks, a group of streets, several office buildings, or a small geographic area)

97   indicates the delivery segment (may be one floor in an office building, one side of a street, specific departments in a firm, or a group of post-office boxes.

4. ***Salutation.*** Traditionally, the salutation, or greeting, is placed on a line by itself following the inside address. Two punctuation styles are used: *mixed,* in which a colon is keyed after the salutation, and *open,* in which no colon is used. Here are some samples of salutations:

Mixed-Punctuation Style	*Open-Punctuation Style*
Dear Ms. Cebron:	Dear Ms. Cebron
Dear Robert:	Dear Robert
Gentlemen:	Gentlemen

5. ***Body.*** The fifth major part of a letter is the body, or message, of the letter. This section represents the reason for writing the letter. The sender is sharing with the receiver of the letter a message on paper in lieu of face-to-face or other form of oral communication. Notice that the body of a business letter is usually single-spaced, with a double space between paragraphs.

6. ***Closing.*** The next part of a letter is the complimentary closing. Again, two punctuation styles are used: *mixed,* in which a comma is keyed after the closing, and *open,* in which no comma is used. The same punctuation style used for the salutation must also be used for the closing. Here are some samples of complimentary closings:

Mixed-Punctuation Style	*Open-Punctuation Style*
Sincerely,	Sincerely
Yours truly,	Yours truly
Very truly yours,	Very truly yours

7. ***Signature Line.*** Following the complimentary closing is the signature line. It includes the first and last name of the individual responsible for creating the correspondence. The signature line is important because many signatures are difficult to read; in responding to the writer of a letter, one wants to spell the individual's name correctly. Since letters may be originated by females or males, individuals are encouraged to use first names rather than initials; appropriate titles may then be used in responding to the person.

8. ***Title Line.*** The next major part of a letter is the title line. Here you will find the business or professional title of the person who has prepared the message of the letter. In some cases, you may find that if a person has a short name and title, the signature and title lines will be combined:

Guy Able, President

Speed and Accuracy Development

It is again time for you to concentrate on further developing your straight-copy speed and accuracy. Key the material below following the instructions shown in the left margin.

Lines 1–5 once—speed
Lines 1–5 again—speed

```
1  trip rest tree ring hire fire hard earn dirt fair   10
2  reign range raise ridge rinse risks art jar right    20
3  stare there their after pride tired far her press    30
4  green greed dress large heart after ran fir eager    40
5  refrain repress release retreat resident register    50
```

Lines 6–10 once—speed
Lines 6–10 again—speed

```
6   Spread the lard in the skillet and grill a treat.   10
7   He risks great danger if he departs after dinner.   20
8   The ship at the pier carried pearls and trinkets.   30
9   The sad intern lingered in the garden and rested.   40
10  The raging giraffe splintered that ringside seat.   50
```

Lines 1–5 once—speed
Lines 1–5 again—speed

```
1  seem seem miss miss made made game game mate mate    10
2  might might metal metal dream dream ram ram small     20
3  admit admit smile smile limit limit mad mad smash     30
4  theme theme remit remit stamp stamp gem gem ample     40
5  ed mashed limped harmed minted melted timed named     50
```

Lines 6–10 once—speed
Lines 6–10 again—speed

```
6   Add ample stamps and mail the letter at midnight.   10
7   The fireman attempted an immense task and missed.   20
8   Did Sammie eliminate all mistakes in the message?   30
9   Jim, is that smashed metal mass a damaged helmet?   40
10  Minne missed the main message as her mind dimmed.   50
```

Timings

Key once at controlled rate.
Take a 1-min. timing.
Take another 1-min. timing.

```
1      As he firmed the damp earth at the tree, the    10
   miser imagined he heard a small sigh.  Mirages in   20
   the misted marsh alarmed him.  Grim fears emerged   30
   as his mindless tramping faltered.                  37
```

Key once at controlled rate.
Take a 1-min. timing.
Take another 1-min. timing.

```
2      Make that simple diagram first.  Then send a    10
   message in the mail.  Tell that salesman that his   20
   latest remarks made the manager mad.  The meeting   30
   impaired the imminent merger.                       36
```

The default margins in the Mastery Software are set at 1 and 66, which allows a 1-inch margin at the left and right of your text when printed. It is recommended that letters be keyed using these default margins. To set margins, follow this procedure:

1. Depress the *F7* function key to bring up the ruler line.
2. Move the cursor to the desired position for the left margin and depress *L*.
3. Move the cursor to the desired position for the right margin and depress *R*.
4. Depress the *F7* function key to return to the display area, and begin keying your text.

BUSINESS LETTERS

Parts of a Business Letter

A business letter has ten major parts.

1. *Letterheads.* Letterheads are preprinted on stationery and come in all types of printing and colors; they can include pictures, symbols, or other designs of varying sizes. Some of the items in a typical letterhead include the following:

   a. The name and address of the firm or individual
   b. Departments, divisions, or sections within the firm
   c. Telephone number(s)
   d. The firm logo, which is a trademark representing the firm

   A *personal* business letter, which is further explained in Session 38, is keyed on plain paper.

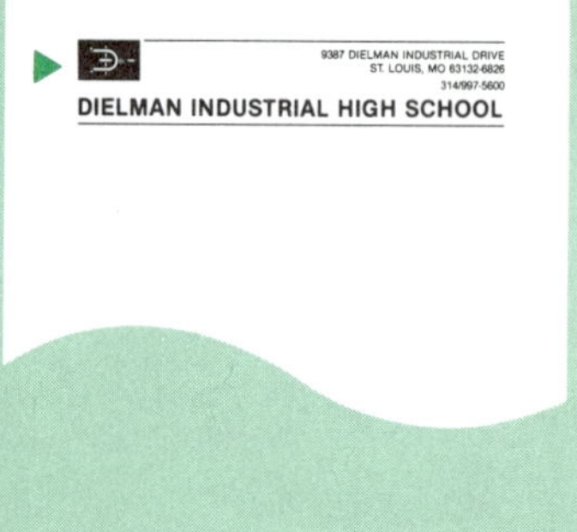

2. *Date Line.* The first keyed part of a letter is the date line. Typically, the date is written as follows: the month, the day of the month followed by a comma, and then the year; for example, January 12, 1990. Some individuals rearrange the order in which these items are presented. They may put the day of the month first, then the month and the year. No commas are required when the date is presented in this manner; for example, 12 January 1990. Some countries, such as Canada, employ the metric system of dating in which only numerals are used. In this system, the date is presented in this manner: 90/01/12 (year-month-day). If uncertain, check with your instructor for the appropriate method in your area. The date is usually keyed 9 to 18 lines from the top of the page. The actual placement will vary, depending on the style of the letterhead and the length of the letter.

3. *Inside Address.* The inside address represents the person and/or organization receiving the letter. Included are the name of the person, the person's title, the department or office, and the name of the organization. This information generally takes two lines. The street address or post-office box number follows. In the United States, the city, state, and postal code (zip code) make up the last line. In Canada, the city and province are on one line and the six-character postal zone appears on the last line. (Many organizations use the inside address as the envelope address by using window envelopes when mailing correspondence outside the firm.)

   In this text, the ZIP + 4 coding system is used for United States addresses, although the five-character ZIP code is acceptable. The ZIP + 4 system allows the postal service to handle mail more accurately and efficiently. The system works as follows:

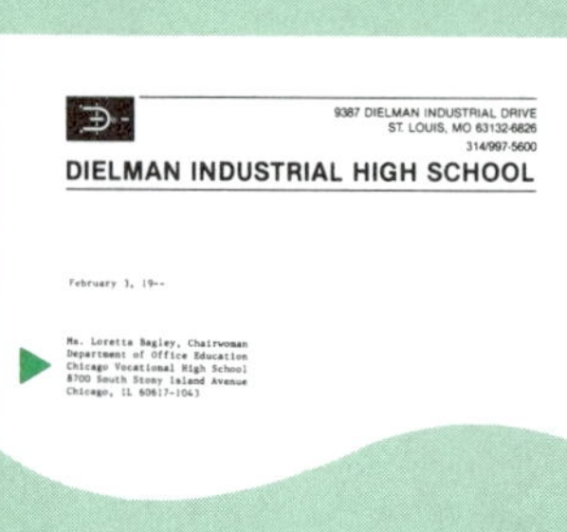

60645-2797   an example of a ZIP + 4 code

     606   indicates the area of the country

3   That overly busy lady is not tidy. She pays 10
dearly for her folly and hasty ways. A sloppy or 20
dirty habit will always imply a lazy personality. 30
In theory, a neatly and correctly done job hardly 40
portrays apathy. The lady is in a hurry and only 50
makes costly errors for her employer.   57

☐☐☐☐ 1 ☐☐☐☐ 2 ☐☐☐☐ 3 ☐☐☐☐ 4 ☐☐☐☐ 5 ☐☐☐☐ 6 ☐☐☐☐ 7 ☐☐☐☐ 8 ☐☐☐☐ 9 ☐☐☐ 1 0

SESSION 24 — !, $, #, &

WARM-UP

1 A violent storm moved along the remote oak grove.
2 He saw few minnows swimming in the shallow water.
3 Billy is ready to carry the heavy load Wednesday.

4 Two-thirds of the computers are here in the room.
5 The new computers--IBM and Tandy--are here today.
6 John asked, "Are you going abroad this semester?"

INTRODUCTION TO THE EXCLAMATION POINT

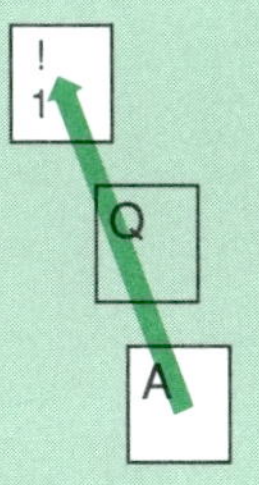

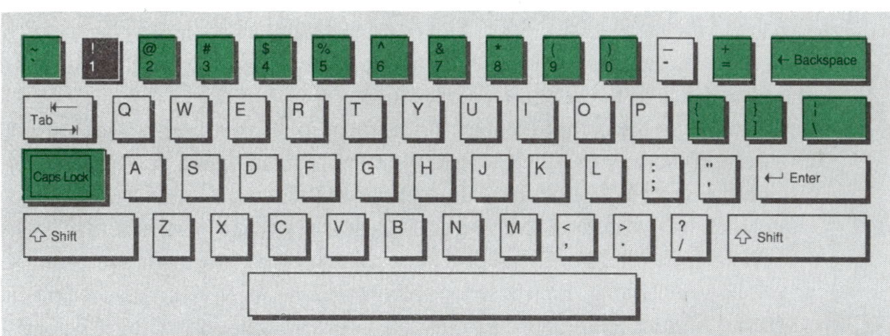

The *exclamation point* (*!*) is located in one of three positions on the typical key-board: (1) it may be the shift of the number *1* key; (2) it may be located to the right of the *p* key; or (3) on a typewriter it may be necessary to construct the exclamation point by keying an apostrophe, backspacing, and then keying a period directly beneath it. Locate the position of the *exclamation point* key on your keyboard. Identify the appropriate reach based on previously learned reaches. Place both hands on the home row and practice the move to the *exclamation point*. Look at your hands and watch your finger make the motion. Do this several times; then look away and try the same motion.

1 a! a! a! a!a a!a a!a a!a! a! a! a!a! a!a a!a a!a!

2 Help! Stop! No! Yes! Go! Wait! Begin! Halt! None!

3 Walter, stop right now! You had all better stop!
4 No, you cannot go right now! Listen to them now!

reading, editing, and language arts skills, which include spelling, punctuation, and grammar.

Finally, you must be able to prepare correspondence in mailable form at marketable production-speed levels. Most people can write in longhand at the rate of 20 to 25 words a minute. Your goal is to reach a rate of over 25 words a minute for correspondence preparation.

Before you can master the keying of business correspondence, you need to read the following material to become familiar with letter styles and the parts of a business letter. The tasks you will be keying will occasionally refer you back to this information. After you have keyed several letters, you will become quite familiar with the necessary format and parts.

Letter Styles

A variety of letter styles are being used today for both personal and business letters. The term *block style* is used to describe the letter format in this section. In the block-style letter, all parts of the letter begin at the left margin. The block-style letter is popular because it is comparatively easy to learn, and it is the fastest letter style to set up. Once you have mastered the block-style letter, you will have little difficulty adjusting to other letter styles.

Vertical Letter Placement

The vertical spacing on letters, regardless of style, is the same. Your goal is to place the letter on the page so that it is visually attractive. If the body of a letter is short, leave more space between the letterhead and the date line and between the date line and inside address. Less space is left in these two areas for medium and long letters.

Following the inside address, double-space to the salutation and then double-space to the body of the letter. The body of all letters is single-spaced except between paragraphs, which are double-spaced. Following the last line of the body, double-space to the complimentary close.

Following the complimentary close, there are four single spaces to the signature line. Next there is a single space to the title line and then a double space to the reference initials. For additional notations at the bottom of a letter to include attachments and copy notations, double-space from one to the next.

With electronic systems, vertical adjustments in placement can be made any time before printing. For those using typewriters, there is another technique that can be used if you should happen to make a poor estimate in placing a letter on a page. After finishing the body of a letter, if you find that it is going to end too high or too low on the page, adjust the closing lines. For example, if the letter is going to end too high, drop down five or six lines to the signature and three or four lines to the reference initials. If the letter is going to end too low on the page, leave fewer line spaces between the closing lines of the letter.

Margins

To center a letter on a sheet of paper, you must provide for horizontal as well as vertical placement. Left and right margins of a letter should be approximately equal. A common practice is to allow for a line of 60 to 70 spaces. (For a 60-space line, margins are set at 20 and 80 for 12-pitch (elite) and 12 and 72 for 10-pitch (pica).) Another alternative is to set left and right margins of 12 to 18 spaces (1 to 1-1/2 inches) for machines with 12-pitch type and 10 to 15 spaces for machines with 10-pitch type.

To avoid the time necessary to adjust margins for long, medium, and short letters, decide on one line length or margin width for all correspondence. As noted in the preceding section, documents of varying lengths can be accommodated without detracting from vertical letter placement.

GENERAL GUIDELINES	1. The exclamation point is used to express a high degree of emotion or strong feeling.

GENERAL GUIDELINES

1. The exclamation point is used to express a high degree of emotion or strong feeling.

2. The exclamation point may be used in any of these situations:

   a. One word

   ```
   What!  You mean the flight has been delayed for
   six hours?
   ```

   b. A phrase

   ```
   How frightening!  The fire broke out only ten
   minutes after we had left.
   ```

   c. A clause

   ```
   The date of the meeting--mark it on your
   calendar!-- is November 10.
   ```

   d. A sentence

   ```
   So there you are, you rascal!
   ```

   e. A quotation that is exclamatory

   ```
   My brother yelled, "Run for your life!"
   ```

   f. A complete sentence that is exclamatory

   ```
   I simply do not believe the fiscal report that
   states, "The absentee rate was increasing by
   500 percent"!
   ```

DRILL

Key each sentence, inserting appropriate ending punctuation.

```
1 Congratulations   You won the first prize

2 Jan shouted   What a mess

3 I emphatically restate my position, I will not
     resort to underhanded tactics

4 Help   Help   I'm locked in

5 Oh, how ridiculous  He's never even seen the
     inside of a bank
```

SYMBOL KEYS

Symbols are located on the number keys that you already have learned. You have mastered the necessary reaches; now all you have to do is learn the location of each symbol. ***Remember:*** Be sure to depress the *shift* key firmly.

Certain symbol keys appear on microcomputer keyboards only. Others appear on typewriter keyboards only. Omit the drill lines for those symbol keys that do not appear on your keyboard.

WARM-UP

Lines 1–5 once
Lines 1–5 again

1 Kevin marked the package of workbooks for the keen speaker.

2 The bookkeeper kept a king-sized textbook in his back room.

3 Karl keeps the workable kayak near a kettle by the kennels.

4 Do not use a whiskbroom on the workbooks or the blackboard.

5 That fickle king is skilled as he tackles the old bulkhead.

Lines 6 and 7 once
Lines 6 and 7 again

6 01 and 02 and 03 and 04 and 05 and 06 and 07 and 08 and 090

7 41,345.51 15,376.78 31,428.27 89,261,500.68 59.63 71.31 897

Timed Short Drills

Turn to pages TSD 1–8 (timed short-drill material) and complete the following:

1. Five 15-second timings for speed
2. Five 30-second timings for speed
3. Five 30-second timings for control/accuracy

MASTERY SOFTWARE

Timed Short Drills are grouped by length. After each set of timings, you will need
to press *F1* to re-select Timed Short Drills from the Session Menu before keying
another set of timings.

Number Timings

Take two 30-second timings on Line 7 above.

Straight-Copy Timings

Take two 1-minute timings on the following material.

S.I. 1.37

Your ability to key at a very rapid rate will be a skill that you 14

will never forget. It will be a skill that you will use almost all of 28

the time if you work with computers. It will be an important skill if 42

you end up using it only for your personal correspondence. As the key 56

to success, the keyboard skill will open many new avenues. It will be 70

the ticket to many new events. Events that you will find exciting now 84

and in the future. 88

CORRESPONDENCE

You are now going to learn to prepare letters, envelopes, and memorandums.
Your first goal is to be able to prepare a document that conveys a favorable image.
To do this, you will need to learn style and format guidelines for preparing
correspondence.

In addition to preparing correspondence that makes a positive first impression,
you must be able to prepare correspondence that is without error in content. To
accomplish this second goal, you will be given an opportunity to refine your proof-

INTRODUCTION TO THE DOLLAR SIGN

The **dollar sign** (**$**) is the shift of the number **4** key. Home-row *f* finger moves up and to the left to the **dollar sign** key. Be sure to depress the *right shift* key with the *semi* finger. Place both hands on the home row and practice the move from *f* to **dollar sign**. Look at your hands and watch your finger make the motion. Do this several times; then look away and try the same motion.

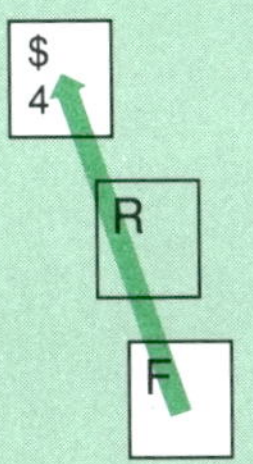

Unless instructed otherwise, use the following margin settings for the entire Symbol section:

12-pitch: 25 and 75
10-pitch: 17 and 67

Key each line once as quickly as you can.

```
1  f4 f4 f$ f$ f4 f$ f$ $$$ f4f4 f$f$ f$f$ f4f f$f$f  10

2  444 f$f$ $4 $4 44 $$44 $4.00 $$44 $4.00 4$ $40.00  10

3  $1 $2 $3 $4 $5 $6 $7 $8 $9 $10 $11 $120 $16.00 f$  10

4  $1.44 $26.80 $17.31 $689.33 $1,640.68 $143,789.00  10

5  Add $1.16, $28.96, $17.44, $18.00, $21.13, $4.26.  10

6  The gifts cost $1.10, $6.90, $19.89, and $101.13.  10
```

INTRODUCTION TO THE POUND/NUMBER SIGN

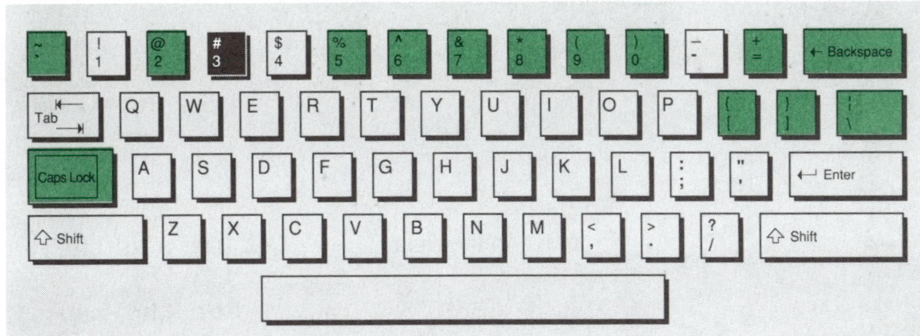

The **pound/number sign** (**#**) is the shift of the number **3** key. Home-row *d* finger moves up and to the left to the **number sign** key. Be sure to depress the *right shift* key. Place both hands on the home row and practice the move from *d* to **number sign**. Look at your hands and watch your finger make the motion. Do this several times; then look away and try the same motion.

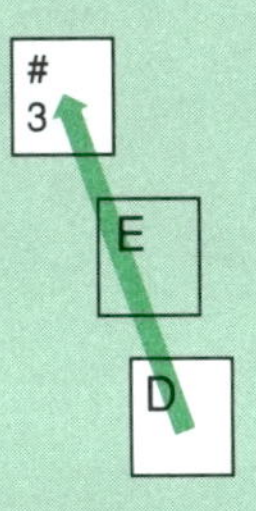

before number = NUMBER

after number = POUND

Key each line once as quickly as you can.

```
1  d3 d3 d# d# d3 d# d# ### d3d3 d#d# d#d# d3d# d#d  10

2  333 3#3# #3 #3 33 ##33 #3 3# ##33 3# #3 d3#d d#d  10

3  #33 33# 39 9# #168 168# #106 106# #3 3#3 21# #12  10

4  Buy 6#, 21#, 13#, 41#, 8#, 3#, 71#, 23# and 14#.  10

5  Items #10, #7, #3, #6, #4, #1, and #19 are mine.  10

6  Get #6 weighing 10# and #2299 weighing 189,756#.  10
```

PROOFREADER'S SYMBOLS

When correcting text that contains errors (rough draft copy), practice marking the necessary corrections with the following standard proofreading symbols:

Symbol	*Stands for*	*Example*
∽ S	transpose (change around)	See the play children. / Second, is the .... / First, is the ....
^ V	insert	Bring me the big tub.
⌢⌣	close up	book keeping
#	add a space or a line	Let usnow begin.
ℊ or /	delete (take out)	Bring me the big tub. *or* Show me the sway.
lc *or* /	lower case (small letter)	Look at Jack Run. *or* Look at Jack Run.
uc *or* ≡	upper case (capital letter)	Look at jack run. *or* Look at jack run.
[	move to the left	[Let me see the paper.
]	move to the right	Let]me see the paper.
ss	single-space	See the man. ss Why should I?
ds	double-space	ds Look at the cars. I see them.
ts	triple-space	Look at the cars. ts I see them.
stet *or*	let it stand (ignore marked change previously made)	See the old man. *or* See the old stet man.
¶ *or* ℙ	begin new paragraph	¶ I see the man.

INTRODUCTION TO THE AMPERSAND

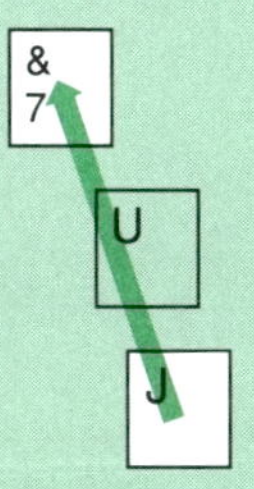

The *ampersand* (**&**) is the shift of the number *7* key. Home-row *j* finger moves up and to the left to the *ampersand* key. Be sure to depress the *left shift* key. Place both hands on the home row and practice the move from *j* to *ampersand*. Look at your hands and watch your finger make the motion. Do this several times; then look away and try the same motion.

Key each line once as quickly as you can.

```
1  j7 j7 j& j& j7 j& j& &&& j7j7 j&j& j&j& j7j& j7j  10

2  777 7&7& &7 &7 77 &&77 j7& j7j& && j&j& j7j& &j&  10

3  17 & 60 & 9 & 16 & 14 & 71 & 77 & 45 & 61 & 9891  10

4  Buy gifts from the J & K store and the R & Sons.  10

5  Jim & Steve & Arlen & Robert were tired & dirty.  10

6  Sally & Donald went to Smithetsers & Sons today.  10
   □□□□1□□□□□2□□□□□3□□□□□4□□□□□5□□□□□6□□□□□7□□□□□8□□□□□9□□□1 0
```

Speed and Accuracy Development

It is again time for you to concentrate on further developing your straight-copy speed and accuracy. Key the material below following the instructions shown in the left margin.

Lines 1–5 once—speed
Lines 1–5 again—speed

```
1  order prove among noise loose store flavor inform  10

2  along avoid drove prior other toast option oppose  20

3  stove movie shove floor front stole region reform  30

4  polite proper report remove lesson shovel opinion  40

5  endorse diamond another visitor develop insertion  50
```

Lines 6–10 once—speed
Lines 6–10 again—speed

```
6   Someone noted the stolen passport photos at noon.  10

7   The senior pilot spotted an airport in the gloom.  20

8   Jo dropped the looped rope at the rodeo and lost.  30

9   A violent storm moved along the remote oak grove.  40

10  Did the florist remove the thorns from the roses?  50
    □□□□1□□□□□2□□□□□3□□□□□4□□□□□5□□□□□6□□□□□7□□□□□8□□□□□9□□□1 0
```

- Proofread technical or difficult material ***at least twice.*** Read slowly; check for spelling and keyboarding errors. Also, read for errors in punctuation and grammar.

- Proofread with another person; one person should read from the original while the other makes proofreading changes on the keyed document. When reading from the original, indicate difficult spelling, paragraphing, format, and decimal points. Read numbers digit by digit; for example, 4,230.62 should be read aloud as "four, comma, two, three, zero, point, six, two."

- Proofread statistical tables by adding the numbers on the material from which you are copying. Then add the numbers on your keyed copy. If totals do not agree, check the figures on your copy with the ones on the original to locate the error.

DRILL E

Key the paragraph shown below. After you finish, ask another student to read the paragraph to you while you proofread your keyed/printed copy. Then you read the paragraph to the other student who, in turn, proofreads his/her keyed copy.

1   Mr. Smythe suggested that our selling price on Item

2 #16-780-32 was entirely too high. He recommends that we

3 reduce the price approximately five percent, from $14 to

4 $13. I feel he has a good idea, but I would like you to check

5 it with Sandra Dennis in accounting. Perhaps she may have

6 some additional recommendations that should be considered.

7 Please get back to me as soon as possible. The new catalogs

8 will have to go to the printers within the next two weeks.

9 If something unexpected comes up, contact me at 734-1617.

10 Thanks. George Aspick

Lines 1–5 once—speed
Lines 1–5 again—speed

1 saving saving eleven eleven selves selves divided 10
2 shelve shelve invite invite savage savage adverse 20
3 private private deliver deliver veteran even even 30
4 prevail prevail seventh seventh arrival vane vane 40
5 negative negative seventeen seventeen advertising 50

Lines 6–10 once—speed
Lines 6–10 again—speed

6 The rival divers tried varied dives in the river. 10
7 Val, deliver that vast velvet divan this evening. 20
8 Marvia served vanilla malts at the private event. 30
9 The driver has a grave fever; give him a vitamin. 40
10 The starved vandal evaded five vigilant servants. 50

□□□□1□□□□2□□□□3□□□□4□□□□5□□□□6□□□□7□□□□8□□□□9□□□1 0

Timings

Key once at controlled rate.
Take a 1-min. timing.
Take another 1-min. timing.

1   Navigate the even trail in life. Derive all 10
things that are pleasant and reap the advantages. 20
Preserve the vital past and evade vile evils. An 30
avid, aggressive striving is needed in all lives. 40
A varied and diverse path prevents grief. 48

□□□□1□□□□2□□□□3□□□□4□□□□5□□□□6□□□□7□□□□8□□□□9□□□1 0

Key once at controlled rate.
Take a 1-min. timing.
Take another 1-min. timing.

2   The vessel vanished in the savage river. An 10
adept diver salvaged several parts. Seven native 20
men assisted him. The added strength gave him an 30
advantage. He saved the silver investment. 39

□□□□1□□□□2□□□□3□□□□4□□□□5□□□□6□□□□7□□□□8□□□□9□□□1 0

Key once at controlled rate.
Take a 1-min. timing.
Take another 1-min. timing.

3   An excursion into an old cave excites expert 10
explorers. The expedition offers mixed anxieties 20
and an extreme joy. Excavating an old cave takes 30
dexterity and complex reflexes to examine ancient 40
examples of a past existence. Some old caves are 50
a hoax and are a pretext to extract extra cash. 59

□□□□1□□□□2□□□□3□□□□4□□□□5□□□□6□□□□7□□□□8□□□□9□□□1 0

DRILL D

Key the text below. If you discover an error as you key, key it correctly.

1   You may not no this storey, but it is told by hunters
2 talking about thier hunting experiences.
3   Every hear, during the deer hunting season, a certain
4 farmer lost one or two cows to overzealous hunters. In their
5 enthusism to bring back a prize buck or doe, some hunters would
6 shoot at anything that moved or didn't mover.
7   It got so bad that the farmer and his family were afraid to
8 come out of their house, for fair of being shoot. At first, the
9 farmer put up signs warning the hunters not to hunt on his
10 propety. This was not very succesful beuse the hunders would
11 shoot at the signs. All that mattered to the poor famer is that
12 he new something had to be done or he would go broke, or get kilt.
13   One year, after a trip to the local hardware stor, the
14 farmer beleived he had the solution to his problm.
15   With the usually excitement, the hunters invaided the area
16 with the thoughts of bagging a prise dear. Of course, the first
17 place they headed for was the the farmer's property. But this
18 time, they were in for a surprise. The farmer had taken the
19 precauiton of identifying everything he owed with large letters
20 painted with bright yellow paint. Each cow had the word "cow"
21 painte on it side, and the house and the bard and the tracter
22 were also marked with yellow paint to identify them
23   Needless to said, the hunters got the massage and the
24 farmer stopped losing his cows.

Lines 1–3 once
Lines 1–3 again

Lines 4–6 once
Lines 4–6 again

WARM-UP

1 It is only your duty to obey every law of safety.

2 John gazed with amazement as Helen won the prize.

3 It is wise to send the news to the waiting child.

4 Buy 6# of #7 & 2# of #8 while the price is cheap.

5 Help! I don't know how to use the laser printer.

6 A new computer operator will make about $900 now.

INTRODUCTION TO THE ASTERISK

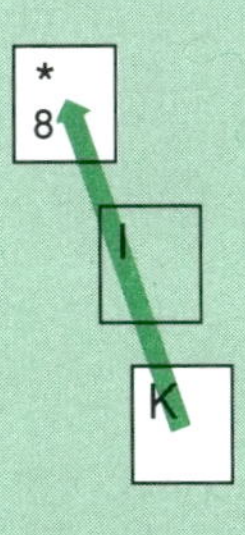

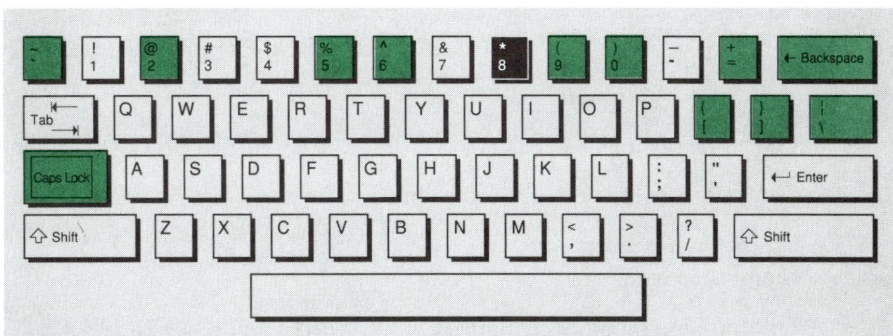

The *asterisk* (*) is the shift of the number *8* key. In addition to being used as a signal for the reader to refer to a footnote or as an indication for spacing, the asterisk is used in some programming languages as a multiplication sign. Home-row *k* finger moves up and to the left to the *asterisk* key. Be sure to depress the *left shift* key. Place both hands on the home row and practice the move from *k* to *asterisk*. Look at your hands and watch your finger make the motion. Do this several times; then look away and try the same motion.

(If your keyboard does not have an *asterisk* key, omit this section.)

Key each line once as
quickly as you can.

1 k8k k8k k8k ki8k ki8k ki8*k k*k K*K k*k k*k *ki*k 10

2 k*k K*K k*k k8*k k8*k k*k*k k8k*k k8*k k*k K*K k* 10

3 8*8 8*8 8*8 k8*k ki8*k k*k 8*8*8 *** 8*8 ki8* k*k 10

4 The check was for $***4.65 and it should be $.46. 10

5 The * symbol is used in programming: A - B * 38. 10

6 The table had the following note: *Source table. 10

☐☐☐☐1☐☐☐☐2☐☐☐☐3☐☐☐☐4☐☐☐☐5☐☐☐☐6☐☐☐☐7☐☐☐☐8☐☐☐☐9☐☐☐1 0

```
 5  keyboards are designed to reduce or eliminate many of the

 6  problems secretaries encounter.  Problems such as restarts,

 7  dedlines, page-end presseres, revisions, and errors lower

 8  productivity.  Magnetic media typewriters are designed to

 9  enable secretaries to key a document at routh-draft speed and

10  correct erros by cbakspacing and striking over the erroor.

11  They assist secredtaries to mroe efficienty process revisions

12  by eliminating the need to rekey eth entire document.
```

• The errors you are most apt to miss in proofreading are shown below. Study each
  one carefully.

COMMON PROOFREADING ERRORS

Conditions	*Examples*
Confusion of similar words	`now/not; on/of/or; than/that; yes/yet`
Confusion of suffixes and word endings	`formed/former; pointing/point; type/types`
Omissions in sequence of enumerated items	`a/b/d/e; 1/2/4/5`
Transposition of digits in numbers	`451/541; 1978/1987`
Transposition of letters within words	`teh/the; tehir/their`
Misspelled names and words that sound alike	`Clark/Clarke; Reed/Reid; knew/new`
Omissions and additions of letters	`thogh/though; wite/write`
Omissions in long words	`recorporate/reincorporate; throughly/thoroughly`
Omissions, additions, and transpositions in headings and subheadings	`Atheletic/Athletic; Devlopment/Development; Introductoin/Introduction`
Errors in words that fall near margins	(Because beginnings and endings of lines are often skimmed more rapidly)
Omission of an entire line when a word appears in the same place in two consecutive lines	`Turning it on is accomplished by moving the lever in.` `Turning it on is accomplished by (turning the dial to the left and) moving the lever in.`
Errors occurring at the bottom of a page	(Because the eye is tired or the reader skims too rapidly at the end of the page)
Omission of short words	(Short words such as *if, is, it,* and *in* when the preceding word ends in a similar letter or the following word begins with the same letter)

INTRODUCTION TO THE PERCENT SIGN

The **percent sign** (%) is the shift of the number **5** key. Home-row **f** finger moves up and to the right to the **percent sign** key. Be sure to depress the *right shift* key. Place both hands on the home row and practice the move from **f** to **percent sign**. Look at your hands and watch your finger make the motion. Do this several times; then look away and try the same motion.

Key each line once as quickly as you can.

```
1 f5f  f5f  f5f  f5f  f5f  f%f  F%F  f5f  F%F5  f%f5  f%f  f%f  10

2 555  5%5  5%5  5%5f  f5%f  f5%f  f5%f  f5%f  f%f  f5%f  f%f  10

3 55%  555%  5%  5%5%  555%  55%  5%  5%  55%  555%  5%,  555%  10

4 Did you know that 5% of 3,000 equals 150% of 100?  10

5 A 6% discount and a 10% reduction will equal 16%.  10

6 They made 55% of their shots and 8% of the fouls.  10
```

INTRODUCTION TO THE LEFT BRACKET

The **left bracket** (**[**) generally is located to the right of the **p** key. Home-row **semi** finger moves up and to the right to the **left bracket** key. Place both hands on the home row and practice the move from **semi** to **left bracket**. Look at your hands and watch your finger make the motion. Do this several times; then look away and try the same motion.

(If your keyboard does not have a **left bracket** key, omit this section.)

Key each line once as quickly as you can.

```
1 ;[;  ;[;  ;[;  ;[;  ;[;  ;[;  ;[;[  ;[;[  ;[;  ;[;[;  ;[;[;

2 ;[  ;[  ;[  ;[;  ;[;[;  ;[;[;  ;[  ;[;[;  ;[;[;  ;[;  ;[;[;
```

- When using a typewriter, another technique to improve proofreading ability is to bring the paper beneath the *paper bail* of the typewriter. As you read a line, move the paper forward. Use the *paper bail* to guide your eyes along the line of typing. When using this method of proofreading, read for context; it will help you identify grammatical errors and words that do not make sense. On the micro-computer, scroll the line up as you proofread it.

- It is quite common to use a word similar in sound but different in meaning and spelling from one that should be used. Here are some examples of incorrect usage:

their	*instead of*	there
your	*instead of*	you're
too	*instead of*	to

DRILL B

Key the sentences below, correcting any errors you find. After you finish keying the sentences, proofread them.

1 He paid me a great complement.

2 Please except our apology for the delay in shipping your order.

3 Many of our correspondence request literature on the subject.

4 In the United States and Canada, each state and province has a capitol city.

5 Far to many errors are made as a result of our failure to listen to directions.

6 The personal in the Marketing Department planned an office party.

7 I strongly advice you to consult your attorney before signing the papers.

8 I do think that their are advantages to be gained from a variety of media.

9 Honesty is it's own reward.

10 The base of the bookend is weighted with led to prevent sliding.

- Locating keyboarding errors is a difficult task for some people. Keyboarding errors include incorrect letters or letters transposed, repeated, or omitted. One method that will help you improve the detection of such errors is to read the copy backwards. Start at the right margin and read each word until you get to the left margin. Then move to the next line down and repeat the process. In reading the material in this manner, you cannot read context; you are forced to read for detail.

DRILL C

Key the paragraph below. If you discover an error as you key, key it correctly. Then proofread the paragraph using the method of reading from right to left.

1   Secretarial and clerical studenst should be provided with

2 the opportunity for more variety and in-depth application

3 traing. They should have knowledge of technology advances in

4 offi e equipment used by business to rpocess typing. Todyas'

(continued on next page)

INTRODUCTION TO THE RIGHT BRACKET

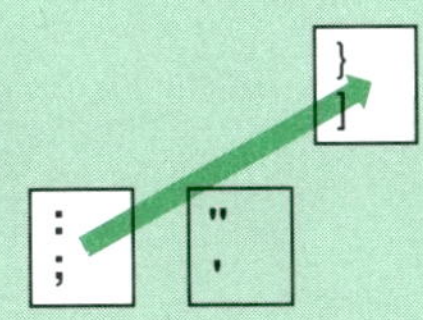

The **right bracket** (*]*) generally is located to the right of the **left bracket** key.
Home-row *semi* finger moves up and to the right to the **right bracket** key. Place
both hands on the home row and practice the move from *semi* to **right bracket**.
Look at your hands and watch your finger make the motion. Do this several times;
then look away and try the same motion.

(If your keyboard does not have a **right bracket** key, omit this section.)

Key each line once as quickly as you can.

1 ;[; ;]; ;[; ;]; ;[; ;]; ;]; ;[; ;]; ;[; ;[; ;];];

2 ;[ ]; ;[; ;]; ;[; [;] [;] [;] [;] [;] [;] [;] [;]

INTRODUCTION TO THE LEFT PARENTHESIS

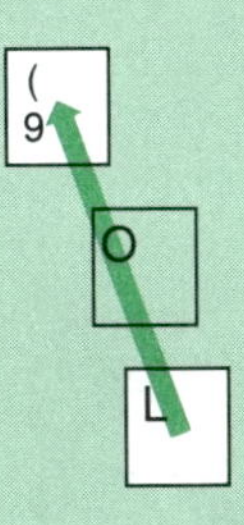

The **left parenthesis** (*(*) is the shift of the number *9* key. Home-row *l* finger moves
up and to the left to the **left parenthesis** key. Be sure to depress the *left shift* key.
Place both hands on the home row and practice the move from *l* to **left parenthesis**.
Look at your hands and watch your finger make the motion. Do this several times;
then look away and try the same motion.

Key each line once as quickly as you can.

1 l9l l9l l9l l9l lo9l lo9l lo9(l l(l l(l lo(l lo9(10

2 l(l l(l l9l l(l l9(l lo9(l lo(l lo9(l l9(l l(l l(10

3 L(L L(L L(L L(LL(L L(L L(L L(L 191 191 191 l(10

4 l(l l(l l9l l9l l9(l lo9(l lo(l lo9(l l9Ll l(l l9 10

5 lo9l lo9l LO(L LO(L LO(L L(l(l L9l L(L l(l L((l 10

6 9(9 9(9 9(9 (9(l9(l 9l9l 9l9l l(l l9l l(l (l (l9 10

□□□□**1**□□□□□**2**□□□□□**3**□□□□□**4**□□□□□**5**□□□□□**6**□□□□□**7**□□□□□**8**□□□□□**9**□□□**1 0**

To master proofreading skills, follow the techniques described here and throughout this section (indicated by bullets •).

- As much as possible, control the environment in which you proofread. Noise and movement are distracting. Be sure there is sufficient light.

- It is best to proofread text immediately after keying. In this way, errors can be corrected before the paper is removed from the machine or the document is printed.

Whether you are using a microcomputer or a typewriter, complete the following drills to reinforce proofreading techniques and to demonstrate the time-saving features of electronic correction.

With electronic document processing, you do not have to print a document prior to proofreading. Therefore, you must develop the ability to proofread text on the screen. With some software packages, you can move the text up or down on the display area slowly so that you can read each line carefully. After discovering an error, correct it before moving on to the next line. Your instructor may request that you print your document and proofread it in the traditional manner.

MASTERY SOFTWARE

Moving Text

Text is moved up or down (scrolled) one line at a time on the screen by using the up and down arrow keys. *Num Lock* must be off in order to use the arrow keys on the 10-key numeric keyboard. The *Page Up* and *Page Down* keys move a full screen of text.

Moving Cursor

The *Home* key moves the cursor to the beginning of the line of text; the *End* key moves the cursor to the end of the line of text.

Deleting Text

The *Backspace* key deletes the character to the left of the cursor. The *Delete* key deletes the character at the cursor. The arrow keys move the cursor without deleting text.

Inserting Text

Text is inserted on-screen wherever the cursor is positioned. Use the arrow keys, *Page Up*, *Page Down*, *Home*, or *End* keys to move the cursor to the space where you want to insert text; then key the new text.

DRILL A

MASTERY SOFTWARE

Key Drills A–E on the Drill Screen provided in the software.

Key the following paragraph, correcting any errors you find.

```
1       The implimentation of Information Proocessing Systems in

2  busniess offices requires secretariel and clerical personnil

3  to haev a greater knowledge of a veriaty of keyboarding

4  applications, since thier responsibility is too process the

5  keyboarding of material from many authors.
```

Proofread and rekey or correct the paragraph, making the necessary changes.

INTRODUCTION TO THE RIGHT PARENTHESIS

The *right parenthesis* (*)*) is the shift of the *zero* key. Home-row *semi* finger moves up and to the left to the *right parenthesis* key. Be sure to depress the *left shift* key. Place both hands on the home row and practice the move from *semi* to *right parenthesis*. Look at your hands and watch your finger make the motion. Do this several times; then look away and try the same motion.

Key each line once as quickly as you can.

```
1  ;0;  ;0;  ;0;  ;0;  ;p0;  ;p0;  ;p0;  ;p0;  ;p);  ;p);  ;0;   10
2  ;);  ;);  ;);  ;);  ;);  ;0);  ;);  ;0);  ;p0);  ;p0);  ;);   10
3  0)0  0)0  00)  00)  00)  00)  ;;)  ;)  ;)  ;)  ;0);  ;0;  ;);   10

4  The price ($5.95) was more ($2 more) than I paid.   10
5  Most of the teams (at least 6) won all six games.   10
6  Mary (the wife) and George (the husband) like it.   10
```
□□□□ 1 □□□□ 2 □□□□ 3 □□□□ 4 □□□□ 5 □□□□ 6 □□□□ 7 □□□□ 8 □□□□ 9 □□□ 1 0

Speed and Accuracy Development

It is again time for you to concentrate on further developing your straight-copy speed and accuracy. Key the material below following the instructions shown in the left margin.

Lines 1–5 once—speed
Lines 1–5 again—speed

```
1  libel fiber broil amber begin labor label algebra   10
2  bread bingo label brave alibi blast debit vibrate   20
3  bargain member harbor blank ballot border benefit   30
4  verbal emblem better before absorb absent tremble   40
5  alphabet basement neighbor remember remarkable be   50
```

Lines 6–10 once—speed
Lines 6–10 again—speed

```
6  Babe is baffled; the beverage bottles are broken.   10
7  Big Bo's banjo is broken; he is bitter and bleak.   20
8  The big battered barrels bent the riverbed barge.   30
9  Barb babbles to her bored brother; she is a snob.   40
10 Barni, the beagle, barks and begs for a big bone.   50
```
□□□□ 1 □□□□ 2 □□□□ 3 □□□□ 4 □□□□ 5 □□□□ 6 □□□□ 7 □□□□ 8 □□□□ 9 □□□ 1 0

WARM-UP

Key each line once.
Then key again.

1 The alphabetic letters are the easiest of all to key today.

2 Ginny and Carolyn are on their way to the cities to browse.

3 Wayne and Mike were exactly four miles from here yesterday.

4 Now that 88 men and 92 women are coming, we must get ready.

5 As 77 cats were chased by 66 dogs, 33 children were crying.

6 The 44 students took 155 trees to be planted in the garden.

Timed Short Drills

Turn to pages TSD 1–8 (timed short-drill material) and complete four 30-second timings. Select the line you feel you can complete. If you complete that line, move to the next one. If you do not complete the line, try it again or drop back one. Select either speed or accuracy as a goal.

Straight-Copy Timings

Take two 1-minute timings on the following material.

S.I. 1.36

Never use a steel hammer to strike a chisel. Utilize either the   14

solid rubber or wooden mallet. You can use the palm of your hand, of   28

course, depending on the particular project. A mallet can be used in   42

cases where the edge to be cut is across the grain. If, however, the   56

cutting edge is with the grain, a mallet could easily split the wood.   70

Remember to angle the chisel slightly when starting a cut. The angle   84

makes smooth or pared cuts easier to do.   92

PROOFREADING TECHNIQUES

Developing effective proofreading techniques is one of the common needs of those who prepare documents. Proofreading requires practice. The document is to be read slowly, word for word. It is best to proofread the document three times: (1) for spelling and keyboarding errors; (2) for punctuation and grammar; and (3) for meaning.

The characteristics that you want to develop to become an effective proofreader include the following:

1. Be a good speller.
2. Know the basics of punctuation.
3. Pay attention to detail.
4. Know and use the various methods of proofreading.
5. Know the types of errors most frequently overlooked.
6. Take the time to proofread.
7. Be conscious of errors.
8. Use the dictionary (or the spell checker available with advanced software programs) when in doubt.

1 sixty extra sixth borax waxen vixen luxury export 10
2 deluxe excise expand export prefix excite example 20
3 oxygen reflex exotic expert boxing expire textile 30
4 explain extinct perplex mixture expense expecting 40
5 explode exhaust toolbox examine anxiety exporting 50

6 Did Baxter excuse the next six tax experts, then? 10
7 Maxim exchanged a box of textiles for a textbook. 20
8 Is the lynx an exotic pet or is it a vexing jinx? 30
9 Fix the exhaust and examine the axle of the taxi. 40
10 That X-ray excluded the existence of an appendix. 50

□□□□1□□□□2□□□□3□□□□4□□□□5□□□□6□□□□7□□□□8□□□□9□□□1 0

Timings

1   Barbi is able to make edible spareribs. She 10
blends the best herbs and parboils the ribs. The 20
ribs are broiled and basted. She adds vegetables 30
and bread to the elaborate meal. The first bites 40
are an unbelievable treat. 45

□□□□1□□□□2□□□□3□□□□4□□□□5□□□□6□□□□7□□□□8□□□□9□□□1 0

2   Bo is indebted to Ben, the able banker. The 10
liberal loan is to brighten a drab sailboat. Big 20
debts are a problem to Ben, the banker. Sensible 30
debtors absolve all debts. Bo might have a habit 40
of breaking his verbal bindings. 46

□□□□1□□□□2□□□□3□□□□4□□□□5□□□□6□□□□7□□□□8□□□□9□□□1 0

3   Exercise an extreme caution before investing 10
in an old duplex. Have an expert examine all the 20
existing details and explain them to you. It may 30
be easier to buy a luxurious and deluxe apartment 40
house. An experienced land expert knows if it is 50
an expensive venture. 54

□□□□1□□□□2□□□□3□□□□4□□□□5□□□□6□□□□7□□□□8□□□□9□□□1 0

Half sheet;
single spacing

Be sure to center *each* line.

MASTERY SOFTWARE

Single-space three times to triple-space.

Full sheet;
double spacing

Be sure to center *each* line.

Headings

To center a heading over a list, key in all capital letters and triple-space before beginning the next line.

1.   POPULAR FEMALE NAMES

```
Amy

Annie

Bernice

Betty

Carol

Cathy

Clara

Connie

Cynthia

Darlene
```

2.   POPULAR MALE NAMES

```
Alvin

Arnold

Ben

Bruce

Charles

Donald

Ernest

Fred

Gary

George

Harold

James

John

Kenneth

Larry

Michael
```

WARM-UP

Lines 1–3 once
Lines 1–3 again

1 He dropped the looped rope at the rodeo and lost.

2 The florist did remove the thorns from the roses.

3 Tom needs a light flashlight if he skis at night.

Lines 4–6 once
Lines 4–6 again

4 Write a check for $****8.88 and send it to Patti.

5 That amount equals 50% of the $2500 already paid.

6 The equation is (A * B) and is almost like (A*B).

INTRODUCTION TO THE CENT SIGN

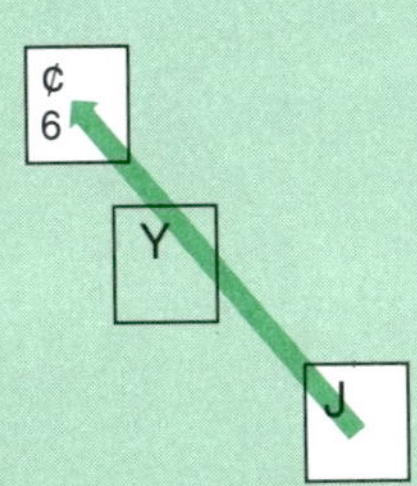

The **cent sign** (¢) will not appear on most electronic keyboards, but it will be on a typewriter keyboard. The **cent sign** is the shift of the number **6** key. Home-row **j** finger moves up and to the left to the **cent sign** key. Be sure to depress the *left shift* key. Place both hands on the home row and practice the move from **j** to **cent sign**. Look at your hands and watch your finger make the motion. Do this several times; then look away and try the same motion.

If your keyboard does not have a **cent sign** key, omit this section.

Key each line as quickly as you can.

1 j6 j6 j¢ j¢ j6 j¢ j¢ ¢¢¢ j¢j¢ j¢j¢ j¢j¢ j6j j¢j¢j 10

2 666 6¢6¢ ¢6 ¢6 66 ¢¢66 6¢ 66¢ 6¢ ¢¢ 6¢6 6¢ 66¢ 6¢ 10

3 6¢ 16¢ 13¢ 89¢ 42¢ 99¢ 6¢ 14¢ 52¢ 80¢ 71¢ 89¢ 11¢ 10

4 Add 6¢, 36¢, 96¢, 68¢, 1¢, 43¢, 71¢, 31¢ and 21¢. 10

5 The gifts cost 12¢, 9¢, 5¢, 7¢, 29¢, 45¢ and 87¢. 10

6 The boy spent 29¢, 6¢, 8¢, 46¢, 71¢, 78¢ and 91¢. 10

□□□□ 1 □□□□ 2 □□□□ 3 □□□□ 4 □□□□ 5 □□□□ 6 □□□□ 7 □□□□ 8 □□□□ 9 □□□ 1 0

MASTERY SOFTWARE

Key Drills A and B on the Drill Screen provided in the software. Use the *F5* key to change the setting for line spacing.

Half sheet; double spacing

Full sheet; single spacing

Note: Insert hard returns at the end of your document until you reach the bottom of the page.

Half sheet; double spacing

Center each of the following problems both vertically and horizontally. Each task will indicate the size paper and the line spacing to be used. *Remember:* You must center *each* line horizontally. Your finished task will *not* look like this.

1.

```
Oregon Technical Institute

Atlanta Christian College

Northern Illinois University

Kilgore College

Saddleback College North

Danbury State College

McGill University
```

2.

```
Kenora, Ontario

Salem, Massachusetts

Monmouth, Illinois

Kentfield, California

Minneapolis, Minnesota

Wakefield, Rhode Island

Coral Gables, Florida

Middlebury, Vermont

Glenville, West Virginia

Omaha, Nebraska

Victoria, British Columbia

Huron, South Dakota
```

3.

Rodney Schmidt
Robert Talmage
Agnes Salzer
Gladys McCabe
Connley Hartman
Ted Faravelli
Manasseh Manoukian

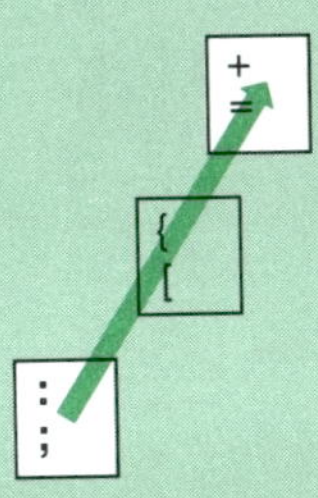

INTRODUCTION TO THE AT SIGN

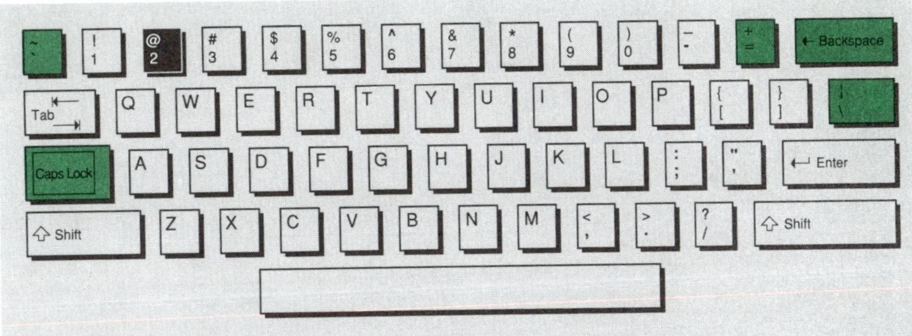

The **at sign** (@) is the shift of the number *2* key. Home-row *s* finger moves up and to the left to the **at sign** key. Be sure to depress the *right shift* key. Place both hands on the home row and practice the move from *s* to **at sign**. Look at your hands and watch your finger make the motion. Do this several times; then look away and try the same motion.

1 s2s s2s s2s s2s s2ws sw2s sw2s s@s s@s s2@s sw2@s 10

2 S@S s2s s@s sw@s S@S S@WS SW@S S@S s2s s@2s sw2@s 10

3 14 @ $2.00, 16 @ $55.00, 1 @ $17.59, 13 @ $124.66 10

4 It is better to buy 99 @ 18 rather than 180 @ 10. 10

5 I will take 4 @ 66, 14 @ 22, 17 @ 55, and 1 @ 33. 10

6 If you add 1 @ 55 and 1 @ 33 it will cost you 88. 10

□□□□ 1 □□□□□ 2 □□□□□ 3 □□□□ 4 □□□□□ 5 □□□□□ 6 □□□□□ 7 □□□□ 8 □□□□□ 9 □□□ 1 0

INTRODUCTION TO THE EQUALS SIGN

The **equals sign** (=) is generally located to the right of the **hyphen** key. The **semi** finger moves up and to the right to the **equals** key. Place both hands on the home row and practice the move from **semi** to **equals**. Look at your hands and watch your finger make the motion. Do this several times; then look away and try the same motion.

1 ;=; ;=; ;=; ;=; ;=; ;=; ;=; ;=; =;= =;= =;= =;= ;= 10

2 a=f s=d s=d ;=; ;=; j=j j=j k=k l=l ;-; ;= ;=; ;=; 10

3 a = b c = d e = f g = g j = j k = k l = l ;=; ;=;; 10

4 A = B C = D J = J K = K L = L A = B C = D E = R =; 10

5 ;=; ;=; ;=; =;= ;=; ;=; ;=; ;=; ;=; ;=; ;=; ;=; ;= 10

6 The = sign is generally used in math problems now. 10

□□□□ 1 □□□□□ 2 □□□□□ 3 □□□□ 4 □□□□□ 5 □□□□□ 6 □□□□□ 7 □□□□ 8 □□□□□ 9 □□□ 1 0

Key each line as quickly as you can.

3. Determine the number of lines that will not be used (subtract "lines used" from "lines available"). Assume you're using the example from the previous page.

	Single Spacing		_Double Spacing_		_Triple Spacing_	
	Full Sheet	Half Sheet	Full Sheet	Half Sheet	Full Sheet	Half Sheet
Available	66	33	66	33	66	33
Used	6	6	11	11	16	16
Unused	60	27	55	22	50	17

MASTERY SOFTWARE

	Single Spacing		_Double Spacing_		_Triple Spacing_	
	Full Sheet	Half Sheet	Full Sheet	Half Sheet	Full Sheet	Half Sheet
Available	54	27	54	27	54	27
Used	6	6	11	11	16	16
Unused	48	21	43	16	38	11

4. Determine how far to space down from the top of the page (divide "lines not used" by 2).

Note: Always advance the paper one additional line.

	Single Spacing		_Double Spacing_		_Triple Spacing_	
	Full Sheet	Half Sheet	Full Sheet	Half Sheet	Full Sheet	Half Sheet
	$\frac{30}{2\,\lfloor 60}$	$\frac{13\text{-}1/2 = 13}{2\,\lfloor 27}$	$\frac{27\text{-}1/2 = 27}{2\,\lfloor 55}$	$\frac{11}{2\,\lfloor 22}$	$\frac{25}{2\,\lfloor 50}$	$\frac{8\text{-}1/2 = 8}{2\,\lfloor 17}$

Note: If a fraction occurs from division by 2, drop it.

MASTERY SOFTWARE

	Single Spacing		_Double Spacing_		_Triple Spacing_	
	Full Sheet	Half Sheet	Full Sheet	Half Sheet	Full Sheet	Half Sheet
	$\frac{24}{2\,\lfloor 48}$	$\frac{10\text{-}1/2 = 10}{2\,\lfloor 21}$	$\frac{21\text{-}1/2 = 21}{2\,\lfloor 43}$	$\frac{8}{2\,\lfloor 16}$	$\frac{19}{2\,\lfloor 38}$	$\frac{5\text{-}1/2 = 5}{2\,\lfloor 11}$

Summary

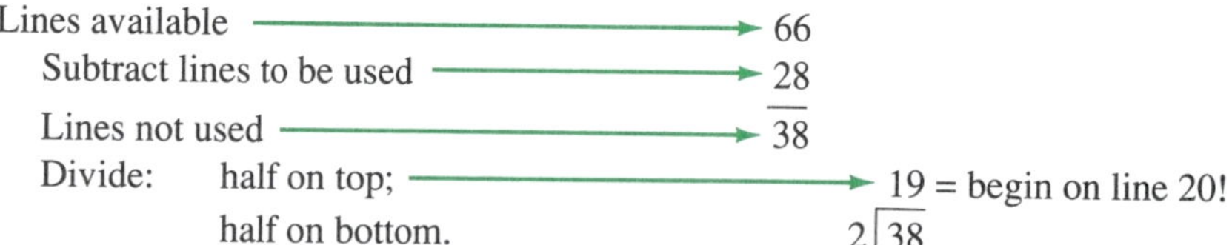

Lines available	⟶	66
Subtract lines to be used	⟶	28
Lines not used	⟶	38
Divide: half on top; half on bottom.	⟶	$\frac{19}{2\,\lfloor 38}$ = begin on line 20!

All typewriters/printers have a point from which to begin counting down to the line on which you want to begin. Check your machine to determine how far you should advance the paper before beginning to count.

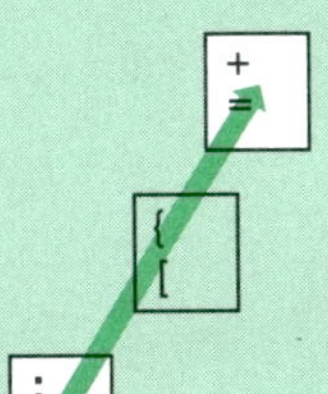

The *plus sign* (+) is the shift of the *equals-sign* key. Generally, it is located to the right of the hyphen key. The semi finger moves up and to the right to the *plus* key. Be sure to depress the *left shift* key. Place both hands on the home row and practice the move from *semi* to *plus*. Look at your hands and watch your finger make the motion. Do this several times; then look away and try the same motion.

Key each line once as quickly as you can.

```
1  ;=;  ;+;  ;+;  ;=+;  ;+:+:+=;  ;=;  ;+;  ;=;  ;+;  ;=;  :+;   10

2  A = B + C + D + F J = K + L + P Y = T + E + R ;=;   10

3  The equations were:  A = D + F + G and E = E + RT   10

4  The equations were:  A = B + C + E and A = A + BC   10

5  The computer program stated A = (B + C + C) * AD.   10

6  The formula C = A + BC is the same as C = (A+BC).   10
```

□□□□1□□□□2□□□□3□□□□□4□□□□□5□□□□□6□□□□□7□□□□□8□□□□□9□□□1 0

Speed and Accuracy Development

It is again time for you to concentrate on further developing your straight-copy speed and accuracy. Key the material below following the instructions shown in the left margin.

Lines 1–5 once—speed
Lines 1–5 again—speed

```
1  white grown waist drown waken swamp elbow welfare   10

2  brown water twine where swell write frown awkward   20

3  review warmer bowler wiring inward wisdom preview   30

4  window follow waiver jigsaw within warmth lawless   40

5  hardware workable followed weakness endowment two   50
```

Lines 6–10 once—speed
Lines 6–10 again—speed

```
6   Is Win wasting water if he washes the new window?   10

7   It is wise to wire the news to the waiting woman.   20

8   The wealth of the world will not wield wiser men.   30

9   He saw few minnows swimming in the shallow water.   40

10  Widen the wooden window and rewire the two bells.   50
```

□□□□1□□□□2□□□□3□□□□□4□□□□□5□□□□□6□□□□□7□□□□□8□□□□□9□□□1 0

If you are using a full sheet of paper (8-1/2 inches wide and 11 inches long), there will be 66 lines available (11 inches × 6 lines = 66). If you are going to use a half sheet of paper, there will be 33 lines available (5-1/2 inches × 6 lines = 33).

MASTERY SOFTWARE

The Mastery Software has 1-inch top and bottom default margins. Therefore, you must center problems vertically based on a 54-line page. Line 27 of the editor is the vertical center of a full sheet; line 14 is the vertical center of a half sheet. Insert hard returns at the end of your document until you reach the end of the page.

---

2. Determine the number of lines required for the text you are going to place on the page (in other words, how many lines will be used). Assume you want to horizontally and vertically center the following:

```
              Welcome!
            Texas Tech's
           Fifth Annual
            Homecoming
             Activities
         October 21, 19--
```

Depending upon the spacing you wish to use, you would determine the number of lines required as follows:

Single Spacing	*Double Spacing*	*Triple Spacing*
1 Welcome!	1 Welcome!	1 Welcome!
2 Texas Tech's	2	2
3 Fifth Annual	3 Texas Tech's	3
4 Homecoming	4	4 Texas Tech's
5 Activities	5 Fifth Annual	5
6 October 21, 19--	6	6
7	7 Homecoming	7 Fifth Annual
8	8	8
9	9 Activities	9
10	10	10 Homecoming
11	11 October 21, 19--	11
12	12	12
13	13	13 Activities
14	14	14
15	15	15
16	16	16 October 21, 19--

MASTERY SOFTWARE

The *F5* function key allows you to set the print feature for single or double spacing. The current setting is displayed at the top of the screen. To change the current setting, press the *F5* function key. ***Note:*** Single space 3 times to leave a

---

Lines 1–5 once—speed
Lines 1–5 again—speed

1 duel shut gulf fund dump bulb hunt must rude true 10
2 build fault under usual until awful insure budget 20
3 vault audit rumor truth about nurse sprung refund 30
4 adjust endure refuge manual fourth versus publish 40
5 fusion lawful nature urgent plural module suppose 50

Lines 6–10 once—speed
Lines 6–10 again—speed

6 Buff found a huge bug on the shrub in the puddle. 10
7 A stout runner shouted and slumped to the ground. 20
8 The group hummed a rousing tune during the stunt. 30
9 Susan put tuna on a bun and built a super supper. 40
10 The pup dug around in the mud and found a peanut. 50

Timings

Key once at controlled rate.
Take a 1-min. timing.
Take another 1-min. timing.

1   Ron is fond of opera. The golden tones of a 10
violin smooth his tense nerves. Visions arise in 20
his mind as the viola responds to the mood. Soft 30
tones float in the air as the piano renders notes 40
of dimension and diversion. 45

Key once at controlled rate.
Take a 1-min. timing.
Take another 1-min. timing.

2   Oatmeal is often a good food to eat. Add an 10
orange, hot toast, and milk to a morning meal for 20
digestion. It is important to eat in the morning 30
to avoid tension. Restore vim and vigor at noon; 40
do not overeat. 43

Key once at controlled rate.
Take a 1-min. timing.
Take another 1-min. timing.

3   Muffin is a genuine bulldog. Although he is 10
a plump pup, he bounds about with a flourish. It 20
is fun to see him plunge around, indulging in the 30
pure pleasure of running. He huffs and puffs and 40
slumps to the ground. No doubt, he will jump and 50
lunge again after a pause and find trouble. 59

WARM-UP

Key each line once.
Then key again.

1 An unfair boss singled out the busy man and gave him money.

2 Equip the ship's cabin with a radio and wire the islanders.

3 Patti marked the package of workbooks for the keen speaker.

4 456 789 125 125 127 124 126 129 125 128 982 982 12

5 242 252 252 262 852 258 158 148 284 282 272 958 94

6 222 224 225 226 227 228 228 822 922 202 202 212 21

Timed Short Drills

Turn to pages TSD 1–8 (timed short-drill material) and complete four 30-second timings. Select the line you feel you can complete. If you complete that line, move to the next one. If you do not complete the line, try it again or drop back one. Select either speed or accuracy as a goal.

Straight-Copy Timings

Take two 1-minute timings on the following material.

S.I. 1.35

Snowshoes add two dimensions to the feet. Snowshoes are big and   14

add a lot of weight. To compensate for size, you must use your eyes,   28

as well as your brain, to pick the way. Normally, in walking through   42

the forests, most of us look ahead about ten feet. When walking with   56

snowshoes, it is best to look ahead about twenty or thirty feet. The   70

size of the shoes requires that a person turn bigger corners and also   84

allow more room to maneuver. Most brush and bramble bushes are a big   98

problem and should be avoided.   104

VERTICAL CENTERING

To center text vertically on a page, you must determine how far to space down on the page before keying the first line. Some software packages have built-in features for vertical centering. However, it is good to know how to center vertically without using the software features. On typewriters, the keyboarder must center text manually. Study the following procedures to determine how to center text manually.

1. Determine how many lines are available on the paper on which you will be keying/printing. On a typewriter/printer, six lines equal 1 inch:

```
xxxxxxxxxxxx
xxxxxxxxxxxx
xxxxxxxxxxxx  } 1"
xxxxxxxxxxxx
xxxxxxxxxxxx
xxxxxxxxxxxx
```

Note: Some printers can print eight lines per inch.

WARM-UP

Lines 1–3 once
Lines 1–3 again

1 The patient is in pain; his left thigh is gashed.

2 Dan tested his stiff ankle and gnashed his teeth.

3 Jim, is that smashed metal mass a damaged helmet?

Lines 4–6 once
Lines 4–6 again

4 Lisa and Patti solved the equation A = B + C now.

5 If you purchased 2 @ $4.00, it would equal $8.00.

6 The = sign is used to show what two values equal.

INTRODUCTION TO THE SLASH (DIAGONAL)

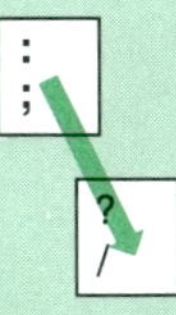

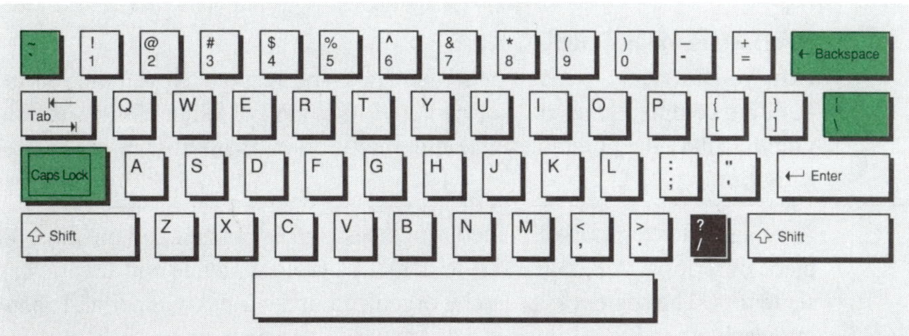

The *slash* (/) is located on the same key as the *question mark*. The slash is used as a division sign in computer programming languages. Therefore, it will be used frequently on the electronic keyboard. Sometimes it is also used to divide characters, such as month, day, and year in the date (i.e., 04/14/83). The *semi* finger moves down and to the right to the *slash* key. Place both hands on the home row and practice the move from *semi* to *slash*. Look at your hands and watch your finger make the motion. Do this several times; then look away and try the same motion.

Key each line as quickly as you can.

1 ;/; ;/; ;/; /;/ ;/; ;/; /;/ ;/; /;/ ;/ ;/ ;/;/ ;/ 10

2 a = b/c d = f/g h=j/l t=k/j r = j / k fgh = rty/j 10

3 The equation: miles/hours will equal speed rate. 10

□□□□1□□□□□2□□□□□3□□□□□4□□□□□5□□□□□6□□□□□7□□□□□8□□□□□9□□□1 0

1. Compose a complete sentence about each of the following items:

a. ballpoint pen   f. fire
b. ice cream   g. rain
c. gas station   h. dance
d. bank   i. apple
e. elevator   j. water

2. Compose a complete sentence about each of the following items:

a. mirror   f. radio
b. television   g. shoe
c. dollar bill   h. building
d. door   i. sunset
e. chair   j. clock

PARAGRAPH RESPONSE

Now you are ready to move on to the paragraph-response level, the fourth stage in building compositional skills. Read the following guidelines for composing paragraphs. Study the guidelines and attempt to follow them in your compositional activities.

GENERAL GUIDELINES

A paragraph is a group of related sentences—an organized and meaningful unit in a piece of writing. A paragraph is to contain a topic sentence and several supporting sentences. The sentences are to be organized in a logical manner and should flow into each other. Transitional words are used to connect one sentence to another.

1. A ***topic sentence*** expresses the main idea or subject of the paragraph. The topic sentence usually opens the paragraph, since most readers like to know what the paragraph is about before they read on. The topic sentence is underscored in the example below.

2. ***Supporting sentences*** describe, explain, or further develop the topic sentence.

   Example: <u>In a small office, the receptionist has a wide variety of duties.</u> Answering the telephone and receiving callers is a primary responsibility of any receptionist. Sometimes an employer will ask a receptionist to take an important client to lunch or to contact a business customer. The correspondence in a small office varies from simple letters to complicated reports, and so the receptionist handles many types of communication.

DRILL C

Compose a short paragraph using the following topic sentence. Concentrate on content; disregard keyboarding errors.

"A shortage of quality paper causes problems."

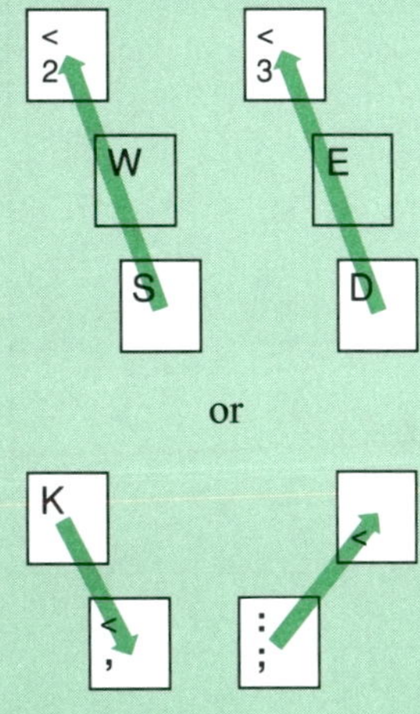

INTRODUCTION TO THE LESS THAN SIGN

The *less than sign* (<) is located in different positions, depending on the layout of the keyboard. The most common locations are (1) as shift of the number *2* key; (2) as shift of the *comma* key; (3) to the right of the *p* key, and (4) as shift of the number *3* key. Locate the position of the *less than* key on your keyboard. Identify the appropriate reach based on previously learned reaches. Place both hands on the home row and practice the move to the *less than* key. Look at your hands and watch your finger make the motion. Do this several times; then look away and try the same motion.

If your keyboard does not have a *less than* key, omit this section.

1 2<7 3<8 4<9 5<6 8<9 1<2 5<7 6<8 k<l k<l 5<6 1<8<9 10

2 12 < 43 16 < 58 17 < 89 15 < 28 123 < 456 17 < 77 10

3 2 < 4, j < k, l < m, K < L; S < Z; K < L; JK < LM 10

□□□□ 1 □□□□□ 2 □□□□□ 3 □□□□□ 4 □□□□□ 5 □□□□□ 6 □□□□□ 7 □□□□□ 8 □□□□□ 9 □□□ 1 0

INTRODUCTION TO THE GREATER THAN SIGN

The *greater than sign* (>) is located in different positions, depending on the layout of the keyboard. The most common locations are (1) as shift of the number *6* key; (2) as shift of the *period* key; (3) to the right of the *p* key; and (4) as shift of the number *7* key. Locate the position of the *greater than* key on your keyboard. Identify the appropriate reach based on previously learned reaches. Place both hands on the home row and practice the move to the *greater than* key. Look at your hands and watch your finger make the motion. Do this several times; then look away and try the same motion.

If your keyboard does not have a *greater than* key, omit this section.

1 f6f f6f l<l l<l ;<; ;<; 6>f 6>f f>f f>f l>l ;>>;; 10

2 F>F L>L ;>; 12 > 43 126 > 78 198 > 48 66 > 55 6>> 10

3 6 > 2 < 6; 6 > 1.2; 78 > 8; 1234 > 678; 56 < 234; 10

□□□□□ 1 □□□□ 2 □□□□□ 3 □□□□□ 4 □□□□□ 5 □□□□□ 6 □□□□□ 7 □□□□□ 8 □□□□□ 9 □□□ 1 0

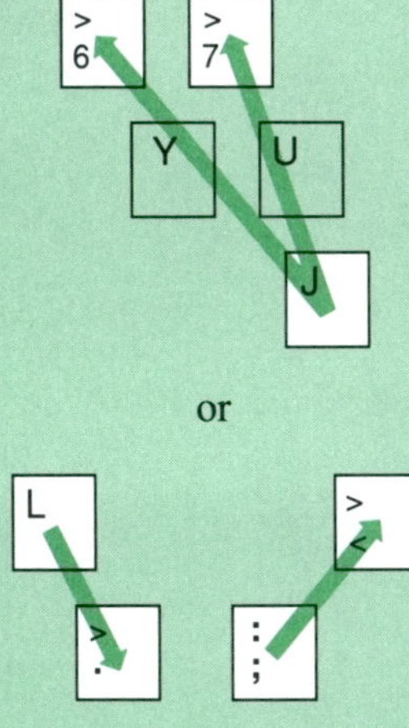

3. *Use the correct word;* some words are often misused.

   Examples:

accept *to take or receive* ⟵	⟶ except *to leave out; aside from*
advice *an opinion*	advise *to recommend*
biannual *twice a year*	biennial *once every two years*
council *a governing body*	counsel *to give advice*
fewer *(use with nouns that can be counted: fewer apples)*	less *(use with nouns that cannot be counted: less noise)*
good *modifies a noun or pronoun*	well *modifies a verb or adverb*
angry at *(things and animals)*	angry with *(people)*
angry about *(occasions or situations)*	

SENTENCE RESPONSE

Now that you have completed the phrase-response level, you can move on to the sentence-response level. Read the instructions for each drill; then compose as quickly as possible. **Remember:** Do not hesitate.

DRILL A

MASTERY SOFTWARE

Key your responses to Drills A, B, and C on the Drill Screen provided in the software.

1. Drawing from your experience and observations, try to think of descriptive words or phrases to make the sentences below more interesting. Key the revised sentences.

   a. The last book I read was good.
   b. Today is a nice day.
   c. My favorite sport is fun.
   d. My favorite color is a nice color.
   e. My best friend is nice.

2. Select the correct idiom from the sentences below, and key each sentence using the correct words.

   a. (Try to, Try and) key the data without any errors.
   b. Juan went (in search for, in search of) a new printer ribbon.
   c. My book is (different from, different than) Harriet's book.
   d. I will try to (comply with, comply to) your wishes.
   e. This (kind of a, kind of) paper is easier to store.

3. Select the correct word from the sentences below, and key each sentence using the correct word.

   a. (Accept, Except) for Henry, the entire class went on the trip.
   b. Our teacher strongly (adviced, advised) us to study for the exam.
   c. There have been (fewer, less) absences this winter than last winter.
   d. We have (fewer, less) flour than we need.
   e. He is a (good, well) student.
   f. Martha doesn't feel (good, well) today.
   g. Sean plays the violin (good, well).
   h. I am angry (at, about, with) my best friend.
   i. I am angry (at, about, with) the rising costs of the textbooks.
   j. I am angry (at, about, with) Whiskers, my cat.

INTRODUCTION TO THE EXPONENT SIGN

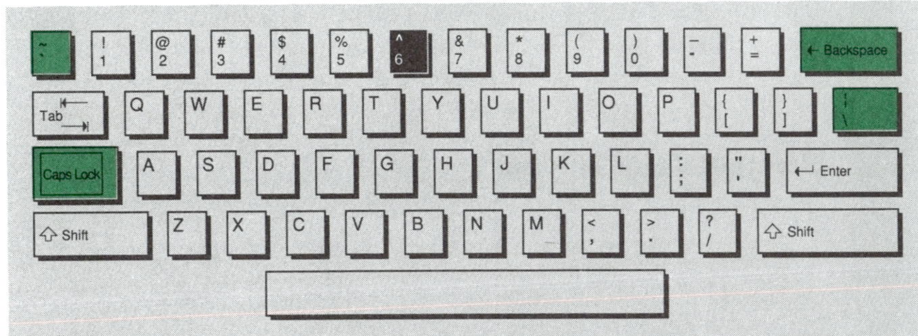

The *exponent sign* (^) is usually located as the shift of the number *6* key. Home-row *j* finger moves up and to the left to the *exponent* key. Be sure to depress the *left shift* key. Place both hands on the home row and practice the move from *j* to *exponent*. Look at your hands and watch your finger make the motion. Do this several times; then look away and try the same motion.

If your keyboard does not have an *exponent* key, omit this section.

Key each line once as quickly as you can.

1 j6j j6j j6j j^j j^j j^j j^j J^J J^J J^J J^J J^J J^ 10

2 The ^ sign is used to raise an integer to a power. 10

3 For example, 2^2 is the square of the numeral two. 10

□□□□1□□□□2□□□□3□□□□4□□□□5□□□□6□□□□7□□□□8□□□□9□□□1 0

INTRODUCTION TO THE BACKSLASH

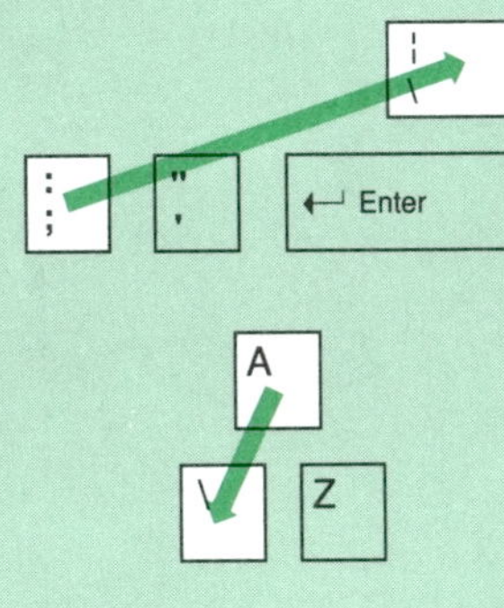

The *backslash* (\) is usually located above the *Enter* key or next to the *z* key. If it is located above the *Enter* key, home-row *semi* finger moves up and to the right to the *backslash* key. Place both hands on the home row and practice the move from *semi* to *backslash*. Look at your hands and watch your finger make the motion. Do this several times; then look away and try the same motion.

If the *backslash* is located next to the *z* key, home-row *a* finger moves down and to the left to the *backslash* key. Place both hands on the home row and practice the move from *a* to *backslash*. The shift of the *backslash* is the vertical line.

If your keyboard does not have a *backslash* key, omit this section.

Key each line once as quickly as you can.

1 The \ sign is used to designate a given file path. 10

2 For example, CD\ will return to the DOS directory. 10

3 The command, MKDIR \TGRADES, made a DOS directory. 10

□□□□1□□□□2□□□□3□□□□4□□□□5□□□□6□□□□7□□□□8□□□□9□□□1 0

Timed Short Drills

Turn to pages TSD 1–8 (timed short-drill material) and complete four 30-second timings. Select the line you feel you can complete. If you complete that line, move to the next one. If you do not complete the line, try it again or drop back one. Select either speed or accuracy as a goal.

Straight-Copy Timings

Take two 1-minute timings on the following material.

S.I. 1.35

```
        At sunset, it is nice to enjoy dining out on a bank of   12

a pond.  Unless uninvited insects and swarms of ants invade     24

the picnic, you will certainly unwind.  As those soft night     36

sounds enfold you, frenzied inward nerves and the decisions     48

that haunt you drain from your mind.  You may enjoy napping     60

on a nearby bench.  Next, swing into action after your rest     72

and inhale much air into your lungs.  Unpack the nice lunch     84

and munch away.  Don't deny yourself this experience.          95
```

    □□□□1□□□□2□□□□3□□□□4□□□□5□□□□6□□□□7□□□□8□□□□9□□□10□□□11□□□12

CHOOSING THE RIGHT WORD

One of the most common problems a writer faces is how to choose the exact word to convey a certain thought or idea to the reader. Writing must be precise; vague words or the misuse of words may change the author's meaning.

CORRECT WORD USAGE

GENERAL GUIDELINES

1. *Use concrete nouns and descriptive adjectives, adverbs, and phrases; do not use vague or abstract words.* Vague words can mean many different things. Words such as **nice, good, bad, thing,** and **work** do not give the reader much information. Read each of the following and note the differences.

   Examples:

   Vague: The lecture was good and I learned a lot.
   Better: The lecture solved two problems for me. I learned how to balance a checkbook and how to calculate interest.

   Vague: a nice color
   Better: an emerald green, a vivid scarlet, a dull black

   Vague: he said
   Better: he shouted defiantly, he muttered, he demanded

2. *Use English idioms correctly.* An idiom is an expression peculiar to a language and is perfectly acceptable if used correctly.

   Examples:

Correct	*Incorrect*	*Correct*	*Incorrect*
acquitted of	acquitted from	in search of	in search for
aim to prove	aim at proving	kind of (+ noun)	kind of a (+ noun)
can't help feeling	can't help but feel	aloud	out loud
comply with	comply to	try to	try and
independent of	independent from	different from	different than

DRILL

You have now completed all the special punctuation marks and symbols. Key each line once as quickly as you can. Key a space for any punctuation-mark or symbol key that does not appear on your keyboard.

Your instructor may also have you complete some timings.

```
 1  Two-thirds of the three-fourths are very gifted.    10
 2  John said:   Data Structures is a great textbook.    20
 3  Jerome's cat ran to Mary's house and said meow!!    30
 4  "Hello" said Billy, "How are you this fine day?"    40
 5  Help! yelled the young man as the bees followed.    50

 6  If the dress is $35.95, why is the coat $125.75?    10
 7  Take #33 and move it to #66.  Move #66 to #1234.    20
 8  Mary & Sally ran to see Johnny & George walking.    30
 9  The check was made out for at least $*******.99.    40
10  You scored 89% on the exam and 78% on the drill.    50

11  Now is the time (11:45) for you (Ginny) to move.    10
12  Perhaps 65¢ is too much.  But 56¢ was not ample.    20
13  Sixteen @ $1.23 and 57 @ $23.45 is far too much.    30
14  If hours = 40 and rate = $5.00 then gross = 200.    40
15  The equation was A = B + C + F + D + G + H + IJ.    50

16  Jerry thought that A < B and F < G and JK < JKL.    10
17  However, Tom knew that A > B and F > G and II>K.    20
18  If you raise 2^2 the answer will be squared now.    30
19  PRINT "THIS IS THE ANSWER:   " A$, TAB(34) " "B$.    40
20  LET B = A + B + C / D * H * (HH - K) + (HH + JJ)    50

21  IF TY$ < > "QUACKER" THEN GO TO READ-AGAIN-RTNS.    10
22  IF GH < AN AND TH > HJ OR TY < TU MOVE TRY TO A.    20
23  LPRINT TAB(42) "TOTAL" TAB(50) "PER GAME AVER.";    30
24  PRINT TAB(17) "PLAYER" TAB(34) "FG PERCENT "; FG    40
25  FIELD 1, 2 AS NUM$, 20 AS NM$, 2 AS D1$, 2 AS Z$    50
        1     2     3     4     5     6     7     8     9    10
```

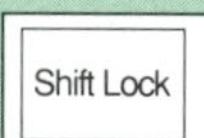

MASTERY SOFTWARE

Use the *F6* centering feature to complete Drill C.

Center each name on a separate line.

For emphasis you may wish to capitalize a whole word or a whole line. To capitalize more than one consecutive letter on the typewriter, use the *shift-lock* key. It is located above the *left shift* key. Depress the *lock* key and the machine will be "locked" so that it will print only uppercase (capital) letters. To unlock, tap the *shift* or *lock* key. On the microcomputer, use the *caps lock* key. As on the typewriter, it is located above the *left shift* key. Depress the *caps lock* key to begin all uppercase letters, and again depress the *caps lock* key to return to normal lowercase keying. Center each line of the following tasks.

1.
```
             YOU

        are Invited

        to Attend the

        First Annual

    STUDENT FORENSICS FOLLIES

        STUDENT THEATRE

        October 17, 19--

        8:00 p.m.
```

2. James Wong   Jack Johnson
Betty Lee   Miguel Ortega
Roman Shipek   Jim Barton
Joe Leipsel

DRILL D

MASTERY SOFTWARE

Use the backspace method to complete Drill D. Key again using the *F6* centering feature.

Center the following information using the backspace method. ***Remember:*** Mentally say each two characters; backspace ***once*** after saying each two.

Line 1:   Your first, middle, and last names.

Line 2:   Your street address.

Line 3:   Your city, state, and zipcode.

Line 4:   Your telephone number.

SESSION 34   COMPOSITION: SENTENCE/PARAGRAPH RESPONSE

WARM-UP

Key each line once. Then key again.

```
1  At one time the typewriter was the tool of choice for them.

2  The desk and chair are in agreement with the decor for now.

3  The color of the room is much too dark to be used as a den.

4  3748 3833 9374 1585 1392 1458 1382 1483 3230 30339

5  4435 4344 3345 3443 2343 2334 4873 4848 3929 26282

6  4844 6673 8733 5663 5543 3323 6788 6733 2343 23343
```

Reminder:
Think of pairs as you key four-digit numbers.

It is again time for you to concentrate on further developing your straight-copy speed and accuracy. Key the material below following the instructions shown in the left margin.

Lines 1–5 once—speed
Lines 1–5 again—speed

1 zing zone zoom zero blaze gauze glaze graze prize 10
2 seize breeze amaze razor pizza hazel zombi wizard 20
3 bronze wheeze frozen nozzle zipper fizzle seizing 30
4 freeze bazaar hazard puzzle zealot zinnia sneezed 40
5 trapeze zealous pretzel drizzle horizon embezzler 50

Lines 6–10 once—speed
Lines 6–10 again—speed

6 It is only your duty to obey every law of safety. 10
7 An early yellow lily may defy a wintry windy day. 20
8 Silly Sally annoys that friendly young boy, Gary. 30
9 Billy is ready to carry the heavy load Wednesday. 40
10 Accuracy at a typewriter keyboard may imply zest. 50

Lines 1–5 once—speed
Lines 1–5 again—speed

1 chain notch chute touch cheap since chase ancient 10
2 career public credit police carpet income decease 20
3 camera notice commit impact circle decide attract 30
4 compute deceive collate finance climate placement 40
5 compare produce consult service council enclosure 50

Lines 6–10 once—speed
Lines 6–10 again—speed

6 Cecelia consumed a rich chocolate ice cream cone. 10
7 The clever client could conceal crucial evidence. 20
8 Carol watched a cautious crow circle the cottage. 30
9 The wicked witch cackles as she concocts recipes. 40
10 Can Cam choose music as a classic school subject? 50

The automatic centering feature will save you time when centering lines of text. To use this feature, follow this procedure:

1. Key the line of text at the left margin.
2. Depress the *F6* function key to center the line of text.
3. Depress the *Enter* key to go to the next line.

DRILL A

Use the backspace method to complete Drill A. Key Drills A–D on the Drill Screen provided in the software.

Practice horizontally centering each of the following lines:

<pre>
                 Getting a Job

              Vertical Centering

              Review and Check

                 Betty Allen

              Frank Bestemore
</pre>

Compare your copy to the example. Does it look the same? Now key the same problem again; attempt to complete it in a shorter amount of time. Compare your second attempt to the example. How does it compare?

DRILL B

Use the *F6* centering feature to complete Drill B.

Practice centering the following tasks. **Remember:** You must center *each* line. Your finished solution will ***not*** look like this.

1.
<pre>
You are

Invited to Attend

the First Annual

Student Forensics Follies

Student Theatre

October 17, 19--

8:00 p.m.
</pre>

2.
<pre>
Plan to Attend

the

Pre-game Pep Rally

Tomorrow (October 19)

3:00 p.m.

Football Field
</pre>

Timings

Key once at controlled rate.
Take a 1-min. timing.
Take another 1-min. timing.

1   Barlow, a shrewd fellow, winked as he waited 10
in the shadows. A whistle warned him of the slow 20
walk of his fellow worker. As he wallowed in the 30
warmth of that workshop, Will worked in the wild, 40
blowing wind. Barlow was worthless. 47

1 2 3 4 5 6 7 8 9 10

Key once at controlled rate.
Take a 1-min. timing.
Take another 1-min. timing.

2   Zelda gazed in amazement as Zip, the wizard, 10
seized a wand. It was ablaze with a maze of fire 20
and lights. He did dozens of hazardous feats and 30
puzzled all at the bazaar. He also was a trapeze 40
whiz and dazzled folks. 45

1 2 3 4 5 6 7 8 9 10

Key once at controlled rate.
Take a 1-min. timing.
Take another 1-min. timing.

3   A lazy bicycle ride in the country is surely 10
a healthy and worthy activity. A sunny sky and a 20
dry day is surely an omen to any type of cyclist. 30
Be wary of cloudy and windy days. A daily remedy 40
for a healthy and spry body is a ride on a cycle. 50
Energy is enjoyed by young and not so young. 59

1 2 3 4 5 6 7 8 9 10

Straight-Copy Timings

Take two 1-minute timings on the following material.

S.I. 1.33

```
        Driving the car is fun to do whether with friends or alone.  Some   14
of the time drivers get careless because they feel that it is funny to   28
show how great they may be behind the wheel.  As you take control of a   42
vehicle, be sure to drive in a manner which would illustrate that your   56
driving habits are to be respected.  Observe traffic laws and be aware   70
of the driving habits of others.  Drive defensively when on the street   84
or highway.  Watch out for children and pets.                           93
```

☐☐☐☐1☐☐☐☐2☐☐☐☐3☐☐☐☐4☐☐☐☐5☐☐☐☐6☐☐☐☐7☐☐☐☐8☐☐☐☐9☐☐☐10☐☐☐11☐☐☐12☐☐☐13☐☐☐14

HORIZONTAL CENTERING

Centering of words and titles is very important in making copy appear neatly on a page. On electronic typewriters and computers, there are features that facilitate the centering of text. However, it is good to know how to center on electronic equipment without using the automatic features. On electric typewriters, the keyboarder must center text manually. Study the following to learn how to center text manually.

To center a word, phrase, or sentence horizontally on a page, follow this procedure:

1. Move the element or cursor to the center point of your line. If you are using a typewriter, insert a tab if one is not present. With 10-pitch (pica) spacing, 42 will be the horizontal center. With 12-pitch (elite) spacing, 50 is typically regarded as the center. The Mastery Software uses a 65-space line as a default; therefore, 33 should be used as the center point if you are using this software. If you are using another software package, consult your instructor or the manual.

2. Backspace *once* for each *two* strokes or spaces in the information to be centered.

   Example: Ca|li|fo|rn|ia

   Important: Remember to backspace *once* for every *two* strokes or spaces.

3. If there is a single character left, drop it (do not backspace for it).

   Example: op|ti|on|al| ac|ti|vi|ti|e|s

4. Efficiency guideline:

   As you press the *backspace* key, mentally say each two characters; backspace *once* after saying each two.

   Example:

   (to be centered) ⟶ Horizontal Centering

   (mentally say) ⟶ Ho ri zo nt al C en te ri ng

ALPHABETIC REVIEW

The time spent building your keyboarding skill must be meaningful and purposeful. Therefore, you must determine your specific goal each time you complete a line of drill. For example, "Are you building speed?" or "Are you working to improve your accuracy?" Remember, you must push yourself to improve your speed. You must slow down and key with control to improve your accuracy. The ABC approach to building speed will require that you complete the following steps:

A **Assess** your skills by taking an initial timing for either speed or accuracy. Determine your assessment score: number of words keyed if speed is your goal, or number of errors if accuracy is your goal.

B **Build** your skill by keying the lines or drills identified within the section. If you are building speed, push yourself to key an increased number of strokes each time you take a timing. Constantly push to key the line faster and faster. If you are working to improve your accuracy, think *control* as you key the lines or drills. Concentrate on the copy and control your speed to improve accuracy.

C **Check** your progress by repeating a timing on the same material you keyed to assess your skill. Be patient and recognize that you will not improve either your speed or accuracy each time you complete a skill building exercise. Improving your skill takes both dedication and continuous practice. Keyboarding accuracy relates directly to concentration. Sometimes you will notice progress on a one- or two-word level or a one- or two-error improvement level. Other times you will notice that progress is made after returning the next day. Diligent practice will lead to improved skill!

ALPHABETIC REVIEW

Ten sentences and one timing are presented for each letter of the alphabet. You may use this material for developing both speed and accuracy.

1. *Accuracy development:* If a particular letter of the alphabet causes you problems (you consistently key another letter instead of the one you want), use this material for reinforcement practice to eliminate the error.

2. *Speed development:* Words in the English language are composed of **digraphs** (two-letter combinations) and **trigraphs** (three-letter combinations). The more fluently you can key these combinations, the faster you will be. Use this material to increase your speed.

The procedure you should follow when using this material is outlined below:

1. Take a 1-minute timing on the paragraph. Determine the total number of words and the total number of errors.

2. Determine your practice goal. Concentrate on SPEED if you had no more than one error, or on ACCURACY if you had two or more errors.

3. Key the ten sentences, **concentrating** on your individual practice goal.

Read a question and then answer it by keying several words. *Remember:* Do not hesitate. Key your answer as quickly as possible.

1.
   a. What does a police officer do?
   b. What does a plumber do?
   c. What does a fire-fighter do?
   d. What does a lawyer do?
   e. What does a teacher do?

2.
   a. What does an auto mechanic do?
   b. What does a medical doctor do?
   c. What does a dentist do?
   d. What does an accountant do?
   e. What does a chef do?

SESSION 33 — HORIZONTAL CENTERING

WARM-UP

Key each line once. Then key again.

1 Store all of the diskettes in the safe with your printouts.

2 All of the software applications are necessary for the job.

3 The tape backup system is nice to have while running tasks.

4 345 636 663 663 663 336 393 393 993 993 339 936 93

5 234 354 345 456 383 838 938 736 373 369 936 963 33

6 568 936 947 373 464 585 484 737 363 922 291 302 30

Alphabetic Sentence Review

Key each line once. Then key again.

1 Silas considers that offensive noise as a passing nuisance.

2 The gentle cattle are too thin; the earth's thaw is timely.

3 I guess that tough guide has taught thousands about values.

4 A savory flavor is evoked in veal by serving anchovies too.

5 The scowling prowler scowled as the dog howled and growled.

6 The extra text on the extractions of textiles is extensive.

7 The style of yellow nylon and vinyl is certainly very ugly.

8 Lazy Fritz is woozy and dizzy from that crazy, zany puzzle.

   1   2   3   4   5   6   7   8   9   10   11   12

Timed Short Drills

Turn to pages TSD 1–8 (timed short-drill material) and complete four 30-second timings. Select the line you feel you can complete. If you complete that line, move to the next one. If you do not complete the line, try it again or drop back one. Select either speed or accuracy as a goal.

4. Take another 1-minute timing on the paragraph. Determine speed and accuracy.
   Compare with your first timing. If you improved according to your goal,
   proceed to another section emphasizing a different letter. If you did not
   improve according to your practice goal, key the ten sentences again.
   Remember: Concentrate on your individual goal. Take another timing on the
   paragraph. Compute the words and errors. Whether you improved or not, move
   on to another section. If you did not improve, return to the section emphasizing
   this particular letter the next time class meets.


```
        That happy play has an amazing climax.  It affects all   12
watchers.  The absorbing last act is majestic with an array   24
of blazing ideas.  Many apt actors who speak well may apply   36
and qualify for a part.  The author is apt and adept; he is   48
ascending toward a lavish share of awards.  He is aware and   60
now aims to avoid mistakes in reaching goals ahead.  He had   72
to fire an agent who made absurd demands and squandered all   84
the cash on large purchases.  He was a fraud and a hoax.      95
```

 1 The actor felt he could adapt to the lead in the first act.
 2 The leak in the rear seal lost the race for the racing ace.
 3 The captain on the sailboat trained the sailor in the rain.
 4 The green jeep had a linkage clamp squeak which alarmed Al.
 5 Jac's amazing kayak, with ample ballast, will always align.

 6 An alarm alerted all the coal miners who ran along a trail.
 7 An antique aqua vase was caked with an opaque lacquer film.
 8 Allen and his daughter toured automobile and sausage firms.
 9 Await that taxi and avoid paying a crazy fee; it is a hoax.
10 Someday, that relaxed weaver might amaze the awful gawkers.

Now that you have completed the word-response level, you can move on to the phrase-response level. Read a question and then answer it by keying several words. Do not make complete sentences—just answer the question. If you do not know the correct answer, invent one. ***Remember:*** Do not hesitate. Key your answer as quickly as possible.

1.
   a. What is the name of a town and state/province that you would like to visit?
   b. What is your instructor's first and last name?
   c. What is the president's/prime minister's last name?
   d. What is the name of this book?
   e. What is the name of this course?

2.
   a. What is your first and last name?
   b. What is your friend's first and last name?
   c. What is the title of your favorite song?
   d. What is the name of the last movie you saw?
   e. What is the name of the last television show you saw?

3.
   a. Where were you born?
   b. Where did you attend elementary school?
   c. Where did you go on your last vacation?
   d. Where are you going after class today?
   e. Where will you be tomorrow at this time?

4.
   a. What are your favorite sports?
   b. What are your favorite colors?
   c. What will you be doing five years from now?
   d. What is the name of your favorite class?
   e. What is the name of your best friend?

Complete these sentences by keying a phrase of two or more words.

1.
   a. Because the clock was wrong, I ____________.
   b. Because the road was icy, I ____________.
   c. Because the team won, I ____________.
   d. Because I was late, I ____________.
   e. Because I cannot drive, I ____________.

2.
   a. If I pass this test, I ____________.
   b. If I finish early, I ____________.
   c. If I get the job, I ____________.
   d. If the price is right, I ____________.
   e. If the beach is crowded, I ____________.

3.
   a. I *do/do not* like loud music because ____________.
   b. I *do/do not* study at the library because ____________.
   c. I *do/do not* obey the speed limit because ____________.
   d. I *do/do not* like math because ____________.
   e. I *do/do not* play sports because ____________.

4.
   a. A hammer is used to ____________.
   b. A lawn mower is used to ____________.
   c. Scissors are used to ____________.
   d. A pencil is used to ____________.
   e. An eraser is used to ____________.

While the boys scrambled about, Barb baked a big batch 12
of bars. The bleak cabin needed a good scrubbing. She had 24
been able to buy a bulb for the amber lamp. The bright and 36
probing beam chased the gloom away. A cheery robin sitting 48
on a limb called to other birds. The tasty leg of lamb and 60
herb dressing would soon be ready. The slight haze of that 72
day made the family feel an abounding sense of peace. Soon 84
they would climb aboard the boat and return to urban life. 96
□□□□1□□□□2□□□□3□□□□4□□□□5□□□□6□□□□7□□□□8□□□□9□□□10□□□11□□□12

1 Bif's big exhibit is a combination of ambition and ability.
2 A big black bear lumbered about a cabin begging for a bite.
3 Ben scrubbed the beaker before he began the riverbed probe.
4 The mobile beam on the bike probed the biased urban battle.
5 Bo scrambles and climbs to noble objectives; he is capable.
□□□□1□□□□2□□□□3□□□□4□□□□5□□□□6□□□□7□□□□8□□□□9□□□10□□□11□□□12

6 The black inkblot is a terrible blemish on that blue table.
7 The ambitious climber needs an ambulance; he took a tumble.
8 That bragging boy is a brat when he grabs and climbs lamps.
9 No doubt, the bow of the boat should be swabbed and rubbed.
10 The business disbursed an abundance of burlap and buckskin.
□□□□1□□□□2□□□□3□□□□4□□□□5□□□□6□□□□7□□□□8□□□□9□□□10□□□11□□□12

EMPHASIS ON C

The chief and the crew did concur. That ocean cruiser 12
could be launched at once. It was a fact, the cursed cruel 24
pirates had discovered their recent acquisition of sacks of 36
gold coins. As the panic arose, the excited crew scanned a 48
curving cedar grove along the coast. Those ancient cypress 60
boards crackled as the excess load caused the boat to crawl 72
and cease almost all movement. The acute crisis excluded a 84
quick chance at a complete escape. 91
□□□□1□□□□2□□□□3□□□□4□□□□5□□□□6□□□□7□□□□8□□□□9□□□10□□□11□□□12

WARM-UP

Key each line once.
Then key again.

1 The steadfast judge pledged his badge to the stodgy widows.

2 A handsome adult cannot have a dull wardrobe or drab shoes.

3 The elder clerks objected to the sleek styles in the store.

4 789 789 456 456 475 678 789 908 908 970 970 987 09

5 890 890 690 690 906 960 978 589 479 690 978 890 89

6 900 909 909 969 969 696 989 797 690 578 589 987 95

Alphabetic Sentence Review

Key each line once.
Then key again.

1 That jumpy jigsaw is jinxed and could injure Jean; junk it.

2 That fickle king is skilled as he tackles the old bulkhead.

3 Lil is willing to duplicate the lists of discipline drills.

4 Mike might mope more if the campus merger is in the autumn.

5 Cranky Nina's nice pink banjo is nicked; she plans revenge.

6 An oldtimer scolds the troops only once, then moves onward.

7 Place the splendid duplicate on the plain plywood platform.

8 The quick quakes brought queasy quiverings to the squadron.

9 A lark ate a kernel of corn in the warmth of the dark barn.

    1   2   3   4   5   6   7   8   9   10   11   12

Timed Short Drills

Turn to pages TSD 1–8 (timed short-drill material) and complete four 30-second timings. Select the line you feel you can complete. If you complete that line, move to the next one. If you do not complete the line, try it again or drop back one. Select either speed or accuracy as a goal.

Straight-Copy Timings

Take two 1-minute timings on the following material.

S.I. 1.29

The news on the network newscast might spawn a winning 12

wealth of followers. If the newsman can draw a wider range 24

of viewers, his rewards are power and wealth. Watchers and 36

followers of a witty newscaster are won when the daily news 48

is written well. It is not a waste to rewrite the worst of 60

interviews when witless words can wreck a well-planned show 72

or review. He who dawdles in the newsroom will not work or 84

write very long. His award will be awful reviews.   94

    1   2   3   4   5   6   7   8   9   10   11   12

1 The scarred cedar canoe is wrecked and anchored on a beach.
2 Chad challenged the champion to an archery match at school.
3 Unpack the clock quickly and see if it ticks or is wrecked.
4 Pick up the tacks and the buckets and climb into the attic.
5 I discovered the lacquered comb on a beach along the coast.
□□□□1□□□□2□□□□3□□□□4□□□□5□□□□6□□□□7□□□□8□□□□9□□□10□□□11□□□12

6 Since that old scow was launched, it has coughed only once.
7 Underscore the escape scene in the manuscript schedule now.
8 Expect an edict from the architect to collect the contract.
9 The policy of that agency is to curb the excess excitement.
10 The fancy motorcycle has a cylindrical cyclometer attached.
□□□□1□□□□2□□□□3□□□□4□□□□5□□□□6□□□□7□□□□8□□□□9□□□10□□□11□□□12

EMPHASIS ON D

Even the steadfast must agree some birthdays are dandy 12
with abundant kindness and others seem to be dark and dull. 24
Adults have undue qualms when adjusting to growing older; a 36
child stampedes through the days with wild abandonment. No 48
doubt a small child full of daring and dynamic energy deals 60
with life in a candid way. All the bedlam and wild dashing 72
dispels any dim attitudes of dour adults. To avoid adverse 84
thoughts on birthdays, spend them with children. 94
□□□□1□□□□2□□□□3□□□□4□□□□5□□□□6□□□□7□□□□8□□□□9□□□10□□□11□□□12

1 The hardboard woodbin held a sandbag, a birdbath, and pans.
2 Denny detected deep dents on the side of the wooden girder.
3 That wildcat withdraws to the ridge on the edge of a hedge.
4 That endless bedlam muddled the kindly landlord needlessly.
5 The widow's abundant kindness is doubtful; she has no dogs.
□□□□1□□□□2□□□□3□□□□4□□□□5□□□□6□□□□7□□□□8□□□□9□□□10□□□11□□□12

6 The stampede at midnight had the doe in a state of sadness.
7 A handsome adult cannot have a dull wardrobe or drab shoes.
8 Don, drag that dull handsaw to the edge of the dry bedrock.
9 Dwight ate a sandwich at the roadway dwelling by the woods.
10 That sturdy bodyguard is steady; he is always ready to run.
□□□□1□□□□2□□□□3□□□□4□□□□5□□□□6□□□□7□□□□8□□□□9□□□10□□□11□□□12

DRILL B

Which One?

Read a question and then answer it by keying one of two responses or key the word "neither." *Remember:* Do not hesitate. Key your answer as quickly as possible.

1.
    a. Would you rather ski or swim?
    b. Would you rather drive or ride?
    c. Would you rather eat or cook?
    d. Would you rather walk or talk?
    e. Would you rather hike or bike?

2.
    a. Are you a female or a male?
    b. Are you right- or left-handed?
    c. Is the instructor of this class male or female?
    d. Would you rather drink milk or tea?
    e. Would you rather dance or read?

3.
    a. Would you rather dance or sing?
    b. Would you rather eat hot dogs or hamburger?
    c. Would you rather write or read?
    d. Would you rather study or play?
    e. Would you rather own a dog or a cat?

4.
    a. Do you like summer or winter best?
    b. Would you rather be short or tall?
    c. Would you rather be dirty or clean?
    d. Would you rather win or lose?
    e. Would you rather run or walk?

DRILL C

Opposites

Read a word and then key its opposite. If you cannot think of an opposite, key the word shown. *Remember:* Do not hesitate. Key your answer as quickly as possible.

1.
    a. day   f. rich
    b. salt   g. war
    c. mother   h. young
    d. uncle   i. love
    e. grandmother   j. hot

2.
    a. clean   f. stop
    b. male   g. no
    c. minus   h. winter
    d. seldom   i. sick
    e. floor   j. true

3.
    a. high   f. beginning
    b. up   g. forget
    c. over   h. stand
    d. few   i. give
    e. wrong   j. short

4.
    a. new   f. come
    b. win   g. child
    c. negative   h. wet
    d. good   i. all
    e. open   j. fast

That eccentric thief scares me. He swears that he did 12
not steal the wealthy lady's jewels. He is either embarked 24
on an evil route of crime, or else he is a cheap cheat. At 36
best, he knows how to effect an illegal entry. Each of his 48
creeping moves suggests a false value. He prizes money and 60
exerts extra effort to obtain it. In any event, it appears 72
that he has the stolen jewelry. He is edgy and tired. His 84
tale may change soon. 88

1 The telecast was technical and reflected the forecast well.
2 The feature of the feast was eggplant and pieces of shrimp.
3 The barge is wedged under the bridge; it's eight feet high.
4 A deceitful neighbor received the weighty heirloom Tuesday.
5 The elder clerk objected to the jeweler's sleek edged case.

6 To enact that epic opera, one is required to erect scenery.
7 Erase the errors and enter the correct equity in the entry.
8 A reunion banquet may reunite Beulah with her feuding sons.
9 A few extra blazers are needed to stop the freezing breeze.
10 That shrewd boxer exhaled deeply; are his eyes glazed, too?

Often, before we face all the facts, our own fears may 12
begin to defeat us. Life seems filled with deep strife and 24
failures. We become inflamed at oneself and fuss in small, 36
futile ways. This is the time to stop fretting and inflate 48
our ego with a firm, fresh start. Swiftly, our spirits are 60
lifted. We have a fine feeling of being free from cares or 72
defeat. 73

When taking timings, your goal will be to improve either your speed *or* your accuracy. ***Remember:*** You must concentrate on one or the other. Your goal will probably change daily—or even during a particular class period.

Straight-Copy Timings

Take two 1-minute timings on the following material.

```
Long ago, pilgrims loved to indulge in blunt folklore.   12
Tales, sometimes false, were told with glee daily.  One old  24
tale included a blazing clash of sailors in balky sailboats  36
on a bottomless lake.  The last sailor alive was a lad that  48
was blind.  As he lay clinging to a slim balsa log in filth  60
and slimy silt, the leader's falcon led help to him.  Balmy  72
days followed as the lad's leg healed slowly and the salves  84
applied to his eyes let the light in.                        91
```

1 2 3 4 5 6 7 8 9 10 11 12

COMPOSITION

Now that you have learned the keyboard and have further developed your skills, it is time to learn to think and compose at the keyboard. While learning the keyboard, you were given the opportunity to "Think—and Key." The next few sessions will provide additional practice in composing at the keyboard.

There are four stages in building compositional skills:

1. Developing skill at the *word-response* level. (You have already begun working at this level.)

2. Developing skill at the *phrase-response* level.

3. Developing skill at the *sentence-response* level.

4. Developing skill at the *paragraph,* or *"complete,"* level.

WORD RESPONSE

DRILL A

Yes or No

Read a question and then answer it by keying either *yes* or *no.* ***Remember:*** Do not hesitate. Key your answer as quickly as possible.

1.
a. Do you like the weather today?
b. Do you like animals?
c. Are you hungry?
d. Do you read the newspaper?
e. Would you like to go into politics?
f. Do you participate in any sport?
g. Do you like to watch television?
h. Do you own a car?
i. Do you ride a bike?
j. Do you like soccer?

2.
a. Are you tired?
b. Do you have any brothers?
c. Do you have any sisters?
d. Do you have a job?
e. Are you a "good" speller?
f. Are you going on vacation soon?
g. Do you like English?
h. Do you like coffee?
i. Would you like to travel overseas?
j. Do you like to cook?

3.
a. Do you like to dance?
b. Would you like to become a millionaire?
c. Do you like hot weather?
d. Do you like music?
e. Do you like to rollerskate?
f. Do you ride to school in a car?
g. Is today Wednesday?
h. Did you get up early this morning?
i. Do you like pizza?
j. Have you watched television today?

1 The effects of the transfer of professors is felt by a few.
2 File all the facts on future films in their fireproof safe.
3 Confirm those official figures on the fifth fiscal profits.
4 Before the fox infects the folks, get a rifle from a shelf.
5 That flag flapped in the infield before that football game.

6 Forty uniformed foresters followed the fox into the forest.
7 The chefs fumed as the fresh fruit on that buffet softened.
8 Lift the fifth rafter swiftly to the rooftop; shift it aft.
9 Buff bluffs and fusses at loafers who are adrift from life.
10 The new furniture is fully functional as well as beautiful.

EMPHASIS ON G

The boy is going to grab a bag of hamburgers after the 12
game. That last game was grim. The team's energy ought to 24
be higher for the rough gripping coughs are gone. The last 36
germs have given way to good health through better hygiene. 48
It is our guess that the girls will get eight goals. Those 60
grounds are genuinely great. The eight dingy lights, which 72
were illegal, glow brighter. When the gala bash is in full 84
swing, the manager will give the guests a grand gift. 95

1 Gail agrees with that judge; vague pledges are not genuine.
2 A cartridge was wedged on the edge of a ledge of the lodge.
3 Eager agents merged in the rugged village to stage revenge.
4 Give the giggling girl a gift that is fragile and original.
5 Eight glad beagles glared at the slight girl on the ground.

6 The grim golfers merged on the driving range by the lagoon.
7 The large gray barge surges and swings against the bridges.
8 Green grapes and grapefruit grow in the good, grassy grove.
9 That guard is anguished as he argues with a fatigued guest.
10 Gail likes the technology of biology, geology, and ecology.

Key each line once.
Then key again.

WARM-UP

1 abide absorb slab babbly jab act actor race bacon react ace

2 bag bar bat bake back batch battle urban debar combat cabin

3 chew chat chief change choice ache much each ditch anchored

4 456 456 456 456 456 456 456 456 456 456 456 456 45

5 444 444 555 555 555 666 666 555 444 444 555 666 45

6 456 456 456 654 654 564 564 654 564 565 564 456 46

Reminder:
Think *four-fifty-six*
as you key 456.

Alphabetic Sentence Review

Key each line once.
Then key again.

1 Jac's amazing kayak, with ample ballast, will always align.

2 Bo scrambles and climbs to noble objectives; he is capable.

3 I discovered the lacquered comb on a beach along the coast.

4 The widow's abundant kindness is doubtful; she has no dogs.

5 The elder clerk objected to the jeweler's sleek edged case.

6 That flag flapped in the infield before that football game.

7 Eight glad beagles glared at the slight girl on the ground.

8 Shall Holly hire Hal to chop those high bushes at her home?

9 Has the existing script been revised--or a new one written?

□□□□1□□□□2□□□□3□□□□4□□□□5□□□□6□□□□7□□□□8□□□□9□□□10□□□11□□□12

MASTERY SOFTWARE

Key the Timed Short Drill
material from the screen.

Key Straight-Copy
Timings using wordwrap
with the default margins.
Drop hyphens at ends of
lines except where noted.

Timed Short Drills

Turn to pages TSD 1–8 (timed short-drill material) located at the back of your book before the *Reference Summary* and complete four 30-second timings. Select the drill you feel you can complete. If you complete that drill, move to the next one. If you do not complete the drill, try it again or drop back one. Select either speed or accuracy as a goal.

MARGIN SETTINGS

Timed Short Drills and some Straight-Copy Timings are shown in a 70-space line format. Setting your margins at 15 and 85 for 12-pitch (elite) or 7 and 77 for 10-pitch (pica) for these exercises will allow you to follow the line endings in the text. This will help you when checking for errors in your keyed copy. You may wish to key all of the drills and timings on a 70-space line to avoid having to change margin settings. If you are using the Mastery Software, key Straight-Copy Timings using wordwrap with the default margins.

SYLLABIC INTENSITY

Beginning with this session, the *syllabic intensity* will be given in the left margin for all 1-, 3-, and 5-minute straight-copy timings. Syllabic intensity (S.I.) is an approximate indication of how difficult material is to key. The lower the S.I., the easier the material is to key; the higher the S.I., the more difficult the material since the words are longer.

Those happy chaps hope to hike to the south shore. It 12
is eighty miles from their homes. If harsh weather hinders 24
them, each has a small, tight tent. When they are enroute, 36
the head chef can prepare wholesome meals. Breakfast might 48
be ham and eggs or hotcakes. A hearty lunch of milk, fresh 60
fruit and sandwiches will be eaten in haste. The plans for 72
night meals include meat, mashed potatoes and other things. 84
They are healthy and hearty. They may catch fresh fish. 95

1 The hardwood benches are chipped; have Herb haul them here.
2 Detach each chain and launch the machine on the cold beach.
3 A head chef is happy when he chops herbs into healthy hash.
4 Hide that thing; it has harsh hooks that hinder his chores.
5 Shall Holly hire Hal to chop those high bushes at her home?

6 Shorten the cashmere shirt and finish washing those dishes.
7 The theft of the cathedral heirloom made their hearts ache.
8 A white whale wheezed and was near death in the south tank.
9 The shutters shuddered and thundered during that hurricane.
10 Hammer another lath on that wharf; that whole booth shakes.

That stadium by the river isn't immune to crime. Last 12
night a thief seized an expensive radio from a taxi driver, 24
who was picking up a rider. The thief ditched the radio in 36
the river. A diver fished it out quickly. The weird irony 48
is that the thief is out of jail on bail. It's likely that 60
he bribed an ignorant civil aide. In spite of this, he has 72
been identified. His alibi is nullified. Irate voices are 84
being raised to swiftly close the issue. 92

2

BASIC LEVEL PRODUCTIVITY

Upon successful completion of the BASIC LEVEL PRODUCTIVITY module you will be able to key straight-copy alphanumeric material at an average rate of 50 words-a-minute with two or fewer errors per minute. You will also be able to key formatted letters, memorandums, tables, and manuscripts at a basic level productivity rate of 15 to 20 words-a-minute (1.5 to 2.0 lines-a-minute).

SESSION CONTENTS

1 Big pieces of ice on the bridge made it slick and slippery.
2 Did that guide brief the alien aide in detail about fibers?
3 Mike and Spike are likely to bike or hike a mile to a dike.
4 Willis will sail daily to build a skill similar to sailors.
5 Has the existing script been revised--or a new one written?

6 The principal ship is equipped with a skipper on this trip.
7 A retired admiral inspired the pair with spirit and desire.
8 In spite of the waiver, Jill will win the elite quiz prize.
9 Fix the sixty mixtures and affix the prefixes to sixty-six.
10 As the pizza sizzles, the organized quiz will be continued.

EMPHASIS ON J

The object of the jury is to judge that subject and to 12
be just. The adjacent jail adjoins the courtroom. A jaunt 24
to the jail is not enjoyable. The judge's job is to remain 36
judicious when the final judgment must be made. All jurors 48
must be adults; juveniles are not allowed on the jury. The 60
jokers who jeer and jest will be ejected. Adjournment will 72
take place after justice has been resolved. 81

1 Jack adjusted the jerky jeep by ejecting the jammed object.
2 Jack jarred his jaw on the jalopy as Jan adjusted the door.
3 Jane's jewel is a jade; she just lost it on the jaunty jet.
4 The jeep project is in jeopardy if jealousy is interjected.
5 That jumpy jigsaw is jinxed and could injure Jean; junk it.

6 John and Jonas enjoy jogging on the journeys to their jobs.
7 Mix a jug of juice with that jelly and pour it in jam jars.
8 An injured juvenile justified his case to a judge and jury.
9 Jason's jealousy just puts the dejected jumper in jeopardy.
10 Jean took a jar of jelly and a jug of juice on the journey.

That wizard of zoology amazes zillions of zoo visitors 12
daily. The dazzling display of puzzling zebras daze people 24
of all sizes. Lazy lizards zigzag into a dizzy speed on an 36
oozing pond. Monkeys puzzle many folks by the crazy antics 48
on the hazardous horizontal bars. The graceful gazelles in 60
brown graze in the park plazas. After a day at the zoo, it 72
is fun to stop at a bazaar and have a zesty pizza. 82

□□□□1□□□□2□□□□3□□□□4□□□□5□□□□6□□□□7□□□□8□□□□9□□□10□□□11□□□12

1 A dozen zesty spices are drizzling and oozing from a pizza.
2 Liza seized the magazine and zipped to the zillion zinnias.
3 The dazed czar gazed at the zillions of lizards and zebras.
4 The zodiac puzzle makes the dazzled wizard dizzy and woozy.
5 Lazy Fritz is woozy and dizzy from that crazy, zany puzzle.

□□□□1□□□□2□□□□3□□□□4□□□□5□□□□6□□□□7□□□□8□□□□9□□□10□□□11□□□12

6 A fuzzy buzzard zoomed crazily on that horizon with a zest.
7 Did Buzzy and Hazel realize the prized magazine was seized?
8 A chimpanzee gazed at a bulldozer in amazement and sneezed.
9 Zeb is a lazy zoologist; he snoozes like a zombi in a haze.
10 A dozen frenzied citizens seized the wheezy zither in zest.

□□□□1□□□□2□□□□3□□□□4□□□□5□□□□6□□□□7□□□□8□□□□9□□□10□□□11□□□12

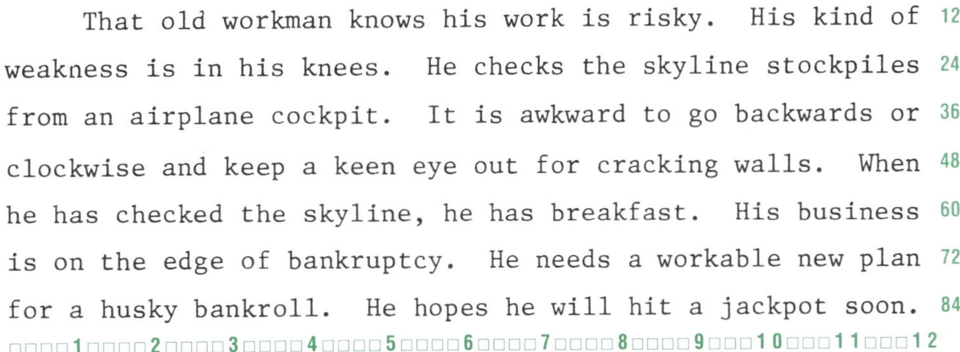

That old workman knows his work is risky. His kind of 12
weakness is in his knees. He checks the skyline stockpiles 24
from an airplane cockpit. It is awkward to go backwards or 36
clockwise and keep a keen eye out for cracking walls. When 48
he has checked the skyline, he has breakfast. His business 60
is on the edge of bankruptcy. He needs a workable new plan 72
for a husky bankroll. He hopes he will hit a jackpot soon. 84

1 Kevin marked the package of workbooks for the keen speaker.
2 The bookkeeper kept a king-sized textbook in his back room.
3 Karl keeps the workable kayak near a kettle by the kennels.
4 Do not use a whiskbroom on the workbooks or the blackboard.
5 That fickle king is skilled as he tackles the old bulkhead.

6 That keen kennel keeper was a keynote speaker last weekend.
7 Hector needs a checkup; his skull was kicked as he skidded.
8 The kindly old skipper took that skinny kid to the kitchen.
9 The markup of the bookmobile's stockpile will be a jackpot.
10 Get a hacksaw from the stockroom and fix the weak backstop.

Long ago, pilgrims loved to indulge in blunt folklore. 12
Tales, sometimes false, were told with glee daily. One old 24
tale included a blazing clash of sailors in balky sailboats 36
on a bottomless lake. The last sailor alive was a lad that 48
was blind. As he lay clinging to a slim balsa log in filth 60
and slimy silt, the leader's falcon led help to him. Balmy 72
days followed as the lad's leg healed slowly and the salves 84
applied to his eyes let the light in. 91

1 Examine the exhaust on the taxi and fix that vexation soon.
2 An executive relaxed as the boxer executed mixed exercises.
3 That exhibitor exhorted the exhausted exercisers to exhale.
4 The sixteen extra oxygen mixtures exploded next to an exit.
5 The extra text on the extractions of textiles is extensive.
□□□□ 1 □□□□ 2 □□□□ 3 □□□□ 4 □□□□ 5 □□□□ 6 □□□□ 7 □□□□ 8 □□□□ 9 □□□ 10 □□□ 11 □□□ 12

6 The excellent boxer put on an exciting exhibition at least.
7 Exquisite taxi rides are a luxury and expensive to experts.
8 The exciting excursion excluded the exasperated executives.
9 Dexter was exhausted after the exhilerating exotic exhibit.
10 The exterior of that exit was exposed to extended freezing.
□□□□ 1 □□□□ 2 □□□□ 3 □□□□ 4 □□□□ 5 □□□□ 6 □□□□ 7 □□□□ 8 □□□□ 9 □□□ 10 □□□ 11 □□□ 12

EMPHASIS ON 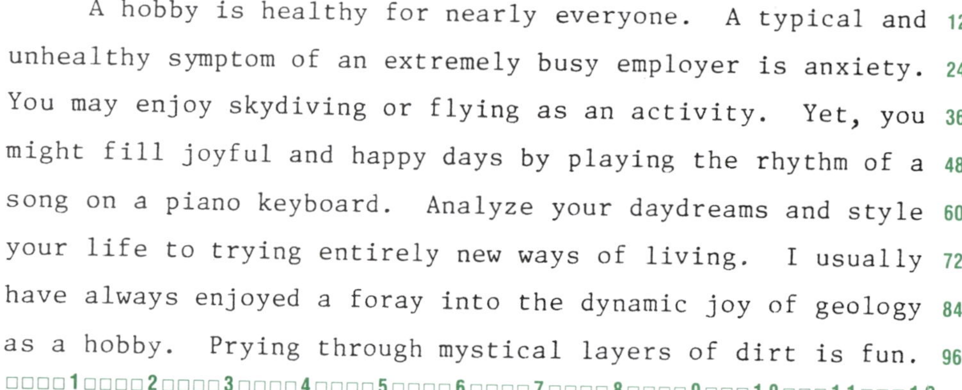

A hobby is healthy for nearly everyone. A typical and 12
unhealthy symptom of an extremely busy employer is anxiety. 24
You may enjoy skydiving or flying as an activity. Yet, you 36
might fill joyful and happy days by playing the rhythm of a 48
song on a piano keyboard. Analyze your daydreams and style 60
your life to trying entirely new ways of living. I usually 72
have always enjoyed a foray into the dynamic joy of geology 84
as a hobby. Prying through mystical layers of dirt is fun. 96
□□□□ 1 □□□□ 2 □□□□ 3 □□□□ 4 □□□□ 5 □□□□ 6 □□□□ 7 □□□□ 8 □□□□ 9 □□□ 10 □□□ 11 □□□ 12

1 The yardarm on the royal yacht is gaudy; boycott the entry.
2 The cyclist will buy a motorcycle or bicycle on the voyage.
3 Yesterday Candy daydreamed about skydiving and hydroplanes.
4 Yes, buy the layers of yellow nylon for the sunny skylight.
5 The style of yellow nylon and vinyl is certainly very ugly.
□□□□ 1 □□□□ 2 □□□□ 3 □□□□ 4 □□□□ 5 □□□□ 6 □□□□ 7 □□□□ 8 □□□□ 9 □□□ 10 □□□ 11 □□□ 12

6 A yearbook is a joyful memory of happy years and busy days.
7 Lily is annoyed at the yipping and crying of the shy puppy.
8 A youngster yodeled in the yonder canyon beyond the valley.
9 That lynx is in that broken shanty beyond the rocky canyon.
10 An eyewitness saw the uncanny mystic obey the crystal ball.
□□□□ 1 □□□□ 2 □□□□ 3 □□□□ 4 □□□□ 5 □□□□ 6 □□□□ 7 □□□□ 8 □□□□ 9 □□□ 10 □□□ 11 □□□ 12

Margin settings
12-pitch: 15 and 85
10-pitch: 7 and 77

Double-space

Five-space paragraph
indent

The material in this section may be used for 15-, 30-, or 60-second timings. You may use it for either speed or accuracy development.

Determine the amount of time you will be keying (15, 30, or 60 seconds). Then identify the appropriate column at the right-hand side of the page. Go down that column of figures and select the words-a-minute rate you think you can attain. Key the material to the left of that rate. If you complete the selection before time is up, it means that you averaged *at least* that many words a minute. Go to the next selection (which is longer) and attempt to complete it before time is up. Keep progressing through the drill material until you cannot complete a selection in the given time.

If you are using the material for *speed* development, don't worry about errors—make your fingers fly. If you are using the material for *accuracy* development, concentrate on accuracy; attempt to finish the selection, but do not proceed down to the next one until you can finish the selection within the time allotment *with no more than one error.*

15–30–60 Seconds

	15 sec.	30 sec.	60 sec.
1 Now is the time to study.	20	10	
2 Move the computer to the room.	24	12	
3 You should eat a healthy breakfast.	28	14	
4 The grass needs to be mowed and watered.	32	16	
5 Place those big tickets in the long envelope.	36	18	
6 The legal people do not want to disagree with him.	40	20	
7 The trouble with those animals is that they need water.	44	22	
8 Staple all sheets of paper together in the left-hand corner.	48	24	
9 Send the second element over to him. I believe he needs it soon.	52	26	
10 Do not wait to phone me. My major responsibility now is to help them.	56	28	
11 This magazine is fairly good. It would be better if it had a harder cover.	60	30	15
12 Please invite both of them. I need to have them determine if they are eligible.	64	32	16
13 That tape dispenser is missing. I believe I know who the low person is that took it.	68	34	17
14 Oil paintings, in many cases, have proven very good investments. We should buy more, now.	72	36	18

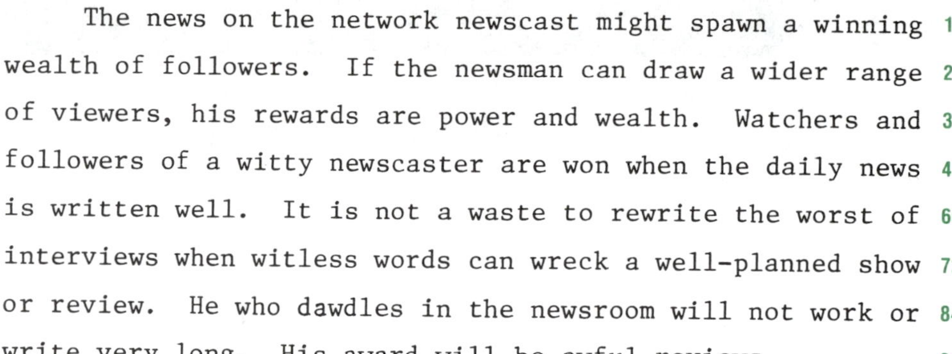

The news on the network newscast might spawn a winning   12
wealth of followers. If the newsman can draw a wider range   24
of viewers, his rewards are power and wealth. Watchers and   36
followers of a witty newscaster are won when the daily news   48
is written well. It is not a waste to rewrite the worst of   60
interviews when witless words can wreck a well-planned show   72
or review. He who dawdles in the newsroom will not work or   84
write very long. His award will be awful reviews.   94

□□□□1□□□□2□□□□3□□□□4□□□□5□□□□6□□□□7□□□□8□□□□9□□□10□□□11□□□12

1 That rowdy crowd swarmed on the west freeway and went wild.
2 Wes was awarded with twelve weeks of rest as a wise reward.
3 Wendy and Will were weary of the unwelcome weekend showers.
4 Who wired the winch to that warship and prowled in the bow?
5 The scowling prowler scowled as the dog howled and growled.

□□□□1□□□□2□□□□3□□□□4□□□□5□□□□6□□□□7□□□□8□□□□9□□□10□□□11□□□12

6 The swift cowhand will win the lawful crown on the weekend.
7 The clown frowned and yawned as he crawled around the lawn.
8 The wry newsman writes wretched words on the wrecked wagon.
9 The newscast shows the views of the snowslide and the cows.
10 Warren browsed with wonder in the sawmill for wood or wire.

□□□□1□□□□2□□□□3□□□□4□□□□5□□□□6□□□□7□□□□8□□□□9□□□10□□□11□□□12

An example of a tedious exercise is the flexing of lax   12
muscles daily. Excess anxieties are exhausting to all that   24
are under extreme pressure. A program of extensive complex   36
exercises are a vexation. Most experts agree that exertion   48
to exhaustion is wrong. A flexible, yet exuberant exercise   60
involves exhaling noxious air and inhaling oxygen. Explore   72
the exotic experience of a brisk daily walk. That expended   84
energy will excite you and extend your life.   93

□□□□1□□□□2□□□□3□□□□4□□□□5□□□□6□□□□7□□□□8□□□□9□□□10□□□11□□□12

15 sec.	30 sec.	60 sec.

15 The typewriter is broken. Have Dick call the repairman as soon as he
returns from the meeting.   76   38   19

16 There are many fine job openings in the business world. A person seeking
one must have good talent.   80   40   20

17 The doctor is quite busy. If you can, be sure to arrange for our
appointment in the very near future.   84   42   21

18 Going to a meeting can be an enjoyable experience. We might go by car
or by plane. Try to go to the meeting.   88   44   22

19 Vacation time can be exciting. You can either travel or stay at home.
Whichever is done, plan to have loads of fun.   92   46   23

20 The electrical wiring in the house is worn out. We must get an
electrician to give us an estimate to repair it at once.   96   48   24

21 Target shooting is great fun. It is exciting to become active in a sport
that one can enjoy. Young and old can participate.   100   50   25

30–60 Seconds

30 sec.	60 sec.

1 In many towns it is difficult to locate a place to rent. You can
usually find something, but it may not be exactly what you want.   52   26

2 The airport is closed because of poor visibility. We had to land at
another city quite a distance away. I hope we get there soon.   54   27

3 The owner is doing a study on revising the furniture in our office.
I certainly hope that we will be able to purchase some new desks soon.   56   28

4 The city youths charted their national tour on the map. They plan very
carefully and in great detail. Each stop is timed exactly for ten hours.   58   29

5 Staplers are a necessity in an office. They come in all kinds of sizes,
shapes, and forms, designed for all jobs. They also are in different colors. 60   30

6 The microcomputers in the lab at the high school are about worn out. I
sincerely hope that there will be enough money to trade them for new ones.   62   31

7 After turning right at the third corner, you will see the site. Spend
enough time analyzing the location so that you will be able to give us a
logical report.   64   32

1 Put lettuce, cucumbers, and zucchini squash on the saucers.
2 Chuck is lucky; that subtle judge is too grouchy in public.
3 Good judgment should be included in any student's attitude.
4 The quiet guy is suffering as that ugly cough gets rougher.
5 I guess that tough guide has taught thousands about values.

6 Biscuits and fruit juices are suitable for lunch or brunch.
7 Sonny's aunt and uncle are both unusually young and unique.
8 A furry and fuzzy squirrel nuzzled the muzzle of the puppy.
9 One executive duty at the institution is computing figures.
10 The author urged the absurd ushers to utilize the ukuleles.

EMPHASIS ON V

A visit to a village in a quiet valley gives vitality, 12
vim, and vigor to the tired individual. Nothing rivals the 24
valuable voyage to revive the spirits. Heavy problems seem 36
to vanish and vexing tribulations evaporate. Vivid visions 48
of a diverse way of living evoke valuable impressive vistas 60
of rest. Save those fevered nerves and prevent grievous or 72
adverse tribulations. Endeavor to take advantage of events 84
which elevate the spirits; you deserve the very best. 95

1 The evil virus invaded the valley of very lively villagers.
2 Elvis invited the evil visitor to see our village vineyard.
3 Is it valid if Van vetoes the valuable division of travels?
4 The silver velvet covering on that davenport is attractive.
5 A savory flavor is evoked in veal by serving anchovies too.

6 The heavy bovine is very vulnerable to the vicious vulture.
7 Violet vows to avoid the vocalist, as his volume is vulgar.
8 A vagabond vacation is available for the clever adventurer.
9 Victor moved Vera's valuable vases to an attractive alcove.
10 Valerie, move the five covered violins to the vacant villa.

8 A shy person tends to stay in the background of social activities. This type doesn't make new friends easily. He or she should try very hard to relax in any crowd. 66 33

9 He thought he would like a beef hamburger for lunch. However, the roast beef looked better. Unable to decide between the two, he finally took the fried chicken special. 68 34

10 That lovely song is a smash hit. Although the lyrics are sad, the haunting melody is easy to remember. Maybe the composer will win an award or a grand prize for that talent. 70 35

11 The old photograph is faded and worn. Can it be restored? It would take an artist many days to fix it. The cost might be expensive. Perhaps that museum curator will restore it. 72 36

12 The winter skating party was a huge success. The roaring bonfire helped ward off the cold. The children enjoyed the hot chocolate and the roasted weiners. A good time was had by all. 74 37

13 The solution to that puzzle is not an easy one. The trick is to analyze all of the numbers first. Then, read the problem carefully before you do the math. Solve it quickly and do another. 76 38

14 Take a dose of that medicine every five hours. Also, rest as much as possible. It is a good idea to drink a lot of liquids and eat plenty of fruit. Your cold symptoms should disappear quickly. 78 39

15 John is fixing up that old cabin. He expects the project to take at least six months. If he shingles the roof and paints the exterior, the results will be amazing. That hillside site is delightful. 80 40

16 Poor Paul was stranded in the airport lounge all night. The plane he intended to take was grounded because of heavy fog. He was not only cold, but also very hungry and weary. He hoped to be home soon. 82 41

17 Hopefully, the child will not have to stay there much longer. A large hospital can be frightening to such a tiny baby. Although the staff of nurses and doctors are quite friendly, she really wants to go home. 84 42

Tenseness while typing causes costly mistakes. Take a 12
gentle tip or two and practice them as you type. Watch out 24
for fatigue--a tired typist tends to clutch at the keys and 36
doesn't tap them with a gentle touch. Twirling or twisting 48
in your seat is a fatal trick at the typewriter. Talking a 60
lot as you type is first on the list of bad techniques. Do 72
not try too hard, as this often turns those keys into some- 84
thing terrible. Don't let the typing mistakes continue. 95

1 Catch that tall, thin teen and tell her to watch the store.
2 The wretched witch tended to foretell fortunes in tea cups.
3 The stern reporter noticed the courteous tennis team often.
4 Tim writes creative articles and practices dramatic acting.
5 The gentle cattle are too thin; the earth's thaw is timely.

6 The strutting entry of the actor stumped the top two stars.
7 Treva tried to trade the trinkets for a treasured portrait.
8 The toiling tutor might try trimming the time of a student.
9 The sturdy cactus in the pasture is a study of true nature.
10 Seventy typical typists typed that tycoon's witty thoughts.

The impulse to judge individuals quickly causes faulty 12
results. It is unwise and unfair to jump to conclusions in 24
a hurry. Actually, a useful guide to a sound understanding 36
of humans is to quietly assess the situation. A subtle and 48
thorough query can subdue doubts and evaluate behavior. An 60
ugly and cruel deduction about another's values could cause 72
undue suffering. You are urged to utilize more time if you 84
are puzzled and used to useless, quick guesses. 93

18   A good health insurance should be a part of our life plans. One is never prepared for a major illness. But if one should occur, good insurance will ease tensions. Money worries are not a problem when getting well.   86 43

19   That fine old estate is elegant. Huge trees surround the entire house. The lush green grass is highlighted by masses of brilliant flowers. Inside, there is a huge collection of antiques. Indeed, it is a unique house.   88 44

20   Because of a severe ice storm, most city residents were without electric power. Many homes had little or no heat. Some people found they were not able to cook meals. The power was restored in most homes by the third night.   90 45

21   That expert pianist has performed in public for fifty years. Critics have said that she plays as well as ever. Few others have duplicated or attempted the feat. The concert next week, however, will be her last. Be sure you go.   92 46

22   Eat three balanced meals each day. Include fresh vegetables, fruit, milk, and meat. Be sure to begin the day by eating a hearty breakfast. Those who skip breakfast usually run out of energy. Be sensible in eating habits every meal.   94 47

23   More and more people are beginning to learn about the delights of taking a trip and camping out. The different types and kinds of camping equipment are almost endless. The cost can be quite low or quite high. Select your camp gear soon.   96 48

24   An automobile can be costly to own. Just to run it requires a tank of gasoline. Other costs such as tires, oil, valves, and minor repairs add to the total bill. Insurance is an added expense. Perhaps it would be wise to take the bus or taxi.   98 49

25   The design in that fabric is unique. Geometric shapes can be seen as the focal point. Tiny circles add to the stunning work of art. Blues and browns blend in harmony. The hues and tints are a marvel. It is truly a fine example of a great artist.   100 50

1 That raven on the curb near the urban arcade is not fierce.
2 Red heard the warden's words that pardoned the tardy guard.
3 The large barge surged in the surf to reach the coral reef.
4 The writer's historical script merits a brilliant critique.
5 A lark ate a kernel of corn in the warmth of the dark barn.

6 Shirley really should burn that pair of torn burlap drapes.
7 The arsonist pursues a dangerous course and a harsh career.
8 A portion of those curious artifacts at the fort was dirty.
9 An abrupt rupture of an eardrum is crucial and frustrating.
10 Worry and hurry will make a person angry, weary, and sorry.

EMPHASIS ON S

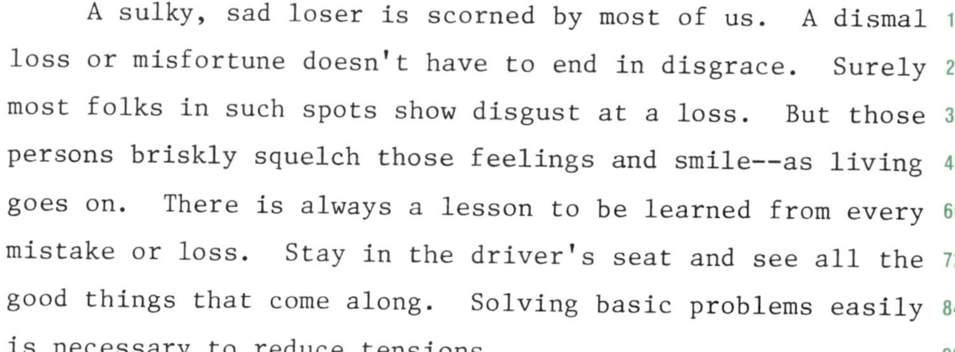

        A sulky, sad loser is scorned by most of us. A dismal 12
loss or misfortune doesn't have to end in disgrace. Surely 24
most folks in such spots show disgust at a loss. But those 36
persons briskly squelch those feelings and smile--as living 48
goes on. There is always a lesson to be learned from every 60
mistake or loss. Stay in the driver's seat and see all the 72
good things that come along. Solving basic problems easily 84
is necessary to reduce tensions.   90

1 Scratch that scene in the script and schedule the newscast.
2 Browse in that immense museum and observe the bird section.
3 The flashy salesroom she visited was a disgraceful mistake.
4 The publisher is shrewdly dishonest and shoddy in his work.
5 Silas considers that offensive noise as a passing nuisance.

6 Ask the skilled skipper to briskly sketch the masked spies.
7 The dismal aspects of some prisons are a dismay to newsmen.
8 A desperate spy responded to the whispering suspect's gasp.
9 The squab stew tasted greasy, as usual; serve salted squid.
10 The swift swallows swooped over the swans in the swampland.

1   A good secretary must be skilled in answering the telephone. A calm and friendly voice puts most callers at ease. Learning to handle calls quickly and efficiently will add to the firm's image. Practice each day on personal calls at home. You can learn.   51

2   On a bright day when you are bored make a visit to the local library. You will find exciting books on varied subjects. Hours of leisure time can be spent among those interesting shelves. You might enjoy browsing among the magazines. Get in a reading habit.   52

3   Many students have great difficulty when taking a test. They simply can't relax. Sometimes a student's mind just goes blank. Studying for a test helps. A good night's sleep is an aid. Just before taking the exam, walk briskly in the outdoors--for a good start.   53

4   Good manners are a must every moment of the day. A polite person thinks of others first. A thank you can brighten the gloomiest day. Please should be used automatically. Excuse me is a phrase that should always be on the tip of your tongue. Concentrate on manners.   54

5   What you want and get out of life depends largely on planning. If you have goals that you want to achieve, you are on the right track. Too many people wander through daily living. Many have no idea of what they really desire or how to achieve. Plan ahead and succeed now.   55

6   Gestures and facial expressions can tell others a lot about you. This silent language has been ignored in the past. People all over are paying more attention to this new and fun subject. Watch the faces of others with whom you converse. You can start to see all those signals.   56

7   A good worker always finishes what he or she starts. Leaving many small duties undone presents a problem. Soon, they will grow and become a huge mountain. If you do a job thoroughly, you will feel a real satisfaction. Get into this habit right now. You might have a surprise soon.   57

8   Many folks enjoy a camping trip in the wilds. Today, gear and equipment used for camping is varied and quite useful. From sleeping in a tent to relaxing in an elegant motor home, the range of choices is wide. What type of person you are will dictate the kind of equipment you will want.   58

EMPHASIS ON 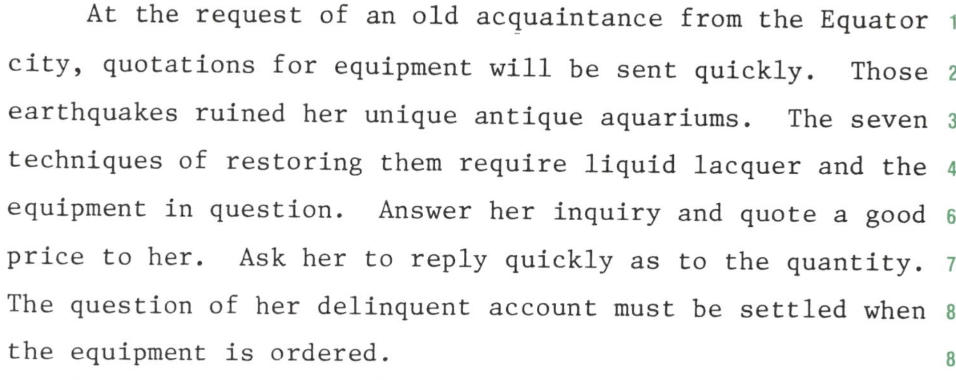

At the request of an old acquaintance from the Equator 12
city, quotations for equipment will be sent quickly. Those 24
earthquakes ruined her unique antique aquariums. The seven 36
techniques of restoring them require liquid lacquer and the 48
equipment in question. Answer her inquiry and quote a good 60
price to her. Ask her to reply quickly as to the quantity. 72
The question of her delinquent account must be settled when 84
the equipment is ordered. 89

□□□□1□□□□2□□□□3□□□□4□□□□5□□□□6□□□□7□□□□8□□□□9□□□10□□□11□□□12

1 The queen questioned the unique request for that equipment.
2 Quentin acquired the liquid lacquer for the quaint antique.
3 The squad questioned and quizzed the quiet delinquent lads.
4 The squadron ate squab and squash after the quick conquest.
5 The quick quakes brought queasy quiverings to the squadron.

□□□□1□□□□2□□□□3□□□□4□□□□5□□□□6□□□□7□□□□8□□□□9□□□10□□□11□□□12

6 A quintet questioned the quality of that squad's equipment.
7 The queen requested a quantity of quinine after that quake.
8 The inquisitive delinquent inquired about the antique vase.
9 That requirement for acquittal is a questionable technique.
10 That quarterly quota of sequoias has been quickly acquired.

□□□□1□□□□2□□□□3□□□□4□□□□5□□□□6□□□□7□□□□8□□□□9□□□10□□□11□□□12

EMPHASIS ON 

A rapid rise in industrial prices is normally absorbed 12
by the consumers. Large firms that need raw materials work 24
hard to realize a profit. It is a marvel that the poor and 36
weary customer can afford to purchase services or products. 48
The grim race to raise prices must be curbed early. Scores 60
of workers who earn small salaries find no mirth in fierce, 72
sharp rises in the market. The rows and rows of bright and 84
sparkling products are a farce to all concerned consumers. 96

□□□□1□□□□2□□□□3□□□□4□□□□5□□□□6□□□□7□□□□8□□□□9□□□10□□□11□□□12

9   Finding a cure for a common cold has eluded scientists for decades. The symptoms can be relieved in a variety of ways, but there is simply no cure available. One would think that a world that sends men to the moon could surely find a quick cold remedy. The only answer is to rest as you wait.   59

10   A career in nursing can be a rewarding experience. The joy of helping the sick get well is a special feeling. The work is hard and the days get long, but the effort is worth the end result. An efficient and kind nurse will go a long way. Both men and women alike are discovering this great field.   60

11   Good dental habits are a must for every person. A thorough brushing at least once a day is vital. If brushing is neglected, plaque and tartar will build on the teeth. This leads to serious dental disease. Your family dentist can show you how to brush properly. Healthy gums and teeth are a necessity.   61

12   Going to the circus is always exciting. The artists who perform provide thrills and chills in their acts. The trained animal acts are fun to watch. Another funny part of the circus is the many clowns who do all sorts of hilarious antics. Along with the acts in the ring, some like to eat good cotton candy.   62

13   Bird watching has become an exciting hobby to a lot of people. To be an avid watcher, you must first study many species. You have to learn how to know the various birds. Early morning is a good quiet time to observe the birds in their natural surroundings. Your own fine interest in bird watching can be joyful.   63

14   In the olden days, there were no streetlights like we enjoy today. The streets were lighted each evening by a person. He lit each individual lamp one by one. As he walked around, he would call out the hour and tell the citizens that all was well. Although the system was not too efficient, many said it was romantic.   64

1 Token office offenses often evoke spoken and pointed words.
2 Oil that boiler at all points to avoid noises and moisture.
3 Take the textbooks and workbooks from that broken bookcase.
4 Omit the olives and onions from the omelet and let it cool.
5 An oldtimer scolds the troops only once, then moves onward.

░░░░1░░░░2░░░░3░░░░4░░░░5░░░░6░░░░7░░░░8░░░░9░░░10░░░11░░░12

6 A snoopy shopper dropped the workshop telescope on purpose.
7 Ora ordered an ornate organ for her house; it's not costly.
8 The boss chose the boring quotes from a book of poor prose.
9 That unknown prowler somehow came in the downstairs window.
10 A dozen prowling crows hovered over that fox's cozy burrow.

░░░░1░░░░2░░░░3░░░░4░░░░5░░░░6░░░░7░░░░8░░░░9░░░10░░░11░░░12

EMPHASIS ON 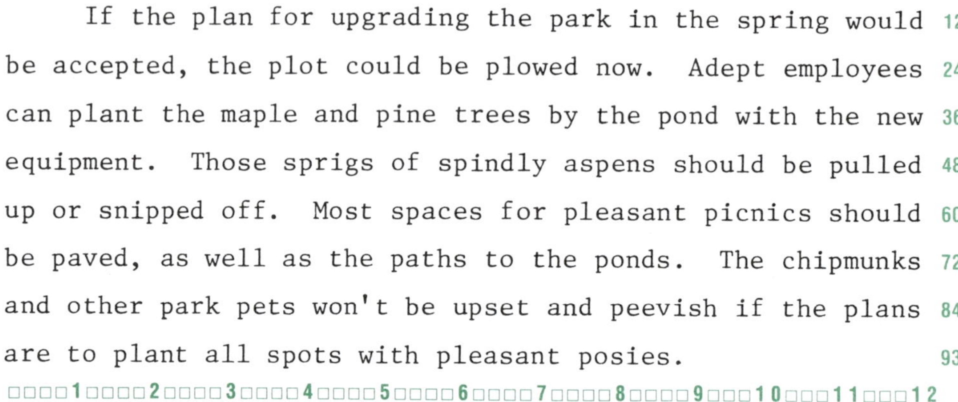

    If the plan for upgrading the park in the spring would 12
be accepted, the plot could be plowed now. Adept employees 24
can plant the maple and pine trees by the pond with the new 36
equipment. Those sprigs of spindly aspens should be pulled 48
up or snipped off. Most spaces for pleasant picnics should 60
be paved, as well as the paths to the ponds. The chipmunks 72
and other park pets won't be upset and peevish if the plans 84
are to plant all spots with pleasant posies.   93

░░░░1░░░░2░░░░3░░░░4░░░░5░░░░6░░░░7░░░░8░░░░9░░░10░░░11░░░12

1 Peg's helpful nephew peered into the topcoat for a red pen.
2 Phyllis can spare a cupful of soap and a pail if Pa phones.
3 His nephew won a trophy for the photograph of the elephant.
4 Peter spoke with poise as the spring prom plans progressed.
5 Place the splendid duplicate on the plain plywood platform.

░░░░1░░░░2░░░░3░░░░4░░░░5░░░░6░░░░7░░░░8░░░░9░░░10░░░11░░░12

6 A report on the possible proposals disappointed the police.
7 Peg peeled the ripe pears as Pete inspected the grapefruit.
8 The campus deputy publicized the purpose of the punishment.
9 Push the pulsing pump upward and stop the ship's equipment.
10 Pepin is happy that the perky puppy is not sloppy or jumpy.

░░░░1░░░░2░░░░3░░░░4░░░░5░░░░6░░░░7░░░░8░░░░9░░░10░░░11░░░12

15   Choosing a painting for your home can be quite frustrating. First, you
must have some knowledge about the world of art. Study various artists and
their subjects. Choose a quality painting that appeals to you, not one that
someone else says is beautiful. Try to pick one that has varied colors
which are enjoyable and airy.   65

16   Owning a dog is indeed a very huge challenge. A responsible owner sees
to it that the animal is fed each day and has an ample water supply. The
dog must be trained to obey simple commands. Training a dog is not too
difficult; you need patience. The joy comes after knowing you really can
have a loving friend in the dog world.   66

17   It has been said that music is a universal language. It is understood
by all listeners. It does not matter if it is classical or light. Studies
have been done in the area of music therapy. It is known that music can
help in emotionally disturbed persons. It seems that the soothing tunes can
ease tense nerves in the worst cases.   67

18   The world of mathematics is fun, once you get to know it. Numbers and
figures can be juggled around to play math games. Puzzles and riddles are
very exciting to do. But, to be a competent math expert, you first must
study very hard to learn basic math concepts. Perhaps you might decide to
explore geometry or algebra as a next step.   68

19   If you face a hard difficult problem, don't waste time thinking of
reasons for not dealing with it. Although it may seem easier to ignore a
problem, in the long run you must eventually face facts. Instead, spend
that valuable time thinking of methods of solving the problem. Then choose
the best one and commit yourself to the final solution.   69

20   A good safe driver should always be aware of all traffic hazards.
Before even starting the auto, you should check the tires and be certain
the visibility is topnotch. A good driver has to know every driving rule
of the road and follow them to the letter. When driving, you have to be
constantly looking for traffic hazards. Are you a good driver?   70

At sunset, it is nice to enjoy dining out on a bank of   12
a pond. Unless uninvited insects and swarms of ants invade   24
the picnic, you will certainly unwind. As those soft night   36
sounds enfold you, frenzied inward nerves and the decisions   48
that haunt you drain from your mind. You may enjoy napping   60
on a nearby bench. Next, swing into action after your rest   72
and inhale much air into your lungs. Unpack the nice lunch   84
and munch away. Don't deny yourself this experience.   95

□□□□1□□□□2□□□□3□□□□4□□□□5□□□□6□□□□7□□□□8□□□□9□□□10□□□11□□□12

1 Nancy and Andy concur; nail the fence to the round benches.
2 Amanda and Randy defended the landfill amendment on Monday.
3 The conference on infectious invasions was confusing to me.
4 The singers sang songs and mingled among the hungry diners.
5 Cranky Nina's nice pink banjo is nicked; she plans revenge.

□□□□1□□□□2□□□□3□□□□4□□□□5□□□□6□□□□7□□□□8□□□□9□□□10□□□11□□□12

6 He enlarged the unlisted analysis of the enlisted men only.
7 The agent insisted that none of the nouns need be censored.
8 A nurse insisted that a ransom note was inserted in a menu.
9 The frenzied inventor unwisely unpacked the bronzed handle.
10 The convicts invaded and conquered a convoy and ran onward.

□□□□1□□□□2□□□□3□□□□4□□□□5□□□□6□□□□7□□□□8□□□□9□□□10□□□11□□□12

An oldtime cowboy often chose a lonely life out on the   12
open range. Hoards of prowling foxes snooped among the old   24
cows and their young ones. Owls often hooted as an obscure   36
and occasional sound annoyed them. The food was often cold   48
and soggy. Cooking his food and boiling his coffee over an   60
orange-hot fire offered some enjoyment, however. Through a   72
long night his mournful songs poured out. He was a proven,   84
loyal worker who overcame obstacles or coped with problems.   96

□□□□1□□□□2□□□□3□□□□4□□□□5□□□□6□□□□7□□□□8□□□□9□□□10□□□11□□□12

21   Learning to write a letter of complaint takes practice. It is never
a good idea to write letters while you are very angry. You should take
some time to cool off. Then, carefully and tactfully explain to the firm
exactly what your complaint is about. Be firm and state specific facts
and problems. Ask for a quick solution and above all, thank the firm.   71

22   Coin collecting is one of the most exciting hobbies in the world.
The study of all the various types and origins of coins can be quite
complicated. It does require time and the desire to learn. Much can be
learned by reading monthly and weekly papers and magazines. It is not too
expensive to buy books and papers about coins. Then, we really enjoy them.   72

23   Almost all of us are guilty of not being a good listener. We very much
like to talk and ramble on, sometimes to the point of becoming a very boring
person. Being a good listener will make others like you and have respect
for you. In addition, you can learn a lot if you listen instead of talk.
Try to develop the habit of listening. You must try to listen more.   73

24   The octopus is one sea animal that has not been understood by mankind.
All of us have heard stories about the creature, with its long slimy arms,
attacking sailors. An octopus is not a terrible monster. Studies have
shown that an octopus is really quite shy. In addition, it has been found
that this animal has quite a brain. This should be an area for further study.   74

25   For anyone wishing to relax, one excellent trick is to let the body go
limp all over. This can be easily done while sitting in a chair or better
yet, by indulging in a quick catnap on the sofa. Try to erase all worries
from your mind as you relax. Leisurely let the calming and soothing
limpness take over. You will find that you are renewed in body and will be
refreshed.   75

1 Lay the toolbox by the mailbox and latch the balcony doors.
2 Evelyn welcomed the clerical classes in the balcony alcove.
3 Leaves engulfed that golfer's cleats; his lead is building.
4 Aldo pleaded with the child to leave the calf in the field.
5 Lil is willing to duplicate the list of disciplined drills.
□□□□1□□□□2□□□□3□□□□4□□□□5□□□□6□□□□7□□□□8□□□□9□□□10□□□11□□□12

6 That bold culprit and a helper stole the wallpaper samples.
7 The pulsating propeller bolstered the cavalry on the hills.
8 Melvin salvaged the twelve shelves and the valuable velvet.
9 I will apply the supply of oil daily to the costly plywood.
10 Did he imply that the filthy blue silt in the gully is new?
□□□□1□□□□2□□□□3□□□□4□□□□5□□□□6□□□□7□□□□8□□□□9□□□10□□□11□□□12

EMPHASIS ON 

The merger of an academy and the campus may take place 12
in the autumn. It might bring mixed emotions from some men 24
and women. The stormy economic issue might make an anatomy 36
class impossible at the academy. Some who must commute for 48
months are not amused; many think that the merger is clumsy 60
and dumb. There is not much warmth among the enemies. The 72
teamwork is not smooth. The amount of stormy mass meetings 84
must be diminished. An amendment must be made. 93
□□□□1□□□□2□□□□3□□□□4□□□□5□□□□6□□□□7□□□□8□□□□9□□□10□□□11□□□12

1 The bamboo limbs were climbing and rambling over the tombs.
2 He made amends for smashing the melons and making the mess.
3 The meal of omelets and melons was welcomed by the farmers.
4 Please move the model and the motor to the armory tomorrow.
5 Mike might mope more if the campus merger is in the autumn.
□□□□1□□□□2□□□□3□□□□4□□□□5□□□□6□□□□7□□□□8□□□□9□□□10□□□11□□□12

6 The champion jumper complained as he stomped from the camp.
7 Cam camped among the remnants of an old chimney for months.
8 The warmth and teamwork of the comrades might make enemies.
9 The smug musician was immune to the muttering and mumbling.
10 That whimsical hamster is amusing as it munches many meals.
□□□□1□□□□2□□□□3□□□□4□□□□5□□□□6□□□□7□□□□8□□□□9□□□10□□□11□□□12

The guidelines provided in this section will help you master the use of proper procedures and formatting rules when preparing business documents. If you need information on topics not included in this section, please refer to the Index.

METHODS OF CORRECTING ERRORS

A skill needed by anyone who prepares printed documents is the ability to select the best correction method for each situation and to correct keyboarding errors so that they are undetectable.

The various methods of correcting keyboarding errors are described in the following paragraphs.

Electronic Error Correction

To make corrections on electronic keyboards (with or without display screens), backspace and strike over the incorrect character. The correct character replaces the incorrect one in the electronic memory of the system. Extensive corrections such as inserting and/or deleting words, phrases, sentences, and paragraphs, moving sections of text, and reformatting documents are examples of the flexibility of electronic editing and revision.

Mastery Software Error Correction

To make corrections on microcomputers when using the Mastery Software, move the cursor to the point of the correction and key the characters to be inserted. Use the *delete* or *backspace* key to remove any incorrect characters.

Typewriter Error Correction

Self-Correcting Typewriters
The lift-off technique of error correction is available with self-correcting typewriters. Instead of covering a mistake with tape or fluid, the lift-off ribbon pulls the ink off the page.

Correction Tape
Correction tape is a continuous strip of white, pressure-sensitive adhesive paper that can be attached to a document and typed on. The corrected document can then be photocopied.

Correction Paper
When a strip of correction paper is placed between the paper and the typewriter ribbon, the force of a key striking the correction paper transfers a chalk-like substance from the correction paper to the paper. You actually rekey your original mistake in order to cover it with the chalk-like substance.

Correction Fluid
Correction fluid can be used with either fabric or carbon ribbons to correct mistakes, or it can be used to correct handwritten errors. Correction fluid may be used on paper in or out of the typewriter, does not damage the paper, and is permanent. The fluid is available in white or can be color-matched to most colored papers.

Eraser
Although erasing is time-consuming, it is an alternative correction method. To erase properly, use the right eraser and an erasing shield. The two basic types of erasers are abrasive erasers, used for originals and ink, and soft erasers, used for carbon copies and pencil.

PREPARATION OF COPIES

The technological advancements in copying machines and the increased use of these machines over the past two decades have been phenomenal. Many of the documents that were once made using the carbon copy process are now made with copying machines.

Many offices today use both copying machines and carbons. Sometimes a carbon copy is made for the file and copies for distribution are made on a copier. Forms may come preassembled with carbon paper or printed on special paper that automatically reproduces information on a second or third sheet.

Electronic Document Processing

One of the biggest advantages of using an electronic keyboard or a software package is being able to produce multiple copies of the original document without rekeying. Because the machines have the capability of storing documents, a document can be printed when needed.

Copying Machines

The primary reasons for the widespread use of copying machines are quality, ease, and convenience.

- The quality of the last copy is the same as that of the original.

- Errors need to be corrected only on the original, reducing correction time.

- The number of copies can be adjusted as needed; additional copies can be made at any time.

Carbon Pack

If you are keying on a typewriter and do not have a copier available, you may be required to use carbon paper to make copies. To make carbon copies, follow these steps:

1. Determine the number of copies to be made. Then take out enough sheets of paper for the copies. Align the pack so that all sheets are even.

2. Place the pack behind the *platen.*

3. Turn the *platen knob* until the pack is caught in the machine.

4. Insert a sheet of carbon paper between each piece of paper. As you insert the carbon paper, the shiny or carbon side should be facing you.

5. Turn the carbon pack to the first line to be keyed and proceed.

6. To correct an error, roll the carbon pack forward or backward, whichever allows you to correct the error without removing the pack from the machine. If you are using correction paper, insert it between the shiny side of the carbon paper and the copy; do this for all copies. Place a piece of correction paper over the error on the original and proceed with the correction process.

   If you are using an eraser, place a card or a piece of metal that can be used as a guard between the shiny side of the carbon paper and the copy. Start by erasing the error on the original and then the error on the carbon copies, beginning with the first copy and proceeding to the last. Be sure to remove the piece of metal or card being used as a shield. When finished, key the correction.

7. After the page has been completed, remove the carbon pack from the machine. With one hand, tightly hold the pack in the upper left or right corner; with the other hand, grasp the carbon paper that extends beyond the pack at the bottom and pull. Put the carbon paper away and distribute the copies.

Personal Business Letter

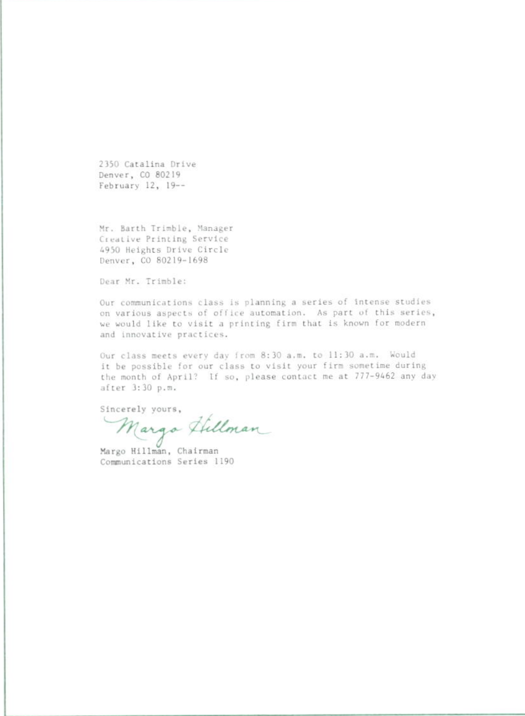

Block Style

Business Letter

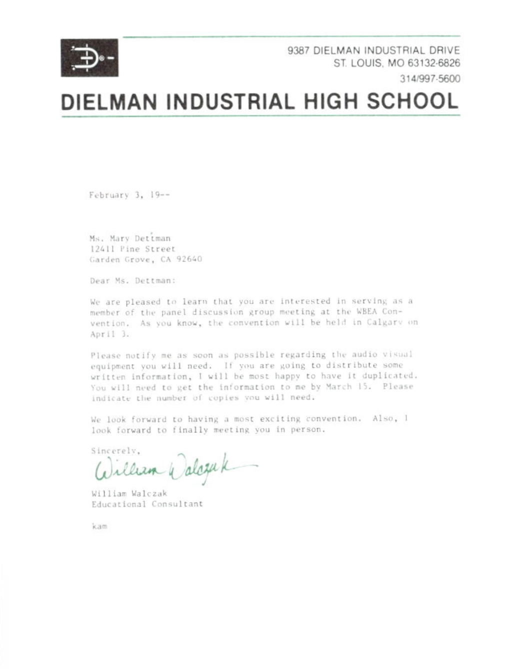

Block Style

Business Letter

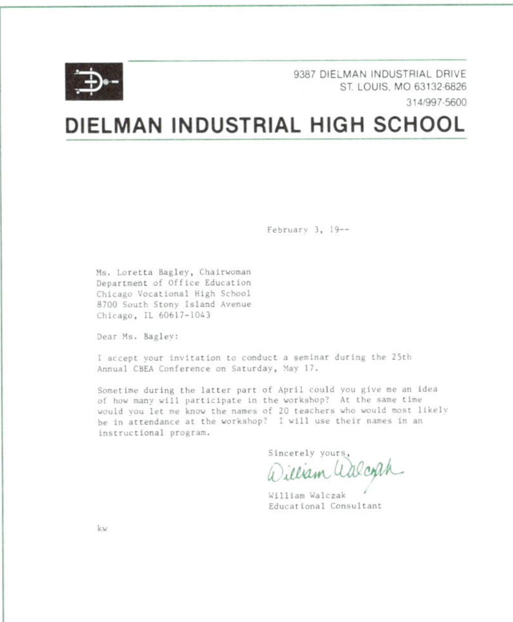

Modified Block Style

Business Letter

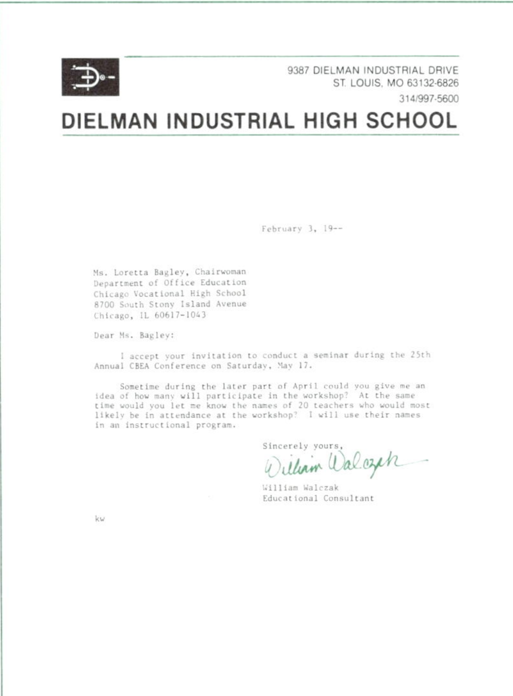

Modified Block Style (with paragraph indentions)

LETTER STYLES (continued)

Business Letter

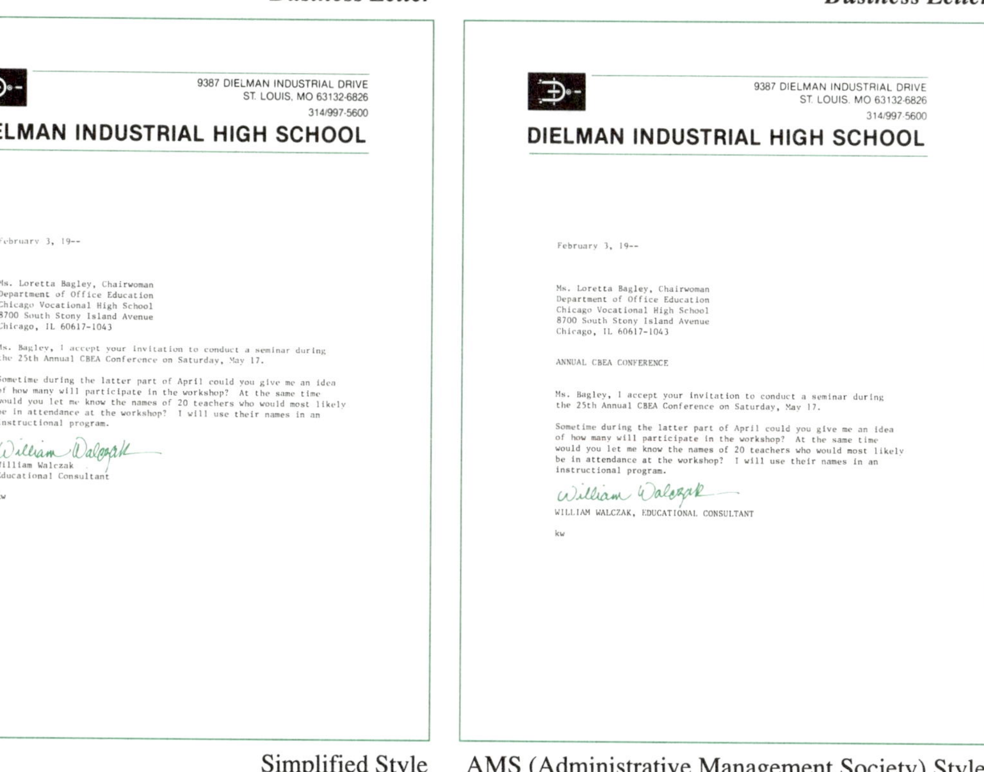

Business Letter

Simplified Style | AMS (Administrative Management Society) Style

PUNCTUATION STYLES

Mixed Punctuation	*Open Punctuation*
Salutations	Salutations
Dear Ms. Bagley:	Dear Ms. Bagley
Dear Loretta:	Dear Loretta
Closings	Closings
Sincerely,	Sincerely
Yours truly,	Yours truly

ENVELOPES

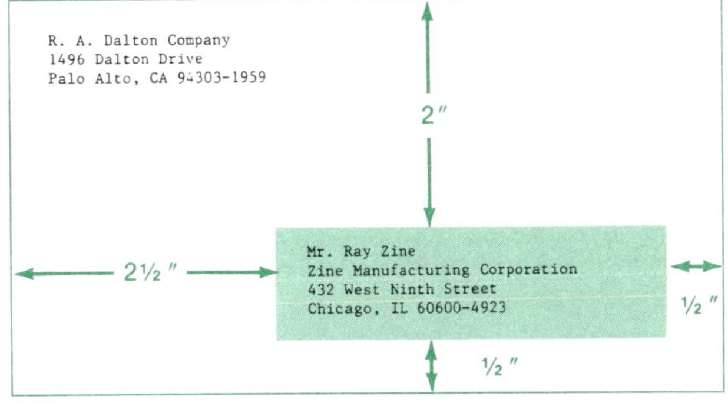

Small Envelope

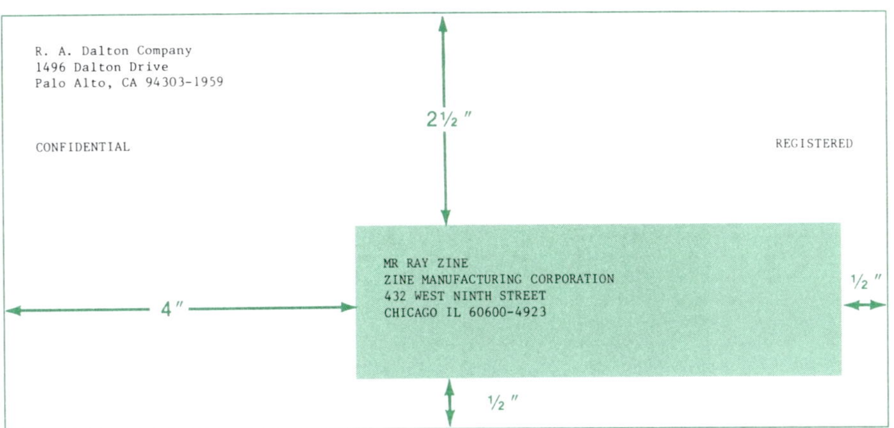

Large Envelope

MEMORANDUMS

Preprinted Memo Form   *Keyed Memo Form (Blank Paper)*

Traditional Style	Simplified Style
WALCZAK CONSULTING CO. MEMORANDUM date: February 9, 19-- to: Ron Decker, Editorial Department from: Bill Walczak, Educational Consultant subject: SEMINAR OUTLINE Ron, attached is the revised seminar outline for the program on Organizational Communication. Ned Ostenso, Bill Sleep, Randy Smith and I collaborated on this revision. Please note that we changed the name of the program. We feel that this is really a better description of the content of the seminar. Please let us know when you are ready to review the program. kw Attachment c: Mark Mitchell Ned Ostenso Bill Sleep Randy Smith	February 9, 19-- TO: Ron Decker, Editorial Department Bill Walczak, Educational Consultant SEMINAR OUTLINE Ron, attached is the revised seminar outline for the program on Organizational Communication. Ned Ostenso, Bill Sleep, Randy Smith and I collaborated on this revision. Please note that we changed the name of the program. We feel that this is really a better description of the content of the seminar. Please let us know when you are ready to review the program. kw Attachment c: Mark Mitchell Ned Ostenso Bill Sleep Randy Smith

Ruled Table

STATES RANKED BY
MEDIAN FAMILY INCOME

Thousands of dollars

State	Rank	Income
Alaska	1	$12,440
Connecticut	2	11,810
Hawaii	3	11,550
New Jersey	4	11,410
Maryland	5	11,060
Michigan	6	11,030
Illinois	7	10,960
Massachusetts	8	10,840
California	9	10,730
Nevada	10	10,690
New York	11	10,620
Washington	12	10,410
Ohio	13	10,310
Delaware	14	10,210
Wisconsin	15	10,070
Indiana	16	9,970
Minnesota	17	9,740
Rhode Island	18	9,730
New Hampshire	19	9,700
District of Columbia	20	9,580

Table with Column Headings

DEPARTMENT SUPERVISORS
OF CLAIRMONT STORES

October 11, 19--

Name	Department	Extension
Lynn Anderson	Personnel	382
Jim Elliot	Treasurer	256
Don Graffe	Shop	371
Lisa Orton	Data Processing	416
Mike Pankratz	Accounting	555
Joan Rosen	Operations	450
Sarah Strauss	Payroll	265
Steve VandenLangen	Safety	370

Boxed Table

RESULTS OF ENVIRONMENTAL PROTECTION AGENCY
GASOLINE-CONSUMPTION TEST

Sporty Cars	Engine	Transmission	EPA Estimates Highway	City
Chevrolet Monza 2 + 2	140-cu. in 4-cyl. 2-bbl.	Manual	30	19
Chevrolet Monza Towne Coupe	140-cu. in 4-cyl. 2-bbl.	Manual	30	19
Pontiac Sunbird 2-Door Coupe	140-cu. in. 4-cyl. 2-bbl.	Manual	30	19
Oldsmobile Starfire Sport Coupe	140-cu. in. 4-cyl. 2-bbl.	Manual	30	19
Buick Skyhawk "S" Coupe	231-cu. in. V-6 2-bbl.	Manual	26	17
Datsun 280 Z Sport Coupe	168-cu. in. 6-cyl. F.I.	Manual	25	17
Toyota Celica ST & GT Sport Coupes	133.6-cu. in. 4-cyl. 2-bbl.	Manual	32	19
VW Scirocco Sport Coupe	97-cu. in. 4-cyl. 2-bbl.	Manual	38	26
Fiat XL/9 Coupe	78.7-cu. in. 4-cyl. 2-bbl.	Manual	31	21
Audi Fox 2-Door Sedan	97-cu. in. 4-cyl. F.I.	Manual	36	24
BMW 2002 2-Door Sedan	121-cu. in. 4-cyl. 2-bbl.	Manual	30	20
Mazda Cosmo Coupe	80-cu. in. Rotary 4-bbl.	Manual	28	17
Porsche 914 Coupe	120-cu. in 4-cyl. F.I.	Manual	31	20
Triumph TR-7 Coupe	122-cu. in. 4-cyl. 1-bbl.	Manual	27	19

Unbound Manuscript

WHERE TO BUY

Most cities have several stores which carry similar, or identical types of merchandise. The people of a particular city, therefore, have a choice of stores in which to buy certain products. Several factors which may influence their decision about where to purchase are quality, style, cost and location. If two items are of the same quality and the same style, people will usually buy the item which costs less; that is, if they know which store is selling the item for less.

Most consumers depend upon advertising for information about sales and bargains. Although pricing is an important consideration, in far too many instances it becomes the only factor in a decision. The consumer forgets that there are two additional factors which must be considered along with price. These two factors are the amount of traveling time required to get to the store and the cost involved in the travel. Most people fail to recognize these added factors.

If a consumer must spend quite a bit of time traveling to the store which has the merchandise for the lowest price, travel time becomes a major consideration. How much is time worth? Each individual must answer that particular question.

The cost of travel, whether by private or public transportation, has continued to rise. Again, if the distance involved is quite far, the consumer may spend more on transportation than would be saved on a "bargain" purchase; thus, he or she will not save any money.

Bound Manuscript

WHERE TO BUY

Most cities have several stores which carry similar, or identical types of merchandise. The people of a particular city, therefore, have a choice of stores in which to buy certain products. Several factors which may influence their decision about where to purchase are quality, style, cost and location. If two items are of the same quality and the same style, people will usually buy the item which costs less; that is, if they know which store is selling the item for less.

Most consumers depend upon advertising for information about sales and bargains. Although pricing is an important consideration, in far too many instances it becomes the only factor in a decision. The consumer forgets that there are two additional factors which must be considered along with price. These two factors are the amount of traveling time required to get to the store and the cost involved in the travel. Most people fail to recognize these added factors.

If a consumer must spend quite a bit of time traveling to the store which has the merchandise for the lowest price, travel time becomes a major consideration. How much is time worth? Each individual must answer that particular question.

The cost of travel, whether by private or public transportation, has continued to rise. Again, if the distance involved is quite far, the consumer may spend more on transportation than would be saved on a "bargain" purchase; thus he or she will not save any money.

2

The intelligent consumer must be aware of all factors involved with purchasing. Too many times the consumer considers difference in prices as only "cents" and not dollars. Yet, "cents" add up to dollars over the duration of a small period of time.

Endnote Reference

the common denominator and the
...ey require more storage space.

...ed productivity and correspondence of businesses of today,
the sheer volume of paperwork has increased beyond one's wildest imagination.
Business records take up more space than any other single item and more money
is paid out for salaries and equipment than for any other single item
(Holbreck and Marcus:1984:2). Not only has the need for additional space
become critical, but the cost of maintaining the records' system has risen.

One expert indicated that if trends continue, the cost of filing just one
document could rise to ten cents (Dane:1983:52). The problems increase, as
one file drawer can hold only a certain amount of items. Not only do the

Traditional Footnote Reference

maintaining the records system has risen.
...indicated that if trends continue, the cost of filing
...ot one document could rise to ten cents.[2] The problems increase, since
one file drawer can hold only a certain number of items. Not only do the
records take up precious space, but the need for higher salaries and
equipment soars. Quite obviously, any time or effort spent by office

[1] Judy L. Holbreck and Vincent T. Marcus, Problems in Record Storage
(Dayton, Ohio: Western Publishing Company, 1984), p.2.

[2] Deborah Dane, "The Rising Cost of Record Storage," Management and
Money (April, 1983), p. 52.

Endnote Bibliography

BIBLIOGRAPHY

Armes, Jane, E. J. James, and Betty Jane Onis. Secretarial Systems.
Cincinnati, Ohio: Poston, Inc., 1983, p. 19.

Onie, George. Control in the Office. Chicago, Illinois: A-Z Publishing
Company, 1984, p. 219.

Prentis, Richard A., and James E. Johnson. Clerical Systems. Dallas,
Texas: Weston Publishers, 1983, pp. 16-20.

"Speed and Quality in Handling Workflow." Office Systems. Vol. 29,
No. 3, January, 1983, p. 4.

Wilson, James. Using Your Skills. New York: Creative Enterpri...
p. 323.

Traditional Footnote Bibliography

BIBLIOGRAPHY

Armes, Jane, E. J. James, and Betty Jane Onis. Secretarial Systems.
Cincinnati, Ohio: Poston, Inc., 1983.

Onie, George. Control in the Office. Chicago, Illinois: A-Z Publishing
Company, 1984.

Prentis, Richard A., and James E. Johnson. Clerical Systems. Dallas,
Texas: Weston Publishers, 1983.

"Speed and Quality in Handling Workflow." Office Systems. Vol. 29,
No. 3, January, 1983.

Wilson, James. Using Your Skills. New York: Creative Enterpri...

Title Page

OFFICE MANUALS

By

John Smith

O.A. 417, Section 01
Administrative Management
T/Th. 2 o'clock
Dr. Johnson
Current Date

Table of Contents

TABLE OF CONTENTS

BUSINESS REPORTS

Memo Report

Current Date

TO: You, the Student

Business People of America

MEMORANDUM REPORT PREPARATION

Reports in business are frequently prepared in different forms from those in education. You are looking at a very popular example, the memo report. Rather than prepare both a report and an accompanying letter or memo, the two are combined. This method is usually used for reports that are fairly short, fewer than three pages. You will notice that the style is the same as shown in the memorandum section of this text.

Many times you will find that the report content lends itself to the use of subheadings as shown below.

Summary. The findings of the survey of advertising at Old London Square Mall are similar to the national trends. All the mall stores use, in addition to local cooperative advertising, some type of outside media. The choice of outside media compares quite closely with national trends, since newspapers are listed most effective and used most frequently, followed by radio, television, direct mailing, and magazines.

Background. Our organization entered into an agreement three months ago with the merchants of the Old London Square Mall to investigate avenues of approach to effective advertising. We assigned methods currently in use throughout the nation, and especially those methods utilized by businesses in some type of physical location arrangement (shopping centers, malls, and so on). After gathering the evidence used throughout the country, a questionnaire was prepared and administered to all the merchants located in the Old London Square Mall. The results of both the nationwide survey and the mall survey were then compared.

Findings. Nationwide merchants agree that individual firms must do more advertising than the cooperative efforts the mall association makes. Cooperative efforts seem to be quite effective when the entire mall conducts some type of sale (usually seasonal), but for the remainder of the time it is the individual firm which must generate sales by individual advertising efforts. The Old London Square Mall merchants agree with this 100%. The national use and popularity of various types of advertising media is somewhat different from what the Old London Square Mall merchants now use.

Page 1

You, the Student
Page 2
Current Date

Types of Advertising Media

Nationwide	Old London Square Mall
newspaper	newspaper
television	radio
radio	television
direct mail	direct mail
magazines	magazines

Ranked according to frequency of utilization

Conclusion. The use of advertising media by merchants at the Old London Square Mall closely follows what is being done on a national scale. The only difference found was in the ranking of television and radio. Television is second in popularity nationwide, and radio is third. At the Old London Square Mall, radio is second in popularity and television is third.

Recommendations. Our agreement called for both a written report and an oral presentation of the findings. This information was given to the merchants at their last monthly meeting. A recommendation was made that the merchants utilize television more than radio in the future. After discussion, it was decided by the members in attendance to follow this recommendation for the next six months. Accordingly, the mall manager was instructed to change the mall cooperative advertising campaign. We were given another agreement to provide a research follow-up report at the conclusion of the trial period.

Follow-up. Jim Lane will be in charge of the follow-up research project. Alice Barnes, June Folton, Bob Arterburn, and Leslie Barth will work with him.

Page 2

Formal Business Report (left-bound format)

RECOMMENDATIONS FOR THE MADISON STREET CROSSING

This report contains the basic data gathered and analyzed to make recommendations regarding the Madison Street crossing. The recommendation made by this committee strongly supports the rebuilding of the crossing as soon as possible.

Purpose

The purpose of this committee was to study possible alternatives to the traffic problem as it now exists at the Madison Street crossing. This includes recommendations for an arterial street improvement which would serve the central part of the city, provide access to the downtown area and the major industrial complex, link U.S. Highway 73 with the east/west arterial street system across the Chippewa River, and eliminate the serious and chronic problem with the Chicago and Eastern Railroad traffic.

The objective of the recommendation is to relieve traffic congestion that affects the business and industrial portions of the city, while also providing for safe and more efficient travel.

The Problem

Existing conditions. Topography and the location of commercial business has primarily determined the character and location of the street network in the immediate area. Because of the steep grades in certain areas, several industries are located on the plateau of the river. As a result, access roads have tended to be located in valleys, where lesser slopes are available. Such locations, however, limit the continuity, which results in many jogs and offsets in the street system.

For instance, when traveling up the hill on Madison Street motorists must travel in a northeast direction (See Exhibit A). Immediately after crossing the railroad tracks--which cannot be seen until the motorist is directly upon them--a seven-degree jog to the right must be made. Right turns onto Dewey Street are permitted, but the effort involved to make such a turn is such that many motorists make it improperly and dangerously. The net result is often confusion, danger to both motorists and pedestrian traffic, and generally bad feelings.

Train traffic, which at this point is the main double track line (mainline) of the Chicago and Eastern Railroad Line with several side tracks south of Madison Street, is a serious barrier to automobile

Page 1

2

traffic and has long been recognized as bad. A separation of grades was planned by the railroad more than 30 years ago, but the expense involved was so great that no steps have ever been taken to carry out the needed reconstruction.

Traffic. The route including Birch Street, Germania Street, and East Madison Street is the only east/west arterial serving the northern half of the city. The use of this particular route has developed due to the industry in the northern part of the city and highway traffic to and from the principally rural areas to the north and east.

Studies have shown travel patterns in the city to be of three basic types: local traffic within the city, travel from outlying regions into the city and returning, and external traffic passing through the city. Industry located in the northern part of the city probably is responsible for the largest part of the traffic. The greatest proportion of traffic to and from these industries originates to the north and east. There are three routes serving the northeast section of the city from Starr Avenue/ Birch Street, U.S. Highway 73/Birch Street, and C.T. Highway Q/Birch Street. Of these, because of the construction of a major interchange and viaduct now in progress, the majority of the traffic naturally travels west on Birch Street from U.S. Highway 73. A good arterial street connection between this route and the downtown area is therefore vitally important.

Traffic studies conducted have revealed the overall average daily traffic using this route is one automobile every 4.5 seconds during the daytime hours, making it one of the highest volume routes serving the central city (See Exhibit B). Only short segments of two other city streets approach this volume. Traffic volume is fairly well distributed, however, with the largest volumes being recorded early in the morning and later in the afternoon, corresponding to local industrial shift changes.

Congestion. In addition to peak hour capacities, congestion is caused by four existing conditions:

1. A major delay is created by the at-grade level crossing of the railroad. Heavy vehicular traffic and 15 regular trains and several locals and switching movements each day make it quite evident that the railroad represents a significant disruption to traffic flow.

2. Due to reasons previously mentioned, sharp turns at the Birch Street/Germania and Germania/East Madison intersections cause a general slowdown of traffic, which often affects traffic flow at the crossing.

3. The combination of steep grades and the at-grade roadway causes congestion, as normal traffic is not able to pass slow-moving traffic. This problem is compounded on East Madison Street where a steep grade is encountered (See Exhibit C).

Page 2

PROOFREADER'S MARKS

Symbol	Stands for	Example
⁀ ⌇	transpose (change around)	See the (play children). Second, is the .... First, is the ....
∧ ∨	insert	Bring me the big tub.
⌒	close up	book keeping
#	add a space or a line	Let usnow begin.
⸱ or /	delete (take out)	Bring me the big tub. or Show me the sway.
lc or /	lower case (small letter)	Look at Jack Run. or Look at Jack Run.
uc or ≡	upper case (capital letter)	Look at jack run. or Look at jack run.
[	move to the left	[Let me see the paper.
]	move to the right	Let] me see the paper.
ss	single-space	See the man. Why should I?
ds	double-space	Look at the cars. I see them.
ts	triple-space	Look at the cars. I see them.
stet or	let it stand (ignore marked change previously made)	See the man. or See the man.
¶ or ⁋	begin new paragraph	¶ I see the man.

PREFERRED SPELLINGS

United States	Canada	United Kingdom
acknowledgment	acknowledgment	acknowledgement
airplane	airplane	aeroplane
analyze	analyze	analyse
catalog	catalogue	catalogue
center	centre	centre
check (bank)	cheque	cheque
color	colour	colour
cooperate	cooperate	co-operate
coordinate	coordinate	co-ordinate
councilor	councillor	councillor
counseled	counselled	counselled
curb	curb	kerb
defense	defense	defence
disk	disk	disc
enroll, enrollment	enroll, enrollment	enrol, enrolment
favor, favorite	favour, favorite	favour, favourite
fiber	fiber	fibre
flavor	flavour	flavour
fulfill	fulfill	fulfil
gray	gray	grey
harbor	harbour	harbour
honor	honour	honour
installment	instalment	instalment
judgment	judgement	judgement
labor	labour	labour
license (noun and verb)	license (verb)	license (verb)
liter	litre	litre
maneuver	manoeuvre	manoeuvre
marvelous	marvellous	marvellous
meter	metre	metre
mold	mold	mould
mortgagor	mortgagor	mortgager
neighbor	neighbour	neighbour
offense	offense	offence
plow	plow	plough
practice (noun and verb)	practise (verb only)	practise (verb only)
programmed (one m permissible)	programmed (one m not permissible)	programmed (one m not permissible)
skeptic	skeptic	sceptic
skillful	skillful	skilful
sulfur	sulphur	sulphur
theater	theatre	theatre
tire	tire	tyre
traveled, traveling (and similar words)	travelled, travelling	travelled, travelling
woolen	woolen	woollen

INDEX